The New Berlin

The New Berlin

MEMORY, POLITICS, PLACE

Karen E. Till

University of Minnesota Press

Minneapolis | London

The publication of this book has been aided by a subvention from the Center for German and European Studies, a consortium of the University of Minnesota, Twin Cities, and the University of Wisconsin–Madison supported by the German Academic Exchange Service (DAAD).

Published by the University of Minnesota Press
111 Third Avenue South, Suite 290
Minneapolis, MN 55401-2520
http://www.upress.umn.edu

Library of Congress Cataloging-in-Publication Data

Till, Karen E.
    The new Berlin : memory, politics, place / Karen E. Till.
      p.   cm.
    Includes bibliographical references and index.
    ISBN 0-8166-4010-6 (hc : alk. paper) — ISBN 0-8166-4011-4 (pb : alk. paper)
    1. Berlin (Germany)—History—1990- 2. Memory—Political aspects—Germany. 3. Holocaust, Jewish (1939–1945)—Influence. I. Title.
    DD881.T55 2005
    943'.155088—dc22

                                                     2004028616

12 11 10 09 08 07 06   10 9 8 7 6 5 4 3 2

*To all German daughters
and their mothers*

Contents

ix   Acknowledgments

A Fence   1

5   1. Hauntings, Memory, Place

A Metro Stop   25

31   2. The New Berlin: From *Kiez* to *Kosmos*

A Flyer   59

63   3. The Gestapo Terrain: Landscape, Digging, Open Wounds

Fieldnotes   107

121   4. Berlin's Ort der Täter: A Historic Site of Perpetrators

A Neighborhood   155

161   5. Aestheticizing the Rupture: Berlin's Holocaust Memorial

A Newspaper Article   189

193   6. Memory in the New Berlin

229   Notes

271   Index

Acknowledgments

I *walk down into my basement. Distracted and somewhat absentmindedly, I look into a box and pull out a familiar object—a coat that once belonged to my now deceased grandmother. It was made by my grandfather Jakob Till, a tailor and furrier, someone I met only once as a very young child. I inhale the coat's musty scent and am overwhelmed by a sense of loss for a past that wasn't mine: a memory of having had grandparents.*

When I was in my late twenties, my grandmother passed away. A box arrived at my parents' house with some of her most valued possessions, and I inherited my grandmother's coat. Years later, as I was immersed in the research and writing of this book, I found it again and began to wear it. Her well-worn coat, and other familial fragments—some sketchy recollections, a few salvaged photos—haunt this project and me. As this book is about revenants, ruins, and returns, I feel compelled to acknowledge the ancestral phantoms that crowd my work.

My father's parents, Jakob Till and Anna Kemp, both born in 1899 in what is now Austria (near the former Yugoslavian border), were to meet later as young adults in Pennsylvania. They married and had two sons, Jack and Joseph (my father). My grandmother emigrated to the United States as a child with her family around the turn of the century for economic reasons, whereas my grandfather left the town of Palanka in the early 1920s to escape recruitment as a soldier. It was only in writing this (and after years of persistently asking relatives) that I discovered our family story about his emigration to escape fighting in World War I was a myth; we all believed him to be ten years older than he was. Both my grandparents had family members living in the United States when they left Europe.

I met my grandparents once, when I was three, shortly after my youngest brother was born. My vague memories of the visit are of bodily sensations: eating candy pills from the toy doctor kit my grandfather had given me; licking my fingers after eating the cookies my grandmother had baked; descending the stairs to their basement and looking at the furnace and the piles of coal that stood near it. When I look at photographs of that visit, my grandparents seem foreign, otherworldly, to me, though they then had already lived in Harrisburg for some time.

My mother's parents, Johann Brause (born 1881) and Leokadia Wardowski (born 1896), raised their five girls, Cäcelia, Theodora, Ursula, Euphemia (my mother), and Gertraut, in the town of Troop, in what was then West Prussia and is today Poland. I know my grandfather only from the recollections of my mother, who came to the United States in the mid-1950s, and of her older sisters, still in Germany. They describe a doting parent, who rubbed their cold feet after they had been ice-skating on the pond and gave them extra sweets from their family-owned store. Their stories always end the same way: their gentle father died in 1939 in a hospital. They say his bleeding ulcer originated from his experience as a prisoner in France during World War I.

Infrequently my mother tells me stories of war. As a young teenager, she, with my four aunts and grandmother, fled from their home on January 21, 1945, to become refugees in what would become West Germany. (My mother always mentions this date precisely when she tells this story, as well as the fact that they escaped advancing Russian troops by a mere day.) Only upon hearing those stories as a young adult did I begin to understand the stubborn, impenetrable silence that surrounded my grandmother. I was seven years old when I met her for the only time, during my first trip to Germany.

In subsequent trips to Germany, many years later as a graduate student and professor, I met many people who shared their lives with me and also shaped this project. They described their complex personal and social relationships to the past, to their nation(s), and to the cities they lived in. They talked about their work and sometimes their families, took me to important places and venues, introduced me to different people and ideas, and challenged my interpretations. In addition to the people I quote directly in this book, I also extend my deepest gratitude to many others who remain unnamed. I have tried my best to represent their insights, and any limitations with interpretation are my own.

The financial support generously provided by a number of institutions, organizations, and universities allowed me to pursue this research for more than a decade. Initial research was supported through an Alexander von Humboldt Foundation Federal Chancellor's Fellowship and an Association of American Geographers Dissertation Research Grant. Later phases were funded through a follow-up research grant from the Alexander von Humboldt Foundation; a summer stipend granted by the Council on Research at Louisiana State University; a summer grant from the McKnight Humanities Board of the University of Minnesota; and a grant-in-aid, summer fellowship, and single-semester leave awarded by the University of Minnesota's College of Liberal Arts and Vice President for Research and Graduate School. The Center for German and European Studies, a consortium of the University of Minnesota and the University of Wisconsin–Madison funded by the German Academic Exchange Service (Deutsches Akademisches Ausstauch Dienst), supported travel funds and research assistance as part of my participation in the research collaborative "Contemporary Germany and the Transatlantic Politics of Memory." The Center for German and European Studies at the University of Minnesota also generously provided a grant to help offset costs of publishing this book.

In addition to the direct funds that sponsored this project, a number of individuals from many institutions in the United States, Germany, and England warmly offered collegial and administrative support. I am especially grateful for the excellent research and editorial help from Heike Alberts, Gundolf Graml, Beth Muellner, Mary Strasma, Kristin Szairto, and Daisaku Yamamoto. Faculty, colleagues, and students in the Department of Geography at the University of Wisconsin–Madison, the Department of Geography and Anthropology at Louisiana State University, and the Department of Geography at the University of Minnesota—my "home" departments during my research and writing— supported my excitement as well as frustrations about my work. My colleagues from the University of Minnesota's Space and Place Research Group (supported by the Humanities Institute and the Institute for Global Studies), the Center for German and European Studies, the European Studies Consortium, the Center for Advanced Feminist Studies, and numerous students in various graduate seminars offered valuable feedback to draft chapters. The history department of the Free University in Berlin, the Department of Geography at Humboldt University in Berlin, and the Department of Geography at the University of California, Los Angeles, also provided me with research and office space, as well as stimulating intellectual exchange during research trips and my semester leave. Finally, new colleagues and staff at Royal Holloway, University of London, kindly supported me in the final production phases of this book.

Many institutions provided access to their archives, libraries, and collections (and xeroxing and related expenses), including the Active Museum for Resistance and against Fascism in Berlin (Actives Museum Widerstand und Faschismus Berlin); Berlin's Senate Offices for City Planning, Construction and Building, and Cultural Affairs; the Foundation Memorial to the Murdered Jews of Europe; Daniel Libeskind's architectural office (Berlin); the Fritz-Bauer Holocaust Center (Frankfurt); the German Historical Museum (Berlin); Partners for Berlin; the Memorial Museum of German Resistance (Berlin); the Oranienburg City Planner's Office; Sachsenhausen Concentration Camp Memorial Museum (Oranienburg); the Topography of Terror (Berlin); the United States Holocaust Memorial Museum Research Center (Washington, D.C.); and the Wannsee Holocaust Memorial Museum Center (Berlin). Staff of the German Historical Museum, Memorial Museum of German Resistance, Partners for Berlin, Topography of Terror, and Sachsenhausen Memorial Museum Center supported (and tolerated) the numerous months over many years that I spent at their exhibitions and tours. The German Historical Museum and Topography of Terror (through the generous financial support of the Berliner Festspiele GmbH) also helped me create, distribute, and analyze visitor surveys of their exhibitions.

I am indebted to the following individuals and organizations for granting copyright permission to reproduce artwork: Paul Glaser; Jürgen Henschel; Historisches Archiv zum Tourismus des Willy-Scharnow-Instituts, Freie Universität Berlin; Horst Hoheisel; Iguana Photos; Karin Joggerst; Landesarchiv Berlin; Munich Bilderdienst/Süddeutscher Verlag; Frieder Schnock and Renata Stih; Senatsverwaltung für Stadtentwicklung Berlin; Stiftung Denkmal für die ermordeten Juden Europas; and Stiftung Topographie des Terrors. The Cartography Lab in the Department of Geography at the University of Minnesota produced the beautiful maps in this book through the talented expertise of Xuejin Ruan.

I am grateful to the many people who were supportive of my work. Some looked at rather drafty drafts of chapters, others offered help with copyediting, and still others provided valuable constructive feedback on my ideas at critical moments. Then there were those who helped create safe spaces for me to write and think. In addition to my family and other close friends, I wish to thank especially Martin Becher, Julia Bleakney, Denis Cosgrove, Michael Curry, Dydia DeLyser, Frank Dingel, Lisa Disch, Lorraine Dowler, Stefanie Endlich, Ben Forest, Gundolf Graml, Joan Hackeling, Leila Harris, Klaus Hesse, Steve Hoelscher, Christiana Hoss, Karen Jankowsky, Tahir Kayani, Gerry Kearns, Britta Klagge, Rudy Koshar, Jack Kugelmass, Sonja Kuftinec, Helga Leitner, Tom Lekan, Thomas Lutz, Rick McCormick, Suzanne Michel, Carrie Mullen, Bob Ostergren, Steve Pile, Miles Richardson, Gerhard Richter, Jani Scandura, Bob Sack, Andreas Sanders, Frieder Schnock, Gunter Schlusche, Eric Shepard, Renata Stih, Kristin Szairto, Mary Thomas, Yi-Fu Tuan, Rhodri Williams, Sharon Zukin, and anonymous reviewers of my proposal and book manuscript. I was fortunate to work with a number of talented individuals at the University of Minnesota Press, who patiently supported me in realizing the concept for this book. My warmest thanks to my editors Pieter Martin and Robin Moir, and also to Doug Armato, Adam Grafa, and Carrie Mullen.

Finally, I would like to mention three people who deserve special thanks. Yi-Fu Tuan was my mentor and guide in the earliest phases of this project, at a time when all I felt I could do was stumble around the theoretical literatures and material and metaphorical landscapes of Berlin. Many years later, after I had completed the first full polished draft of the book, Steve Pile provided me with the courage to cut it in half. His encouraging suggestions allowed me to focus my arguments about the complex spatialities and temporalities of Berlin (and its ghosts). Jani Scandura helped me find my voice and give life and rhythm to my stories. Through our numerous conversations and editing sessions, she challenged me to pay attention to the performative and spatial nature of narrative and language, and in so doing helped me refine my arguments about place making, memory, and the city.

Minneapolis, 2004

Berlin, 1997. Photograph courtesy of Karin Joggerst.

A Fence

June 1999

In the center of Berlin is a wooden fence. It was erected to protect the 4.2-acre construction lot destined to become the central Memorial to the Murdered Jews of Europe. Plastered on the most-trafficked corner of this fence is an ever-changing montage of posters, political graffiti, and enlarged newspaper articles that either support or oppose the memorial. This fence is a temporary structure in the landscape that marks long-standing contested social identities.

Large posters put up by the citizen group responsible for the memorial announce, "Here is the place!"[1] On one, a familiar historical photo depicts a bedraggled elderly man wearing a thick coat stitched with a Star of David. A lonely figure, he reminds onlookers in the present about the unjust death he and others suffered; his image haunts the city and the imaginations of onlookers. It is a familiar face, one that some tourists walking by would most likely recognize, perhaps having seen it before in black-and-white photographs at museum exhibitions or in historical films. As a historical document, this (reproduced) photograph provides evidence that he existed, and that necessarily, given the history of Jews in the Third Reich, he was persecuted. Still, he remains nameless. It is not clear who captured the image (Nazi soldiers? German citizens?), why he was photographed (documentation? propaganda?), or where he was when the photograph was taken (a processing center? a train station? a street in a Jewish ghetto in another city? a neighborhood here in Berlin?).

Printed on a small band at the top of another poster, a different citizen initiative invokes the authority of Theodor Adorno: "The past can only be dealt with when the causes of the past are removed."[2] Viewing the memorial as yet another attempt to "draw a final line" with the past *(Schlußstrich),* this citizen group advocates discussion about the continued presence of anti-Semitism and xenophobia in contemporary

1

"Memorial for the Murdered Jews of Europe: Here is the place!" Förderkreis zur Errichtung eines Denkmals für die ermordeten Juden Europas eV (Association for the Establishment of a [Holocaust] Memorial for the Murdered Jews of Europe). Photograph courtesy of Karin Joggerst.

"6,000,000 minus 54 years of 'we didn't know anything' minus 1 Germany minus 1 war minus 1 memorial = ⊠." Initiativkreis gegen den Schlußstrich (Initiative against Drawing a Final Line with the Past). Photograph courtesy of Karin Joggerst.

Germany. For them, the past is always constituted by the present; the violent history of National Socialism and the Holocaust should be left open to interpretation and debate indefinitely. They see this memorial as symptomatic of contemporary Germans' desire to put an end to discussions about their social responsibility for the past.

Someone else has posted a handwritten sign that declares: "The discussion IS a memorial!" Another asserts, "The memorial is already there," only to be emended to read: "The memorial is already *here*." These proclamations point to the very real presence of the memorial in Berlin and in Germany's national imaginary despite its lack of a sculptural form in 1999.

The fence protects an empty lot.

Maybe it's this feeling, the internationality, the cosmopolitanism, that brings people here, as well as the market because of its proximity to Eastern Europe. Berlin changed its geographical location, from the margins to the center of Europe. That is important for young people.

—*Interview with spokesperson for Partners for Berlin, 2000*

1 | Hauntings, Memory, Place

> Berlin is unlike every other city because it is new. There is so much
> construction and change going on now, and it won't be the case
> ten years from now.
> —*Interview with marketing company spokesperson for Partners
> for Berlin, 2000*

The "New Berlin" represents the promise of Germany's future. The unified
national capital now includes sleek corporate buildings, a federal government district, new regional transportation and communication links, a renovated historic
district, gentrified neighborhoods, urban parks and riverfronts, and a growing suburban
ring. This cosmopolitan city of the twenty-first century is also an international cultural
center, ranked above London in a recent *Condé Nast Traveler* magazine for its numerous
symphonic orchestras, opera houses, choirs, galleries and museums, theaters, alternative
art scene, and buildings designed by internationally famous architects. "With 3.5 million inhabitants, Berlin has as many theaters as Paris and more symphony orchestras
than London, both metropoles of some 10 million inhabitants and contenders for the
title of Europe's cultural capital."[1]

Just as the New Berlin has been given a radiant material form through buildings
and districts designed by world-famous architects, so places and landscapes throughout
the contemporary city embody new Berlins imagined in the past and historic Berlins
imagined today. As the capital of five different historical Germanys, Berlin represents
the "unstable optic identity" of the nation[2]—for it is the city where, more than any other
city, German nationalism and modernity have been staged and restaged, represented
and contested.[3] Berlin is a city that cannot be contained by marketing representations of
time, of the "new."[4] It is a place with "heterogeneous references, ancient scars," a city that
"create[s] bumps on the smooth utopias" of its imagined futures.[5] Even the marketing

Advertising Berlin, 2000.

images that now adorn city billboards to promote the New Berlin as a cosmopolitan beauty queen, surrounded by corporate power and wealth and bejeweled by cultural icons, are haunted by former hopes for the future of Weimar, National Socialist, and Cold War Berlins.[6]

While Berlin may be unusual in Europe because of the sheer scale of construction and renovation that has occurred since 1990, it remains distinctive because of the array of places that have been (re)established that convey both the desires and fears of returning to traumatic national pasts. The specters of the past are felt in the contemporary city when groups or individuals intentionally or unexpectedly evoke ghosts, such as when they plan and market another "new" Berlin, identify artifacts and ruins as culturally significant, "discover" and mark formerly deserted landscapes as historic, claim a national heritage and dig for past cities, establish museums and memorials, or visit places of memory through tours.[7] Even postunification urban landscapes continue to be defined by presences from the recent past. Recently built corporate buildings and consumer spaces designed by internationally known architects, including O. M. Ungers, Philip Johnson, and Aldo Rossi, characterize Germany's aspirations toward being a "normal" European nation-state[8] and are squarely located at sites of former East–West Bloc confrontation: Potsdamer Platz, Friedrichstraße, and Checkpoint Charlie. The glimmering Daimler-Benz and Sony towers in the center of the city at Potsdamer Platz grew out of the former "death strip" between the two Berlin Walls—a no-man's-land that existed as a result of the trauma of National Socialism.[9]

Historic Berlins are also part of the new city; some places that once existed in the distant past have been proposed for reconstruction after unification, such as the

THE INTERNATIONAL CITY
BEHIND THE IRON CURTAIN

Advertising Berlin, 1950. Tourism brochure cover, published by Verkehrsamt der Stadt Berlin. Courtesy of Historisches Archiv zum Tourismus des Willy-Scharnow-Instituts, Freie Universität Berlin.

Hohenzollern City Palace. A newly reconstructed city palace would satisfy nostalgic longings for royal (i.e., pre-Nazi) European pasts previously denied to the Cold War Germanys but would necessitate the erasure of other pasts, in particular the demolition of the East German Palace of the Republic, a former government and cultural center.[10] Other new "historic" places proposed before unification, such as the German Historical Museum, were established under the former Kohl administration to ameliorate that national trauma, to "master" the past and promote a positive understanding of German identity.[11] Now located in the historic district near the museum island, the postunification historical institution is housed in the Prussian armory building, or Zeughaus—the same place where the East German Museum for History was located only years earlier—with a new extension designed by I. M. Pei. At the same time that these places are being made to contain undesirable pasts, a cosmopolitan memory of the Holocaust has become hypervisible in the center of the city. An emerging memory district will soon be completed near the new federal district and corporate skyscrapers at Potsdamer Platz that will include the Jewish Museum (designed by Daniel Libeskind); the Memorial to the Murdered Jews of Europe (designed by Peter Eisenman); and the Topography of Terror International Documentation Center projected to be finished in 2008 (designed by Peter Zumthor). These new, yet historic and commemorative, places communicate conflicting social desires—to remember and to forget violent national pasts that still linger in the present.

Much has been written about Germany's attempt to master the National Socialist past *(Vergangenheitsbewältigung)* and about the controversial politics of memory in Berlin.[12] In these works the city, as well as place more generally, is treated as a stage on which the drama of history—represented as contested negotiations between key political figures, historians, philosophers, and artists—is performed.[13] But places are never merely backdrops for action or containers for the past. They are fluid mosaics and moments of memory, matter, metaphor, scene, and experience that create and mediate social spaces and temporalities.[14] Through place making, people mark social spaces as haunted sites where they can return, make contact with their loss, contain unwanted presences, or confront past injustices.

This book focuses on the practices and politics of place making, and how those practices mediate and construct social memory and identity by localizing personal emotions and defining social relations to the past. It explores how particular places of memory narrate national pasts and futures through the spaces and times of a city that is itself a place of social memory. Berlin is a place haunted with landscapes that simultaneously embody presences and absences, voids and ruins, intentional forgetting and painful remembering.[15] If the Holocaust and its memory still stand as a test case for humanist and universal claims of Western civilization,[16] one might argue that these place-making

German Historical Museum (Deutsches Historisches Museum). Extension designed by I. M. Pei, 2004. Photograph courtesy of Iguana Photo.

processes in Berlin are central symbolic and material sites of the crisis of modernity, uniquely embodying the contradictions and tensions of social memory and national identity in the late twentieth century and the early twenty-first.

The places of memory I explore in this book were made to confront and contain the lingering legacies of a violent national history. But each embodies a different narrative of the past and imagined future. All were controversial: the Topography of Terror International Documentation Center, the Bavarian Quarter memorial, the Memorial to the Murdered Jews of Europe, a proposed memorial called *Bus Stop!,* the Jewish Museum, and Sachsenhausen Concentration Camp Memorial Museum. Each was established or proposed before reunification, and each was subsequently relocated in the space-times of the New Berlin after 1990. While these memorial, museal, artistic, and educational sites may be interpreted in a number of ways, the controversial debates that accompanied their making point to the distinct ways that Germans continue to negotiate their contradictory feelings of being haunted by a dark national past in the present. The stories about them indicate how dominant understandings of place may simultaneously constrain, direct, and enable the mourning and commemorative practices of a nation.

When people feel personally and culturally haunted by the past, they may evoke ghosts by making places that commemorate, question, remember, mourn, and forget. According to Avery Gordon, the ghost is a social figure through which something lost can be made to appear before our eyes, a way of coming to know the traumas that accompany modern life, even though those traumas may be socially repressed.[17] One way people make ghosts appear is by selectively remembering particular understandings of the past through place.[18] As Steve Pile writes, "to haunt is to possess some place."[19] Although places are understood to be materially real and temporally stable, that is, they give a spatial "fix" to time, their meanings are made and remade in the present. Places are not only continuously interpreted; they are haunted by past structures of meaning and material presences from other times and lives.[20]

Places of memory are created by individuals and social groups to give a shape to felt absences, fears, and desires that haunt contemporary society. Traditionally national places of memory were created and understood as glorifying the pasts of "a people."[21] But such places are also made today to forget: they contain and house disturbing absences and ruptures, tales of violence. Places of memory both remember pasts and encrypt[22] unnamed, yet powerfully felt, absences—absences that might be considered modernity's ghosts of the nation. People speak of historic sites as eyewitnesses to the past or describe landscapes as original artifacts and traces *(Spuren)* from another time; they believe that by visiting these places they can experience, and perhaps work through, their contradictory emotions associated with feeling haunted by the past, including fear, anger, guilt, shame, sadness, longing, and unease. By representing places in these ways, people create social spaces defined by contemporary needs and desires; they emplace their social dreams and hopes for the future.

When people make places of memory, they often give evoked ghosts a spatial form through landscape.[23] Through the material authority of a landscape and the metaphor of archaeology, a particular understanding of the past is believed to be uncovered and made visible. Simon Schama writes that some myths about landscape endure through the centuries, functioning like a "ghostly outline . . . beneath the superficial covering of the contemporary" and accessed by "digging down through layers of memories and representations toward the primary bedrock."[24] The archaeological metaphor is often used to give a spatial form to the past: it locates time in neatly defined vertical layers. Representing place as an archaeological site, an unchanging, materially embodied past, is a discursive-material practice: the past is organized and structured through place to create a chronotope, or time-space formation, through which contemporary narrations and performances of subjectivity and authority are inscribed.[25] People believe that a deep underlying "essence," an unchanging reality from the past, exists underneath the sedimented layers of history. But as they dig, the past becomes a ghostlike presence. The past is never settled, sedimented, neatly arranged in horizontal layers. Similarly, places do not have an essential set of qualities resulting from an internalized history, even though we may construct them to function in this way. Places are unique due to the lingering imprints of particular interactions that transpire: "nowhere else does this precise mixture occur."[26] But those same imprints and interactions will result in new (and often unexpected) spatial, social, and temporal effects.

Places of memory give a shape to that which is metaphysically absent through material and imagined settings that appear to be relatively permanent and stable in time. According to Walter Benjamin, memory is the "scene" *(Schauplatz)* of the past as well as "the medium of what has been experienced the way the earthen realm is the medium in which dead cities lie buried."[27] As the scene of the past, social memory and its outcomes are fluid and changing with the needs of the present. A scene implies making

Topography of Terror, 2002.

particular actions, actors, and events visible by situating them, giving them a context. *Schauplatz* in the German also refers to the place from which one can see and be seen, a location imbued with power relations. For Benjamin, memory is not just information that individuals recall or stories being retold in the present. It is not layered time situated in the landscape. Rather, memory is the self-reflexive act of contextualizing and continuously digging for the past through place. It is a process of continually remaking and re-membering the past in the present rather than a process of discovering objective historical "facts."

And yet there is always a tension when marking absence and loss, longing and desire. Representation is impossible without the play of the trace, of absence and presence, of stories told and not told.[28] In Berlin, it was precisely the question of what ghosts should be invoked, what pasts should be remembered and forgotten, and through what forms, that led to heated public debates over what and where these places of memory *should be*. People made memorials, created historical exhibitions, dug up the past, and went on tours to represent, confront, and ignore a violent national past and to define and forge possible national futures. They made places as open wounds in the city to remind them of their hauntings and to feel uncomfortable.[29] And while these places of memory gained authority as landscape markers from the past, they were nonetheless powerful *as* places of memory because they were also traces of the *future*. Traces from the past are constructed as "figures strained toward the future across a fabled present, figures we inscribe because they can outlast us, beyond the present of their inscription."[30] The promise of a resurrected past through symbols and material objects gives us hope. For some, it is a promise of redemption.

As a geographer and ethnographer, I am intrigued by the ways people construct places to narrate time and embody the past and future. I am interested in the stories people tell about the places they make. As Michel de Certeau and Luce Giard surmise, without those stories, places are empty. "Through stories about places, they become inhabitable. Living is narrativizing."[31] In this book, I use different narratives and representational forms to tell stories about places of memory and to retell the stories about place making that Berliners, Germans, and Americans described while I conducted research (through interviews, informal conversations, and printed documents).[32] My research approach—what I call a geo-ethnography—draws from qualitative and feminist traditions in ethnography, and from critical and humanities traditions in geography.[33] It is an approach that focuses on why people make places to create meaning about who and where they are in the world, and how, in the process of place making, they communicate feelings of belonging and attachment.

Central to the ways that people create meaning about themselves and their pasts is how they expect places to work emotionally, socially, culturally, and politically. How do people make places to delimit and represent time (past, present, and future)? How, in turn, do those places define social relations? Often a dominant set of culturally place-based practices—what Linda McDowell calls "regimes of place"—comes to define how people think about a place's location, social function, landscape form and aesthetics, about international commemorative display, and even personal experiential qualities.[34]

But those regimes of place may be questioned during times of social and political transition. When practices at one locale are challenged, understandings of how places are supposed to work elsewhere (locally, in the city, nationally, or even internationally) may be disputed. During times of social change, people may wish to return to the past and search for a mythic self through place making as a means of confronting inherited legacies of national violence that haunt and influence their everyday lives.[35] Their place-making activities and stories teach an important lesson, one that Shakespeare and Freud knew all too well: we must learn to take our ghosts seriously.

Hauntings: Of Places and Returns

I remember when I decided to become an educator in this field the fear I had when I began to look through archival materials. I kept searching through the documents, and especially the photos. It is an awful feeling not knowing whom you might find. I remember studying each photo, looking for the image of my father or uncle.
—*Interview with German seminar leader and tour guide for the Memorial Museum of German Resistance, 1992*

What does it mean to say that the spaces of the nation are haunted or that ghosts are evoked through the process of place making? How do social hauntologies and personal hauntings intersect?[36] Often unexpectedly, many of us feel the presence of ghosts in our

Memorial Museum of German Resistance (Gedenkstätte Deutscher Widerstand), historical exhibition, 1993.

everyday lives. Ghosts are real and imagined, intensely personal and emotive, and haunt our social spaces when we are open to their presence.[37] Not only do individuals feel haunted by the past; they sometimes feel *the need* to be haunted.

Being haunted involves the desire and repetitive practice of returning to a past time and self that never was. People create homes for their ghosts through telling stories about places and returning to the places that haunt them.[38] Returning to places that haunt our imaginations folds and warps imagined times and selves (past, present, and future), yet the ritual practice of returning creates a sense of temporal continuity and coherence. When someone goes back home (and each of us may have many homes), he or she may experience such vivid memories that it may appear (even if only momentarily) as though the place and the person returning are exactly the same as they once were. Time stands still. Such moments are actually quite rare, but it is in pursuit of those moments and rediscovering the emotions tied to them that individuals engage in such pilgrimages.[39]

When we return to a place, remember an experience in a place, and perform a rendition of the past through a place, we may feel haunted by that which appears not to be there in material space but is, in fact, a powerful presence.[40] When people speak of ghosts, they use a metaphor to describe their feelings of being haunted. As de Certeau describes, "there is no place that is not haunted by many different spirits hidden there in silence, spirits one can 'invoke' or not."[41] He argues that people can only live in haunted places, where, to quote T. S. Eliot, "Time past and time future / What might have been and what has been / Point to one end, which is always present."[42] People set aside ruins, wastelands, or fragments as belonging to some other time and protect them as places that are haunted and somehow lost or stuck in the temporalities of the present. Through place making, people try to contain the past.

But even these places are haunted by our social needs in the present. Dydia DeLyser argues that one reason people make and go to ghost towns is because they can see what they want to see about the past, believe what they already know is true about the American West or about themselves as Americans.[43] From a secure place in the present moment, people create places as eyewitnesses to the past. They may preserve ruins. They may archive documents. They may exhibit artifacts. They try in some way to give a form to the past and to their feelings of being haunted. In so doing, they engage in *social memory*, an ongoing process whereby groups map understandings of themselves onto and through a place and time.

Material remnants haunt our imaginations and performances by materializing social relations. We collect and make photographs, buildings, scrapbooks, films, archives, memorials, tourist pilgrimage routes, and other artifacts to document and save the past, as outcomes and sites of memory.[44] Through the juxtaposition, interpretation, and representation of these sites in the cultural spaces of their production, we try to localize meaning about what we think the past is. Marita Sturken argues that the outcomes of memory are always entangled with the very technologies and processes of their production.[45] But why the obsession with *material* traces? Individuals and groups may try to validate their recollections and their myths of self through an anxious saturation of "bygone reliquary details, reaffirming memory and history in tangible format."[46] Although we may think the past exists, without textualized and material remains we may feel uncertain about the "reality" of the past.

People become obsessed with material remnants because *the past* is a fiction: what remains are memories that are defined by our mourning for that which can no longer be present.[47] We try to preserve memory by creating traces of a past that by definition can never be present. When places are made and understood in this way, their perceived material or emotive presence may seem comforting in the present moment because they are interpreted as giving the past a material form. Euclidean science tells us moderns that no two things can be simultaneously in the same location; hence place has come to signify a fixed quality, of being situated, of locational and temporal stability.[48] We often assume that these rules of located site also apply to time. Because we think of places as stable, we often understand them as having a timeless quality.

However, if the past is a construction, if our understandings of time change with our needs in the present, then what is being made? Why do people spend so much energy giving the past a form through place making? When people make places as stable sites that materially embody the past, they are attempting to give form to their search for a mythic self, a coherent, timeless identity. Moreover, in the process of locating and mapping the past through place, social groups and individuals give a shape to their desire to be connected to that which is no longer metaphysically present, but that which continues to have an important presence in their contemporary lives.

Personal and social memory are experientially punctuated and fragmented and reflect the needs and desires of individuals in the present. When people remember the past, they are physically located in contemporary social and spatial contexts;[49] through the experience of being in certain kinds of places, they may wish to (re)imagine the past and themselves. Memories are unexpectedly triggered by smells, songs, stories, people, travels, and places. When in the presence of a familiar place, recollections may cascade back, mixed with imagination, hopes for the future, and desires for knowing a "true" self. When individuals "go back home," they go to a place because they feel a need to visit a familiar past. One visits a childhood home or school or returns to a well-known neighborhood in a city; these places become thresholds through which an individual may experience intense memories that become fleeting moments of returning, reexperiencing, remembering.

Stories about the self are always situated; they have a particular time and place.[50] People may find comfort in at least believing that the places to which they return are more or less unchanged, for they house experiences and memories from and about other times through their materiality and spatialities. Yet every return also includes those confusing and shocking moments when the places are not the same as the places so fondly remembered: the twenty-story-high building in one's mind is really only three stories high, the expansive wooded lake is actually a small pond, one's childhood hiding place is just a small bush. Equally shocking are those moments when a place from one's childhood memory is no longer there, like the neighborhood dairy in my hometown—with its small pasture, cows, and drive-through milk pickup under the giant plaster cow—that had become a parking lot and minimall when I returned home for a visit from college one summer. In these moments, the sense of time and decay is nostalgic, reminding us of our own lives: "'Oh yes, that's where the old cinema used to be,' we say, or 'do you remember, that's where those houses were all squatted, before they were pulled down.'"[51]

When people tell stories and fictions about their pasts, they also constitute places as significant contexts and as actors that define who they are and who they may become. Returns narrate time yet are not placed in time. Returns narrate self yet remind us that there are many selves. Elizabeth Wilson suggests that when one returns to a city in which one has lived for a long time or has often visited, that person is not only aware that he or she is returning to a place that has changed since last visited (for most know that cities are in continual change); one is also aware that one is returning as a different person. A person is someone else when returning but may want to remember what it was like to be the person that once lived in that city.[52] Visiting past places brings a sense of nostalgia for the past and for past selves.[53]

Sometimes, through the ritual of returning, one may experience a transformative moment and confront personal and social hauntings. This may be true when one returns to familiar place-times to which one has affective attachments but has neither experienced nor visited in person. Through memories of listening to stories of parents and grandparents, watching films, looking at old photographs, engaging or making art, or visiting places that have special personal or cultural meaning, people evoke social ghosts that communicate yet other people's past experiences. Those ghosts are familiar through the images and stories that circulate in the popular imagination as well as in families. Through these encounters, through these returns, the past is not defined by recollections of "firsthand" knowledge but rather creatively imagined through the reconstructions and repetitive viewings of images, stories, and other representations by second or later generations.

Marianne Hirsch and Andrea Liss use the term "postmemory" to indicate the process whereby knowledge about past events, and in particular violent pasts, is mediated through the circulation of representations of other people's memories in popular domains.[54] Second, third, and future generations may seek to bridge their experiential distance to an "empirical" past (History) through familiar images and stories and in the process may feel closer to that past or even their ancestors through imaginative space and postmemorial practice.[55] They may also embark on pilgrimages, sometimes to places that are social symbols of trauma for their cultural nation or contemporary era, such as Auschwitz or Hiroshima. They "return" to a place that is known to them through representation (popular films, narratives, family stories). Often individuals who go on a pilgrimage will upset the sacred image known through their imaginations, for the experience of visiting a place may disturb their ideal of what the place should be or, even worse, the emotional attachments they believe they should have in the presence of a sacred past/site haunted by ancestral ghosts. In the documentary film *Peace of Mind* coproduced by Israeli and Palestinian teens, for example, Bushra, a Palestinian woman living in a West Bank refugee camp, travels to what was once Iraq al-Manshiyya, the ancient homeland of her family's village.[56] Her family instructs her to "see everything," to visit the tomb of a holy man, and to bring back soil from this sacred place. The stories of village elders depict a rich and fruitful land, an imagined future for a Palestinian nation-state. Bushra travels to this place, now an Israeli neighborhood called Qiryat Gat, to find a deserted area and destroyed tomb. As she looks at the site not knowing how to respond, one of her film coproducers, an Israeli youth, awkwardly states, "At least it is still there." Past and present collide. This is not the homeland she had imagined. Bushra prays at the site and brings back the sacred soil for her family and elders but remains silent about her experiences.

Postmemorial returns like Bushra's are motivated by an intense desire to know who one is. But there are no answers. Nothing can be recovered because the past one attempts to visit is haunted by someone else's ghosts and secrets, even as those ghosts continue to haunt and define social spaces of belonging and attachment. Such returns are different from returns to places associated with personally experienced pasts, for the former is a quest to make a connection to past lives, and the latter (re)constitutes traumatic recall. In traumatic recall, individuals compulsively repeat acts, repress the memories of what happened, or create multiple stories of what happened to continue living an ordinary life in the present.[57] Being in a place where one experienced violent events may cause a person to relive memories of one's pasts, even if only for a moment. Rearticulating what happened through narrative form may be too difficult for some individuals due to the intensity of the event(s) experienced, such as the horrific events associated with the Holocaust.[58] In these instances, people may make places to supplant narrative and locate their loss. They return to emplace their traumatic memories of the past and relive part of that past as a little death in the present.[59]

These (post)memories and returns, created by and forming personal and social hauntings, are thus always spatially situated. As such the practices of place making may be one way that people work through trauma. As phenomenologist Edward Casey describes, "To be embodied is *ipso facto* to assume a particular perspective and position; it is to have not just a point of view but a *place* in which we are situated. It is to occupy a portion of space from out of which we both undergo given experiences and remember them."[60] Through performance and cultural reenactment, an individual may use his or her body to communicate memories of the past, to connect with the dead, to confront guilt or anger, and to work through past traumas in the present. Sonja Kuftinec, for example, describes how place-based theater in the war-torn and haunted streets of Mostar, Bosnia, has helped youth of different ethnic groups to work through fear, hate, and grief.[61] They theatrically enacted their memories of a place, their longings for a past that no longer exists, in the context of a conflict-ridden present. The actors and audiences of this theater had to confront their own realities of a haunted present by moving through divided territories and urban spaces to enact and witness the performance. Through these artistic sites, the performers and audience created new spaces through which to experience their pasts and remade personal attachments to the places they called home.

Individuals perform their identities in particular places and through their bodies; by acting, speaking, dressing, and interacting in certain ways at different locales, they cite who it is they are supposed to be.[62] In so doing they create bodies/places through which they experience, remember, and imagine the world, and through which they fashion an identity.[63] While each person is physically and socially embodied in distinct ways, through routine and repetitive actions a person situates himself or herself in social spaces. Through those repetitive acts, each may experience a reassuring (or distressing) fiction: it is the fiction of the self, that there is some coherent person underneath all of their confusing actions (past and present), that there is someone that remains at least in some respects more or less the same. It is a fiction, of course, because a person is always a different self with each return and with every performance, a self styled according to specific needs and the particular contexts of the present moment.

Memory-Work and the Politics of Memory

> As a professional planner, I know that you need a transparent and
> structured process of planning if you want to have results. This
> process has had to be open and inclusive of new findings. The
> debates [about the Holocaust Memorial] have to continue, and
> many people should participate in them. . . . This sensibility is
> especially important when memory is built, when cultural values
> are represented.
>
> —*Interview with Günter Schlusche, urban planner and Holocaust
> Memorial Foundation building coordinator, 2001*

Cultural practices of social memory take place and define a public space through which groups debate their understandings of the past and contemporary social relationships to that past. This planner emphasized that "memory is built," that its forms are negotiated rather than inherent to a place. To establish a memorial, for example, a society agrees to set aside a parcel of land, build a social site for ritual and tourism, sculpt an aesthetic form, name a place, and inscribe what and who is to be remembered and in whose name. This open and inclusive process in Berlin is, for Schlusche, not only a critical part of constituting the cultural and political meanings of a controversial place of memory (in this case, the Holocaust Memorial); it also creates a public realm, a "sensibility," that inscribes what a democratic nation and its citizens should be.

The legacies of National Socialism in contemporary Germany continue to be negotiated through parliamentary debate, media representations, public art competitions, tourism, and popular protest actions. This negotiated "politics of memory" (*Erinnerungspolitik*) narrates national and transnational belonging through the practices of foreign policy decisions, legal institutions, educational reform, party politics, and place making.[64] In this book, I focus on the establishment of public places of memory that call attention to the inherent contradictions of remembering the period of National Socialism, mourning the aftermath of the Holocaust, and claiming a democratic nation in the so-called land of the perpetrators. That these places of memory remain controversial years after reunification demonstrates just how politically fraught national imaginaries in Germany continue to be, despite—or more likely because of—the increasing temporal distance between contemporary German society and its National Socialist past. In his comments about the proposed Holocaust Memorial in Berlin, for example, Jerzy Halbersztadt, the director of the Museum of Polish Jews in Warsaw, stated that the memorial may have "national importance" but will not be critical for (international) Jewish memory because the historic sites of the Shoah are far more significant.[65] Halbersztadt reminds us that social memory and place-making activities tell us more about the people building a memorial than the peoples and pasts being commemorated.

Two social place-making practices in particular were critical to the establishment of all the places described in this book: public art competitions and citizen actions. In Germany, public art competitions are a venue through which federal and local officials, city elite, experts (historians, artists, art historians, and others), and citizens negotiate how to represent the histories and legacies of National Socialism and the Holocaust. The Association of Artists and Architects and other urban planning and architecture organizations formally administer these competitions, and expert juries evaluate the projects submitted by artists and architects.[66] These competitions are often expensive, take a long time, and are highly politicized. But they are also interpreted by many politicians, social groups, and citizens as an important part of the democratic process. In Berlin, when competitions are not held, people become suspicious of the political motives of a project, and media debates, public controversies, and popular protests often ensue.[67] During the 1970s and 1980s in West Berlin, a distinctive culture for public art competitions emerged: they were used to explore and discuss different possibilities for memorials as a type of place, and to rethink the possibilities of using art to create public spaces that would encourage residents and visitors to remember and question the past.[68]

Another way that the past was negotiated through the places discussed in this book was through the activist work of citizen groups, survivors' groups, human rights activists, historians, artists, politicians, and others. These groups and individuals called attention to the ways that political figures and elite normalized the histories of state-perpetrated violence after World War II. By the 1980s and 1990s, many grassroots initiatives remapped urban topographies and uncovered past terrains and pathways of power that had intentionally been silenced and forgotten by public officials. In Berlin, a number of individuals and social groups used landscape practices to communicate their understanding of the social responsibilities of being German in the present and future. Rather than deny or encrypt past losses, these citizen groups, artists, social groups, and politicians gave a form to what they called the "wounds" of their nation. They engaged in a critical process of *memory-work* by acknowledging what was forgotten, what was not seen, what was lost in the process of remembering and constructing the past.

Memory-work *(Erinnerungsarbeit)*, a term used by many memory experts with whom I spoke, is the process of working through the losses and trauma resulting from past national violence and imagining a better future through place. It is a powerful, albeit difficult, way to live with the ongoing presence of modernity's ghosts. Artists as well as citizens have made "haunting reminders" in their everyday settings to acknowledge their social responsibility for the past, as well as remember the remarkable lives that constitute their social world.[69] They make places to which they can return to confront

"The past can be dealt with only when the causes of the past are removed." Berlin, 1997.
Photograph courtesy of Karin Joggerst.

what it means to feel haunted as German citizens at the same time that they explore new possibilities for thinking about and representing national belonging in the future.

Two Moments—*die Wende*—and the Chapters to Come

> It was simply too painful to remember the significance of Berlin and its historic buildings following the war. . . . "Historic" buildings were removed to forget about the past and boxlike buildings were erected to reflect the modernism of the day. Now the reverse is true. People [today] are sad that so many buildings were destroyed and blown up during and after the war, and so historic preservation exists in an exaggerated form in Berlin.
>
> —*Interview with public relations staff member of German Historical Museum, 1991*

During times of political and social transition, taken-for-granted meanings and social functions of places may be questioned. As spatial and temporal contexts change, so do the possibilities for place making and memory-work. Two such moments of transition and social instability punctuate the place-making activities described in this book. The media, scholarly accounts, and citizens' everyday speech referred to these moments as *die Wende,* quite literally the change or turn. People would talk about their jobs, homes, or nation in terms of before or after the change (*vor* or *nach der Wende*) to indicate how different their everyday worlds and spaces became as a consequence of these ruptures.[70] Both transitions were accompanied by heated public debates about whether German national identity should be defined by contemporary acknowledgments of its responsibility for the Holocaust.

The first followed a period of social upheavals and violence in the Federal Republic of Germany (FRG or West Germany) and was accompanied by a switch from a liberal Social Democratic Party (SPD) to a neoconservative Christian Democratic Union (CDU) federal government administration headed by chancellor Helmut Kohl in the early 1980s. The second transition was German reunification in 1990. At the national and local scales, both moments were recognized as significant turning points that created new social spaces. These two moments of transition were defined by changes in international geopolitical relations. In response to *die Wende,* places of memory were proposed, remade, and questioned in ways that resulted in heated debates about belonging and citizenship in Berlin and Germany. Some people engaged in social returns to places and times where absences were previously entombed and pasts were selectively forgotten. Others made or proposed places as sites of resolution and redemption through which Germany could move toward a better future.

Although these transitions were relatively recent, they were premised on the changes that accompanied new social and geopolitical relations after World War II. In particular, the memory of Nazi crimes in the East legitimated the imposition of a second German dictatorship, whereas in the West, silence about the crimes of the Third Reich and German society was seen as necessary to establish a then fragile Western democracy.[71] Jeffrey Herf argues that it was not until the 1960s and 1970s, during a time of social upheaval in West Germany, that political leaders and a significant part of the population in the Federal Republic came to argue that more memory and justice (rather than silence) were needed to build a stable democracy. This shift in political and popular relationships to the National Socialist past in the FRG resulted in the first *Wende* or time of transition. In West Germany, the long period of instability from the 1960s to 1970s, resulting from environmental, cultural, and political crises, civil unrest, and even domestic terrorism, led to social anxiety about the future and a perceived lack of German national identity. A number of places of memory were established in the 1980s to provide a sense of stability and continuity, such as the museums and memorials proposed by conservatives and officials in Berlin and Bonn who wanted to provide a positive image of German identity for younger generations. New kinds of places were also created during the 1980s as grassroots movements and artists throughout West Germany confronted the history of National Socialism through progressive educational centers, history workshop movements, neighborhood tours, and more radical projects. This emerging decentralized form of social memory explicitly questioned the politics and legitimacy of national (centralized) places proposed by state and federal officials.[72]

In Berlin, the Topography of Terror was established in 1987 as a temporary exhibition, memorial site, and historic terrain located at the former Gestapo, SS, and Reich Security Service headquarters (chapters 3 and 4). It resulted from many years of intense debate, citizen initiative activism (at local, national, and international levels), and support by some politically left-leaning to liberal politicians, city elites, and historians. The Topography also opened at a time when there was interest and financial support for innovative cultural and historical programs in the city, and was one of many special projects and events celebrating Berlin's 750th anniversary. Although initially made as a temporary place of memory, the Topography of Terror became known as the "open wound of the city," a metaphor that reflects the history of activist memory-work and digging. This place embodies a decentralized culture of memory in its emphasis on the specificity of locale, commitment to a "postnational" politics, and insistence on returning to a traumatic national past in the spaces of a continuously interpreted present. Moreover, in contrast to defining citizens (or the public) as normal Europeans, the Topography of Terror represents Germany as a society of perpetrators. Through this site, the possibilities of a more democratic and humanitarian future are imagined.

The second transition, or *Wende,* was the collapse of the East-West geopolitical world system. The fall of the Berlin Wall in 1989 was quickly followed by unification, the establishment of Berlin as the national capital, and the relocation of the seat of government from Bonn to Berlin. Narratives of the self and of national belonging changed to accommodate the new territory, relative location, and political structures of the state. Because of Germany's divided history of working through the National Socialist past, after unification the legacy of two authoritarian regimes had to be confronted. Addressing these pasts meant returning to the so-called Jewish question. According to Herf, representations of the Holocaust in the two Germanys, and in particular of Jewish suffering, were tied explicitly to Cold War geopolitics that were in turn defined by selective restorations of anti- and non-Nazi traditions suppressed after 1933.[73] These hauntings were materialized in the very creation of the New Berlin (chapters 2 and 6); the building of new places of memory, such as realized and proposed Holocaust memorials (chapter 5) or the innovative Jewish Museum (chapter 6); the remaking of existing places of memory, including the Topography of Terror in the former West (chapter 4) and Sachsenhausen Memorial Museum just outside Berlin in the former East (chapter 6); and the relocation of these new and existing places of memory in urban, national, and international commemorative spaces through new trends in public commemoration, such as Berlin's nascent memory district (chapter 6).

The Memorial to the Murdered Jews of Europe (hereafter the Holocaust Memorial) is a place of memory in the center of a new postunification landscape (chapter 5). Yet it is a contested field of West German public memory that did not include much participation from East German citizens.[74] The debates about the memorial began before unification and continued after 1990 by predominantly West German citizen groups, politicians, memory experts, American and international experts, and representatives of the local and international Jewish community. Although a number of innovative artistic proposals were submitted through two public art competitions, the memorial design chosen reflects the project's history. It embodies aspects of West German public cultures of social memory, most notably the traditional *Mahnen* (admonishment) approach to national guilt that requires public ritual performances and aesthetic and emotive approaches of mourning for, and dismay toward, Jewish suffering in particular

(Betroffenheitskultur). To a lesser degree, it includes the more recent approach of confronting the past *(Aufarbeitung der Vergangenheit)* through its new educational center. It is also defined by a cosmopolitan understanding of Holocaust memory that represents a global moral order according to the categories of good and evil. Through its symbolic location and monumental size in the center of the new capital, the memorial is intended to show shame at the same time that it signals Germany's place as a democratic nation in a post–Cold War moral order.

By the late 1990s, this cosmopolitan Holocaust memory was given a new kind of visibility in the New Berlin through the emergence of a national memory district (chapter 6). The memory district will include the Jewish Museum, designed by Polish American architect Daniel Libeskind (who lived in Berlin for ten years and is now working on the World Trade Center site in New York); the Holocaust Memorial, designed by the American architect Peter Eisenman; and the future permanent center of the Topography of Terror, designed by the Swiss architect Peter Zumthor. While it is hard to know how the introduction of a memorial mall in the New Berlin will influence the existing national commemorative landscape, some experts are concerned that this new centralizing trend—which they associate with a global Holocaust industry and its easily consumed, popular representations of "the Holocaust"—will detract attention and cultural significance from the existing national decentralized network of authentic historic sites that emerged in the 1980s in West Germany. This network includes important sites of suffering and perpetration, such as Sachsenhausen Concentration Camp Memorial Museum, located just outside Berlin in the former East. For second- and third-generation educators, historians, directors, and citizen initiatives, such authentic historic sites are places where future generations should bear witness and confront the histories and consequences of National Socialism. The emergence of a memory district, as well as criticisms of it, raise important questions about the moral economies of (post)memory, authenticity, and Holocaust tourism at local, national, and international levels.

Hauntings: Stories and Images

> Before the conference started, early in the morning I went to the special court [at Auschwitz]. . . . When I arrived, the cleaning lady was wiping the windows and dusting the gas chamber. That was the first thing I saw. The second thing I saw was an elderly lady who was a survivor from the United States. She herself was not in Auschwitz, but lost most of her family there. I saw this woman standing in front of the crematorium and approaching the oven. You could literally see how something formed in her throat, how she couldn't breathe anymore. She gasped for air and then started crying. After she had cried she came closer to the ovens, touched them, looked through this hole, put her head in. She was no longer touching this oven as an instrument for murder, but touching it like

a shroud, like a thing that touched the dead in their last minutes of living.

You have this ambivalence in Israel and everywhere else where the context [of social memory] is dominated by the survivors. You have the ambivalence between the instrument of murder and the last thing of the beloved people. That is true for everything they exhibit in Washington [at the U.S. Holocaust Memorial Museum]. Somehow you have that ambivalence. [pause] But where shall that come from in Germany?

—Interview with Hanno Loewy, director of the Fritz Bauer Research Institute, 1993

The process of selectively calling forth the dead and the past through place is one way individuals and groups try to fill absence and represent loss in the present. To talk about ghosts means to interrogate the reasons people feel haunted, or even feel the need to be haunted, in the present. It means to take affect seriously as a part of politics of place making, memory, and social identity.

To represent these complex social relationships, I have written and organized the narratives, images, and spaces of this book in somewhat unconventional ways. Because my research and writing spanned roughly a decade of time (1992–2003), I did not want to create an artificial narrative coherence defined by an ethnographic present. My voice changes in this book in ways that reflect my shifting positionalities (as geographer, ethnographer, and humanities scholar; as student, "Frau Doktor," and tourist; as a young woman, American of German ethnic descent, and adopted Berliner) in the different times and places in which I lived, researched, and wrote this book.[75] I have also written the book in a way that I hope will make sense to scholars and students in various fields in the humanities and social sciences, as well as to memory experts and interested citizens. By attempting to speak to a broad audience, I wish also to question institutional academic and disciplinary boundaries that, while increasingly permeable, remain marked by distinct practices that legitimate certain narrative forms as "valid knowledge."

The structure of the book reflects and questions the process of ethnographic research. First there are the formal chapters, beginning with this introductory chapter, and followed by another about the context of this study: memory in the New Berlin (chapter 2). I then explore the case studies (chapters 3 through 6) and end with a discussion of the memory district in the New Berlin (chapter 6). Between these chapters, interlude pieces, which loosely take the form of fieldnotes, work to connect chapters, undermine the narratives and claims to authority I make, or introduce new case studies. They are set off in a different font; I ask the reader to interpret my experiences and the significance of the everyday, the mundane, through these fieldnotes. The images in this book, including photographs, advertisements, and maps, also represent place differently than do my formal narratives. I ask the reader to think about how these images and texts work (or not) as sites of ethnographic authority ("I was there"), visual data, and postmemories.

Engaging in a geo-ethnography means to take ghosts seriously as a contradiction of social life.[76] One must talk and listen to those individuals who wish to connect their actions, feelings, dreams, desires, and social relationships in some way to past worlds through place. For this reason, I distinguish my words from those of the people I worked with and interviewed—memory experts including historians, preservationists, urban planners, city marketers, museum and memorial directors and exhibition authors, artists and architects, politicians, representatives of various victim and survivor groups, citizen initiatives, residents, tourists—even though I recognize the uneven power relations that accompany the performances of researching, writing, and editing. These ethnographic texts, set off by quotes or a different font, work as both evidence and fragment, words offered to the reader to suggest the multiple and nuanced ways people struggle with, confront, deny, and celebrate being German citizens and residents of Berlin. Their words have haunted me, my research, and how I wrote and revised this book.[77]

The ghost is one way to make "the injustices of life walk amongst the living—a way of calling for justice."[78] Through the process of conducting my research and working with numerous individuals and groups, I have learned that it is important to take our hauntings seriously.[79] By following ghosts, I have perhaps overemphasized place-making activities that advance progressive political agendas in this book. Americans, as well as citizens from other countries, have a lot to learn from the German experience, particularly in the contemporary political context of renewed aggression that defines a world order through exclusion and fear. Unless we consciously remember the ways that absences constitute the (violent) histories of nations, there will always be a gap, a willed amnesia, inherited phantoms that will continue to haunt.

A Metro Stop

July 1997

I take the metro to the "world's largest urban renewal site" in the center of Berlin and arrive at an underground stop partially sealed off behind temporary metal and wooden structures. Naked lightbulbs dangle overhead. For years, trucks and helmeted workers have been laboring underground to reconnect old metro networks and create new ones. They are also making a five-mile tunnel through which trains, cars, and shoppers will circulate under this emerging city center.

I think of the stories that *Wessis* (West Germans) have told me about this place, when Potsdamer Platz was located in the GDR, and how they would pass through the station without stopping, only catching a hushed glimpse of border guards holding their leashed, muzzled German shepherds in one arm and rifles in another. It was the only way to traverse the "death strip" *(Todesstriefe),* the West German term for the area between the two Berlin Walls that was chemically treated, filled with land mines, and heavily guarded by dogs, lights, barbed wire, and guns. I also think of the hostile tone in people's voices whenever I ask why the Wall was removed so quickly; I assume *Wessis* feel this new Berlin will be better than the gray "island" (a term commonly used to describe West Berlin). No longer contained by Cold War division, the seductive promises of capitalism—its sparkling baubles and lustrous bodies—now spread beyond former boundaries and thrust skyward in architectonic displays of global power and wealth. The underground metal barriers seem to promise the anticipated pleasure and excitement of a future shimmering city, a "cosmopolitan" Berlin more like London, Paris, or New York.

My own memories and American presence define my experiences here. As I travel to this metro stop, I think of images of the city I have seen in history books and documentary films or imagined through novels. And therefore these construction tunnels

Checkpoint Charlie, 1992.

also evoke images of dystopian futures. The dim lights and underground settings for me trigger a strange nostalgia for 1970s and 1980s science fiction films that were defined by Cold War images of urban Armageddon, continual warfare, and destroyed worlds. Above ground, the nascent cityscape proclaims an American occupation of a different sort. Large buildings designed by Philip Johnson or the extra-wide security buffer demanded for the American Embassy (annexed from the space designated for the Holocaust Memorial) overwrite and wrap earlier American presences (from Weimar, World War II, the Cold War) as they create a new American facade for this aspirant global city *(Weltstadt)*. Hungry American tourists, perversely curious about Germany's spectacles and secrets, come to Berlin to experience the drama of modern history writ large (World War II, National Socialism, the Holocaust, the Cold War) "over there." Like me, they search for places that exist but are not marked, such as Hitler's driver's bunker, which was sealed shortly after it was discovered. They indulge in Cold War tourism and walk the path of the no longer standing Berlin Wall and make the pilgrimage to Checkpoint Charlie. Visiting Americans solemnly go to memorials out of a sense of duty, all the while never questioning how much of what they see in this city is haunted by American specters, of which they and I are part. We are all voyeurs here, the researcher, the tourist, the architect.

As I walk up the exit steps I stop. I am bombarded by the noise of a frenetic construction zone, the size of twenty-four football fields outside. Gigantic yellow mechanical limbs—a "forest of construction cranes" according to city marketing ads—lumber slowly day and night to erect the metal frames of the new city. Underneath these oversized arms, dump trucks and tractors move about like busy ants creating and

Checkpoint Charlie, 2002.

Potsdamer Platz, 1997.

relocating ponds, dirt piles, and iron rods. There, in the center of this moving landscape, stands a bright red oversized construction trailer propped atop silver struts:
the INFOBOX.[1] In this high-tech cabinet of technological curiosities, visitors play with
sound boxes, interactive models, and virtual reality simulations, hurling their bodies
and imaginations through Berlin's staged future landscapes. It is then, standing partially below ground and partially above on the exit steps of the Potsdamer Platz metro
station, that I realize I am in the city's Roman *mundus,* a site connecting the fertility
and hopes of a New Berlin with the buried traumas, tragedies, and social imaginaries
of new Berlins from the past.[2]

You are welcome to come into the construction sites. Daimler Benz/Debis, 2004.

2 | The New Berlin: From *Kiez* to *Kosmos*

Journal name: Wait a minute, was I really in Berlin?
Guide pen name: Mr. Wonka
Type of trip: Pleasure
Date created: 3/5/2003
Description: Nazis. Hitler. The Wall. These images have
                        always been what came to mind when thinking
                        of Berlin. But after spending a mere four days
                        in this vibrant city, I realized those dark days
                        are long gone, replaced by a cosmopolitan,
                        laid-back vibe that permeates every facet of
                        Berlin's infectious personality.
                        —*http://www.igougo.com/planning/journal.asp?JournalID=17895*

In the early 1900s, Siegfried Kracauer bemoaned the loss of streets, buildings, and a city that seemed to vanish before his eyes.[1] His nostalgic descriptions of the old Berlin portrayed corner stores that had disappeared, vistas that no longer existed, and his unease about the new Berlin (and Germany) to come. In the first decade of the twenty-first century, not many people would feel Kracauer's sense of sadness for the lost city, nor would they feel apprehensive about the future. While most would admit that the Berlin Republic is far from perfect, few would want the Cold War city back.

Shortly after reunification, city marketers described the city under construction as a stage on which the performance of the new city could be watched; by 2000 the New Berlin was represented as a spectacular architectural exhibition. City officials, real estate developers, planners, and marketers encouraged this way of visualizing the city through virtual reality shows, live displays at construction sites, and exhibitions of the hundreds of architectural models and sketches submitted for different renovation and construction competitions. Curious visitors and residents could visit a room-size white model of the existing and planned city to find out about newly built and planned urban blocks and districts.[2] Tours organized by a private-public marketing firm brought locals to the "behind-the-scenes" reality of construction sites to watch experts and construction workers finish innovatively designed buildings and new city centers, gentrify courtyards

[Tour of Isosaki Building, Potsdamer Platz, 1999.] We want
to bring the idea of Berlin into people's minds. . . . We
don't want to ignore them [Berlin residents] in our marketing concept. They should feel comfortable in their city.

—*Interview with spokesperson for Partners for Berlin, 2000* and blocks, and renovate nineteenth-century buildings in the historic district.[3] Called Schaustelle Berlin (Showcase Berlin), these tours represented Berlin "as the largest urban renewal construction site of Europe." For former Berlin mayor Eberhard Diepgen, through these tours, "Berliners and their guests have an unusual chance to participate in this exciting process of planning and construction. In front of the eyes of the public, a capital city that was once divided for decades grows freely together, the worksite of unification."[4]

Such representations of the New Berlin were juxtaposed with images of the city's past.[5] Planners celebrated the city's "second founding time," suggesting parallels to Berlin's first *Gründerzeit,* a time roughly beginning after the Franco-Prussian War and the establishment of the first unified German nation-state (1870), and ending sometime in the Weimar period of the 1920s. Advertisements for the new business centers at Potsdamer Platz similarly played with historic images to represent Berlin (again) as a turn-of-the-century "shock city." In the 1990s and after 2000, just as the visitor gazed at past Berlins depicted in historic photos, sketches, ruins, and buildings, so the future city was literally being built up around him or her.

These planning visions, marketing representations, and architectural fragments were sites through which the "new" was visualized. When removed from historical contexts and displayed in a city in transition, those sites appeared as exhibitions that displaced the present-past and recent-past from the representational frames of the contemporary city. The stagings of the new city were largely located at sites of former division or in the former East. The north–south stretch that formerly stood between the two

Tour of Neues Museum, Museum Island, Historic District, 1997.

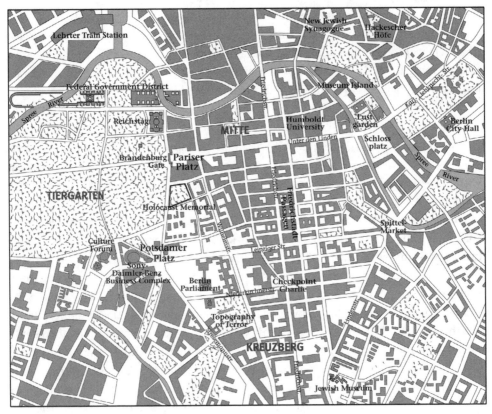

Central Berlin, 2002.

Berlin Walls in the center of the city, for example, has become the new fifty-hectare, $5 billion Potsdamer Platz business-entertainment center with buildings designed by internationally acclaimed architects such as Arata Isozaki, Rafael Moneo, and Richard Rogers. One sixteen-building complex was developed by Daimler-Benz/Debis and designed by Italian architect Renzo Piano; another large complex was developed by Sony to function as its European headquarters.[6] An estimated 100,000 people will walk along these privately owned streets and squares each day to work and play in offices, high-end apartments, cinemas, restaurants, indoor shopping malls, or attend cultural events at Marlene Dietrich Platz, but few may be aware of the history of past postwar division that too is part of this site. The only indication of a "former West" is the Cultural Forum (Kulturforum), originally designed by Hans Scharoun in 1956, which includes the golden-tiled Philharmonic concert hall, the state library (Staatsbibliothek) (where Wim Wenders's angels, who could walk through the city's walls, listened to the thoughts of anxious Berliners in *Wings of Desire*), and the Chamber Music Concert Hall.[7] The original designs of the forum were only recently completed with the addition of the new $140 million Gemäldegalerie (Painting Gallery), designed by Heinz Hilmer and Christoph Sattler, which displays European art from the thirteenth to eighteenth century.

Potsdamer Platz, 2000. "I am trying to understand why whole generations shaped by the violence of the long and dark years of pain, dictatorships, wars, bombing, and occupation, have the will to forget. . . . For somebody who comes from a different reality, the anger shown toward a city, which is guilty only of having been a silent witness and the innocent scene of a whole string of successive catastrophes, seems to be a crime. Today's last remaining rubble is equal to precious archaeological finds of the present" (Giorgio Muratore, "Forget Not Berlin," *StadtBauwelt* 154 [2002]: 48).

Just north of Potsdamer Platz stands the new federal belt. The historic Reichstag, once left empty in the former West as the promise of a unified Germany in the future, was renovated by Sir Norman Foster (for roughly $382 million) and is Germany's new parliamentary building. It anchors the new government quarter, close in size to the Washington Mall, which runs symbolically from west to east along the Spree River, the location of former division, where, along its former "Eastern" banks a Wall once stood. The nearby transportation hub at Lehrter Bahnhof to the north (in the former East) is also heralded as a unifying symbol; it will be Germany's largest train station and function as a gateway connecting the cardinal points of the new Germany and Europe.

To the east of the federal belt, once standing behind yet another Wall, is one of the city's historic icons: the Brandenburg Gate. A newly interpreted, and now open, historic Pariser Platz functions as a formal entrance into the historic part of the city. As one tourism company's Web page described,

> the pristine flower-beds and gushing fountains which fill historic
> Pariser Platz lend a touch of rural elegance to the urban jungle.
> Once known as "the Emperor's reception room," Pariser Platz

has been the first stop on visitors' itineraries since the 18th century. Located at the end of Berlin's grandiose boulevard, Unter
den Linden, wartime destruction left much of Pariser Platz flattened, with only the Brandenburg Gate left standing. Yet money
has flooded into Berlin since reunification and the square is being
slowly restored to its former splendour.[8]

The original rectangular form and building density of Pariser Platz has been reconstructed
with nostalgic yet modern reconstructions of historic buildings, such as Hotel Adlon, as
well as more contemporary (and inspired) postmodern structures, such as the Academy
of Arts designed by Frank Gehry.

Further east, the elegant baroque and neoclassical buildings and cultural institutions, opera houses, and universities that grace the grand boulevard of Unter den
Linden are also renovated and embellished. The $1 million renovation of the historic
Museumsinsel (Museum Island), now classified as one of UNESCO's World Heritage
sites, includes the restoration and modernization of five museums originally built between 1830 and 1930 (Alte Nationalgalerie, Altes Museum, Neues Museum, Pergamon Museum, and Bode Museum), which will be connected by underground walkways according
to the master plan designed by British architect David Chipperfield.[9] At the same time that
these buildings are being renovated in the historic district, architectural fragments from
Berlin's early royal past are displayed. Just across from the new/old Museum Island,
visitors will find the foundations of the historic City Palace (Stadtschloss), surrounded
by pictures, maps, and texts that describe the past royal residences of Brandenburg
margraves and electors, Prussian kings, and German emperors. A citizen and business
group has created this outdoor exhibit of Berlin's past as well as its imagined future, one
that would include a modern reconstructed palace with a historically accurate exterior
and a modern conference and cultural center inside.

The New Berlin's staging also includes a revitalized cultural scene in the former
Eastern residential district of Berlin-Mitte, now home to "Europe's SoHo," where "New
Berliners" frequent the district's numerous art galleries and institutions.[10] The new
Museum of Contemporary Art, for example, opened in 1996 in a renovated abandoned
railroad station, the Hamburger Bahnhof, and now displays major works by artists such
as Joseph Beuys, Anselm Kiefer, Andy Warhol, and Roy Lichtenstein. Artsy professionals
frequent the avant-garde galleries and architecture studios that have emerged in renovated historic residential blocks known as the Hackesche, Sophien, and Gips Höfe. These
turn-of-the-twentieth-century gentrified courtyards, with their trendy cafés, movie
theaters, galleries, bars, and entertainment blocks, provide a taste of the alternative art
scene for hip Berliners who consume and are consumed by the arrogant gaze of those
who enjoy this street-courtyard culture, reminiscent of both Greenwich Village and an
imagined cosmopolitan Berlin from the early 1900s. Even the dilapidated buildings of
Tacheles along Oranienburger Straße, the site of a postunification squatters movement,
is being gentrified by the Fundus Group and Johannishof Project Development Inc.
Previously, artists created courtyard "gardens" of refuse and mechanical art and made

City Palace, Historic District, 2000.

studios, exhibition galleries, and performance spaces from these buildings with no back walls. Spontaneous discos, film viewings, alternative events, and local bars also took place here. Soon it will become the city's first New Urbanism project, complete with a master plan by Miami-based Duany Plater Zyberk and Company. Located in the vicinity of the renovated Jewish Synagogue, the new Tacheles is being marketed as an "open ensemble of spaces, courtyards and streets" that will offer a mix of "traditional" architectural elements, retail outlets and restaurants, a "designer" five-star hotel, office space, apartments, and a series of courtyards run by the artists of Art Forum Tacheles.[11]

Other areas of reconstruction to the south include the historic shopping district along Friedrichstraße, where more than six thousand million German marks were invested since 1995 on 800,000 square meters of high-end retail and office space. The Friedrichstadtpassagen, a few blocks from Checkpoint Charlie, connects the new buildings (by O. M. Ungers, I. M. Pei, and Jean Nouvel) filled with luxury boutiques and office space connected by underground courtyards, shopping areas, a gallery, escalators, and bodies continuously in motion. Nearby, a building by Aldo Rossi presents a facade of differently sized and textured surfaces with ornaments from various epochs, behind which stands a single block-shaped building.

Berlin's contemporary city planners and marketers, like other urban professionals elsewhere, selectively borrowed urban forms and lifestyles of imagined past Berlins to "remember" a new global city for the future. Planners known as "critical reconstructionists," for example, argued that their job was to bring back the historic texture of the city that was destroyed by poor postwar urban design; they described their approach as the "counter-position to the urban landscape of the contemporary."[12] Through rigid

[Interior courtyard, Hackesche Höfe, 2000.] Other cities are completed; you know where everything is. Berlin is not a complete city
yet. In ten years probably I could show the finished product. We
want to say that Berlin is a large architectural exhibition. Each and
every year things change.
           —*Interview with spokesperson for Partners for Berlin, 2000*

planning guidelines based on nineteenth-century building facades and densities, planners intended to restore a unified vision of the authentic city. Marketers represented
the city as a spectacle and drew from images of Weimar cosmopolitanism. Such contemporary stagings of the New Berlin located Cold War and National Socialist Berlins
elsewhere, into the undesirable spaces of the "old" (often assumed to be in the former
East), or mapped as consumable objects in the spaces of global tourism.

   Nostalgias for the imagined "historic" royal city or the projections of a modern
world-class city *(Weltstadt)* revealed a strong dissatisfaction with, and anger toward,
the pasts embodied through National Socialist and Cold War Berlins that continued to
define Germany's place in the contemporary world even after unification. Planners'
disdain for the postwar period and its alleged destruction of the real city also suggested a desire to return to a dignified place and time, where Germany was no longer
a special case for modern European nation-states. Yet the very possibility for Berlin to
be created as new—in terms of material landscapes, economies, politics, and of course
through symbols—was itself a historical outcome of previous modern attempts (during
the Weimar, National Socialist, and Cold War periods) to reimagine the city as new,
and through those visions to stage national futures. These past desires and lingering

hopes for Germany's modernity are as important to the historic texture of the city as are Berlin's gentrified nineteenth-century courtyards or unearthed seventeenth-century ruins. Indeed, the persistent presence of the recent past in the city and in the minds of Berliners may explain why city elites and planners feel a need to remember the future in the ways that they do today.

Visions or prophecies of the Berlin that is yet to come—both historically and in the contemporary period—can be understood through a memory structure that Michael Perlman defines as "remembering the future." Psychologically, images of the future can only have a resonance with what appears to be familiar, with known experiences from the past and present. As Perlman describes,

> Images of past and present inevitably point to future possibilities. . . .
> If we recall and explore childhood memories, as in psychoanalysis,
> we see that these fantasies of the past speak too of what is and will
> be in our lives (including transformative possibilities), for we are
> remembering foundational complexes. So too with collective me-
> morial fantasies, which "present" the cultural psyche and its future
> possibilities. When we address remembrances of Hiroshima and
> Nagaski [or of Berlin], we will discover ways in which these images
> tell not only of the past but also of the present and (the imaginal
> presence of) the future.[13]

Through the act of recalling and situating the past through place-based images, the presence or endurance of imagined futures is made possible ontologically. Places are remembered in one's imagination, and through that memory the future is located in the past. Modernist utopian visions of society, the nation, and global power in Germany (and in other nations) have been staged through contemporary historic urban land-scapes and architectural fragments understood as standing for times gone by—and for times to come.[14]

Because Berlin represents the imaginal presence through which Germany's hopes for the future are performed, city planners, architects, and promoters have always played an important role in representing the nation through material and symbolic reconstruc-tions of the city. In the following sections, I explore past and contemporary visions of remembered new Berlins that narrate a history of national hopes for the future—desires that continue to haunt the spaces of the New Berlin today.

Past New Berlins: Politics, Architecture, and Urban Design

The ideal of a remembered new Berlin that symbolizes the nation-state and a modern German society is not new in the history of the city and has been tied to phases of eco-nomic reconstruction, political (re)representation, and symbolic and functional change. Berlin has changed many times and quite rapidly at different moments in time; it was al-ready marketed as a new, world-class European city of the twentieth century by the turn of the last century, if not earlier. Figures responsible for building the new city included officials, politicians, elites, planners, artists, and architects who believed that the forms, material presence, and representations of particular buildings and urban designs would communicate political ideals and worldviews. They also believed that by building a new city they could create a new society.

Hitler's New Berlin

The most dramatic and obvious example of remembering the future through Berlin is Hitler's fantasy of Germania. His idea for a new Berlin was to supersede ancient Rome and stand as a model of German supremacy for centuries to come:

> Nothing will be too good for the beautification of Berlin. . . . One will arrive there along wide avenues containing the Triumphal Arch, the Pantheon of the Army, the Square of the People—things to take your breath away! It's only thus that we shall succeed in eclipsing our only rival in the world, Rome. . . . Let [the center of the new Berlin] be built on such a scale that St. Peter's and its Square will seem like toys in comparison![15]

Hitler's national imaginings were given a form through the mythic past of the Roman Empire on which he based his grandiose plans for Berlin. By evoking Rome, Hitler wanted to remember a timeless, monumental city that would "outlast the centuries" and "speak to the posterity of our times."[16] Hitler's sketches for Berlin were translated through the designs, models, and buildings of court architects Albert Speer and Paul Ludwig Troost, among others, and indicated that he viewed these buildings as performances of his political project and the future Germany. The built environment was to represent the "purity" of the National Socialist state and its "people," which meant that "the style of its architecture would, by necessity, be classical—not only for the use of heroic forms, but because the Greeks and the Germans were racially linked."[17]

Contemporary accounts of Berlin's National Socialist architectural history tend to emphasize the monumental and fantastic visions Hitler had for the future. The most familiar image used is the designs for the Triumphal Arch or the Grand Hall located at one end of the planned *via triumphalis,* the vast north–south axis of the future city. The Grand Hall, for example, was to be so large—accommodating up to 180,000 people— that Albert Speer anticipated the problem of clouds forming beneath the vaulted ceilings of this massive structure. Such descriptions are perhaps pleasurable to imagine in the present day because they seem so unreal, so insane, and so dystopian. Scholars often use such historical evidence and imagery to encourage readers to visualize the "imperious nature of the Nazi state and the megalomania of its head."[18] Recent scholarship has demonstrated, however, that planned or existing monumental built environments do not provide much evidence of coherent political agendas or of a state's popular appeal. John Agnew's discussion about Benito Mussolini's Rome, for example, demonstrates how the aesthetic "overproduction" of monumental places under fascism denoted the regime's ideological incoherence.[19] Using monuments as evidence to understand the quest for power by elites also does little to interrogate critically the geographies established in their making. These include complex relations between cultural and economic systems, state institutions, and the social-spatial relations of power created through everyday routine.

While Hitler's writings are filled with metaphors of construction, these literary and theatrical stagings had material and social consequences. At the most mundane level, large areas of streets and buildings were demolished to make room for the new Berlin and its grandiose buildings, plazas, and boulevards. In terms of the larger infrastructure needed to build the city, new social and economic geographies were created and supported through social relations of slave labor and genocide. As Jan van Pelt has described, an important but understudied part of Nazi architecture and urban design was the regime's modern industrial projects and related systems of concentration, death, and work camps.[20] Building materials from nearby and distant quarries were brought to the capital city through the use of forced labor, such as the stones and tiles made by concentration camp inmates at Sachsenhausen just outside of Berlin that were sent to build Hitler's Germania.

Architecture, art, and urban design—elements contributing to the built environment—may not convey inherent political meaning but are often used to justify political needs in the present. The "glass and steel modernism" used in the construction of the Bundestag building in postwar Bonn under a democratic Federal Republic, for example, was also used in Mussolini's Casa del Fascio (House of Fascism) in Como, Italy.[21] In Bonn, "transparent" glass was understood as representing democracy, whereas in Como, it was a symbol of fascism, "a glass house into which everyone can peer."[22] The use of the built environment to justify political agendas was also an important part of the making of post–World War II new Berlins.

Cold War New Berlins

Plans and images for a new Berlin after the war reflected and contributed to fears that the legacies of National Socialism would continue to be part of Germany's future.[23] As early as 1947, fears of the past were encoded in competing urban-planning designs for a "new world class city" that demonstrated "the inner necessity, after . . . Auschwitz and Stalingrad, to completely redefine Berlin."[24] Although the vast destruction of the city during the war—including the loss of more than one-third of Berlin's housing and the presence of 75 million cubic meters of rubble in the city center—provided the material space to redesign the city, additional buildings and streets were intentionally destroyed to rid the city of any remnants of the "Nazi disease" and to create a new slate to build the future.[25]

Although both Germanys (founded in 1949) claimed to build a new city through a new architecture, how they interpreted the past to design Berlin was quite distinct. Deborah Howell-Ardila describes how the "eastern and western ideals for the 'city of tomorrow' diverged greatly in their approaches to historicism (such as classical ornament), the use of stone cladding, and the mixed-use city fabric (which combined living and work environments)."[26] Thus different forms and building materials were used to legitimate the political ideals of their respective new states. Each Germany pointed out those differences to assert that its "new city" broke from the fascist past, whereas the buildings and designs of the "Other Germany" reflected continuity with National Socialist ideology.

Howell-Ardila argues that urban landscapes functioned as rhetoric, providing the material appearance of having moved beyond the recent past toward a better future. In East Berlin, the construction of the neoclassical 2,300-meter Stalinallee (formerly Frankfurter Allee and now Karl-Marx-Allee) in the 1950s was a symbol of the "city of tomorrow."[27] Modeled after Moscow's Gorki Street, the grand boulevard of classical Greek proportions and mixed-use design was said to embrace local architectural traditions and adhere to socialist-realist tenets of urban design and the newly drafted "Sixteen Principles of Town Planning" (also known as the anti–Charter of Athens). The traditional city fabric was considered the "culturally richest form of settlement for community life"; neoclassical design was considered an appropriate model for the GDR because of its "origins" in the French Revolution (a misleading claim that Howell-Ardila argues was used by East German officials to restore selected imperial buildings).[28] In the words of the Socialist Unity Party's (SED) leader Walter Ulbricht, Berlin's historic structure and "monumental edifices" corresponded "to the significance of the capital."[29]

West German critics, in contrast, viewed the boulevard as "Speerish" rather than as expressing the "liberation of our people from Hitler's fascism."[30] Responding to the hype surrounding the Stalinallee, FRG chancellor Konrad Adenauer promoted a "Rebuilding Germany" campaign in 1954 that would clearly locate German cities in a Western tradition of modern, democratic architecture and open urban design.[31] Yet even this campaign was far from consistent within postwar West Germany, as Gavriel Rosenfeld demonstrates. In cities like West Berlin and Frankfurt, modern architecture and design were used to represent democracy, whereas in Frieburg or Nuremburg, officials advocated nineteenth-century traditional architecture to promote local agendas while distancing themselves from the National Socialist past.[32]

An example of the new modern German design in West Berlin was the Hansaviertel, comprised of high-rise buildings of glass, steel, and cement with no ornamentation, designed by architects Walter Gropius, Klaus Müller-Rehm, and Gerhard Siegmann. These buildings, according to the Hansaviertel designers Willy Kreuer and Gerhard Jobst (with coworker Wilhelm Schliesser), were to lie in "open naturalness" surrounded by "free areas" of lawn in contrast to "buildings designed for dictatorial needs."[33] They felt that the scale of their project, located at the edge of the Tiergarten, "spoke of a world class city *(Weldtstadt)*."[34] The new Hansaviertel was the showcase of the Interbau 1957 architectural exhibition and was considered the "most famous example of the NEW (West-) BERLIN of the 1950s established on the grounds of the nineteenth century city."[35] Not surprisingly, planners in East Berlin argued that the functionalist, capitalist, and imperialist international style of architecture at the Hansaviertel had much in common with National Socialist design.[36]

Perhaps the most important project that came to represent West Germany's new

Berlin was Hans Scharoun's Philharmonic Hall.[37] For Scharoun, no place in Berlin represented the presence of a *Weltstadt*; the new postwar open architecture had to "consider the meaning or significance for art in our space/area [in] the middle, between east and west, between north and south."[38] In 1956 he designed the Kulturforum (Cultural Forum), consisting of a major music hall, library, and arts museum, to stand in an "open" urban landscape—the antithesis to the uniform regularity of nineteenth-century Berlin.[39] According to Alan Balfour, Scharoun's vision for the future was heavily influenced by Martin Heidegger. Scharoun viewed the Kulturforum as a spiritual and "symbolic home of German music with the power to renew life and order at the center of devastation, to renew and yet reject the past history of this place."[40]

The bright gold tentlike building of the Philharmonie (completed in 1963) was the foundation stone of the Kulturforum that later included the Staatsbibliothek (1978), the Chamber Music Concert Hall (completed in 1987), and Gemäldegalerie in 1998. Scharoun designed the Philharmonie as a challenge to the "lurid theatricality of Nazi performance space" by creating a "revolutionary, democratic asymmetrical organicism."[41] Drawing from a range of pasts to imagine the future, his expressionistic design for the building blended socialist and naturalist ideals.[42] Although the orchestra and conductor visually stand in the middle of the hall, Sharoun wanted no segregation of "producers and consumers." Rather, he wanted a "community of listeners" (up to 2,200 people), who would sit in intimate, orchestra-sized sections that ascended in tiers around the central podium, to cocreate a musical experience with the performers.

Architecture and urban design, imagined pasts and remembered futures, are always interpreted by contemporary spatial, cultural, and temporal values. Although Scharoun's designs were intended to create a cultural center for a devastated city, by opening night the golden Philharmonie stood adjacent to the newly erected Wall and was interpreted as a political challenge to the GDR, now located at the borders of West Berlin. In the divided city, each Germany constructed objects, buildings, and spaces in opposition to its "Other."[43] These material and symbolic landscapes were, of course, a legacy of the National Socialist past, one that every postwar German administration has tried to normalize through geopolitical and cultural relations since 1945. The tension between the simultaneous renewal and rejection of the past, and the difficulties of remembering the future after National Socialism, continues to be central to the processes of place making and social memory in Berlin today.

Remembering the New Berlin: "From *Kiez* to *Kosmos*"

After unification, planners, architects, and city boosters sought again to create a new world-class European city. Their marketing and planning strategies have been rather similar to those pursued in many contemporary European and North American cities. As Linda McDowell describes for central London, for example, a new city was created and marketed through scenographic built environments designed by internationally known architects. Business practices were pursued to entice international investors that produced corporate landscapes of privatized public spaces.[44] New city spaces, buildings, and bodily performances were contrasted to the old London at the same time that they blurred traditional distinctions between work and leisure for international professional middle classes. Similarly, Berlin officials have pursued an economic development strategy to transform the city into a European service center through its architecture, new business and cultural centers, and marketing strategies, in particular for investors.[45]

The sheer scale of renewal and construction in Berlin after 1990, nonetheless, was unprecedented. According to one Debis public relations director, rebuilding Berlin's center was "an experiment of building an entirely new city from scratch, an experiment similar to and on the scale of Brasilia."[46] Similarly, Berlin's director of Building Affairs, Hans Stimmann, described the city as "the only place in the world where the center is empty."[47] Since 1990, hundreds of billions of dollars have been spent to renovate the once divided city and erect a new capital city for Germany.[48] In 1994 there were more than two thousand building sites, for which $25 billion was spent on construction investment alone. Development at this scale usually occurs not at city centers in Europe but rather at urban edges in new suburbs and edge cities, such as La Defense just outside Paris, a high-tech office high-rise complex connected to the metropolis through high-speed rail. Most major European cities have dense urban cores with landscapes reflecting their uneven growth from the thirteenth century to the twentieth. City and state ordinances have historically regulated land use and restricted building heights, and urban land markets have influenced the location, scale, and pace of development. But because of Berlin's particular and peculiar modern history—the attempts by National Socialists to create a new urban center through grandiose architecture, the physical destruction of those centers during World War II, and subsequent Cold War division, destruction, clearing, and rebuilding—the new city after 1990 was built largely at these central sites of former power and division, in addition to a growing suburban ring.

Berlin's postunification economic development strategy was also unusual because city officials had to create an economy from scratch. Using marketing and planning tools outside usual public-sector channels, local and federal governments encouraged private investment through nonpublic task forces that liquidated East German property to package sites for national and international real estate and commercial developers.[49] These developers typically build corporate high-rise centers in world cities offering mostly office space but may also include high-end apartments and shopping and entertainment districts.[50] City officials also hired city planners and marketers, two groups of urban experts directly involved in the capitalist real estate and development markets, to influence the production of Berlin's postunification material and symbolic landscapes.

Even though Berlin's planners and marketers both evoke historic images to imagine and represent the new city, they have different understandings of what the "new" means. Planners largely understand the "new" as a term that signifies the recent past, in particular the Cold War modernist "open-city" designs. They see their job as returning Berlin to its pre-1933 status as a classical European world city and do so by advocating a neotraditional approach to urban density and contemporary social and spatial relations. They, with marketers and city elite, promote the nostalgic concept of the *Kiez*: compact urban neighborhoods that have a European vitality and are defined by distinctive

Berlin architecture, density, and street design. Unlike planners, however, city marketers celebrate the new as a signifier for a better future. They represent the New Berlin as a cosmopolitan, open, youthful city using images and terms that allude to Weimar Berlin of the 1920s. They define "new" in normative terms, as a positive category of progressive modernity defined in opposition to "the old." Marketers feel their job is to create an image of the new city as a dynamic place to replace dominant images of the gray, Walled Cold War Berlin or the dark Nazi Berlin.

Neotraditional Critical Reconstruction

In 1991 the Berlin Senate created a new position called "city architect" and appointed Hans Stimmann to handpick expert commissions that judged the numerous architectural and development competitions in the city.[51] Stimmann exerted enormous power over the form of new emerging Berlin by advocating a planning approach of critical reconstruction, also known as "the new simplicity."[52] Critical reconstruction, or "a modern interpretation of the model of the European city," was first advanced during the 1980s in West Berlin by the International Building Exhibition movement (Internationale Bauausstellung). The IBA was created by a group of architects, planners, and historians who conducted research and "rediscovered" the urban ground plans and architectural heritage of the city, particularly in the nineteenth and twentieth centuries.[53] The goal of the IBA's critical reconstruction program was to "establish a dialogue between tradition and the modern . . . [to] find the contradictions of modernism not in a break, but in a development that remains visible over stages of place and time."[54] While postunification critical reconstructionists may have borrowed the IBA's technical, rational approaches and designs, they do not share in its social agendas.

City planners and architects today who promote a vision of contemporary Berlin as a traditional European city of the twenty-first century revived the traditional image of Berlin's historic "urban house," which they nostalgically called *Kiez*, a late-nineteenth-century term used to describe local neighborhoods typical to Berlin. The mixed-use, high-density block form of the *Kiez* was destroyed, according to contemporary planners, not only by World War II bombing and urban guerrilla warfare but also by poorly planned, rapidly constructed postwar urban redevelopment projects.[55] Critical reconstructionists therefore distinguish their vision of Berlin from postwar open-city designs, such as those for the Hansaviertel, that typically included high-rise modern buildings surrounded by open spaces and serviced by automobile transportation. According to Stimmann, postwar planners in West Berlin

> consciously declared war on the surviving texture of the city. They replaced the density of the old city with spatial disintegration. . . . The goal was to replace the old Berlin with its historical and political rejections with new images. As a consequence of the division of the city, Berlin became the showcase for ambitious urban planning and architectural competition between the [GDR

and FRG] systems, the protagonists of which in both east and west
felt themselves to be committed to the dictates of the modern, car-
friendly city.[56]

To maintain Berlin's traditional form and avoid the destruction of "the centre of
Berlin [as] a European metropolis," contemporary planners strictly regulate the materials, lot sizes, and forms of new developments; some new business centers and buildings,
including those at Potsdamer Platz, were approved before these planning ordinances
went into effect.[57] Because they view architecture as communicating the form of "the
historical city plan," critical reconstructionists in general reject deconstructionist and
postmodern forms, arguing that radically new designs have previously destroyed the
urban fabric of Berlin and would only add to the "aesthetic noise and chaos" of the contemporary city.[58] Instead they attempt to re-create these late-nineteenth-century urban
forms and spaces by enforcing rigid city block building and development restrictions.[59]
They define Berlin's traditional form through the "strict division between public streets,
squares and parks on [the] one hand and private lots on the other." New buildings are
required to maintain consistent frontage lines along streets and squares, use traditional
stone for their facades, and maintain block height restrictions of twenty-two meters to
the cornice and thirty meters to the ridge. To gain approval, new buildings developed
for office and retail space must also provide at least 20 percent of the overall floor area
for housing.[60] "The aim of the new development is the urban house on one lot; the maxi-
mum admissible lot size is the block."[61]

These strict regulations were based on "an extensive analysis of the existing and
historical traces" of the city. City planners developed a series of what they call "black
plans," or snapshots of built-up areas (represented by "footprints" of buildings) in
black—"irrespective of any other architectural or topographical differences"—and non-
built-up areas as white.[62] Stimmann argues that through these plans, "Berlin urban planning and architectural history, and by extension, an important part of German history,
can be read more easily than ever before."[63] The idea of the black plan originated with
postwar West Berlin IBA planners such as former critical reconstruction director Josef
Paul Kleihues, who argued that the ground plan was the "permanent gene structure
of the city" and communicated the "spiritual and cultural idea of the foundation of a
city . . . the 'fundamental' character of the place."[64] Similarly, Stimmann's black plans assume that Berlin's "spiritual" foundation can be read through its legible "gene structure"
and traceable "footprints."

The black plans, which have been drawn up for the entire Berlin inner-city area at
different historical moments, are a visual data bank for the planners and are considered
to be the "building memory" of city residents.[65] In exhibitions at planning conferences
and in published articles, for example, black plans are displayed next to historical photos
as a time sequence of the changing city. A special 2001 issue of *Foyer,* a planning and
marketing journal, reprinted a series of black-and-white photos from 1900 through the
1920s, the 1950s, and the present day. Below these images were black plans for Berlin
around 1940, 1953, 1989, and 2000. This time series communicated a narrative of loss.

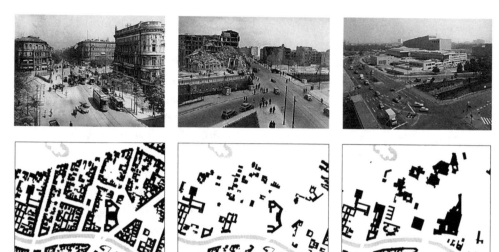

The black plans (*below*; *from left*, 1940, 1953, and 1989) depict "this process of extinguishing, the transformation of a historic city and the changes to its physiognomy" (Hans Stimmann, "The Texture of the City," *Foyer: Journal for Urban Development* [2000]: 10). Kulturforum black plans courtesy of Senatsverwaltung für Stadtentwicklung Berlin. The photographs *(above)* of Potsdamer Straße were taken in *(from left)* 1913, 1952, and 1979. Courtesy of Landesarchiv Berlin.

The first image depicted Berlin's "authentic" form and social life with a visually interesting photograph and a map filled with footprints of former buildings. With each subsequent pairing, the urban texture decreased, until the final map is represented as largely white "empty" space. The visual authority of maps and black-and-white photographs, understood as historical documents, demonstrates how Berlin became a "nonplace" during the Cold War: they record a history of loss. At the same time, these images legitimate the expertise of planners who claim they can return the city to its "natural" status as a world-class city through good urban design.

Critical reconstructionists interpret the city as a subject whose genetic structure and true essence can be observed and documented by the all-knowing expert. They also represent the city as an object, as a text that the city planner can and should edit: "the planner, urban developer and architect must, therefore, repeatedly revise his city, examine it for spelling mistakes, add a new chapter at some points, shorten other bits, read the text from the angle of social and political guidelines without however completely rewriting it."[66] These metaphors of the city have been commonly used in the history of European urban planning.[67] The city is an object located in Cartesian space that can be surveyed and mapped; its essence can be known through the objective and masculinist gaze of the expert planner who is both scientist and social visionary. The all-seeing urban expert surveys the city to find its true, natural form (such as through black plans and other historical documents) and carefully adjusts the buildings, streets, and urban elements (the text) to realize that ideal form.

The story of urban decline and renewal presented by Stimmann and other critical reconstructionists is also similar to more contemporary recovery myths typically found in European and American neotraditional planning narratives. The recovery myth follows the narrative structure of the Judeo-Christian story about the fall from the Garden of Eden and the promise of redemption through a return to "natural" states.[68] For example, royal Berlin, as the classical European city, fell from its civilized status during the "bad modern" Nazi and Cold War periods. After unification, the heroic planner promises to return the city (and the nation) to its dignified historic status and protect further destruction from happening in the future. Implicit to planners' claims to return the city to its "true" status are nostalgia for a lost city and fears about continued damage in a rapidly changing present.

Such a narrative about modern decline and contemporary redemption through past forms has been a defining part of neotraditional planning and social movements in the United States and United Kingdom since the 1980s.[69] Considered a set of conservative reactions to contemporary economic and social changes, neotraditionalism is a postmodern urban development typified by the search for past authentic forms to imagine better futures.[70] For neotraditionalists, the place of the modern "new" (as radically Other from the past) is not warm and comforting: it is mechanical, cold, militant, and impersonal. The modern new also signifies the loss of a more innocent age, of what is represented as the real self, home, or neighborhood (Kiez). Neotraditional planners blame modern urban designs, codes, and planning approaches, and high modernist international architecture for the destructive, alienating, chaotic, and environmentally unsound cities and landscapes that urban citizens currently live in.

That neotraditionalism should appear after unification in Berlin is not surprising. The end of the Cold War created a significant temporal break for Germany as a nation that allowed planners and other groups to search for usable pasts. In other countries, however, the modern city that neotraditionalists rejected was not part of a national inheritance of National Socialism. Contemporary neotraditionalism in Berlin indicates a hostile rejection of the Cold War city as well as anger toward the National Socialist past that always haunts the possibilities for remembering Berlin's future. The controversial "Architects' Debate" that erupted in 1993 demonstrates how central National Socialist history continues to be in defining acceptable or appropriate architecture and urban design in the city.

In these public controversies, critics called Stimmann and a small group of local officials the "Taste Dictators" because of the "authoritarian" manner in which their nostalgic ideals limited what would normally be a creative and democratic process of urban design and innovation.[71] Supporters of critical reconstruction rejected such vilification. Vittorio Magnago Lampugnani, for example, stated that a "provocative conventional architecture" inspired by archetypical models from the past was possible within the new city guidelines.[72] This new architecture, he argued, would provide precision and order for Berlin's residents in the face of a chaotic contemporary world and draw from classics such as Weimar Republic housing projects, the works of "heroes Le Corbusier, Gropius, and Mies" (who "rescued" architecture from late-nineteenth-century historic eclecticism), and even aspects of National Socialist architecture. While acknowledging its megalomaniacal classicism, Lampugnani argued that "the Nazis also produced an architecture of exceptionally solid, detailed buildings."[73] In response to Lampugnani's provocative article, a heated series of discussions ensued, with the so-called Chaotics labeling Lampugnani and other critical reconstructionists as reactionary conservatives and fascists, and the so-called Guardians of the Block defending themselves against such staunch criticisms. Architects like Hans Kollhof who supported critical reconstruction stated simply that using stones in Berlin didn't make a person a fascist. Further, he stated that the 1930s shouldn't be put off limits for contemporary inspiration, noting that many important European buildings were erected at that time.[74]

What was notable about these debates was not the titillating or moralistic use of the National Socialist past to gain authority for contemporary understandings of the city. Rather, what is surprising is that the debates did not revolve around the history of, and associated problems with, selectively using past urban forms to solve contemporary social problems. Neotraditionalists believe that modern interpretations of model historic cities offer a solution to contemporary social ills. But nineteenth-century urban forms also displace contemporary ways of knowing about and living in cities. As M. Christine Boyer describes, when architectural fragments that were originally built as expressions of nineteenth-century needs are manipulated for present uses and inserted into contemporary contexts, not only does the city feel distant, but new social problems may emerge.[75] The architectural critic Cengiz Bektas describes his response to a blending of facades and fragments in the New Berlin.

> Around Friedrichstraße, I get suspicious of anything that looks
> as if it were real. Just a couple of blocks from this underground
> "Passagen," I confront Aldo Rossi's last work. . . . As I entered one
> of the octagonal courtyards, I approached a wall that seemed to
> have been plastered with a technique used in the previous century.
> I knocked on it. From the hollow sound I could tell that there was
> nothing beneath this surface. No, this is not real plaster. Is it fake?
> This kind of "plaster" may have its virtues economically and in
> terms of insulation. But why should it look as if it was from the
> previous century?[76]

Not only do these fragments seem oddly placed and contrived as "traditions," but when past forms of the city are used to displace the recent past, they become problematic sites through which to imagine contemporary and future social relations. For Boyer,

> Engulfed and enframed by a set of new constraints forged in con
> temporary times, these fragments from the past appear denigrated
> by nostalgic sentiments that fuel their preservation or reconstruc
> tion, while our collective memory of public places seems under
> mined by historicist reconstructions. When juxtaposed against the
> contemporary city of disruption and disarray, the detached appear
> ance of these historically detailed compositions becomes even more
> exaggerated and attenuated.[77]

One of the few people who raised the problem of the contemporary meanings and forms of public space and citizens' rights to the city in the Architect's Debate was Daniel Libeskind. Libeskind, considered a Chaotic and a deconstructionist, yet also a respected figure in Berlin for his design of the Jewish Museum, stated that the early postunification rapid-development strategies were targeted for profits and did not consider the associated declines in the quality of life for city residents. He also argued that critical reconstruction would ultimately ruin the unique historical qualities of the city, including its divided legacy. Rather than rid the city of its Cold War past, he recommended leaving Potsdamer Platz as a large, abandoned field and advocated preserving some GDR buildings.[78] For Libeskind it made no sense to

> romanticize the past and become nostalgic for anything, either for the pre-unification of Berlin or some 19th century Berlin or some 1930s Berlin as the planners do. . . . History is not something you can just choose. We see it from all the people who have tried, usually dictators, and never succeeded. They choose a certain history, but it fails miserably because people need a reality. Making all these schemes in somebody else's stencil has not helped Berlin in my view and has not helped it to become a truly public city, with places where people can really sit and talk and where events can take place.[79]

Despite claims to save the city's building memory for its inhabitants, it is striking how infrequently residents appear in planners' representations of the city. Nor were local residents included in the actual process of planning and debate. In this respect, Stimmann's understandings of critical reconstruction break sharply from the progressive social goals of the IBA. While IBA practitioners may have also viewed the city as "ruined" and looked to the past for inspiration, they believed that local residents could "create possibilities of repairing part of the city" and identify "deficits of modern urban development."[80] For the "careful urban renewal" program in particular, IBA planners tried to include local residents in the planning process, an approach "based on collective democratic decisions, not on measures pushed through from 'above.'"[81] Critical reconstructionists today, however, justify the development of office space, hotels, department stores, and scenographic enclaves—rather than subsidized housing—because of the new economic and urban needs that accompanied unification.[82] And while the creation of a new economy was necessary, other pressing social needs, such as affordable housing, were ignored. While planners claim to return Berlin to its rightful European status, locals were not included in discussions about defining that postunification status. Many cannot even afford to live there.

As Libeskind suggests, imagining the city through an idealized, selective past is destructive to the range of meanings, times, and social spaces that make Berlin a unique and complex place. The city's historic texture emerges from ever-changing spaces, representations, economies, and political systems made and remade by people in the past and present. Berlin is a city of multiple modernities, each typified by different desires for the future, including the future-oriented (now hip retro) modernism of the Weimar period, the romantic and reactionary modernism of National Socialism, the socialist utopian modernism of the GDR, the Cold War capitalist modernisms of the FRG, and now post-modern neotraditionalism. There is no singular past that can be reclaimed by planners, for the past is continuously defined by and defines the city. Residents and visitors also deploy different pasts, narratives, and remembered futures to constitute the place and idea that is Berlin. By continuously remaking the past through everyday routines as well as through more dramatic material expressions, people live in, confront, and define their city in the present and future.

Marketing the Cosmopolitan New Berlin

A cultural icon of West Berlin is juxtaposed with one of the new. Scharoun's yellow sculptural Philharmonie is framed at dusk by images of an emerging Potsdamer Platz: a bluish glow of the Mercedes Benz neon icon sits atop a skyscraper, a construction crane looms in the background, and blurred traffic moves in the foreground. A banner on the building proclaims "Welcome, Sir Simon!" to indicate the cosmopolitan flair, creative genius, and youthful vitality of the New Berlin.[83] On the back of this postcard advertising the city, we read that Berlin "has 150 theaters, 880 choirs, 3 opera houses, 8 large orchestras, 160 museums, 200 galleries, and 260 exhibitions daily and an alternative scene that is always in motion and enables that motion."[84]

Advertising the New Berlin.

This advertisement is part of the New Berlin marketing campaign that began in 1998. *Das neue Berlin* was depicted as a capital city, creative city, cultural metropolis, "perfect place to live," and an East-West metropolis.[85] Throughout the city, bright red logos and posters promoted the new city through advertisements on billboards and magazines, promotional tours, and investors' newsletters; even the bodies of corporate sponsors wearing New Berlin lapel pins on their executive suits became walking advertisements for the city. The New Berlin was represented as a place of artists, youth, creative energy and experimentation, and a node of corporate savvy: "everything doesn't just happen anywhere but rather directly here."[86] As a cosmopolitan city, Berlin is a *Kosmos* (world) attracting people, ideas, and investments from other places.

The agency responsible for these images and the New Berlin marketing campaign is Partners for Berlin, founded in 1994 with the support of former Berlin mayor Eberhard Diepgen.[87] Partners for Berlin is subcontracted by the city-state of Berlin (Land Berlin) and is primarily financed by private corporate sponsors (the partners). In 2000, Partners received about DM 8 million from Berlin and DM 15 million from corporate sponsors in fees and material services, including transportation and advertising.[88] Rather than focus on one niche market, Partners markets the city to a diverse group that includes corporate investors, potential business owners and residents, locals, and tourists. Another goal is to change Berlin's old image by educating people about the material and functional changes of the new city. According to one Partners director, "someone has to communicate information about the new opportunities and the new city, and the old marketing organizations did not feel responsible for that. We inform people who are new to the city about the city. We have lots of information on the Internet, in brochures, and so on" (interview, 2000).

Given such a broad target audience, the concept of "new" makes sense. It can mean many different things but always creates a distance from negative images of the old city. For corporate investors, the New Berlin is represented as a global city of youthful bodies, flows of capital, and innovative ideas. In one ad, young, hip women (white corporate managers by day and exotic Asian cyborg designers by night) represent the beautiful surface of the "creative city" (through their bodies as well as the urban images they produce) and frame the "real" (economic) city inside: male managers, scientists, high-tech researchers, and executives making business deals.[89] In another ad, the New Berlin is described as the "perfect place to live," with an edgy avant-garde cultural scene, classical historical districts, flashy new architecture, sports centers, and numerous parks and waterways. This ad describes Berlin as a place where European peoples and pasts meet:

> Germany's largest city is open and cosmopolitan, allowing for
> every kind of life style. The inexhaustible urban diversity of
> Berlin makes for a quality of life that is particularly appealing.
> Berlin is rich in signs of its history and its present, in inner city
> landscapes and urban closeness, in big city life, and in peaceful
> places.[90]

The general marketing themes of the New Berlin campaign—an emphasis on the future, a good quality of life, and centrality (the city as gateway)—are common to post-industrial city makeovers in North America and Western Europe.[91] Such campaigns are intended to attract and retain investments, consumers, businesses, and residents. Yet Berlin's economic and geopolitical status is fundamentally different from other Western cities trying to renovate their image after a decline in manufacturing and heavy industries beginning in the late 1970s. By the late 1950s, West Berlin had already become postindustrial: companies left for safer investments elsewhere because of Cold War divisions. Both East and West Berlin were subsidized geopolitical showcases that emphasized high culture, shopping districts, and, in the West, an alternative scene. Berlin was largely isolated from larger global economic structural changes until 1990, when its subsidies were suddenly cut and the federal funds earmarked to help integrate the city proved to be only temporary.

The New Berlin marketing campaign intentionally distances contemporary images from dominant postwar images of division, economic decline, and isolation. In 2000 one Partners spokesperson, responding to my question "What's wrong with the 'old' Berlin?" stated that the prevalent images of the city for locals, tourists, and investors were negative, based on understandings of the Cold War city. She said that people think of the history of National Socialism, of the Wall that one couldn't pass through, and of division. When asked about the history of National Socialism in contemporary Berlin, she immediately mentioned the existence of the memory district in the center of the city (the Jewish Museum, the Holocaust Memorial, and the Topography of Terror), even though these places of memory were not part of Partners for Berlin's marketing campaigns. More important for city marketers was to replace the Cold War metaphor of Berlin as an island city *(Inselstadt),* an idea that evoked the walled city with no productive or innovative industry (with the exception of tobacco firms and coffee production) and few connections to the outside world. Immediately following unification, Berlin was often in the news as a result of its economic devastation, record unemployment rates, industry shutdowns in the former East, and technological problems with communication and travel. "No wonder no one wanted to invest in the city!" This consultant, while acknowledging economic problems, pointed out recent changes in that trend, noting the new economies related to the rise of smaller innovative companies in the information and communications, biotechnology, medical technology, and transportation sectors. In 1999 the major media and press firms moved from Bonn to Berlin with the German Parliament. In addition, during the mid- to late 1990s, before the collapse of the dot-com markets and the aftermath of September 11, 2001, start-up Internet firms also proliferated in Berlin.

Another way marketers downplayed Cold War images was by emphasizing the central status of Berlin as a European gateway and cosmopolitan city, evoking new Berlin marketing campaigns from the 1920s. In Weimar Berlin, just as today, marketers sought to promote Berlin as a world-class city on par with London, Paris, and New York; they represented the city as a modern metropolis, a cultural center, and a livable city.[92] The 1928 guidebook to the city, for example, described Berlin as

The *Weltstadt* [world-class city] of order and beauty,
the city of work,
the most active *Weltstadt* of the continent,
the European center of economics and transport,
the city of music and theater,
the great city of sport,
the metropolis with the most beautiful surroundings.[93]

City boosters at the time highlighted Berlin's cultural life, its museums, theaters, and concert halls, and its centers of alternative artistic creativity. Berlin was represented as a city of the future, illuminated by lights, moving with trains and trams, and sparkling with the display of shop facades, modern architectural forms, and female bodies. The guide also described Berlin's cosmopolitan stature through its different "foreign colonies," with foreign street names, restaurants, and places of entertainment, which offered visitors "a taste of the exotic."[94] The new Berlin was "the liveliest city in Europe," with a dynamic West End (around Kufürstendamm) and other areas that offered visitors an Americanized, youthful commercial center typified by its quick tempo and energetic nightlife.

Both Weimar and postunification city marketers promoted new Berlins through an ideal of cosmopolitanism and openness, and through sites of foreign encounters and Americanized youth and energy. Yet the futures to be remembered were fundamentally different because of the distinct pasts from which planners wished to depart and reject. Urban developers, city elites, officials, artists, politicians, and residents celebrated the world-class status of Berlin at the beginning of the twentieth century as a way of breaking sharply from their Prussian military and monarchical heritage. They wanted to forge an open, democratic, artistic, and commercial modern city. However, that break with the past was never entirely complete. City elites, while promoting the idea of the new Berlin, also wished to contain the new, as evidenced in debates over art and urban social life at the time. Paintings and writings about the rapidly modernizing Berlin published in *Der Sturm* after 1910 contributed to a new way of viewing and experiencing the city. The city was depicted as a restless, nervous place, and as a place in motion with circulating fashion, commerce, advertising, and bodies.[95]

Some authors and artists also expressed fears about the shadows and dark sides of the "city of lights," fears of the Other, and fears about the possible loss of social order. Marketing images of the new Berlin in the 1920s that claimed to combine the best of the United States and Europe distinguished the city from New York through its order and cleanliness. Unlike its American competitor, Berlin was neither socially nor architecturally chaotic. It was a city that maintained an elegant Wilhelmine presence. The cosmopolitan ideal of the new city meant that in practical terms, Jews were increasingly allowed to participate in and contribute to the secular sphere, but "in this Prussian city of the royal household . . . cosmopolitanism also lent itself to exploitation by those for whom terms like internationalism and alien art became racist code words."[96]

In contrast, postunification Berlin draws from the long-standing stable democracy of the FRG—which now includes a history of trying to work through two authoritarian regimes. Contemporary marketers reject the Cold War city to imagine the future and celebrate the new. Yet this diverse and cosmopolitan Berlin is not advertised through its well-established communities, such as Turkish and other immigrant communities. Rather, foreign ambassadors and educated professionals symbolize a particular foreign status and elite understanding of cosmopolitanism. According to Elizabeth Strom and Margit Mayer, the presence of privileged international people is a desirable form of diversity for well-paid professionals who work in the information, media, and service sectors and will come into contact with diplomats and foreign professionals when they shop at boutiques, eat at expensive restaurants, or attend cultural performances. Officials who pushed for the relocation of the national capital from Bonn to Berlin hoped that such a move would bring this corporate and international elite to the city. "Berlin's policy makers rushed to accommodate office builders not only to balance the budget, but because these developers promised to deliver the kind of city [and bodily presence] Berlin's elites long for: corporate, international, and clean."[97]

Memory in the New Berlin

Some scholars, like Peter Marcuse, are wary of the proud new buildings, rigid design codes, and establishment of the Holocaust Memorial, signs that he feels indicate a renascent German nationalism and anti-Semitism. Others, like Scott Campbell, point out that nostalgia for the lost city indicates a longing for a time when the Left had a clearer identity and agenda in Germany. The image of an edgy, polluted, corrupt, gray, and abandoned Berlin at the heart of the Cold War geopolitical conflict signified a time and place from which it was easier to identify capitalism and related evils.[98] These different responses to the New Berlin suggest that every "new" finds legitimation through what it excludes.[99] Given Berlin's history, the idea of the new is a complicated one, a temporal category that is used in distinct ways to realize political agendas in the present moment.

For planners and marketers in the contemporary city, the postwar past of 1945 to 1990—itself a temporal category defined by the legacy of 1933 to 1945—is a period that is rejected in favor of other pasts through which to remember the future city. These experts use the category "new" to distance the Cold War (and hence National Socialist) past from their visions of the future for different audiences. City planners, in their attempts to combine modern and traditional approaches, associate the new with postwar modernism and arrogant architecture. The neotraditional expert claims authority in planning circles by recovering the genetic code of Berlin through historical documents (the black plans) and strict design codes. Yet such an approach prevents public participation in the future city and may lead to the destruction of important landscapes of the recent past. In contrast, city marketers promote the New Berlin as a youthful city in motion, as an architectural stage on which the new city is performed. They wish to replace negative images associated with the walled city for investors and visitors by emphasizing Berlin's cosmopolitan heritage. Their marketing campaign is reminiscent of claims made in the late 1920s, such as those made by city councilor Walter Behrendt, who wrote an article entitled "Berlin Becomes Capital—Metropolis in the Heart of Europe." In the pages of a 1929 urban planning journal *The New Berlin*, Behrendt claimed that Berlin combined the best of European tradition with that of American modernity.[100]

Discussions about the proposed architecture for the new capital indicate that officials as well as many citizens are resentful about the expected humility that they believe outsiders think Germans should have for their future.[101] Many officials and boosters felt it was appropriate that the new federal buildings express "ambition and pride" rather than "the modest discretion of its former capital, Bonn."[102] One architectural adviser to former chancellor Helmut Kohl argued that German "citizens want their government to be located in a fixed place, not hidden in sackcloth and ashes. They want to be proud. . . . Perhaps not proud. But they don't want the government to have to creep away into any old mouse hole."[103] Similarly, Kohl's building minster stated, "We Germans must finally take off this tattered Cinderella's dress and find our way back to a healthy self-confidence."[104] The cultural editor of the popular national magazine *Der Spiegel* boldly proclaimed, "We should finally dare to be great again in our state architecture. The dream of representative buildings . . . is neither fascistic nor *Grossdeutsch*. It is as European as urban capitals like Vienna, Florence, Paris, London, Stockholm, and Berlin."[105] In response to these discussions, the cultural critic Jane Kramer aptly noted that Berliners continue to believe in architecture

> theologically, the way Paris believes in bread or Los Angeles
> believes in plastic surgeons. They live in a capital from which the
> worst of Germany's history was decreed, and now that the govern-
> ment is moving back to that capital they have convinced them-
> selves that the right buildings will somehow produce the right
> attitudes in the people inside them.[106]

Discussions about architecture in the new Berlin Republic foreshadowed, even created the possibility for, debates about the appropriateness of German patriotism. For perhaps the first time since 1945, there is a general sense that German nationalism is not a bad thing, a taboo category. The new German self-confidence stems from more than forty years of stable democracy and the critical role of its state in transnational organizations, such as the European Union and more recently the United Nations peacekeeping forces. Mainstream politicians now claim they "are proud to be German" despite recent anti-immigrant attacks and the use of this slogan by xenophobic right-wing parties.[107] In March 2001, for example, chancellor Gerhard Schröder declared himself "a German patriot, who is proud of his country," resulting in calls for his resignation. Guido Westerwelle, the general secretary of the Free Democratic Party, criticized German president Johannes Rau, who stated that Germans should be "glad" or "thankful," but not "proud," to be German. Westerwelle argued that "we must not allow neo-Nazis and skinheads to define what national pride is. We democrats, from conservatives to social democrats, must show pride in our country."[108]

My sense is that this (Western) search for defining national pride relates to conservative nostalgic impulses to restore the national capital to a time of grandeur, even if it is at the cost of ignoring citizens' needs in the present, including housing, jobs, and public spaces. Nostalgia of this sort is often motivated by a desire to replace apprehension about change in the present and future through the pleasures of remembering a known place in the past.[109] The contemporary search for the "essence" of Berlin and the hostility articulated toward the Cold War period, when understood as reactionary nostalgic impulses to control time through place, also indicate a desire to find a mythic, untarnished Germany. Nostalgia need not necessarily be reactionary, however. As Elizabeth Wilson suggests, it may be used to promote *awareness* and even ultimately acceptance that cities are always in a process of change,[110] that their spaces and times cannot be controlled by design, or their essence captured by maps, photographs, or advertisements. Urban nostalgia, as a process, as a reaction, as a kind of mapping of time onto place, for example, can be used constructively to help residents, urban experts, and scholars understand how normative (and sometimes negative) meanings of the "new" and "historic" city are created to pursue socially exclusionary nationalist agendas in the present based on utopian visions for the future.

Hostility toward the old city and the recent articulations of national pride suggest unresolved anger about the haunting presence of National Socialism even after reunification. These tensions between utopian hopes for the future and nostalgic desires to return to a golden age, between keeping some pasts buried while calling forth others, between wanting to feel proud of one's identity yet feeling angry at one's shame for national histories of violence, are central to the experience of modernity and national belonging. According to Rudy Koshar,

> modernity is the experience of growing asymmetry between
> dominant hope and marginalized but still resonant memory. . . .
> The nation has defined this asymmetry, seeking to control its more
> radical and unsettling effects and striving to make it explicable to
> subject populations through both force and aura.[111]

The contemporary staging of Berlin through architecture, urban design, and marketing images projects aspirations for a new, yet historic, cosmopolitan city, a European cultural center. It also proposes design solutions for a still lingering violent national past. Yet, as Jeff Kelley reminds us, the present is always littered with "anticipations of futures that never happened, and layered with the natural and social landscapes that happened instead—landscapes that are usually vernacular, subversive, and sometimes chaotic adaptations of a failed master plan."[112] As I explore in the following chapters, when remembered futures encrypt other pasts and social presences from the lived experience of the city, new social traumas may emerge. Rather than return to an idealized time to contain what feels like an unwieldy past and present, places can be made to confront the nation's multiple historical legacies, both positive and negative; through place, people may imagine different possibilities for national, social, and even transnational belonging in the future.

A Flyer

The Lustgarten, 1994–2000

One day, walking along Unter den Linden in the vicinity of the Museum Island, I picked up a flyer. It offered me what seemed to be an obvious choice: "How should the Lustgarten look?" it asked. "Like this?" (under which was a sketch for a city-approved redesign of a concrete garden). "Or would it be better like this?" (It showed a nineteenth-century photograph of a lush and stately garden.) On the back of the flyer, I could sign my name and send in a petition to Berlin's cultural affairs senator (at the time Peter Streider) to oppose the construction of a new concrete garden and support the historic reconstruction of the square.

In the midst of all the building and design controversies that embroiled Berlin in the 1990s, the future of the Lustgarten was hardly a concern for most Berliners. Although the Lustgarten was the site of two failed public architecture competitions, these were among hundreds of other mundane renovation projects. None of the media drama, public uproar, or accusatory debates accompanied those contests, unlike, for example, proposals to reconstruct the City Palace (Schloss) or tear down the GDR Palace of the Republic (just across the boulevard). Most city residents avoided the construction zones, cranes, and scaffolding in the former Eastern district of Berlin-Mitte, where the Lustgarten is located, and many would not have bothered to pick up this flyer if they had walked by. I always considered the Lustgarten to be an innocuous, if rather large, cement plaza.

So I wondered why the citizen group responsible for the flyer—Stadtbild Berlin, eV, or literally City Image of Berlin (formerly the Society for Historic Berlin)—would care about its restoration. The Lustgarten had many histories. Originally it was the kitchen garden for the City Palace in the seventeenth century; later it was transformed into a Prussian royal garden (complete with orangery and teahouse), and then into a parade

Lustgarten and Altes Museum, Historic District, 1994.

ground for Friedrich Wilhelm I. By the nineteenth century, a modified version of Karl Friedrich Schinkel's design for the plaza would set off the splendor of his neoclassical masterpiece, the Altes Museum. With the establishment of a memorial to Friedrich Wilhelm III, the Lustgarten plans changed again. In 1918 this space served as a site of political demonstrations. Paved with concrete and granite in 1935, it became a National Socialist military marching ground. Retaining this form after World War II, the Lustgarten was used for GDR military-political parades and as a meeting place for locals. Which of these Lustgartens did Stadtbild want restored?

Stadtbild offered me only two choices, of which one was "historical." The flyer suggested that they wanted to restore green space and fountains, build something regal rather than modern, create a Berlin without guilt: "We can't let the National Socialist configuration have the last word, nor do we need a parade grounds for the military in the classical middle [of the city]. . . . Historical renovation is not reactionary. They know that in Munich, where they have done a lot for their historical image."[1]

In 1998, the Lustgarten had become a construction zone.[2] Attached to a mesh wire construction fence were two historical photos, one of the nineteenth-century historic garden and one of the National Socialist parade ground in the 1930s, filled with soldiers. When this reconstructed Lustgarten was later finished, it was described in tour books as "the only public square alongside the water and one of the most beautiful in Berlin."[3] Yet it was not a "pure reconstruction"; this new, yet historic, Lustgarten was based on Schinkel's original nineteenth-century vision, not the Lustgarten that was actually built. Only a small commemorative stone, established during GDR times, noted the National Socialist history of the site.

Lustgarten, 1998.

In 2000, walking down the boulevard, I was relieved to see that the statues of Marx and Lenin were still standing near Alexanderplatz. They looked like historians, not revolutionaries, Western historic preservationists had reasoned, standing and sitting calmly, clutching their books rather than raising socialist clenched fists.

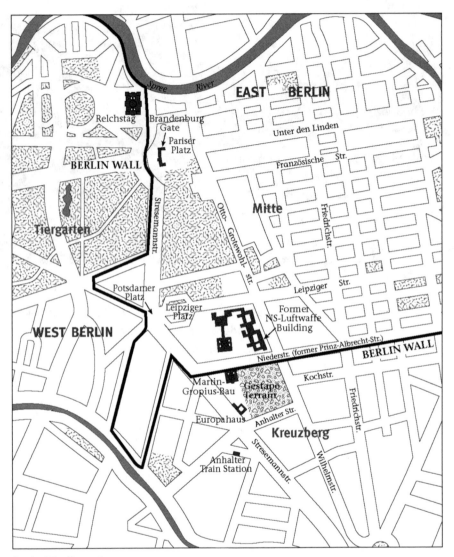

Central Berlin, 1969.

3 | The Gestapo Terrain: Landscape, Digging, Open Wounds

I n the 1970s, a crumbling and bombed-out shell of what used to be a grand neo-classical structure stood in the middle of abandoned fields filled with rubble and over-grown bushes. Known as the Martin Gropius Bau, this nineteenth-century building was located between Anhalter Straße, Stresemannstraße, Niederkirchnerstraße, and Wilhelmstraße, an area at the margins of West Berlin. A narrow stretch of barren land lay north of this building, between the West and East Berlin Walls. On either side of that patrolled chemical desert stood remnants of once ornate buildings from prewar years, a couple of modern, boxy buildings from the 1920s, and a solid, fortresslike building from the 1930s. The Martin Gropius Bau and these urban fields became the topic of a series of heated debates about national identity that began in the late 1970s and would continue well after reunification.

During the late 1970s and 1980s, urban renewal and historic preservation projects flourished in West Berlin and Germany as part of a larger popular "memory boom."[1] Officials proposed restoring the Martin Gropius Bau to create a new cultural center and in 1981 sponsored a well-attended exhibit, "Prussia: An Attempt at Reappraisal," as a trial run for the center. But specters from other pasts also lurked in these ruins. Architectural historians and architects involved in different urban renewal projects found that the buildings that had once stood adjacent to the Martin Gropius Bau were the former administrative headquarters of National Socialist power: this was where the so-called desktop perpetrators of the Nazi Gestapo (Secret State Police), SS (Schutzstaffel, or storm troopers), and SD (Sicherheitsdienst, or Security Service) had issued orders for genocide and managed the Nazi police state. Once this information was made public, a number of people became outraged that an exhibition about Prussia could be housed at this locale; protests were organized to pressure city officials to commemorate the memory of victims of Nazi persecution at this historic site.

Throughout most of the 1980s, numerous public debates took place about the future of this terrain and what should be built there (if anything). These discussions included a diverse group of participants, in terms of age, political leaning, and educational and professional background, who told a number of different stories about this landscape through formal documents (urban renewal plans, historical research), exhibitions, public events (formal debates, protest actions, art competitions), media representations, and personal recollections and conversation. Through their stories, individuals and groups negotiated their personal and social relationships to a difficult national history, enacted landscape practices, and in the process performed what it meant to be German. To borrow the words of John Berger, when they "saw" the landscape, they situated themselves in it.[2]

The discovery of this area was at the end of the 1970s. I can remember well . . . back then the Gropius building was under reconstruction—it was not in use. I remember going home and telling my parents that the Prussia exhibition I was wor king on would be displayed in the Gropius building; it was not called that then but the "ehemaliges Kunstgewerbemuseum" [former Museum

The Gestapo Terrain in West Berlin, 1981: empty fields, piles of rubble, parking lot, and tracks from the Autodrom. Buildings in background are in the GDR. Photograph courtesy of Margret Nissen/Stiftung Topographie des Terrors.

of Industrial Arts and Crafts]. Well, that was at Prinz-Albrecht-Straße, now called Niederkirchnerstraße. My mother, who had survived the Third Reich hiding in Berlin, said that this is one of the worst addresses in Berlin because that was where the Gestapo was. I became interested, and a couple of other people also tried to discover what was there because of the reconstruction of the building. This is how a group of people got together—I do not claim to have discovered this area—others did that at the same time or maybe a bit earlier. . . . Several people came together and formed a citizens' initiative that argued that when you reconstruct the Martin Gropius Bau, you cannot ignore the history of the adjacent places. You can see their work in connection with the larger move-ment of the Geschichtswerkstätten [history workshop movements] at the time—the slogan was "act, dig where you stand."
    —Interview with Andreas Nachama, historian, Berliner Festspiele GmbH, 1993[3]

By 1983 (the fiftieth commemorative year of the rise of National Socialism) there were vastly different understandings of this landscape being communicated in public realms. One journalist described this area as bizarre and liminal, consisting of

> hopeless mounds of an "earthworks salvage company" [located] on . . . the east side of the [Martin] Gropius Bau: the rubble is from the demolition of buildings [during the 1950s]. Next to it, on Wilhelmstraße—whose [northerly] course is interrupted by the Wall and is half-buried by undergrowth and bushes—is the playground of a license-free "Autodrom" [a field where people pay to drive cars around without a license]. . . . Ads of cigarettes on billboards stand atop a rotting fence, and the advertisement for the midnight show of a transvestite bar transports the Autodrom-drivers to another place.[4]

Citizen initiatives began to call this otherworldly place the "Gestapo Terrain" *(Gestapo Gelände)* to invoke the feared authority of a violent national past and the ghosts they felt haunted these ruins. For example, in public debates about the future of the site, two groups, the Active Museum of Resistance against Fascism in Berlin and the Berlin History Workshop, represented the deserted fields and rubble as a metaphor for the postwar German desire to forget. They argued that German officials allowed weeds, grass, debris, and Autodrom to cover this former headquarters of Nazi terror and thereby silence a violent national past. Other individuals saw this landscape as a site of a much-longer-standing national heritage. Some city officials, journalists, and elites who supported urban renewal projects in this district understood the Martin Gropius

Bau and its surroundings as embodying the rich history of the German nation, a history dating back to eighteenth-century royalty and to the first unified nation in the late nineteenth century.

When the debates about the future of this terrain appeared to come to a stalemate, groups like the Active Museum began to work with other activists, historians, artists, and politicians to communicate their view of this landscape as the contemporary debris of National Socialism and an inherited legacy of the German nation and of modernity to a larger public. They began to dig through the detritus. They excavated what it meant for them to be German and in the process began to articulate their understanding of "a society of perpetrators" through the materiality and metaphor of the abandoned landscape. Such a process of place making and memory-work is similar to Walter Benjamin's notion of digging, an embodied, ongoing repetitive performance in which the past and the present coincide through place. For Benjamin,

> He who wishes to approach his own buried past must act like a man who digs. . . . Facts of the matter are only deposits, layers which deliver only to the most meticulous examination what constitutes the true assets hidden within the inner earth: the images which, torn from all former contexts, stand—like ruins or torsos in the collector's gallery—as the treasures in the sober chambers of our belated insights. And, in order to dig successfully, a plan is certainly required. Yet just as indispensable is the spade's careful, probing penetration of the dark earthen realm; and he who only keeps the inventory of his finds, but not also this dark bliss of the finding itself, cheats himself of the best part. The unsuccessful search belongs to it just as fully as the fortunate search. This is why memory must not proceed by way of narrative, much less by way of reports, but must, rather, assay its spade, epically and rhapsodically in the most rigorous sense, in ever new places and, in the old ones, to delve into ever deeper layers.[5]

As these groups "delved into ever deeper layers," they unearthed feelings of anger, frustration, loss, rejection, mourning, and hope. Through the landscape, they envisioned creating a place of "active" memory that would reveal how the fascist state perpetrated crimes against humanity and document how a contemporary democratic state repressed that violent past. In the process they confronted their social hauntings and sought to create a space for their ghosts: this was a place to which they would continuously return, where they imagined future generations choosing also to confront inherited pasts and to forge a different nation.

After numerous years of citizen activism, public discussion, and city support, an entirely new type of place was made at this terrain called the Topography of Terror. The Topography of Terror was a compromise solution: it was part museum, with a historical exhibition (called a documentation) about the National Socialist and postwar history of the site; part memorial, commemorating those who died in the Gestapo prison cells and those who were murdered by the National Socialist state; part archaeological, with an open terrain of excavation sites and information placards; part educational, offering tours and seminars; and part meeting locale, becoming a central meeting point for political rallies. Initially built as a temporary exhibition for the city's larger 750th anniversary events of 1987, the Topography of Terror was so well received that it was left open indefinitely, and formal discussions for a permanent center were held in 1989.

Such place-making activities were not unique to West Berlin. By the late 1980s, the landscape practices of citizens, particularly those of the generation born shortly after the war, resulted in new environments, places of memory, and cultures of commemoration in the Federal Republic. The result of this memory-work would leave a permanent mark on Berlin's and Germany's social spaces, as a decentralized national network of historic sites, memorial museums, and public art began to give a material shape to the ways activists felt haunted by the past. Of these places, the Topography of Terror was one of the few that would become an established national institution. Today it is still described as the open wound of the city and nation, the zenith of a larger European web of historic sites of perpetration. While different groups and individuals will interpret this area in distinct ways, diverse publics now come to the Topography of Terror to visit a contemporary landscape haunted by the legacies of National Socialism. This chapter is a story about how such a place came into being.

Landscape as Palimpsest: Terrain Stories

In West Berlin during the late 1970s and early 1980s, city politicians, historians, architects, survivors' groups, citizen initiatives, and others "rediscovered" the Martin Gropius Bau and its surroundings by narrating landscape histories. Through these histories, they constructed the materiality of the landscape as evidence for (their interpretations of) the past and what should be understood as the contemporary heritage of the German nation. Landscape representations are often used by individuals and groups to frame contemporary claims to the past and communicate understandings of social identity.[6] Descriptions of material settings are often central to the narrative structure of stories, as both scenes that localize time, mood, and affect and as symbols of key turning events or relations between characters. Landscapes in this way signify social relations that take place in an unresolved future, such as multiple unfolding plots (often occurring simultaneously) or complex social and emotional interactions (of love, jealousy, anger) between the main characters of a story. The materiality of a landscape can also be narrated to represent place as an eyewitness to past events and social interactions, a silent figure that may nonetheless speak to other characters in the story. In this way landscapes become central characters in stories that symbolize the past as well as the future. Their presence may represent and renarrate different memories of times and places (that may collide in representational space), and their haunting imprints may enable people to enact their fears, hopes, and desires.

Several different "scripts" about the Martin Gropius Bau and its environs coexisted during the late 1970s and early 1980s. When heated debates emerged about how to interpret the materiality of this landscape, the social practices of different groups and individuals—including public debates, land use planning, public art competitions, historical maps, historic preservation, excavations, and media discussion—erased, overwrote, and performed existing and new understandings about the past and present. These landscape stories and material presences created and produced cross-temporal and spatial (re)inscriptions and (re)interpretations of belonging, written by people alive and formerly living.[7] No one landscape that was "seen" or represented was any less "real" or "historical" than any other. But because different groups claimed the same material site as evidence of their rendition of the past, intense debates and negotiations over the future use of this area ensued.

In this chapter I have reconstructed some of these preunification stories about this area to indicate the array of political and personal agendas that motivated people to narrate their understandings of past and future through the contemporary landscape in particular ways. Their conflicting stories resulted in place-making activities, both metaphorical and material, and framed particular understandings of the landscape according to political visions for the future.[8]

Urban Renewal and Beautifying the City

In 1978 the Berlin Senate voted to renovate the Martin Gropius Bau as part of their larger urban renewal strategy to beautify an otherwise gray city. The building is elegant and not overly grandiose, embodying the proportions and detail associated with neoclassical design of the late nineteenth century, when Germany first became a nation-state. The Senate's interest in urban renewal through historic preservation was rather typical at the time, growing from a larger national trend typified by a broad environmentalism. In the 1960s and 1970s, West Germans not only became concerned with the preservation of their forests but also wanted to safeguard the built environments of their *Heimat,* or home/nation. Artifacts, songs, ecosystems, neighborhoods, and buildings that were viewed as authentic or quintessentially German were classified as historic and preserved. The emergence of a Green political movement also reflected the array of possible meanings associated with the new environmentalism, a trend that included antigrowth socialists to liberal ecologists to conservative heritage fanatics.[9]

The Berlin Senate intended to establish a cultural center in the renovated building, a proposal that also reflected a pressing demographic problem. The city had a lopsided population age-structure: by the mid-1970s there were twice as many pensioners in Berlin than the average for the FRG. After 1970, many more young people began leaving West Berlin than arriving, contributing to a net out-migration of about 15,000 people a year (from 1970 to 1987).[10] Young professionals came on a so-called hardship posting to further their careers, escape the draft, or partake in the more radical student culture, but would often leave after a couple of years. One obvious reason people left was because of increased unemployment and poverty. After 1961, Berlin's economy diminished dramatically, capital investments continued to fall, and emigration to the West became a serious problem, even though the West German government subsidized more than 40 percent of West Berlin's budget in the 1970s. In addition to these economic problems, people stated that they left the city to escape the claustrophobia of living in an "island," an unattractive, walled gray city, with buildings still pockmarked by bullet holes from World War II.

Politicians, some journalists, and urban investors wanted to enhance the livability of the city by creating an aesthetically pleasing and attractive place to live through urban renewal and historic preservation. They also promoted Berlin as a cultural city, emphasizing its distinct economy based on creative exchange. Using images from the classical royal history of the city, the Weimar years, and the alternative postwar scene that had developed in West Berlin, these elites promoted the city as a place of culture and the arts and funded museums, theaters, and artistic venues. The restoration of the Martin Gropius Bau was part of this agenda, envisioned as a future center for fine arts, and creative and experimental artistic productions, and as a site for collaborative projects developed with other art institutions in the city. Renovation began in 1978 and was planned to be finished in time for Berlin's 750th anniversary celebration (in 1987). The 1981 "Prussia" exhibition that opened in the Martin Gropius Bau was considered a trial run for the center.

"Careful Urban Renewal": Discovering a Silenced History

While many people agreed that historic preservation would help make West Berlin a more desirable place to live, some groups felt that urban renewal should include the needs of local residents. In the late 1970s, the progressive International Exhibition of Construction and Design in Berlin (hereafter IBA), a group of historians, architects, planners, and other urban professionals, conducted what they called careful urban renewal that paid attention to the human scale in building and block design, and to local neighborhood history. When possible, they tried to incorporate local residents into the planning and design process. In the late 1970s, the IBA team conducted historical research about residential areas in need of urban renewal in Berlin, one of which was Kreuzberg, a district largely ignored by earlier city development plans because of its location in the "shadow" of the Wall on three sides.

In the process of examining zoning and land use maps from before and after the war, the IBA, with other architectural historians, claim to have "discovered" the National Socialist history of Kreuzberg and where the Martin Gropius Bau was situated. During the Third Reich, the central institutions of the National Socialist police and security state were headquartered there, along Prinz-Albrecht-Straße and Wilhelmstraße. Next door to the Martin Gropius Bau (then the Museum of Prehistory and Early History, originally built as the Museum of Industrial Arts and Crafts) was the former School of Industrial Arts and Crafts at Prinz-Albrecht-Straße 8. This building became the most feared address in the city and throughout Germany, housing the administrative headquarters of the Gestapo, including its notorious house prison, the Reich's director of the SS, and the Reich Security Service Main Office (Reichssicherheitshauptamt). At

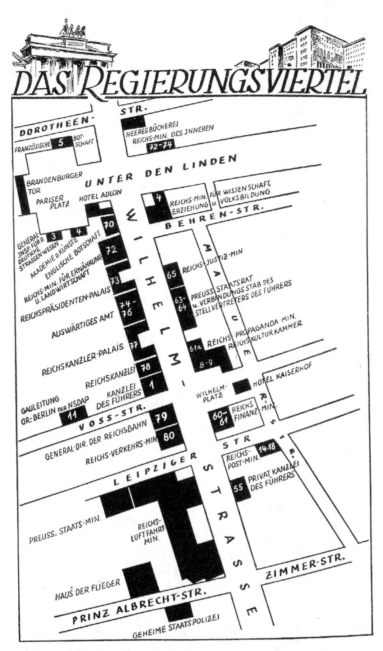

[The National Socialist Government Quarter of Berlin, 1936.] City maps produced during the Third Reich clearly indicated where the National Socialist government district was located, along Wilhelmstraße, and included the exact location of the Gestapo headquarters—even though it was the "Secret" Police. These maps were made perhaps intentionally to create fear in the minds of residents and visitors.

—Frank Dingel, *Topography of Terror guided tour,* 1993

Prinz-Albrecht-Straße 9 was the Hotel Prinz Albrecht, where Heinrich Himmler, the "inspector" of the Gestapo and the SS, relocated his administrative branches from Munich. Reinhard Heydrich and the Sicherheitsdienst (SD) of the SS Reich leadership were located in the neighboring Prinz-Albrecht-Palais (at Wilhelmstraße 102).[11] From these buildings, the National Socialist leadership coordinated and ordered the genocide of European Jews, the persecution of political opponents, the murder of Soviet prisoners of war, and the "Germanization" of occupied territories in Poland and the Soviet Union. This was where the Wannsee Conference was organized and where the secret police units *(Einsatzgruppen)* were assembled.[12]

The IBA team also found existing city plans for an expressway that would cut across this historical terrain scheduled for construction in 1980. The plans for the expressway dated to the late 1950s, when most of the buildings in the area were destroyed (or designated for removal). After the war, planners and architects proposed modern functionalist designs and new uses for city centers, including this former Nazi seat of government. First, a modern heliport was proposed at the site, and then a 1957 urban renewal contest, Capital Berlin, was held. At the time, urban experts and politicians did not anticipate the escalation of an emerging East–West conflict and included both the American and Soviet occupation sectors in competition guidelines. The winning plan for the Capital Berlin competition proposed a new transportation hub in the city

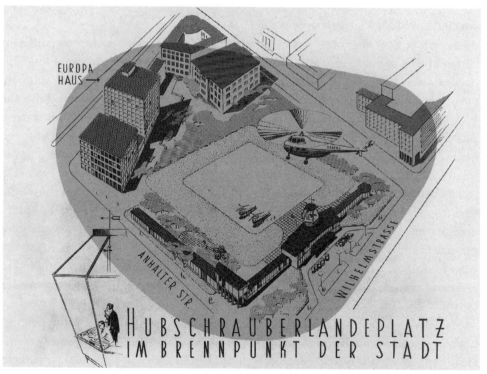

The Capital Berlin public competition was a "spiritual task . . . to fashion the center in such a way that it will become a visible expression of Germany's capital and that of a modern metropolis" (Capital Berlin contest invitation, City of Berlin, 1957). Courtesy of Stiftung Topographie des Terrors.

center, with a modern network of expressways and *Autobahns* connecting different city sectors. This technical-rational approach to urban space was defined by the then dominant economic discourse of recovery and future growth: the area was seen as an empty container in space and time that planners could efficiently design to build a modern city. With the erection of the Berlin Wall in 1961, these visions for the city were postponed but in 1965 were incorporated into a municipal land use plan that projected a construction date of 1980.

The IBA team began to publicize the forgotten history of this area just as the Berlin Senate began renovating the Martin Gropius Bau. In 1978, at the "Do-Nothing Congress" meeting of Berlin environmentalists and anarchists, architectural historian Dieter Hoffman-Axthelm offered a guided tour of the history of National Socialism in the area. He argued that this place could not be used in the present day for everyday activities because it was an "antisite," a material reminder of the perpetration of Nazi crimes. The IBA also protested the plans for the expressway. Although it was unclear if the land use plans from the 1950s and 1960s were actively part of the city planning goals in the late 1970s or simply overlooked, the IBA team and other concerned citizens protested the use of modern zoning to repress and overwrite the area's history. They demanded that public officials rethink their relationship to the National Socialist past by acknowledging the political uses of legal and planning documents.

Haunted Landscapes: Calls for a Memorial

As a result of IBA efforts to draw public attention to the history of the area, different citizen groups began to organize demonstrations in 1980 and 1981. Many of these individuals were survivors and human rights advocates of an older generation who were politically affiliated with a radical antifascist to left stance. They were outraged that the Prussia exhibition could open in a building adjacent to the former Gestapo headquarters without acknowledging the National Socialist history of the area. In a 1980 letter to the Berlin senator of internal affairs, E. M. Koneffke of the Anti-fascist Committee of the International League for Human Rights wrote, "When in 1981 old historic Prussia is commemorated with considerable public display, who will then remember those who were degraded and insulted and were made to suffer untold torments within the immediate neighborhood?"[13] These activists felt a sense of obligation to give those who were persecuted and murdered a place of honor. They called for a memorial to be built in 1980 to lay the forgotten dead to rest respectfully, indicating their understanding of this place as a cemetery haunted by the ghosts of those who had suffered and been forgotten after the war.[14]

As individuals and social groups began to mark this history through signs, descriptions, and other symbolic means, they began to associate their political and personal identities with the landscape. Some were outspoken in their call to build a permanent memorial to honor and acknowledge those who had suffered at the site. A member of the Association of Persecuted Social Democrats (Arbeitsgemeinschaft Verfolgter Sozialdemokraten, or AVS), an international survivors' group, wrote to the Berlin senator of construction and housing in 1980, stating that "the Social Democratic resistance fighters and victims of the Nazi Regime expect that at the spot where the ruin of the Prinz-Albrecht-Palais once stood, i.e., the site where the Gestapo had its headquarters and tortured people, a dignified memorial be put up in remembrance of the National Socialist reign of terror."[15] These activists proposed a memorial (Mahnmal) for the victims of fascism who suffered at the site. Their understanding of a memorial was a place of mourning and public admonishment, a site that would acknowledge the consequences of National Socialist history in the present day. Their views of German society, this landscape, and the future of the area came into sharp contrast with opinions held by some city elites.

A Royal National Heritage: Calls for a Museum

Although a number of social groups began to call for a memorial in 1980, the move to establish a history museum in West Berlin—which had first been voiced in the early 1970s—became quite strong after the success of the Prussia exhibit.[16] So much so that, in 1981, West Berlin mayor Richard von Weizsäcker organized a commission of historians and experts to look for an appropriate building for such a museum. The commission recommended the Martin Gropius Bau, explaining in 1982 that the building "occupies the center of the old capital, [and is] surrounded by the cities of Prussian history, of Reich history, and of the Third Reich, directly located on the Wall. Nowhere else is the connection of the museum to German history so meaningfully ascertainable than here."[17] Von Weizsäcker, in response to citizen calls for a memorial at the site, argued that a large memorial at this locale would do little to remember the complex national history of the area, including the history of National Socialism. A museum, in his view, would be an especially appropriate type of place for the Martin Gropius Bau and this residential district that had a rich history dating back to the seventeenth century.[18]

Museum supporters included public officials, city elites, historians, and conservatives from an older generation who emphasized the longer-standing history of this area in public debates.[19] This residential district was once southern Friedrichstadt, established in 1690 and part of the royal residence since 1710.[20] At the time, Friedrich Wilhelm I commissioned city planners to extend the existing Friedrichstadt district and establish a street pattern of three main thoroughfares (Wilhelmstraße, Friedrichstraße, and Lindenstraße) running north to south and meeting at the Hallesches Tor.[21] By the 1730s, many aristocratic palaces or mansions (Palais) were located in northern Friedrichstadt, including one built on southern Wilhelmstraße by Baron Vernezobre de Laurieux in 1737. The baron's mansion was later acquired in 1830 by Prince Albrecht of Prussia (son of Friedrich Wilhelm III), who had it remodeled by the renowned Berlin architect Karl Friedrich Schinkel. When the German nation-state was established and Berlin became the national capital in 1871, many of these palaces and mansions were used as government buildings.

With the exception of the elaborate Prinz-Albrecht-Palais, however, southern Friedrichstadt was considered a working-class part of the city settled by Bohemian immigrants.

As Berlin grew and new public transportation systems and networks developed, southern Friedrichstadt soon became a new center just south of bustling Potsdamer Platz. The completion of the architecturally innovative entrance hall to the Anhalter Bahnhof in 1880 and the new hotels built in the vicinity,[22] including the elaborate Hotel Prinz Albrecht, attracted both visiting tourists and government dignitaries. After 1880, southern Friedrichstadt also became known for its new museums and government buildings, forming a new cultural district in the national capital. The Martin Gropius Bau, designed and built by Martin Gropius and Heino Schmieden between 1877 and 1881, was originally called the Museum of Industrial Arts and Crafts and became an important building in this emerging national district. Its presence signaled a high quality of German artistic production and an internationally competitive applied arts industry. In 1886 the Museum for Ethnology opened next door, exhibiting objects from distant and more "primitive" cultures acquired in the first German colonies. In 1905 the School for Industrial Arts and Crafts was built on the other side of the Museum of Industrial Arts and Crafts to accommodate the museum's growth and provide classroom and library space. With these three buildings, southern Friedrichstadt was transformed into a new museum district, second only to the museum island located on Unter den Linden along the Spree River. These modern institutions were symbols of the greatness of the new German nation-state and its status as a European colonial power.

With the inauguration of the Prussian Chamber of Deputies in 1889 just north of this

School of Industrial Arts and Crafts, Prinz-Albrecht-Straße 8, Berlin, 1932. Photograph courtesy of SV-Bilderdienst, DIZ München GmbH.

museum district, a modern government quarter was also established nearby. In southern Friedrichstadt, revolutionary rallies, demonstrations, and important elections of the early twentieth century took place. The German Communist Party was founded in the Prussian Chamber of Deputies from 1918 to 1919 (just north of the Martin Gropius Bau), resulting in bloody fighting shortly thereafter. Other changes soon transpired. In the mid-1920s, the Museum of Industrial Arts and Crafts moved out of the Martin Gropius Bau and into the City Palace on Unter den Linden; the Museum of Prehistory and Early History became the new occupant of the building. The School of Industrial Arts and Crafts relocated to the Academy of Fine Arts in Charlottenburg, to be replaced by the State Library for the Arts and a private firm.[23] Part of the nearby Prinz-Albrecht-Palais was sold; the modern Europahaus was built from 1926 to 1931. In 1932, Hitler, Goebbels, and National Socialist delegates frequently began using the Hotel Prinz Albrecht for their rallies and meetings and later used the former School of Industrial Arts and Crafts and the Museum of Prehistory for their state security and police operations.

During the later years of the war, the National Socialist government district became an important target for the Allies, and much of the area was heavily bombed and destroyed in April and May of 1944. After World War II, the Allied powers drew a new political map of the city, dividing the former administrative center of the National Socialist state—and the historic district of southern Friedrichstadt—into two districts. To the north, Berlin-Center (Mitte) was designated as the Soviet sector, and to its south, Berlin-Kreuzberg was designated as the American sector. With the further partitioning of Berlin's municipal administrations, the beginnings of an East–West confrontation and the Cold War become apparent. In 1961 the Berlin Wall was erected.

Considering this complex national history and the cultural heritage of this former museum island, it was not surprising that the group of historians and experts commissioned by the Berlin mayor suggested the Martin Gropius Bau for a history museum. Few eighteenth- or nineteenth-century buildings existed in West Berlin, limiting the possibility of locating the museum in a historic structure. Further, because the Martin Gropius Bau had originally been designed as a museum, it had naturally lit, spacious interior rooms for exhibitions, unlike other buildings under consideration, such as the Reichstag.

Other individuals, including survivors, historians, and activists, however, were to argue that the creation of a national history museum would continue to disregard the memory of those who suffered from the criminal actions of the National Socialist state. They argued that because the Nazi past had been ignored after the war, proclaiming the rich heritage of the nation at this historic site would constitute another form of denial. They continued to push for a memorial.

Forgetful Postwar Landscapes

At a public hearing sponsored by the Academy of Arts about the future of the Martin Gropius Bau in 1983, Roland Stelter recalled standing in front of the rubble of the former Gestapo building after the war as a child. Only later did he find out what had actually happened in that building. He stated that "one cannot so easily, when one speaks about a Museum for German History, move away [from the reality of] where this Gropius-Bau stands: namely, right next to the prison cells where witnesses were persecuted during this time, many of whom are still living."[24]

Stelter's personal memories indicate a sense of belated guilt after learning about the violence of this place and his anger about contemporary proposals for museums that might continue to silence this landscape and the memory of those who suffered. At this site, activists felt the need to honor their memory; they also wanted to research the National Socialist history of the area, and document the postwar erasures that resulted in a contemporary landscape of abandoned fields. Citizen groups and IBA activists pointed out how contemporary land uses, such as parking lots, building reclamation uses, or proposed museums, covered up the presence of a lingering National Socialist past and offered another kind of material evidence of official attempts to forget.[25]

Rubble. Overgrown fields. Debris. Attempts to rid the city of the Nazi presence at the terrain began shortly after the war, when southern Friedrichstadt was divided into Soviet and American occupation zones. Streets were renamed to reflect the ideologies of the occupying troops, and many buildings were destroyed.[26] Western Allies, in particular Americans, supported this utilitarian approach of destruction to deal with the past. The more horrific reminders of the Third Reich, such as at concentration camps like Dachau, were razed in the American sectors during the 1950s to "avert the spread of disease." Even after the area was transferred to German authorities, material remnants of National Socialism were destroyed, and the recent past was represented in ways that did not trouble citizens.[27]

Most of the buildings along Prinz-Albrecht-Straße and Wilhelmstraße were blown up and razed in the 1950s, and in the new western district of Kreuzberg, the former Gestapo headquarters (formerly the School for Industrial Arts and Crafts), along with other buildings used by the Gestapo, the SS, and the SD, appear to have been intentionally singled out for demolition.[28] Even though some of these buildings could have been renovated in some form, the official reason given for their demise was their extreme state of dilapidation. Reinhard Rürup, professor of history and Judaic studies at the Technical University of Berlin (later the academic director of the Topography of Terror), argues that city officials used legal means to actively destroy buildings according to their association with the horrors of the Nazi Regime.[29] The Building Inspection Authority of Kreuzberg wrote in 1948, for example, that the ruined buildings on Wilhelmstraße 98–107 constituted a public hazard.[30] The Martin Gropius Bau, however, was not classified as a public hazard, even though it was more severely damaged than the School for Industrial Arts and Crafts.

Rürup also pointed to the indifference of Berlin citizens to the preservation of buildings formerly used by the Nazi state, such as the Prinz-Albrecht-Palais used by Heydrich and the SD.[31] In 1949 there was little public attention in the Western occupied districts when the Palais was blown up, even though it was built in 1737 and was one of Berlin's last remaining buildings redesigned by Karl Friedrich Schinkel during the 1830s and 1840s. Art historians like Johannes Sievers would later argue that even if the Palais had to be razed, which was questionable, at the very least its monuments and art pieces should have been salvaged. In 1954 he wrote that "the history of the Albrecht Palais with its abundant and constantly changing destinies ends on a dark note: the demonstration of human thoughtlessness and deficient sensibility for the proprietary possession of ir-retrievable cultural values."[32]

Berlin residents of the Western zone, however, were outraged when the GDR demol-ished the Hohenzollern residential city palace along Unter den Linden in the 1950s for overt political reasons, namely, to get rid of the remnants of Prussian militarism in the state.[33] Part of the difference in the public's response to the Palais and city palace *(Schloss),* of course, reflected the growing tensions between the East and West in the early 1950s and the fact that the city palace was a symbol of the city's historic (and royal) center. However, from a supposedly neutral or objective historic preservationist stance, the two structures were similar in age and architectural significance. Both the Palais and the Schloss, it seems, were destroyed for political reasons, despite (Western) suggestions otherwise.[34]

After 1961, with the building of the Berlin Wall, this terrain was an empty lot, except for the Europahaus and the partially destroyed neoclassical Martin Gropius Bau. Given the district's new relative location in West Berlin—at the edge of the Western part of the city and at the center of Cold War conflict—it became worthless as property. No firm invested in the area, except for a building materials reclamation company that sorted and processed West Berlin's rubble there in the early 1970s. Another interim use was the Autodrom, where people could practice driving around in cars without a license; a parking lot was later built behind the Europahaus. This "useless" piece of real estate, next to the no-man's-land adjacent to the Wall, reflected the overall lack of investment in Kreuzberg. One of the least desirable residential places to live in West Berlin, Kreuzberg was largely ignored during the reconstruction boom of the 1960s and 1970s and became a haven for socially marginalized groups, including students, artists, Turkish guest work-ers *(Gastarbeiter),* senior citizens, and squatters. By 1980, foreign guest workers consti-tuted nearly half of Kreuzberg's inhabitants.[35]

Central Berlin, 1980. *Left foreground*: West Berlin, site of former School of Industrial Arts and Crafts (later known as the Gestapo Terrain), with Martin Gropius Bau in far left background. *Center*: Berlin Wall. *Center right*: GDR House of Ministries, formerly Hermann Goering's Reichs-Luftfahrt-Ministerium (Air Force Ministry) and today the federal Finance Ministry. Photograph courtesy of Paul Glaser.

View of terrain from Martin Gropius Bau in the direction of Wilhelmstraße, 1981. Photograph by Gerhard Ullman; courtesy of Stiftung Topographie des Terrors.

Rubble. Overgrown fields. Debris. For a younger generation born shortly after the war, these urban fragments symbolized their fears, guilt, and frustration. The ongoing debates about the terrain for them demonstrated a deep-seated desire by their parents' generation to deny responsibility for that past. Andreas Nachama, who helped research and design the 1981 Prussia exhibition and would later became the managing director of the Topography of Terror, recalled in 1993: "We had one room in the Prussia exhibit . . . that dealt with National Socialism. There was a viewing station where you could see the [surrounding] area through a window. And there were [historical] plans exhibited so that you could see the area's [former] topography. At the time, there was a machine for recycling construction debris at the site. It was a very spooky area. And then we had a large sign that announced in four languages that the torture basements of the Gestapo were here. This was the beginning. Then the citizens' initiatives continued their work." The recycling machine, empty spaces, and debris created a spooky place for the second generation of survivors, like Nachama, who learned about national histories of violence and postwar forgetting through stories of their parents. But it was also haunted for the children of bystanders, perpetrators, and accomplices, many of whom learned about this history through books rather than from their parents and were searching to understand their personal relationships to that past.

The Eichmann process took place and the Auschwitz process [oc-curred] in Frankfurt, so that the press was full of reports about Auschwitz all of a sudden, and pictures. There was a large report in the Frankfurter Allgemeine Zeitung *[newspaper] every day. People had this on their breakfast tables every single morning, after it had not been a topic in the news for a long time. When the topic came up, the young people did not get any answers to their questions because their parents blocked it out. . . . That teenager fighting with his parents intersected with the parents blocking out this topic. These two things reinforced each other. Why should the parents admit something to their children when they fight against them?*

—Interview with Hanno Loewy, director of the Fritz Bauer Institute for Holocaust Research, Frankfurt, 1993

Many of these second-generation activists self-identified as the so-called '68 genera-tion, a label indicating their involvement in the earlier student and social revolutions and their attempts to draw continuities between past and present German "nations." Although the political leanings of this second generation (born in the late 1940s and 1950s) varied—better-educated Germans held left-wing and radical left political views, and individuals with lower levels of education leaned toward conservative, right-wing, and even radical right positions—the '68 generation scrutinized the activities of their parents, community leaders, and politicians.[36] They wrote fiction and autobiographies, they produced films, they organized local history workshop movements. Some resorted to domestic terrorism. In the process of trying to understand their past, they were continually faced with their personal relationships to their relatives and national leaders who silenced the National Socialist past. They increasingly came to care for places in their everyday settings that they understood as being haunted by a violent national past.

> *The 1968 generation started dealing with cultural histories . . .*
> *everything was thought about in a local way, specific to certain*
> *professions or generations. People went deeper into concrete mat-*
> *ters. In the beginning they did that to prove theories . . . [but] at the*
> *moment when this concretization process set in, you always realized*
> *that you were a continuation of the perpetrators. Through local*
> *history, the history of professions, cultural histories—hundreds of*
> *books were published about the cultural history of the German city*
> *square, the Autobahn, the garment industry—all that together with*
> *this "Holocaust effect". . . pointed toward your own history again.*
> —Interview with Hanno Loewy, 1993

By researching the National Socialist and postwar histories of the terrain, citizen groups also began interpreting this past archaeologically, searching for debris in abandoned fields, looking through city plans and historic documents, listening to survivors' stories. They began calling this area the "Gestapo Terrain" (Gestapo Gelände), a name that evoked dark personal memories for an older generation but for this second generation stood for those memories, social hauntings, of a traumatic past that could never be known to them personally. The name signified the second generation's emotional search for a past that would always be unknown; the landscape embodied what it meant for them to be German.

Situating Terrain Stories

These terrain stories suggest how distinct emotional, political, and generational relationships to the past were represented through landscape. Proposals for historic renovation, IBA research, marking the terrain with signs about the Nazi past, protest actions, formal calls for a memorial, city plans, discussions about possible locations for a history museum, and other activities framed and reframed the locations, histories, and meanings of a parcel of land. The material reality of the landscape was interpreted through particular histories and contemporary practices that communicated selective understandings of German identity.

These landscape stories, while particular to West Berlin, reflected larger shifts in public cultures of memory in the Federal Republic during the late 1970s and early 1980s. At the time of these debates, a booming and profitable "memory industry"[37] was producing popular representations of the recent past that contributed to German tourism and place-marketing economies at the same time that it helped create a more general interest in discussions about National Socialism. In 1979, for example, 20 million German viewers were glued to their televisions watching the American miniseries *Holocaust.* In the 1970s and 1980s, there was an immensely popular "Hitler wave" of books, films, and other cultural products. Autobiographies were written about the German *Heimat,* or homeland. Filmmakers creatively used the trope of childhood memories to criticize German traditions, including, for example, how postwar gendered spheres of *Kinder, Kirche,* and *Küche* (children, church, and kitchen) exacerbated "Germany's amnesiac tendencies" by reproducing the authoritarianism and xenophobia of the National Socialist period. Citizen initiatives and so-called barefoot historians (of the history workshop movement) established local memorial centers *(Gedenkstätte)* and organized neighborhood tours to confront the history of National Socialism in their communities. Schoolchildren were encouraged to write essays about the history of their neighborhoods during both world wars for national competitions. These films, books, exhibitions, tours, and school projects circulated in the public imagination at a time when upcoming national and international commemorative events were being planned for the fifty years after Hitler's rise to power and the book burnings in 1983, and the fortieth anniversary of the end of World War II in 1985.[38]

Given the range of popular forms and political agendas tied to the West German memory industry at this time, it was not surprising in hindsight that the 1981 Prussia historical exhibition and the proposal to renovate the Martin Gropius Bau were simultaneously well received and the object of extreme reproach. But because these projects were situated in West Berlin, the debates about landscape and place making were contentious because they also represented domestic cultural and political agendas. The terrain stories not only depicted social and political understandings of national pasts; they also narrated the social functions that places of memory should have in contemporary and future Germany. To generalize, survivors, antifascists, and activists of an older generation demanded a memorial to mourn for and commemorate the memory of those who suffered under the National Socialist terror regime. Conservatives of an older generation, some of whom also believed in confronting the Nazi past, supported a traditional approach to the past—a national history museum—to promote positive images of the nation during a time of perceived social instability and crisis. Younger, second- and third-generation activists, with some individuals from an older generation, began calling for completely different types of places, such as a *Denkstätte* or an active museum, to highlight the unique significance of this historic site in Germany and Europe. These understandings of place framed national aspirations for the future and were debated through conflicting proposals for the terrain.

As I describe in the following section, the debates about a 1982 public art competition for the terrain indicated how different postwar places of memory were interpreted as representing West German identity. The Berlin Senate, which sponsored the competition in an attempt to explore the range of possibilities for the site, awarded a winning design in 1983. But it would never be built. No one solution could be agreed on by officials and citizen groups, leading to a stalemate and continued debate. One of the reasons why a consensus about the terrain was difficult to reach was because dominant understandings of memorials—and hence the histories, aesthetics, pedagogies, and politics associated with these places—were in the process of changing in the early 1980s. Because the Gestapo Terrain was just one site through which national and local public cultures of memory were being renegotiated at this time, I now make a brief digression to discuss hegemonic understandings of Holocaust places of memory in postwar West Berlin.

The Memorial Competition: *Mahnmal,* Museum, *Denkstätte?*

In response to citizen protests, the Berlin Parliament, led by the Social Democratic Party, formally debated the future of the terrain in 1982 and voted to establish a memorial that would remember those who died and suffered as a result of National Socialist tyranny. Berlin mayor Richard von Weizsäcker announced the memorial public art competition for the Gestapo Terrain, stating: "As we go about reconstructing this area, it will be our task to proceed with contemporary history in mind while also providing a place for contemplation. Yet at the same time we must not miss the opportunity to give the Kreuzberg District a terrain where life can unfold and leisure is possible."[39]

In the guidelines, the mayor mapped the terrain in the past and present as "the central region as part of southern Friedrichstadt with its enormous challenges to city planners" and "situated in Kreuzberg and alongside the Wall." At different points in the competition guidelines, he also outlined the social functions of the area in the future, listing the different expectations voiced by groups and public officials in earlier discussions: it should be a place for historical reflection (a place of contemplation, or the memorial), provide livable urban space (parks, playgrounds, and leisure space), and represent history (explicitly through a planned national museum located nearby). Yet the mayor was vague about the social task of the memorial in his introductory remarks, stating simply: "The contest is of vital importance for our goal to attain Berlin's future without losing its past or repressing its evil features." Elsewhere in the guidelines, the district of Kreuzberg suggested (not required) that participants consider the establishment of an "active" memorial museum *(Gedenkstätte)* with exhibition space and an archive for historical documents.

One reason city officials may have been ambiguous about the future function of the area was because existing public cultures of memory for memorials were in transition, a response, in part, to the widespread popular interest in the history of National Socialism.[40] In German there are many words for memorials; further, many particular types of memorials represent the history of National Socialism and commemorate the memory of the Holocaust. Survivors' and human rights groups that demanded a memorial at the Gestapo Terrain specifically called for a *Mahnmal,* literally a memorial of admonishment. This type of memorial was distinct from the more generic *Denkmal* (a celebratory monument memorial) or *Ehrenmal* (a memorial of honor), the latter of which had negative connotations after the National Socialist period. Other types of places also commemorated the memory of those who died as a result of Nazi persecution, including the *Gedenkstätte, Gedenkfriedhof, Gedenktafel,* and *Gedenkstein* (memorial museum center, memorial cemetery, memorial plaque, and memorial stone).[41] Emerging and new types of places included the *Denkstätte, Denkort, Begegnungsstätte,*

Lernort/stätte, and *Dokumentationszentrum* (roughly translated as thinking site, place of contemplation, international youth site of encounter, learning place, and documentation center, respectively). Each of these memorial places was associated with particular aesthetic forms, landscape designs, symbolic locations, cultural practices, political agendas, and socially sanctioned spaces for performances of guilt, trauma, victimization, and shame.[42]

The Mahnmal

While *Denkmal* is the general term for memorial in German, when used in specific contexts it refers to the classical monument-memorial: a sculptural form on a pedestal that commemorates national heroes or great events.[43] After World War II, new types of memorials and commemorative places were established to remember the victims of National Socialism, including the *Mahnmal,* a public place of admonition where the message "Never Again!" was communicated. Most often located at historic sites of persecution and suffering, such as at concentration camps, former synagogues, or train stations, the *Mahnmal* bears witness to past crimes. It may also be located at central symbolic sites, like town squares, as a public reminder. Other types of postwar places of commemoration include memorial museum complexes, *Gedenkstätten,* or educational sites with historical exhibitions, most of which were established at historic sites of suffering. These memorial museum centers provide information about labor and death camps through historical exhibits that include texts, reproductions of legal documents, black-and-white photographs, eyewitness accounts, and artifacts and privilege victims' and survivors' perspectives.[44] Original and reconstructed landscape features, such as camp barracks, are often present, and different memorials and commemorative spaces mourn for those who died and suffered at the camp.

The *Mahnmal* that survivors' groups and activists called for at the Gestapo Terrain would have brought to mind a monumental, abstract sculptural form that called attention to itself in a public setting. It would have communicated universal messages of suffering and pain and represented German guilt through emotive, abstract modern art. By the late 1970s and early 1980s, a number of these types of memorials were already established and communicated what Dariuš Zifonun calls a Christian-humanist discourse of dismay *(Betroffenheitsdiskurs).*[45] Visitors going to the *Mahnmal* were expected to become moved emotionally *(Betroffen),* to experience intense anguish over the torment and pain endured by those persecuted by the Nazi regime, and to feel shame and guilt for the unjust murder of millions of people made in the name of the German state. The aesthetic focus of the *Mahnmal* in the FRG was almost always on the suffering of the victims, in particular on Jewish suffering. Pain and suffering were represented as a necessary stage through which humanity must go to be reborn into a new world of brotherly love (from a Christian perspective, modeled after Christ's suffering and resurrection) or into a new socially just society (from a Western liberal humanist perspective). If perpetrators were represented at these memorials, they were depicted in universal terms as "evil," often through the form of Nazi elite.

The international *Mahnmal* at the concentration camp memorial Dachau, for example, is a large, horizontal, abstract sculpture of intertwined bodies with heads and elbows sticking out to form the shape of barbed wire.[46] This art form symbolizes the bodily pain and suffering of the Holocaust, as well as the strength and courage of the community of inmates and others who gave their lives in the fight against the Nazi regime. It may also be interpreted as representing victims as heroic and noble martyrs. Such artistic interpretations made strong statements about the past and intentionally sought to remind visitors, and more specifically German citizens, of the horrors of National Socialism. Through the public articulation of dismay, those who remember this suffering and show repentance for the past are morally allowed to identify with the victims and move toward a more humane future. The problem with this discourse, in addition to its obvious Western and Christian bias, is that the social groups who were actually persecuted in the past continue to be stigmatized in the present: contemporary Germans, in their articulation of dismay, do not accept social responsibility for the past but identify with the status of victims.

This discourse of dismay emerged in the FRG during the late 1960s and was associated with both the political shift from a conservative to liberal federal administration and the social revolutions of the 1960s and 1970s. Numerous *Mahnmäler* were established as a result of calls to bear witness by survivors, as well as by the contradictory emotional and political relations that second generations of Germans had to their parents and understandings of the nation. These place-making activities in the 1970s resulted from a moralistic, and at times self-righteous, rejection of Adenauer's postwar economic and political agenda of recovery and silence.

> *The process of politicization sunk in [in the 1960s] and . . . people read that Vietnam was worse than Auschwitz and I don't know what else. The topic [of social and personal responsibility for the past] then was very far away—it was capitalism's fault. The past was represented in an abstract political way that didn't have anything to do with oneself. Above all you could identify with the [morally and politically] right thing in Germany: resistance, the resistance of the Third World against the First World. All of a sudden you could be on the right side. Collective identities were created which made it possible to identify with the victims, not the perpetrators. It worked for ten years. And then everything came at the same time,* Holocaust *[the television miniseries] was shown [in the late 1970s], the ideology no longer worked—all these abstract identities that people had taken on started oscillating in every breeze.*
> —Interview with Hanno Loewy, Fritz Bauer Institute, 1993

Because the *Mahnmal* in the FRG was politically associated with the Left and with antifascist traditions, this type of memorial may also have been associated with GDR practices. In East Germany, the *Mahnmal* was a centralized state memorial, defined by a socialist-humanist and antifascist discourse of dismay, monumental forms, and staged antifascist state rituals. The main memorial complex at the former concentration camp Buchenwald (near the city of Weimar), for example, was (and still is) rather extensive. At one end of the camp periphery, a large clock tower with an eternal candle extended upward from the top of a hill, looming above the countryside. At the base of the tower—always surrounded by memorial plaques and wreaths—steps led to a large sculpture of the camp prisoners breaking free from their bonds, with fists raised high to the sky. This sculpture represented the prisoner uprising in 1945 (a struggle historians today say is part myth and part reality). Here, children would come, don a red necktie, and make the Buchenwald pledge to become Thälmann pioneers. At such occasions, concentration camp survivors gave long and dramatic speeches. Candles were lit, and the bell in the clock tower would toll. From the sculptural plateau, more steps led down to a large circular depression, framed by low walls. The depression was one of a series of mass graves linked by an "international path of freedom" running along the base of the hill and perpendicular to the clock tower. Along the path near the mass graves, large columns and torches bore the names of countries from which prisoners were interred. At the path's end, another set of stairs traversed back up the hill, parallel to the first set of stairs from the clock tower. Stelae with engraved friezes of camp scenes on the one side, and quotes on the other, graced either side of the stairway. *Mahnmal* complexes such as these were the sacred spaces of GDR rites of passage.[47]

This description suggests the differences in the political, cultural, and social meanings for memorials in East and West Germany. Because West Germany supported a state-based, federal approach to emphasize the country's democratic traditions, each state or *Land,* including Berlin, had its own set of cultural institutions. When memorials were built, they were established through this regionally based financial and legal structure. In terms of content, memorials and educational work in the FRG mainly focused on the persecution and suffering of Jews, at least until the 1980s, which resonated with larger geopolitical agendas of the West Bloc. In contrast, the GDR had few, selected central state places of memory. These celebrated the memory of heroic communist resistance fighters, some of whom became the political leaders of this new German state. Memorials of admonishment were part of the socialist discourse of antifascism that legitimated the East German Socialist Unity Party (SED) rule by representing state leaders through the memory of concentration and death camp prisoners at these sites of resistance and suffering. Victims of National Socialism were thus defined by their political identity (as communist or socialist resistance fighters). It was only during the 1980s that they began to be identified in terms of their ethnicity, religion, or other social categories of identity (such as Jew, Sinti and Roma, homosexual, handicapped, or Jehovah's Witness).[48]

By the early 1980s, hundreds of *Mahnmäler* and other types of memorials dotted the German landscape at different historic sites, depicting Jewish suffering in the West and the struggle of communist resistance fighters in the East. In the FRG, while Holocaust memorials resulted from one generation's tendency to ignore or repress the National

Socialist past and another generation's attempt to compensate for that lack, paradoxically, the aesthetic form of the *Mahnmal* often encouraged forgetfulness or complacency. Until the late 1970s and early 1980s, these memorials were frequently established through invited, not public, competitions and did not usually include the participation of local citizens. After creating an initial wave of interest, these memorials soon became part of the local milieu and faded into the background of routine daily experience, except on days of commemoration. At their worst, these memorials—in both the former East and West—endorsed a mea culpa attitude, reinforcing the trope of "Germans as victims" rather than encouraging critical reflection about social responsibility and history.

Responses to the Mahnmal: Calls for a Museum

Ian Buruma argues that the generational and political backlash in the late 1960s and 1970s to official silences in the 1950s resulted in "a fretting over memory, a neurotic fear of amnesia, an obsession with casting the past in stone."[49] By the early 1980s, many people—from both the political Left and the Right, but for different reasons—had begun to feel that the *Mahnmal* monuments of warning created other types of problems. Conservatives felt that this form of duty memory reflected a failed Brandt administration liberal approach to the past, as well as an outmoded form of war retribution, or *Wiedergutmachung,* that was grudgingly allowed because of the need for international acceptance. Liberal and left-leaning individuals of the '68 generation felt these memorials did *too little* to promote a critical coming to terms with the German past and the meanings of the nation.

In the public discussions about the Gestapo Terrain, Berlin journalist Rudolf Stiege argued in 1982 that the "inflation of outer memory doesn't help" and stated that "no new, pompous memorial site for victims of National Socialism's inhumanity should be allowed." Professor Wilhelm Kewenig, then the Berlin senator of science and cultural affairs (CDU), agreed, stating that large memorials were always controversial symbols and therefore inappropriate for such a historical site. Mayor von Weizsäcker supported the establishment of a history museum as a "dignified" way to address the entirety of Germany's past, rather than build yet another Holocaust memorial that would soon be forgotten.[50] Implicit to these comments are comparisons between the *Mahnmal*—represented as emotive, subjective, politically volatile, and inappropriate—and the history museum, represented as objective, factual, and democratic. Indeed, the museum is understood as a place of historical research, education, and archival work. In contrast, the memorial is associated with dramatic ceremonies that honor the dead or salute the actions and deeds of heroes; they inspire the sort of social veneration as does a grave marked by a family tombstone.[51] Memorials represent memories of trauma and symbolize death through artistic forms in accessible public spaces, imbuing them with an authority of consternation, of moral righteousness and permanence.[52] Perhaps this is why the memorial also has the potential to be a site of transgression. Groups may take over memorial space at specific times to call attention to their needs or challenge understandings of the nation.

The museum is not associated with protest actions or dramatic public performances that challenge the existing status quo, at least not in West Berlin of the 1980s. Although museums are still seen as public temples that house artifacts and cultural treasures, their work is done inside, including scientific research, classification of objects, and historical education. Visitors are expected to read, listen, observe, and (more recently) interact with artifacts to learn about the past, and move quietly through the interior spaces of a building and along a prescribed path through exhibitions.[53] For museum supporters, this conventional, interior cultural landscape was perhaps a politically safer space to represent a controversial and traumatic past in a divided city than a memorial.

Yet the call for a history museum by public officials, city elites, historians, and others also reflected a larger political domestic agenda that emerged in the early 1980s.[54] Conservatives of an older generation understood the nation and citizenship in terms of a shared ethnic-cultural heritage and were politically committed to a reunification of "all Germans" as constitutionally upheld in the Basic Law. They were concerned that a younger generation had grown up as *West Germans* (rather than "Germans") and accepted the status of the divided nation. Indeed, surveys indicated that West Germans were the least proud of their national belonging of any citizenry in Europe; politicians and cultural leaders reacted negatively to this "negative nationalism," which they thought was reinforced by a public culture of shame and guilt. Conservatives felt that a national museum would provide younger Germans with a sense of historical continuity in what was then considered to be a socially uncertain present. At a public hearing about the proposed museum in 1983, for example, Hagen Schulz, professor of history at the (West Berlin) Free University, stated:

> The economic lull and new constellations in world politics are
> alarming the Germans: restlessness, fear, doubt in identity and a
> loss of orientation disturb society. The more uncertain the pres-
> ent, the darker the future, the stronger the need for an orientation
> based on history. . . . There is no future without history, and what-
> ever [past] was worked through without remembering manifests
> itself as a neurosis or hysteria.[55]

For Schulz, a museum would provide Germans with a positive sense of history and identity and help them get over a critical period of cultural self-doubt.

The museum, unlike the *Mahnmal,* was represented as a place that would help Germans move through their "neurotic" obsession, their "hysteria," with National Socialist history into a normal future. As Berlin cultural senator Volker Hassemer argued, the Martin Gropius Bau should be situated within a larger national historical landscape so as not to bracket out the Nazi past or represent it as an aberrant one in German history.[56] And while Hassemer's comments can be interpreted as an acceptance of National Socialism as part of German national history, in the context of the neoconservatism of the 1980s, particularly under the Kohl administration, these comments were interpreted as revisionist. By the mid-1980s, during the well-publicized Historians' Debate

(Historikerstreit), conservative historians would provoke a national controversy by contending that the National Socialist period was "typical," although extreme, of other violent and genocidal acts perpetrated by other state regimes in the twentieth century. Already in the early 1980s, a number of historians and politicians began arguing that representations of National Socialism as a unique period of world history created an insurmountable barrier to establishing a positive sense of national identity.[57]

New Types of Places: A Site of Perpetrators

Citizen initiatives, and some SPD, Green, and Alternative List politicians, disagreed with conservative agendas of promoting a positive national image. Instead they proposed new types of places for the terrain that would actively confront the National Socialist past, such as a *Denkstätte* (site of contemplation), *Dokumentationszentrum* (documentation center), and *Lernort* (place of learning). One of the first pleas for a *Denkstätte* was articulated at the public debates about the future of the Martin Gropius Bau sponsored by the Berlin Academy of Arts in 1983. Heiner Moldenschardt (professor and architect in Berlin) defined a *Denkstätte* as a site "where active history-work, active political education is carried out." Other individuals also argued for an "active site of memory-work" to, in the words of artist and the Active Museum citizen initiative member Roland Stelter, "carry out an active confrontation with this history on this site," "where the perpetrators loomed large."[58] These alternative places would be educational sites for future generations, where they could confront and work through the past *(Aufarbeitung der Vergangenheit)*. Activists hoped that the physical experience of being emplaced in a setting that was directly touched by the history of National Socialism might promote a personal coming to terms with the significance of a violent national history in contemporary society.

Their vision for a new type of place was contrasted to the model of the existing educational centers, or *Gedenkstätten*. For Moldenschardt, the *Gedenkstätte*, or memorial museum, educates the public about the consequences of National Socialist persecution and about the history of the Holocaust at historic "sites of victims."[59] A *Denkstätte*, in contrast, was located at a "historic site of perpetrators," where murder was centrally planned and organized by the National Socialist Terror Apparatus. Further, because there was only one such location in the National Socialist state, activists interpreted the Gestapo Terrain as a site of international significance. Orders for persecution and genocide were issued from the desks of these offices for the entire Reich and its occupied territories. This was where state bureaucrats organized terror and mass murder without witnessing the violence of their orders; they never saw, face-to-face, the people that they sent to unjust deaths.

As Moldenschardt argued, "sites where victims are, and must be, commemorated are, unfortunately, quite numerous; however, there is only one such location [of perpetrators] in the entire world. Therefore there can be no solution by establishing a *Gedenkstätte* here; what we need instead is a *Denkstätte*."[60] Moreover, Andreas Nachama, who later became managing director of the Topography of Terror, recalled in 1993 that at this place, "you cannot come up with a large design and transform the history of the site into a *Gedenkstätte*—we could have done that in the early 1960s, but by the 1980s and 1990s, it was too late for that. The history is part of the area. That is why we [the Topography of Terror exhibition historians and designers] kept the two piles of debris, which we had to buy from the recycling company, to make visible how nature works against us: things get overgrown and can no longer be seen. That is what happens over time" (interview, 1993). Both Moldenschardt's and Nachama's comments suggest that the 1980s were transitional times for public cultures of commemoration, education, and historical research. Because activist calls for a new type of place were contrasted to the memorial museum, it is important to understand the representational, pedagogical, and cultural practices of the *Gedenkstätten*.

Most people who go to memorial museum centers are tourists, school groups, survivors and their families. In Germany, schoolchildren and adult groups, such as military and police officers, visit memorial centers as part of their "political education" and professional training, which, in the early 1990s, included around fourteen curriculum hours (plus seven optional hours) on "National Socialism and World War II," beginning in fifth or sixth grade.[61] Political education is a concept that emerged with postwar denazification and reeducation programs, as Allies instituted school reforms to help students learn what it meant to be a citizen in a democracy through "civics" courses.[62] Allied attempts at reeducation were initially met with resistance during the 1950s, when there was a relative lack of ideological commitment to democracy in the Federal Republic but support for the transitional ideology of anticommunism.[63] By the mid-1960s, empirical studies demonstrated the ineffectiveness of Cold War political education concepts: anti-Semitism was on the increase (as expressed by graffiti with swastikas and defaced Jewish cemeteries in West German cities), and neo-Nazi parties were elected at local and state levels in Bavaria, Hesse, Schleswig-Holstein, Rheinland-Pflaz, and Baden-Württemberg.[64] With the election of an SPD-led federal government in the late 1960s, a greater public awareness emerged about the need to teach students what it meant to be citizens of a democratic society. Willy Brandt promoted domestic social reforms and pursued new foreign policy agendas under the banner of "more democracy."

In the 1960s, part of the political education program was to take school classes to memorial museums. At this time, exhibitions about National Socialism and the histories of the camps were quite graphic, reflecting what one interviewee described as a "terror pedagogy." In classrooms, students learned about political institutions and processes through rational choice theory and other approaches influenced by the critical theory of the Frankfurt school of sociology and liberal and Marxist traditions. But by the late 1970s and early 1980s, educators began to argue that "real" political education occurred in localized contexts, not through abstract theories. Instructors pointed to the range of political activity in the FRG, including citizen initiatives, self-help groups, the women's movement, ecologically oriented actions, the peace movement, as well as elections and more traditional arenas, to analyze and educate about the political process. They began to encourage students to learn about the past "at the site, where they [problems] *take place,* where they can be directly seen, studied, taught."[65] These spatial and embodied approaches to learning would increasingly come to include "theater work, learning and communication role playing, working group reports, and project exhibits."[66]

Harald Marcuse suggests that the new, "hands-on" or pragmatic pedagogical approaches, particularly those that emphasized empathic as opposed to cognitive, rational teaching, were associated with a younger "1979" generational cohort (born around 1954–1966) who embraced the grassroots-based history workshop movement (Geschichts-werkstätten) as well as new theoretical approaches to understanding historical processes.[67] In the 1970s and 1980s, Geschichtswerkstätten organized to tell the untold social histories of a particular community or district, including the histories of women or of the working class, by researching everyday histories of National Socialism in local neighborhoods. Informal tours of residential districts were organized, and other low-budget, low-tech activities were sponsored to encourage residents to become interested in what had happened in their community, and learn about what they inherited at home. The German history workshop movement was inspired by similar developments in Sweden, with the mottoes "Dig where you stand" and "We stand upon graves." In German universities, moreover, new theoretical approaches also emerged in history, including the history of everyday life (Alltagsgeschichte) and feminist approaches. Structural historians also became interested in researching the histories of "perpetrators." These developments in popular and professional German historiography influenced how the National Socialist past would later be represented at memorial museum exhibitions.

Activists in Berlin promoted this situated and embodied confrontation with the past, treating the learning process as one that included rational thought as well as personal experience and emotions.[68] Rather than an authoritative representation of the past that is not questioned, in this new approach, Germans are expected to work through the past self-critically at historic sites where particular events transpired to move toward more humane futures. Such an understanding of the past, while in some respects similar to the Christian-humanist discourse of dismay, introduced what Zifonun calls a "discourse of reappraisal" (Aufarbeitungsdiskurs).[69] Rather than identify with the historical suffering of victims, Germans were encouraged to accept social responsibility for the past in the present day.[70] In the 1980s, this shift in educational philosophies resulted in the establishment of new types of places, such as international youth centers of encounter (internationale Begegnungstätten).[71] Calls by activists to establish a new type of place at the former site of the Gestapo headquarters, a Denkstätte, were part of these pedagogical, discursive, and representational changes. Citizen groups argued that younger Germans would learn about the rise and consequences of the history of National Socialism—at the site of one's national ancestors—and be encouraged to evaluate, rather than take for granted, their contemporary democracy.

The Public Art Competition: Memorial Outcomes

These dominant and emerging understandings of memorials, historical research, and political education influenced the tone and wording of the memorial competition guidelines put forth by the Berlin Senate and the proposals that were submitted. Recall that artists and architects were required to provide a place of reflection and leisure space for city residents while keeping in mind that a museum would be built nearby. Many activists became quite critical of the public competition guidelines, pointing out, to borrow James Young's words, that "an all purpose terrain for memory and recreation" was inappropriate to the historic site of the former National Socialist headquarters of terror.[72] Although an SPD Senate pushed through the memorial competition in 1982, after state and federal elections were held in 1983, the political climate of Berlin and the Federal Republic had also changed. During the time of the competition, therefore, memorial supporters became increasingly nervous that a national history museum would be built at the Martin Gropius Bau without recognizing the National Socialist history of the area or the memory of those who suffered.

Of the 194 proposals submitted for the memorial competition, however, very few acknowledged the museum stipulation in the guidelines. Instead, participants focused on the demands for a park and some kind of memorial. In addition, because of the size of the terrain (6.2 hectares), some proposals were monumental, including gigantic historical re-creations that were seen as inappropriate to the site. Others, argued Hoffman-Axthelm, "give the impression as if nothing whatsoever had been on that site. Forty years of post-war history mark the place—but what has happened to them?"[73] The jury awarded the first prize to an innovative proposal designed by the Berlin landscape architect Jürgen Wenzel and the Bavarian artist Nikolaus Lang. They viewed the terrain as an antiterrain, an *Ungelände,* and envisioned a flat plane of cast-iron plates, set off by chestnut trees, imprinted with reproductions of original documents "of anguish, inhumanity, injustice, and plain brutality" and the footprints of the original buildings, including the Gestapo headquarters. Wenzel and Lang also recognized the historical significance of the site and later incorporated an educational center in their plans. They described their proposal as an *überschreitbare Dokumentationstätte,* a site where documentations had to be physically traversed and confronted by the visitor.[74]

Although this antiterrain was an alternative to the traditional *Mahnmal,* the artists adopted a modern rational perspective to space and time, smoothing a horizon and fixing a moment of time.[75] As Nachama recalled, "the winning plan proposed to seal off the whole area with concrete, to plant trees in a regular fashion. And some of these concrete plates would have enlarged documents from the Nazi era—letters, regulations, and laws. This plan was soon rejected because it was an engineering dream—I don't think it would have worked" (interview, 1993). Their proposal called for leveling of the grounds to make the Nazi past visible, but in the process, Nazi artifacts and postwar landscapes of erasure would be entombed under cast-iron plates. Activists did not want to lose the tangible evidence of German identity—the abandoned fields—to the bulldozer.

About a year after the competition, West Berlin mayor Eberhard Diepgen (CDU) informed Wenzel and Lang that their proposal would not be built. But no concrete proposal was made for what would happen next. According to Hoffman-Axthelm, "No memorial was [then] put there because one wanted to be rid of the site altogether." The president of one citizen group, Gerhard Schoenberner, speculated that officials stopped the memorialization process in order to save the site for the German Historical

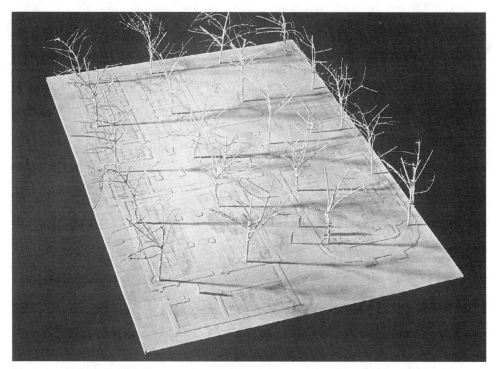

Photograph courtesy of Stiftung Topographie des Terrors. "If we proceed from a scenario of administered death as it was conceived, invented, planned, and organized on this terrain, then the site eludes all traditional, customary, 'normal' criteria of design" (Berlin landscape architect Jürgen Wenzel and Bavarian artist Nikolaus Lang, commenting on their winning model for the public art competition for Gestapo Terrain memorial in 1983, quoted in Reinhard Rürup, Topography of Terror: Gestapo, SS, and Reichssicherheitsamt on the "Prinz-Albrecht-Terrain"; A Documentation [Berlin: Willmuth Arenhövel, 1989]).

Museum. Many who engaged for years in these discussions suddenly felt left out of the decision-making process.[76] Some organized protest actions, including the Active Museum against Fascism and for Resistance in Berlin (Aktives Museum Faschismus und Widerstand in Berlin, eV, hereafter Active Museum).

The Active Museum: Archaeological Approaches to Memory

The Active Museum is a dynamic citizen initiative that organized in 1983, following the success of collaborations among groups working on projects commemorating the fiftieth anniversary of the National Socialist rise to power.[77] Sabine Weißler, a prominent founding Active Museum member, noted in 2003 that a range of activities were organized by groups that were not part of official events, including oral histories, the Ways to Dictatorship (Wege zur Diktatur) exhibition, and other related protest actions. The current Active Museum president, Christine Fischer-Defoy, recalled in 1998 that "several organizations cooperated and we made a program with exhibitions and events. . . . We said that this is not a task that can be fulfilled with an anniversary—it is a permanent task to remind [the public] of this time and what happened." And so these groups formed the Active Museum, an initiative, according to Fischer-Defoy, that included a "very wide spectrum" of "cultural institutes, the evangelical academy, even the German-Soviet friendship society. It was a mixture of political and cultural groups; there were also a few individuals."[78]

The political affiliations associated with Active Museum members ranged from liberal to left to radical left to antifascist positions; West Berlin parliamentary members who joined were predominantly from the Green–Alternative List (AL) members, a coalition party that emerged in response to the more widespread disillusionment by the so-called New Left within the Social Democratic Party in the late 1970s.[79] Their presence reflected a larger national movement, as the Greens gained 5.6 percent of the vote and twenty-seven seats in the Bundestag (House of Parliament) in the 1983 national elections. For younger Germans, the Greens represented the "anti-party party"; they tried to implement grassroots democratic structures and had more women active in the party and represented as parliamentary members than any other national party. The Green-AL party, as a local Berlin phenomenon, also promoted grassroots participatory structures. By 1983, the Alternativler (AL) ran for Berlin state elections and received 7 percent of the vote and nine seats in the Parliament. The AL was an odd amalgam of activists that included ecologists, feminists, gays, liberals, Marxists, and anarchists.[80] Christiana Hoss, the Active Museum's managing director, mentioned in 1997 that because of the support of the AL, the Active Museum would later receive funding for its activities through the Berlin Senate.[81]

While left-leaning politically, Active Museum participants were diverse in age, roughly split into two to three generational groups. The first group was older, born in the 1920s or early 1930s. These individuals had some direct connection to, or experience with, World War II and the National Socialist regime and tended to pursue a socialist or antifascist political agenda. The second, younger generational group was born between the late 1930s and early 1950s and in interviews self-identified as belonging to the '68 generation. Another smaller group came from a transitional generation, the "1979ers," who began to research Nazi history in the 1980s.[82] These two younger generations were well educated, most with university diplomas and some with graduate degrees. They were educators, artists, architects, historians, and art historians.[83] Many Active Museum members were women, some of whom participated in second-wave feminist movements of the 1970s. The first Active Museum president, Gerhard Schoenberner, was from the older generation; former president Leonie Baumann, current president Fischer-Defoy, and current managing director Christiana Hoss all have advanced degrees in history and art history and were from the '68 generation.

This newly established broad-based coalition of eighteen groups and associations focused their energies on establishing a new type of place at the Gestapo Terrain. Their goal was to create an "active museum," described by Hoss in 1997 as an interactive communications center that would have changing exhibits, a documentary center with materials and documents about the history of National Socialism, and a space for visitor-initiated projects. Fischer-Defoy emphasized the center's educational function for youth. An active museum, she mentioned, would provide a "school class that is addressing the history of Jewish persecution in their neighborhood" with an "opportunity to work on a 'project week.' They would get material and a worker who can help them with the technical things like enlarging photos, and after one week they have an exhibition they can present in their school. This was what we wanted. [An active museum means] that it is not a museum you go to, pay entrance fees, walk through an exhibition for an hour and return home. An active museum means that you should work out something for yourself. You could do this in a group or as an individual—you can come and read in the library, and can return home with photocopies. Or you could have the opportunity to speak to witnesses and survivors, watch films . . . a much wider spectrum of activities. That was what we imagined because we said that this topic of National Socialism, at the place of the perpetrators, at the place where the bureaucracy committed crimes, thought them out—you cannot create an authoritative museum, but you can only respond by encouraging and enabling people to discover their own history" (interview, 1998). Active Museum members also mentioned the influence of the *Geschichtswerkstätten* on their concept. For Fischer-Defoy, it was important to "make traces of history visible and work with concrete things" (interview, 1998). Baumann and Weißler stated that through the history workshop movement, they learned to become suspicious of abandoned spaces in German cities (in conversation, 2003). Hoss mentioned the *Geschichtswerkstätten* motto: "We stand upon graves" (interview, 1997).

"Let's Dig"

In 1985, when there was still no official word about the future of the Gestapo Terrain, citizen groups began staging protest actions to gain public support for their demands. The Active Museum and the Berlin History Workshop organized Let's Dig, an "illegal excavation" and "symbolic act that forced the city government to take action."[84] Repressed, negative, and imagined memories of the past, as well as hopes for the future, were brought into lived, experiential spaces of the present through digging. They unearthed the top layer of rubble and grass at the location where the former Gestapo house prison was located. They posted collages of historical texts and National Socialist maps at the terrain and on flyers distributed to residents throughout the city announcing their protest action. With their motto "Let no grass grow over the site!" they dug up a future that would prevent "fertile ground" for potential postwar forgetting and denial.

Theirs was an archaeological approach to memory, one that interpreted and created meanings of landscape, time, and identity through existing public discourses of memory. Like Michel Foucault's use of the term to describe his methodology for the history of ideas, an archaeological approach to social memory delves into the genealogies (contexts, histories, and totalities) in which a word, text, or action was made and used. "Where, in the past, history deciphered the traces left by men, it now deploys a mass of

Let's Dig, West Berlin, 1981: "a commemorative operation on the site" by the Active Museum and the Berlin History Workshop to honor "the resistance fighters who at immense sacrifice offered opposition to the Nazi regime" on the fortieth anniversary of the "liberation from Nazi fascism." Photograph courtesy of Jürgen Henschel.

elements that have to be grouped, made relevant, placed in relation to one another to form totalities."[85] At Let's Dig, activists questioned officials' use of the landscape as evidence of national history, at the same time that they symbolically dug for traces *(Spuren)* from the past. Their goal in this protest action was not to interpret or cite the landscape objectively as a historical object but rather to resituate and recombine texts, signs, things, and locations, and create new meanings, new opportunities for the future. This was a multilinear way of thinking about time, in which past, present, and future were understood as co-constituitive.

For Foucault, historical traces are produced through particular systems of meaning and cultural norms that have distinct genealogies. Because representations of landscape as material evidence obscure as well as articulate lived human experience, the archaeologist must pay attention to the waste, ruins, rubble, abandoned spaces—leftover matter—that have no place in dominant representational systems of meaning.[86] Activists also challenged common understandings of history as locatable in the landscape through the performance of digging. The dig, as a social practice, questions the taken-for-granted ways that landscapes "are read, and how they act as a mediating influence, shaping behavior in the image of the text."[87] Connections between and among these fragments, as well as contradictions in ways of viewing the landscape, are explored. Social spaces, locations, and material objects are materially, discursively, and symbolically unearthed, redefined, and newly mapped, only to be interpreted and critically analyzed again. This is an ongoing process of landscape production, one that, Walter Benjamin reminds us, keeps open the process of interpretation.[88]

Operation Let's Dig spatially relocated the landscape through historical maps, collages, texts, and bodily performances. The dig created a different material present and presence through the excavation of "forgetful" history. Activists' diggings produced the overgrown grass as a symbol of postwar German repression and as a visible material layer of the landscape. In the process of constituting the grass as "real," they used the same positivist ontology deployed through official discourse: that the landscape was material evidence of the different epochs of national history. At the same time, however, groups pointed to the inherent contradictions of official representations of national History as layers of the past that could be objectively narrated and measured. They physically unearthed sedimentation to reveal those layers (grass/histories of repression) not officially seen and narrated. In other words, traditional interpretations of history as neatly sedimented layers of the past on top of a solid seventeenth- and eighteenth-century bedrock were used to make new layers of the past visible (the grass) and in the process created new histories as well as new opportunities: "Let no grass grow over the site!"

Through their illegal diggings, the Active Museum and Berlin History Workshop resituated memories, objects, and official History in new contexts and (re)mapped the site. The dig exposes orientations, positions, and relationships among artifacts, structures, and historical sites; through the performance of the dig, past and present collide and are coconstituted through landscape. The landscape, as a permanently open site of investigation, invites residents and visitors to situate their bodies in relationship to the past and future. Through digging, new temporal constellations and social relations are experienced such that a person may become inspired to start the dig yet again.

Their protest action, together with the pressure by a number of AL representatives in the Berlin Senate, led to formal requests to excavate the terrain as part of Berlin's 750th anniversary events scheduled for 1987. While some speculated that building foundations existed, the Berlin senator of construction initially rejected the request for excavations, noting that a firm had been hired in the early 1950s to clear the site of all ruins above and below ground.[89] By the end of 1985 there was still no word about the city's future plans for the terrain. Only in January 1986, in a *Berliner Tageszeitung* article, did mayor Eberhard Diepgen promise West Berliners "a more beautiful city" for the upcoming anniversary. When asked about the future of the terrain, he stated that a decision would be made early in the year, but also indicated that he favored the proposal to reconstruct the Prinz-Albrecht-Palais.[90] These remarks led to renewed pressure by activists, and the city finally agreed to formally excavate the terrain.

Apparently the firm hired to rid the earth of building remnants had done only a superficial job: Gestapo house prison cells and foundations of buildings used during the Third Reich were found. A commemorative ceremony was sponsored by the Berlin College of Art and the Academy of Arts on September 1, 1986, and a broad coalition of initiatives, organizations, institutions, and some city politicians laid wreaths on the unearthed floors of the Gestapo prison cells, finally establishing an informal memorial. Activist demands to remember the past apparently struck a raw nerve in West Berlin, for the next evening the wreaths were destroyed and the ribbons stolen. Although the terrain was included as part of the formal 750th anniversary events, the defacement of the makeshift memorial probably strengthened the resolve of these groups and other supporters to press for a permanent center.

The Gestapo Terrain as "Open Wound"

After the terrain was excavated, the Berlin Senate established a special authority to create a solution for the site in conjunction with the 1987 Berlin-Berlin historical exhibitions and anniversary events at the Martin Gropius Bau. A group of historians pursued the concept by archaeologist-architect Dieter Robert Frank of "provisional restoration" and, working closely with activists who had long been involved in the public discussions about the terrain, created the Topography of Terror. It was not a memorial park, nor was it a permanent interactive center.

The Topography of Terror became known for its historical exhibit in a temporary hall of wood and glass that "accentuated the special historic significance" of the site during the period of National Socialism and included, as part of this history, the postwar "efforts to render invisible and to repress" the Nazi past.[91] According to exhibition authors, the main goal of the documentation was to present the historical facts and let the visitor take responsibility for his or her interpretation of the material. The low-tech exhibition had numerous texts (historical information), black-and-white photos, reproductions of documents, and maps mounted on placards. The information displayed included a survey of the area before the Nazi rise to power and focused on the organization of activities conducted at the Gestapo and Security Reich headquarters through a structural history of the site. The exhibit also included biographies of persons imprisoned at the Gestapo house prison. Unlike a traditional museum, no artifacts or historical re-creations were displayed. Instead the exhibit was integrated with the site, and at various points along the terrain, signposts indicating past uses of the terrain turned the contemporary landscape into a historical exhibit.

But the Topography of Terror was more than just an exhibition. It was described as the "open wound of the city" and as a "place of commemoration and reflection about the origins and consequences of National Socialist domination."[92] Once at the center of Berlin's national glory, the excavated foundations and "forgotten" fields in a divided city were represented as a gash in the body politic. The open wound was a metaphor for the extreme pain, grief, and anguish caused by the actions of Germans working at this historic national administrative center before, during, and after the war. It also referred to the postwar neglect of this national history, a silence that also created pain by hiding the ancestral secret of suffering, violence, and perpetration. The layers of denial had to be lanced so that the nation could see the exact nature of the injury, of its self-inflicted damage. The Topography of Terror, as open wound, exposes the scars of history, as well

West Berlin, 1986. View from Martin Gropius Bau (toward Wilhelmstraße) of excavated ruins of Gestapo house prison cell floors. Photograph courtesy of Margret Nissen/Stiftung Topographie des Terrors.

Topography of Terror temporary exhibition hall and unearthed cell ruins, 1987. Photograph courtesy of Margret Nissen/Stiftung Topographie des Terrors.

as the contemporary consequences of destruction to the ideal of the nation, and asks visitors to confront this past (and this pain), to keep the wound open in the present, to continue the work of memory.

The metaphor of the open wound draws both from Freud's theory of memory and trauma and from the artwork of Josef Beuys, in particular his project *Show Me Your Wounds (Zeige deine Wunde)*.[93] In the late 1970s and 1980s, other artists also came to understand urban public art in terms of this metaphor, such as Horst Hoheisel's memorial in Kassel's main city square.[94] Hoheisel replicated a historic monument and fountain of a neo-Gothic twelve-meter-high pyramid fountain, originally erected in the early 1900s by Sigmund Aschrott, one of Kassel's Jewish city founders. The artist then inserted the replication upside down into a gaping hole. While the competition guidelines called for the historic reconstruction of the fountain—destroyed by Nazis as the "Jewish Fountain" and later filled by locals with dirt and flowers and called "Aschrott's Grave" (referring to the more than 3,400 deported and murdered Jews from Kassel)—Hoheisel felt that erecting a replica fountain would blur the boundaries between victim and perpetrator. Ordinary people, not some anonymous tyranny or war machine, argued Hoheisel, had demolished the fountain. Further, the repression of the past needed to be confronted, as Kassel's old-timers recalled that the destruction of the fountain was a result of Allied bombings.

For Hoheisel, a great hole in society's fabric resulted at the site where the fountain once stood, "a wound that we can't close through the renovation of the fountain's sculpture.

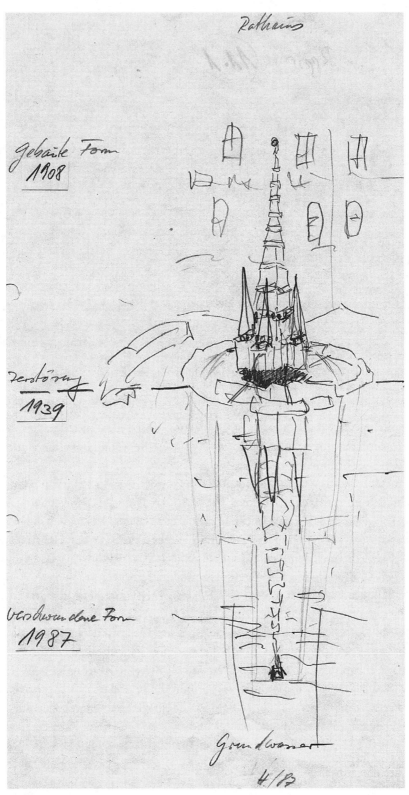

Concept for Aschrott-Brunnen memorial, 1987. Courtesy of Horst Hoheisel.

The place must simply remain open for contemplation and mourning." Hoheisel's sketch of his project inverts the traditional chronological layering of history. At the top he places 1908, when the original form of the fountain was built, under which he labels the date of its destruction (1939)—depicted as a large black gash—under which he includes the inverted fountain (1987). At the bottom, this "wounded form" irritates the city's "groundwaters" of time, forcing the repressed history of violence and loss to resurface to the lived experience of the contemporary moment.

> The sunken fountain is not the memorial. It is only history . . . [offered] to bypassers so that they will take notice and look for the memorial *(Denk-mal)* in his or her mind.[95] Only then will memory-work take place at the fountain. With the water plunging down, one's thoughts can be pulled down into the depths of history, and perhaps a feeling of loss, of the destroyed place, of the missing form, will be made tangible. And then, after the contemplation, together with the feeling of loss, mourning can occur.[96]

Open wounds in the cities of Kassel and Berlin create an irritation in everyday space through which past collides with present. These commemorative sites are "out of place" in the contemporary urban setting, for they are defined by (re)surfacing and repressed

Aschrott-Brunnen, Kassel, 1987. Photograph courtesy of Horst Hoheisel.

memories of violent pasts. The open wound asks visitors to confront their feelings of being haunted (or not) by violent national histories that remain present, yet invisible, in the city. The resident of Kassel, for example, may inadvertently walk over the inverted fountain and be surprised by the sound of the cascading water underfoot. Looking down, the visitor may see the inscribed history, recognize where he or she is standing, and experience a range of personal feelings (loss, defilement, consternation, guilt, anger) as he or she walks across the square. Or visitors to the Topography of Terror—who often accidentally come across the site—become curious about the excavations, read the markers, and even go to the exhibit. The visitor may be surprised to find that the field was actually the site of the Gestapo headquarters.

The open wound relies on what Walter Benjamin called a "shock experience" to re-awaken memory. By shifting the routine line of vision, sound, and touch, the landscape becomes a context through which visitors unexpectedly (re)experience dream images, memories, fantasies, and imagined postmemories that result in a more critical awareness of past and present.[97] Visitors physically become part of this landscape; they must do the work of discovering and confronting the history of this location, and their place in that history. Through these enactments, the wound is kept open as an uncomfortable critical site of experience, interpretation, and meaning.

The Topography of Terror: Past and Future

Although the Topography of Terror was intended to be open only for a few months, more than 300,000 people visited it in the first year, and it was left open indefinitely

Topography of Terror exhibition hall, 1993.

after the Berlin-Berlin anniversary exhibitions closed.[98] Posters of a historical city block, carved out of a muted gray cityscape, with the words "Topographie des Terrors, Gestapo, SS und Reichssicherheitshauptamt, Eine Dokumentation," began to adorn underground metro stations in West Berlin. The temporary exhibit, with the excavations and landscape markers, soon became included on guided city tours, was added to political education programs, and appeared on tourism and city maps. It also became a symbol of a new decentralized public culture of memory, a grassroots movement that represented the nation as a landscape littered by graves bespeaking violent histories. The decentralized network of site-specific museum memorials that emerged during the 1980s, of which the Topography is part, reflected an attempt to confront that past in order to move toward more humanitarian, even postnational, futures, a theme I explore in the following chapter.

The Topography of Terror as a place of memory was powerful because of its ambiguity as a place: it combined different existing and emerging practices of commemoration, critical historical thinking, and pedagogy to create a "site of perpetrators." Even among those who participated in the discussions about the terrain, there was no clear agreement about the role or function this place of memory should have in the city. Should it be a memorial park? An active museum? A *Denkstätte*? It had a documentary exhibit, a memorial, and a mapped topographical terrain—a landscape that, to use Stephen Daniels's words, was "an ambiguous synthesis whose redemptive and manipulative aspects cannot finally be disentangled, which neither can be completely reified as an authentic object in the world nor thoroughly dissolved as an ideological mirage."[99] The different uses and possible interpretations of what the place is and should be make people curious and want to visit the site.

With its history of activist interventions, the Topography also became a site of political contestation in the city, serving as a beginning and end point for different kinds of rallies. On the forty-third anniversary of the end of World War II (May 8, 1988), citizen groups involved in the discussion about the Gestapo Terrain organized a large gathering in front of the Martin Gropius Bau to commemorate the memory of those persecuted. Antiwar rallies were held, and exhibitions, informal discussions, and protest actions were also organized at the terrain. Unlike other places resulting from grassroots initiatives, however, the Topography of Terror never stemmed entirely from the political intentions of local initiatives and activists only. The terrain was always managed by the city-state through formal discussions, public competitions, party politics, and appointed commissions that organized the special 1987 anniversary events.

Following the success of the Topography of Terror, discussions about a permanent center were sponsored by the city at a time when West Berlin was celebrating its status as the "European cultural center." At public discussions organized by the Senate in 1988, a number of different ideas were suggested for the terrain, including a monumental *Mahnmal*, a research center *(Forschungszentrum)*, an antifascist educational center *(anti-faschistische Bildungsstätte)*, a house for human rights *(Haus der Menschenrechte)*, and simply leaving the terrain alone as an "open wound."[100] As a result of these public discussions, Berlin's cultural senator (Volker Hassemer, CDU) named an eight-person expert commission to organize discussions, consider suggestions, and submit a set of recommendations to the Berlin Senate for a future permanent center.[101] The expert commission organized two invited roundtable discussions, one that included representatives of groups involved in earlier debates and national organizations interested in the site's future,[102] and a second with experts from memorial centers and museums in Israel, Poland, Austria, Holland, the United States, the GDR, and FRG.[103] The commission submitted its interim report for the Berlin Senate days before the Wall fell in 1989, and formally filed the final report, with minor revisions, in 1990.[104]

With a (West) Berlin Senate that (for the first time) had a majority red-green (SPD-Green) coalition, in 1989–1990 they approved recommendations made for a future international center by the expert commission. Twelve architects were invited to submit concepts for the center that would also preserve the idea of an open wound; in 1993 the conceptual design by Peter Zumthor, a Swiss architect, was selected.[105] Zumthor proposed an elongated, four-story structure, with milk-glass walls, located close to the temporary exhibit and extending along the two piles of rubble.[106] He viewed the building as an abstract shell or outer casing *(Gebäudehülle)* that is "pure structure, [and] speaks no other language than the building materials, construction, and the unique purpose [of the site]."[107]

As part of the Topography's tenth anniversary events, a ground-breaking ceremony for the new center was celebrated in 1997, and an interim exhibition, based on the temporary exhibition of 1987, was placed along the excavated foundations parallel to the Wall. Several months later, construction abruptly came to a halt: city officials proposed

Model of Topography of Terror International Documentation Center. Design by Peter Zumthor. Photograph copyright Atelier Hofer; courtesy of Stiftung Topographie des Terrors.

closing the center owing to escalating projected costs of Zumthor's design. More than five years later, the future opening date of the permanent center was far from certain. After years of discussion, Zumthor agreed to modify his designs slightly to meet the new budget. Once the long, white, skeletal building is completed (projected for 2008), it will become the orientation point of the terrain, communicating a sense of permanence and creating an expectation of museum exhibition space, as it will be similar in height to the Martin Gropius Bau. Visitors will have multiple spaces through which to learn about the National Socialist past.

The new building will house the main exhibit about the history of the Secret Police and SS, which may be integrated artistically into the excavated ruins. There will also be changing exhibitions, for example, about the history of different occupied countries during National Socialism. The remaining three floors will be used for the visitor, research, and documentation center and will include research facilities and seminar rooms; a library (with specific emphasis on the SS, Gestapo, Reich Security Office, and the crimes committed by these Nazi organizations throughout Europe); a media library (with audio, film, and photographic documents on the history of National Socialism); and an electronic database about the history of National Socialism in Berlin and Europe. The research center will continue to offer public lectures and special events and house the Memorial Museum Department, which organizes international seminars. Next to the main white four-story building, another permanent exhibition about the Gestapo house prison will be located in a smaller pavilion that will in some way integrate the ruins of the cell floors. To the north of the building, in the excavations running along the Wall, a new open-air exhibit about the history of Berlin is being planned. The National Socialist history of the larger terrain will also be documented through information placards, photos, and maps at thirteen locations, with an audio-guided tour available in multiple languages. One of the academic staff members, Andreas Sanders, speculated in 2000 that the overall response to the new Topography of Terror will be positive: "There will be a reaction to the melting together of the architecture, the building, the new definition of the site, and the variety of exhibition and research offerings. Through the reaction to the symbolically charged 'architecture of meaning,' we will get a stronger visitor response."

In the next chapter, I describe the new challenges and opportunities the Topography faced during the 1990s as it slowly shifted from being a grassroots city institution to a national one. Although its relationship to other places in the national commemorative landscape would change after unification, the vision for this "open wound" remained the same. This was a historic site of perpetrators that would confront and document the history of National Socialism through the contemporary urban landscape. It was also a place through which activists, educators, and directors imagined a postnational future.

Fieldnotes

Author's note: The following edited fieldnotes (1992–1994) on the Topography of Terror were written when the 1987 exhibition hall and terrain were still open. *[Edited reflections on these fieldnotes and notes taken after the new temporary outdoor exhibit was installed in 1997 are set off by italics and brackets.]*[1]

The Topography of Terror, 1994 and 2002

1994: To get to the Topography of Terror, tourists take either the bus or a combination of underground metro (U-Bahn) and streetcar trains (S-Bahn) to the Anhalter Bahnhof, where the crumbling, classic, monumental facade of the historic station stands in front of a barren field on the southwest corner of Stresemannstraße. That lone facade is rather typical for this part of Kreuzberg. Every now and then you see a remnant from the past, a ruin in a lone field, standing quietly, out of time, in the middle of the city. Residents walking by or waiting for the bus don't seem to notice this odd fragment looming heavily in the background; it has faded into the background of their everyday milieu.

[2002: People going to the Topography of Terror are much more likely to take the faster and more direct metro to Potsdamer Platz and walk south on Stresemannstraße, rather than taking a bus or streetcar to the Anhalter stop and walking north. Most nineteenth-century architectural fragments in the city no longer stand unnoticed. The

Anhalter Bahnhof facade remains but is no longer in front of an empty field, making its presence seem less unusual, less like a remnant and more like part of the newer structures and buildings that have begun to fill the spaces around it. The (re)development of this area has resulted in more shops and cafés, especially in the direction of Potsdamer Platz.]

1994: In front of the Martin Gropius Bau, a small billboard announces the different exhibits on display. In the spring and summer, a beautiful field of roses, with their dramatic and fragrant blossoms, stands in front of the pink historic building; a lone abstract, silver sculpture offers a contrast to the building's neoclassical design. On any given day (except Mondays), people wander in and out of that old building to visit exhibitions, smaller galleries, including the Jewish Gallery, and public lectures and discussions. In the summer and spring, people sit outside in the museum's café.

[2002: The vibrancy of the social and material landscape I noted here was exaggerated by the dramatic contrast between the colors and uses of buildings in former West and East Berlin. At least for me, even in the early to mid-1990s, it was like comparing technicolor to black and white. The beauty of the Martin Gropius Bau was enhanced by the gray backdrop of what became the Berlin parliamentary building (now yellow), the former National Socialist Luftwaffe building (now the polished Federal Ministry of Finance building), and a fragment of the Wall. Once renovated, the buildings in the former East no longer were empty; they too attract tourists, professional men and women, and state officials. Some social events once held at the Martin Gropius Bau shifted to the Jewish Museum, also located in Kreuzberg, after it opened in 2002.]

1994: If you were to walk behind the large, elegant Martin Gropius Bau, you would

Martin Gropius Bau, 1994.

Topography of Terror exhibition hall, 1994.

see a banner, a metal turnstile, and a small white structure that looks like a trailer. The banner, in white, black, and gray, announces *Topographie des Terrors* and describes the history of the site. It provides information about opening and closing times of the terrain and ground rules (dogs must be on leash; no riding bikes or playing ball). To the right is the temporary exhibition hall, a small, long, white structure that hugs the ground. Its glass walls, punctuated by white painted wooden beams, give the illusion of openness. (Visitors often peek through the windows to look inside before going into the building.) In front of the fragile, painted wooden trailer is a dedication stone and information placard about the history of the exhibit hall's site. To the left of the trailer is a small wooden pavilion, behind which is a hill; another hill is behind the trailer. Both are about fifteen feet high; bricks, bits of concrete, and other building materials stick out of the dirt mounds, which are also partially covered by grass, bushes, and small trees.

[2002: This entire area is now a large construction zone for the future permanent center, expected to open in 2008. Two walls of the building under construction, designed by Peter Zumthor, jut out behind a construction fence. Visitors now enter the Topography to the north, near one of the only remaining fragments of the Wall in the city. Just south of that 1961 fragment, a temporary exhibition was placed outside in one of the 1987 excavation areas in 1997. Because of financial and other controversies surrounding the new building, this new temporary exhibition became more permanent than expected. Even in 2002, it was unclear when the Zumthor building would be finished.]

1994: The exhibit is low-tech, consisting of large, wall-length horizontal placards of black-and-white photos, blown-up reproductions of original documents, and accompanying texts in German written in a fairly dry, factual tone. In addition to black, white, and shades of gray, the other colors in the exhibit are red and the occasional lilac or faded yellow of reproduced historical documents and maps. An individual can spend all day in this exhibit and not read everything, even though exhibit designers, working on the assumption that most visitors would spend about one to two hours in the exhibit, limited the information presented. Some tourists seem to take their time as they study certain photos and parts of the exhibit; others quickly move through the building, as if to "collect" another site on their list of places to visit in Berlin. Faces of tourists range from intensely furrowed eyebrows, to those with shocked and dismayed eyes, to bored expressions with uninterested gazes.

The documentation is displayed in two levels, an upper level that appears to float above the lower level of unearthed ruins. Wires, cables, and metal beams organize the space on the top level and suspend the exhibition placards, arranged in a snakelike pattern along a narrow corridor. At many points in the exhibit, information is displayed on all sides of the visitor, and on busy days, the physical space of the top floor can be a bit constricted. Yet the exhibit appears to open outward because of the glass walls; the terrain becomes a visible part of the exhibition. From above, the visitor can look down into open excavations of the basement cellars and see people moving through them. When the foundations and walls of a former storage unit and cafeteria were accidentally unearthed as the temporary exhibition hall was being built, planners and architects of the Topography of Terror decided to incorporate these ruins to emphasize the "direct relationship that exists between the terrain and the historical documentation."[2]

The first and second thematic sections of the exhibit, "Administrative Center of the SS-State: Addresses and Institutions" and "History of the City District and Its Buildings," surround a small, three-dimensional, all-white model of the historic district that depicts the relative locations and spatial relationships of buildings that once stood here. Tour guides use the model, as well as the terrain outside, to orient the visitor to the historical topography. One tour guide pointed through the exhibit hall windows/walls to the bullet holes still visible in the Martin Gropius Bau from World War II. The same guide often explained that even though the former Gestapo headquarters was left in better structural condition than the Martin Gropius Bau following the war, it was destroyed by German officials in the 1950s and 1960s. Photographs and maps are also used in this section to orient the visitor to historic southern Friedrichstadt and the National Socialist government district on Wilhelmstraße.

The third section, "Institutions of Terror," consists of a wall of charts, documents, and photos that explain the structure and divisions of power in the National Socialist terror apparatus. Photos of storm troopers in action during the early 1930s are displayed, and farther down the corridor, brief biographies and photos of individuals who were interned in the Gestapo prison from 1933 to 1939 are presented. Many of those individuals were members of Communist and Social Democratic political parties, and others belonged to labor unions, socialist youth movements, and other resistance groups. The information is written in a factual tone, listing when and where the person was born, what his or her educational background was, what groups the person became involved with, when that person was interned in the Gestapo prison, and what happened to the person. Kurt Schumacher, Ernst Thälmann, and Erich Honecker are perhaps the best known of these individuals. Lesser-known individuals include Edith Walz, Heinz Schröder, and Heiner Pevka. The last part of this section exhibits information about concentration camps, including maps and the symbols used to classify (dehumanize) prisoners.

After looking at a European map of the location of concentration camps, the tourist heads down small, crumbling steps to the underground level, where the fourth section begins, "Persecution, Extermination, Resistance." The history of groups defined and targeted for extermination by the Nazis is presented, beginning first with German Jews and followed by European Gypsies. The theme of persecution is examined according to a geographic focus, looking at the consequences of National Socialist rule in Poland, the (former) Soviet Union, and other countries. *[2002: Academic staff working on the new exhibition for the permanent center will expand this section and provide historical research with documents made available after the collapse of the Soviet Union.]* The fourth part ends with an examination of political resistance and exhibits biographies of individuals interned in the Gestapo prison from 1939 to 1945.

Downstairs, it is darker. The air has a musty scent. Wires and beams stick out of crumbling walls. One has to duck to go into some of these rooms. Placards hung in darker corners are illuminated with fluorescent lights. When walking down the stairs to this level, one feels immersed in the depths of the Nazi netherworld. It doesn't matter that the ruins below were not torture cells or gas chambers; the weight of the past feels heavy. This heightened experience "brings the past not only to life, but into simultaneous existence with the present, making it appear closer than the present, which it both haunts and hypnotizes."[3] There is a possible danger in this hypnotic feeling, which James Young describes as "forgetful," because the viewer may mistake the "rhetoric of a memorial for the nature of the events it commemorates."[4] The tourist may be haunted by his or her expectations and preconceptions of what a "Topography of Terror" might mean, and may imagine that these dark, dusty ruins were once a site of brutality rather than banality.

Some guides confront this hypnotic quality with their tour groups in the basement level, asking what images visitors had before coming to the exhibit. One guide refers to Hannah Arendt's concept of the banality of evil to explain why exhibit designers used these cafeteria ruins as part of the exhibit. "State employees," the guide mentions, "worked at this site from nine to five. These employees, just like you or I, prepared meals or ate them here. Sometimes these employees would eat lunch in this cafeteria after signing orders that sent thousands of individuals to concentration camps, and ultimately to their deaths." These bureaucrats are known as *Schreibtischtäter* in German, literally "desktop perpetrators." This German term distinguishes between the managers of death and those who actually did the killing. *[2002: Recent research has shown that some of the staff and office directors of the Reich Security Office were directly involved with the violent activities of the Einsatzgruppen in occupied countries.]*

The themes addressed in the basement are emotionally upsetting. A number of the black-and-white images on display are frequently used by the media to communicate the horror of the Holocaust—the picture of running women and children with their hands raised, their eyes filled with terror as they were herded by soldiers after the Warsaw Ghetto uprising in May 1943; or the photo capturing the fear and resig-

Interior of Topography of Terror exhibition hall, 1994.

nation of civilians who are about to be murdered, kneeling before their own mass grave while a group of German soldiers looks on. Such familiar images are part of an iconography of the Holocaust. These photos are known to us through the technologies of mass production and communication. We see certain photos over and over again, in history books, in museum exhibits, in films. They haunt and terrify us, yet we are drawn to them because they are familiar: these faces captured by Nazi film signify the Holocaust.

Although many Holocaust scholars and educators in Germany with whom I spoke described the difficulty of representing the unimaginable, that is, the horror and magnitude of the Holocaust, the visitor is attracted to these well-known photos precisely because of the immensity and overwhelming nature of these historical events. At former concentration camps and other historical exhibits, these images both terrify and reassure. The act of recognizing these photos, however horrible the image, may allow some kind of comfort to the visitor by providing a sense of security about his or her knowledge about the subject, however limited that knowledge may be. *[2002: Is this another "distance of post-memory" that must be traversed? What does it mean to come to know about the Holocaust through the filmic eye of the perpetrator and yet be comforted by those images?]*

[2002: In a group interview with the Topography of Terror academic staff in 1998, we discussed the exhibit's aesthetics and narrative forms. Klaus Hesse, responsible for the photography research division, stated that because so many Gedenkstätten already existed before 1987, "we could make such a clean, aseptic exhibition about the center of the 'Schreibtischtäter,' about the place where things were planned." Academic staff were also able to assume that visitors had some prior knowledge about the history of persecution and genocide. But on reflection, Hesse made a surprising comment, noting that the exhibit might have "spared" visitors too much. "Even ex-Nazis can go through without becoming angry. They have to walk fifteen meters before they see the first execution. . . . When we show Auschwitz we always show what is easiest to stand. I don't know if this is always good, but I want to raise aesthetics as a question. Maybe the success [of the Topography] had something to do with that as well—it spared people who did not need to be spared, people who otherwise might have complained." I realized that while the exhibit in the basement was for me rather upsetting, it was not as graphic as other exhibits I have seen in Germany and Poland. How does photography work in these exhibitions?

Topography experts also commented on the narrative sequence of the exhibition. According to the academic staff member Andreas Sanders, responsible for biographical and oral history research on the Gestapo house prison, it is organized "to give people the opportunity to understand how the end product [organized persecution and murder] developed—which is why we don't begin the exhibit with a photo of an execution—that was really the last thing that happened. When you walk through the exhibit in the right order, you understand where it [the historical development of the National Socialist SS and police state] led to. Then you can talk about it."]

1994: The area devoted to political resistance does not have this same hypnotic quality because it is not located in a dark corner of the basement ruins, and because the photos are qualitatively different. Rather than being confined to a small, dark, dusty area, the visitor is in an exhibition space that opens up overhead and provides a mental breathing space. Should the material become too heavy, the visitor can pause simply by looking upward, at the outside terrain through the above-ground windows to the left, or at the people moving through the exhibit above. The individuals pictured in this section are also smiling and relaxed. Adam Kuckhoff, a member of the Red Orchestra resistance movement, appears to have been photographed by friends at a festive event, rather than classified through the Gestapo lens. These photos seemed to me to be the most human, the most real, in the exhibit. *[2002: Kuckhoff does not confront the camera with defiance, anger, fear, or submission. His image has not been violently "captured" on film; it is not an image produced by someone collecting a picture of death.]*

The exhibit's final section, "From Destruction to Rediscovery," begins in the lower level and ends above ground. Large, wall-size aerial photos illustrate how damaged the city was immediately following the war. Information about "history made invisible" and the "return of a repressed past" is presented above ground.[5] The first time I went through the exhibit, I could only spend a few minutes in this section; I needed to go outside after spending time with a disturbing exhibition in the basement. Only after a number of visits did I carefully examine these photos and documents from the very short section on the postwar history of the site. This section makes clear that the National Socialist past didn't simply "end" in 1945 but is part of present-day realities of Berlin.

I conducted a visitor survey in the summer of 1993 with the help of the Topography of Terror staff and funding from the Berliner Festspiele. Of the 696 visitors who voluntarily submitted surveys, 67 percent of the German-speaking and 48 percent of the English-speaking visitors felt that the exhibition fulfilled their expectations (either completely or for the most part). Seventy-three percent of German-speaking visitors and 51 percent of English-speaking visitors thought that the amount of information presented was "just right." Most visitors agreed with the interpretation of the terrain as a "site of perpetrators" (87 percent of German-speaking and 74 percent of English-speaking) and supported the educational work of such places; 92 percent of German-speaking visitors and 89 percent of English-speaking visitors felt that memorial centers were socially important. Many people (64 percent of German-speaking and 61 percent of English-speaking visitors) also felt this postwar history of the site was important.

Outside the exhibition hall, a series of signs are located along a path that winds around the edges of the terrain and up a hill of rubble. The signboards provide information, maps, and historical photos about the buildings used during the Third Reich. Although one need not view these signposts in any particular order, they are numbered from one to fourteen in the upper left-hand corner. It takes a little over an hour to move through the terrain and read the information signboards.[6] The signposts document the location of a particular building or architectural feature and include

Topography of Terror, terrain with historical placard and excavation site, 1994.

an enlarged black-and-white photo of what the landscape looked like before or soon after World War II. Next to the photo, a short summary describes the function of the pictured building during the National Socialist Regime. The visitor consequently has the unique opportunity to physically experience a "before and after" series, viewing the black-and-white photo of, say, a bombed-out building and then looking at the three-dimensional color perspective of the area in the present. Below the photos, a stylized map of the terrain during the Third Reich outlines the footprints of various historical buildings (in royal blue) relative to the Martin Gropius Bau, the Berlin Wall, and different streets (Wilhelmstraße and Anhalter Straße). A large red dot indicates "you are here." The terrain's photos and maps frame the tourist's view of the present; however temporary, visitors come to see and interpret an otherwise dull landscape as historically significant. *[2002: After construction on the permanent exhibition began, the terrain and its signboards were no longer open to the public. When the new center opens, an audio tour of the terrain at thirteen locations will be available.]*

Because most of the buildings mapped no longer exist, the signposts are most effective at excavation sites. At those locations, the past seems more tangible, not reduced to black-and-white images or maps. At the edges of the terrain, uncovered ruins are protected by wooden structures; a remnant of the (West) Berlin Wall runs from east to west to the north of the exhibition hall, casting its shadow on the descriptions and artifacts unearthed in the terrain. These unearthed sections of building foundations, or parts of cellar walls and floors of rooms of various buildings, are unusual in an urban setting. *[2002: Usually a city is defined by new buildings replacing old ones, newly developed sites at the edges, and preserved buildings and districts. It is unusual to see a place so centrally located defined by dissections of past constructions.]* Even if you are walking quickly through the field en route to another location, chances are that you will take notice of these spaces.

But when you stop to look, the exposed artifacts are rather uninteresting and difficult to see. Many unearthed sections are covered by wooden structures to protect the grounds from environmental damage resulting from acid rain. The most interesting excavation site, which also serves as a memorial, is currently covered with sand: the cell floors of the Gestapo house prison, which were unearthed in 1986, are located across from the temporary exhibit hall under a small white pavilion. Some tour guides explained that after 1988, sand was placed on top of the ruins to protect the cells from further damage. The covered-up ruins unfortunately take away from the drama of the site. Unless the tourist reads the placards adjacent to the wooden structure, he or she may be confused as to why that particular location is set off with a protective roof. *[2002: The cell floors will become integrated in some way in the new center and set off by a smaller structure adjacent to the new four-story building.]*

The most striking excavation site is at the northern part of the terrain, directly below the Wall *[2002: which is probably why the 1997 temporary exhibition was placed there]*. Here, the layering of history is most obvious; the tourist can look into a trench at unearthed tiles, at the graffiti of the Wall above ground, and at the gray buildings of the former Nazi Luftwaffe building just beyond the concrete barrier. The presence of the Wall provides an especially powerful aura of authenticity at this site. After 1989, that physical divider came down so quickly that today only a few sections of the Wall still stand in their original position. Consequently, and perhaps accidentally, the Topography of Terror has become a point along Wall tourism routes. It is now located between two other new (postunification) tourist attractions—Checkpoint Charlie along Friedrichstraße (southwest of the Gestapo Terrain), which proclaims in four languages, "You are entering the American section," and Hitler's drivers' bunker, which

was discovered in the death strip just north of Potsdamer Platz in preparation for a
Pink Floyd concert in 1990.[7] Tourists heading past Checkpoint Charlie en route to the
bunker (which was quickly resealed after it was discovered to prevent neo-Nazi pilgrimages) will stumble onto the Gestapo Terrain and find it worth stopping for. *[2002: It
now is also a central stopping point for tourist buses and part of a new tourist trek moving from north to south from Brandenburg Gate to Potsdamer Platz.]*

In addition to the unearthed ruins, another unusual, yet rather mundane, feature is
the two large hills of rubble, meant to function as reminders of the postwar history of
forgetfulness. These piles are the remnants of the activities of the building reclamation company that leased the site during the 1970s and early 1980s. These two heaps
of stone, dirt, and shrubs look like oddities and may provoke curiosity or indifference.
James Young describes the two hills as mounds of *tel,* a Yiddish word for piles of stones,
which refers to the Jewish tradition of laying stones on graves.[8] As one Israeli visitor in
1992 wrote:

> There is no way to describe how it feels for anyone, let alone a
> Jew, to stand on top of the rubble of the Gestapo. There is a small
> sense of victory, perhaps, but a bitter one. A sense of completion,
> maybe, but incomplete. A feeling, somehow, that a small right has
> been applied to a great wrong. And an unpleasant frisson that
> comes from standing on a place where you know what happened
> but see little sign of it left. You sense that the stones of this rubble
> somehow hold the moans and screams of decades ago.[9]

Topography of Terror, terrain with mounds of rubble, 1994.

At the base of the larger hill of rubble behind the exhibit hall, wooden steps lead up to an observation platform, where information tablets situate the historic site in relation to the larger city space of Berlin. You get a pretty good 360-degree view of the city, since ordinances in Berlin restrict the height of buildings; like many other European cities, Berlin's city centers do not have the verticality of metropolitan sky-lines like New York or Hong Kong. Soon, however, Berlin will have new high-rise busi-ness complexes, including one that will be built just north of the terrain. *[2002: These hills of rubble are currently not accessible to the general public. They will be located (in somewhat modified form) on either side of the new building, providing movement and texture to the lower levels of the new Zumthor building. It is hard to know what skyline will be visible from atop the completed new building.]*

When I talked to some tourists about the hills, they didn't understand the symbolic meaning of postwar forgetting. This was especially true for non-German speakers who may not have understood the exhibition. When I asked one thirty-year-old American visitor what he thought, for example, he shrugged and asked what the hills were and why they were there. To him, they seemed out of place. After I explained what they were and symbolized, he asked in a rather frustrated tone, "Well, why don't they put up a sign explaining this? Otherwise they really don't make any sense being here." His comments draw attention to the fact that the signboards on the terrain map only the National Socialist features (present or missing) in the landscape, whereas postwar features are left undocumented, except in the last part of the exhibition.[10]

One day I was watching visitors who entered the terrain from the east via Wilhelm-straße and noticed a small group of young adults, in their early twenties, moving west toward the Martin Gropius Bau. They had British accents, were wearing jeans and backpacks, and had the telltale sign of tourism: cameras in hand. Once they saw the Wall and the section of unearthed ruins, I watched them wander around for about twenty minutes and overheard them trying to figure out exactly where they were. I finally asked them if they knew what this place was. They said no, and said that they were coming from Checkpoint Charlie and were looking for Hitler's bunker *[2002: which at the time had not yet been unearthed; they confused it with Hitler's driver's bunker]*. Perhaps because the bunker was below ground, they were drawn to the excavation sites. But they were also curious enough to ask me more questions about the area, for example, about the tiles and buildings. Although they didn't stay and go through the exhibition, they did read a number of the signboards before moving on.

[2002: Tourists now stumble onto the new temporary exhibition, a place perhaps better visited than the 1987 exhibition. Because tourists can access the new exhibit in two directions, they can read the placards from past to present or from present to past. Tourists can now check out headphones to accompany their readings of the exhibition and learn additional information. As before, tourists seem to take their time, reading each placard and listening to additional recordings, or walk through the exhibition more quickly.

Because of the outdoor setting, the aesthetics of an otherwise stark exhibit feels less overbearing. The documentary, black-and-white placards are still there. The basic

Topography of Terror, temporary exhibition, 2002.

organization is the same. But it feels less hypnotic. The analytical, distanced tone of the text feels less authoritative. The drama of the previous exhibition's narrative— experienced by going underground to see the consequences of the National Socialist terror apparatus and moving above ground to learn about the terrain's rediscovery— is downplayed. For these reasons, the new exhibition was a more powerful exhibition for me.

The psychological meaning of the basement is also experienced differently here. The visitor is always submerged, but not quite. He or she does not have to move through dark spaces with damp concrete, wires, and fluorescent lights overhead. At any point in the exhibition, the visitor can take a physical break from the dry tone of the historical narrative or the images displayed by looking up or across terrain, or sitting on the bank behind the exhibits (when it is not too cold). Yet these escapes are never complete; one is always aware of being submerged, surrounded, by the exhibition, the excavations, other tourists, and one's thoughts.]

Topography of Terror brochure cover.

4 | Berlin's Ort der Täter: A Historic Site of Perpetrators

> The Topography was the first project, the first exhibition focusing on perpetrators that accomplished so much. Before, exhibitions focused on the perspective of the victims. . . . The Topography had an influence by introducing this change into the culture of commemoration. So the topic, which means perpetrators, was new. . . . Second was the place, the approach through the place. That was new back then. Third, the form of representation [a documentation].
>
> —*Andreas Sanders, Topography of Terror academic staff, in focus group interview, 1998*

After 1990, the Topography of Terror was quite suddenly relocated from the real estate margins of a walled city to what has become a central location in the New Berlin. With its preunification success and postunification location, the Topography has become an important tourist destination; in 2002 it was the tenth most visited "museum" in Berlin. According to academic director Reinhard Rürup, the Topography's postunification centrality also resulted in new national roles, as a kind of central Holocaust museum for some politicians and as a service center for the existing decentralized national network of memorial museums. Although these specific functions emerged in the late 1990s, largely in response to debates about the Holocaust Memorial, the social agenda of the Topography was already specified before unification. In 1989, at discussions organized by the expert commission appointed to make recommendations for a permanent center, numerous suggestions for the future of the terrain were voiced. But there was always a clear consensus that this location should primarily be understood as a site of perpetrators, or *Ort der Täter*.

How does a "site of perpetrators" define contemporary social relationships to a violent national past and understandings of German citizenship? As Andreas Sanders describes at the beginning of the chapter, this *Ort der Täter* differed from other commemorative sites and memorials through its approaches to the past. After unification, the landscape was preserved as an artifact of National Socialist history and of postwar denial. This historic site mapped a larger European network of National Socialist terror through the terrain and its historic relation to other sites of perpetration in Berlin, Germany, and Europe. And the existing historical exhibition, or documentation, represented the past through a distanced and objective structural history comprised of documents, maps, and photographs for visitors to interpret on their own. These preservationist, topographical, and documentary approaches to representing a violent past reflected both political ideals and practical responses to what were perceived to be cultural and social problems at the time, including the value of the terrain as property after unification, Holocaust denial, an increase in popular-cultural productions of the Holocaust, and a German social desire to understand the National Socialist era from the emotive perspective of victims.

Implicit to these approaches to the past, and to the concept for an *Ort der Täter* in general, is an understanding of Germany as a society of perpetrators, a representation of collective identity that reflected political agendas in the 1980s and located social accountability for the National Socialist past in the present and future. In a society of perpetrators, the history of National Socialism, as well as that of the Holocaust, must be communicated to future generations of Germans. This distinction, between victim and perpetrator social identities and spaces, is important to educators in other memorial museum centers in Germany as well. In the words of Hanno Loewy, director of the Frankfurt Fritz Bauer Holocaust Foundation, "The Germans as a collective are first of all perpetrators. This is of course not true for all individuals, but as soon as you speak about identity—and identity is always something that is not individual but collective—in the moment where an individual German deals with identity he is confronted with the perpetrators. You cannot identify with that. In educational work you try to identify with the victims. You can only do this cognitively by reading diaries and trying to take on the perspective of the victims in an intellectual, cognitive way, and thinking what you would have done in the situation, 'What options would I have had?' But this is not an identification that has something to do with the heart" (interview, 1993). From this perspective, contemporary Germans inherit a violent national legacy as perpetrators but cannot identify with that heritage morally.

The Topography of Terror documentation represents a structural history of the so-called National Socialist terror apparatus and includes a short postwar history of the denial and rediscovery of this past. It documents the past and defines German responsibility for past crimes. At the same time, educators believe that by confronting their difficult national history, Germans may come to imagine a postnational future. Postnationalism, as a left to liberal (in the West German sense) utopian ideal, constructs a geopolitical space in which political affiliations are defined by an international democratic community that promotes humanitarian agendas; cultural identities and attachments are formed by citizens through their ethnic and regional ties. In the 1980s and 1990s, some conservatives reacted negatively to this postnational political agenda, arguing that it rejected the possibility of a positive German national identity. As late as 1998, Heinrich August Winkler argued that "Auschwitz had long been transformed into the negative symbol of a new, 'post-national' West German identity. It was used as an argument not only against a new German nation-state, but also against the idea of a German nation of any kind."[1]

In this chapter, I describe the cultural approaches to the past at the Topography of Terror and the political agendas tied to the establishment of a site of perpetrators. I also outline the challenges and opportunities that accompanied its transition to becoming a national institution in the 1990s. Although the underlying political goals of the Topography challenged official agendas of representing Germany as a "normal" nation in the 1980s, by the late 1990s those political goals were downplayed. With the election of Gerhard Schröder's neoliberal SPD administration that acknowledged the National Socialist past, the Topography of Terror Foundation would establish its central role in Germany's commemorative culture and in the New Berlin in different ways. Topography foundation directors proposed the idea for a national memory district in the new capital constituted by the Jewish Museum, the Holocaust Memorial, and the Topography of Terror. In doing so, they continued to define a site of perpetrators as different from the Holocaust Memorial—which would represent German guilt through the perspective of mourning for victims—and as central to the ongoing memory-work of German society. As I describe in chapter 6, this nascent memory district embodies a neoliberal agenda of publicly recognizing national guilt to claim membership in an international moral (Western) society. Yet the district will also emphasize the importance of memory-work in the present through the presence of this historically unique site of perpetrators.

Preunification Debates

In preunification discussions, when activists and Topography staff used the word "site" (Ort) to refer to the Gestapo Terrain, they specifically referred to the historic location where past acts to be remembered took place.[2] They interpreted this location as uniquely one where the so-called desktop perpetrators loomed large: from this headquarters, persecution orders and actions were issued for all groups, including political opponents, Jews, Sinti and Roma, homosexuals, Jehovah's Witnesses, physically and mentally handicapped individuals, and others deemed unfit by the National Socialist state. They also viewed the landscape as embodying a postwar history of collective denial about the existence of this site and its legacies of national violence.[3]

Other views of the terrain were also articulated at public discussions in 1989, however, including a proposal by a new citizen initiative, Perspektive Berlin, eV (hereafter Perspective for Berlin), to establish a traditional Holocaust *Mahnmal* to mourn the loss of European Jews at the Gestapo Terrain. The idea for the memorial emerged after the spokesperson for the group, Lea Rosh, a television journalist and public personality living in Hannover, returned from a trip to Yad Vashem.[4] Rosh was outraged that no national Holocaust memorial mourned for the suffering and persecution of European Jews, and with support of the group, she advanced a proposal to establish such a memorial in Berlin. In 1989, Perspective for Berlin began to gather petition signatures and donations for the memorial in public city squares. They also sponsored and participated in public forums and discussions about this topic and used media support for their cause.[5] Petitions were published in high-profile newspapers with signatures of prominent people such as Willy Brandt, Günter Grass (who later withdrew support), Beate Klarfeld, Walter Jens, and Christa Wolf. Because of its high media profile, American cultural critic Jane Kramer described Perspective for Berlin as a "celebrity version" of a German citizen initiative, with members who consider themselves to be politically left of center and are morally indignant.[6]

In many respects, the proposal for a central Holocaust memorial at the Gestapo Terrain made sense. Perspective for Berlin, like other liberal to left activist groups, was highly critical of Kohl's cultural politics of "mastering the past" and was politically opposed to postwar German denial.[7] The Gestapo Terrain was quickly becoming recognized as an important social symbol of Germany's repression of the National Socialist past and was used locally as a political space of resistance, so it seemed an ideal location for such a memorial. Yet Perspective for Berlin's approaches to place, memory, history, and public art were quite different from those of the local activist groups engaged in Gestapo Terrain debates. Because identities are always relationally constructed, these distinct spatial claims to place were influenced by the ways that different social groups constructed the past and understood German identity in the present and future. These public debates between Perspective for Berlin and other groups, such as the Active Museum, about who should be commemorated, where, and in what form, also indicate important differences within West German mainstream liberal to left perspectives in the 1980s.

Perspective for Berlin pursued the goal of confronting German denial about the past through international approaches to Holocaust memory and commemoration. Rather than narrate the national (and international) past through a local site, as did groups like the Active Museum who were inspired by the history workshop movement, Perspective for Berlin started with the premise that the persecution of Jews and the Holocaust was a unique event in global history. The group also publicly identified with the political agendas of liberal to left groups in other Western countries. Thus while the Gestapo Terrain was recognized as a unique historic site, Perspective for Berlin saw it as a symbol of Nazi evil as well as of German guilt. For this reason, the group felt that establishing a monumental memorial at this location would acknowledge German guilt to an international (Western) public by mourning for the suffering of those who had died. Such mourning work in the present might begin to make amends for crimes of the past and indicate how Germany as a society had changed. By admitting guilt to the international community in this way, Perspective for Berlin also believed Germany would make clear its commitment to the Western "civilized world" and its cosmopolitan humanitarian values, a theme I explore in chapter 5.

Perspective for Berlin was thus also committed to a liberal postnational ideal in the future, but how the group envisioned that future was based on a narration of the past through place that other groups had rejected in previous debates over the Gestapo Terrain. In the next chapter, I describe in more detail Perspective for Berlin's proposal for a national memorial after unification. Here I briefly sketch some of those differences, because it was in opposition to Perspective for Berlin's proposal that the concept for a site of perpetrators was delineated in public discussions and the expert commission's report for the establishment of a permanent center at the Topography of Terror.

Perspective for Berlin supported a West German form of commemoration typical for the *Mahnmal,* associated with a culture of dismay *(Betroffenheit).* At the same time, the group drew inspiration from memorials in other countries, in particular Israel and the United States. For example, the group initially advocated a memorial that would be similar in form to Yad Vashem or the Vietnam War Memorial, such as a monumental wall engraved with the names of 150,000 murdered German Jews. Later, to gain publicity for their project, Perspective for Berlin held its own invited art competition for a memorial at the Gestapo Terrain that stipulated that the seventeen countries occupied by Germany and the corresponding number of Jewish victims in each country had to be named or represented.[8] It was important that the memorial represent the Holocaust by naming victims and also by communicating universal messages of human suffering and hope for a humanitarian future; aesthetic forms of memorials in other democratic countries could be drawn on for inspiration. What would be particular to Germany would be the size and location of the memorial—spatial forms that would function as visible public proclamations of guilt, mourning, and repentance.

There were at least three related reasons why most groups already involved in the Gestapo Terrain debates rejected Perspective for Berlin's proposal. First (as I explore in more detail in the next chapter), in the late 1980s, public memorial art in West Germany, just as in other countries, began to be understood as a set of relationships between place, audience, and art, rather than an object. Rather than emphasize art as the creative expression of an inspired artist-genius, public and conceptual artists more generally viewed their work as a productive outcome of the relationships between art, space, time, and the people experiencing the art. Speaking of this international shift in public art, Jeff Kelley explains that "the place, not the art, is the metaphor. In another place, one would need another art."[9] Public memorial artists conceptualize the memorial as an artistic performance of encounters between visitors and the past, a site through which a society begins to negotiate its relationships to a (haunted) nation. Thus, while the aesthetic forms of Holocaust memorials around the world influence one another through geopolitical relations, political economies of Holocaust memory, and artistic networks at the transnational scale, the memorial, as a particular form of public art, also offers the opportunity for citizens to create and question national public cultures of memory through their particular local contexts.[10] In West Berlin during the public debates about the Gestapo Terrain in the late 1970s and early 1980s, both aesthetic and site-specific problems associated with monumental memorials and a related national culture of dismay were raised, leading to suggestions for alternative types of places that would encourage a confrontation with the past through local contexts.

Indeed, citizen initiatives involved in the Gestapo Terrain debates, particularly of the '68 generation, emphasized the singularity of this particular historic site: it was a place where the German state bureaucratically organized and instituted mass murder. For these citizens, this historic center had a significant meaning in Germany, the "land of the perpetrators," one that demanded a different approach to commemoration and political education. This was a second difference. Because those advocating a new type of place of memory interpreted this historic location as the administrative center where orders for murder and persecution were issued for all groups persecuted under National Socialism, they took issue with Perspective for Berlin's historical interpretation, namely, that the memorial should commemorate Jews only. As Active Museum president Christine Fischer-Defoy recalled in 1998, "The debate was about the location of the Holocaust Memorial. . . . First of all, this is the place of the perpetrators, and if it were also a place for commemorating the victims, we have to commemorate them all—the Gestapo headquarters was responsible for the murder of political opponents, homosexuals, and all groups, not just the murder of Jews. . . . Then she [Lea Rosh, head of Perspective for Berlin] came and said that . . . the Jews are the most important victim group and therefore they have priority. And we said that this place is not primarily the place of the victims. It is the place of the perpetrators and of their crimes, and the structures that led to that. The victims should be commemorated in the concentration camps, or at other authentic places. . . . But not at this place. Not here, at the place of the 'extermination bureaucracy.'"

In the context of debates over who were the "real" victims, activist groups and other individuals raised the most serious concern with Perspective for Berlin's proposal: that such a memorial would lead to a "hierarchy of victims" in Germany and define the Holocaust according to Jewish suffering only. If the memory of Jews was privileged at the Gestapo Terrain, they feared that such a hierarchy of victims would result in anger by other victims, and survivor groups would then (rightfully) demand their own national memorials, a process that could lead to competition for the most central location, the most monumental design, the largest state and federal budget, the most elaborate commemorative events, and so on. Indeed, in response to Perspective for Berlin's proposal, the General Council of Sinti and Roma in Germany published a newspaper advertisement in 1989 addressed to Chancellor Kohl and Berlin mayor Diepgen that called for a memorial for all victim groups.[11] (After unification, when it became clear that the Holocaust Memorial would commemorate Jews only, the Sinti and Roma demanded their own memorial. The foundation stone for it was ceremoniously placed in the vicinity of the Reichstag in 2000).[12]

In the late 1980s and early 1990s, opponents of Perspective for Berlin's proposal felt that a chain of Holocaust memorials standing next to one another in the center of Berlin would do little to help Germans confront their National Socialist past, respectfully mourn those who died, or communicate a positive message to the international community that Germans are confronting their past. Publicly recognizing Jews as the only victim group worthy of commemoration at the Gestapo Terrain meant willfully ignoring the suffering of other victims groups. It was also historically inaccurate. To Perspective for Berlin, naming the victims was a way to raise the ghostly presence of those who had suffered and to honor their memory. They also argued that the suffering and persecution of Jews was unique.

Rosh responded to criticisms of Perspective for Berlin's proposals through publicized media debates.[13] She stated that the group only "dared" to have a different view from the Active Museum about the uniqueness of Jewish persecution and murder. She further accused the Active Museum of claiming to be the only organization trying to address the history of the Gestapo Terrain and defended her group's aesthetic proposal for the memorial. Active Museum members, in response, criticized Perspective for Berlin for using the terrain to advance their political agendas and argued that such a proposal would be a "step backwards to the state of knowledge [about memorials] in 1983." According to Fischer-Defoy, for example, it was a question not only of who and where but also of how: "AM distrusts the pedagogical function of 'memorials' as such" (personal communication, 2003). For the Active Museum, a monumental memorial working within a discourse of dismay and guilt would encourage Germans to situate themselves in the emotive spaces of victims. The Active Museum, other engaged groups, and Topography staff felt that the role of a site of perpetrators is to encourage Germans to engage in the difficult work of confronting a violent national past and accepting social responsibility for that past in the present.

Delimiting Victim and Perpetrator Spaces and Narratives

In these discussions, educators, historians, and other memory experts stressed the importance of distinguishing between victim and perpetrator categories of identity. They argued that this distinction was critical in Germany, unlike the United States or Israel, because Germany was a society of perpetrators, which meant that the pedagogical work and social function of places of memory had to be different. From this perspective, to be German means to occupy a particular social category as perpetrator in historical space, a social location that requires a distinct historical narration of the past. According to Hanno Loewy, "The problem is that the Holocaust is a concept that does not really exist in Germany. When I say 'Holocaust' I mean anti-Semitism, I mean the laws of 1933 and the boycott in April, I mean the 1935 Nuremburg Laws, then the 1938 Reichspogromnacht, the 1939 invasion of Poland, the executions in 1941, the 1942 Wannsee Conference and the gassings, the creation of Auschwitz, Treblinka, Sobibor in 1943, the execution of the Hungarian Jews in 1944, the 1945 evacuation transports and liberation of the camps, and 1945—the return to life. That is the Holocaust. When I talk about the Holocaust, that's what I mean. I don't know anybody who means anything else—the Sinti and Roma construct it in the same way. What does that have to do with Germany? What does that have to do with the German perspective?" (interview, 1993). At the same time, accepting the social identity of perpetrators is understood to be a personal and moral obligation, for it means to assume responsibility for the consequences of this violent past in an ongoing present. Although I am critical of defining German (and non-German) identity in such exclusive ways—in opposition to a "victim" category—during the late 1980s this social and spatial separation of victim and perpetrator identities was tied to a postnational political agenda that helped define new public cultures of memory in Germany.

Why is this separation [between victim and perpetrator] so important?

CHRISTINE FISCHER-DEFOY, Active Museum president: Maybe because the commemoration of the victims would divert attention away from the perpetrators. The responsibility is important for us—to keep an awareness of the perpetrators in the city and to deal with the people who did it. For German politicians, as well as for the German public, it is "easier" to identify with the victims than to deal with the fact that their grandparents were perpetrators. When you mix the educational work about the history of the perpetrators with the commemoration of the victims, it becomes the "Kohl politics" of "we are all so sad, and let us forget that we were the criminals who did it." The mourning hides that, and the perpetrator is put in the background.

When you make such a distinction between the places of the victims and the places of the perpetrators, does that mean that Jews or Sinti and Roma will never be seen as Germans? When you make such a strong distinction it means that . . .

FISCHER-DEFOY: They are Germans as well. It is important that we are the country of the perpetrators and the country of the victims as well—Germans were also victims. I think that there are two different processes in your mind that you have to deal with [with respect to the history of National Socialism in Germany]: the crimes and the consequences, and the mourning for the victims—they are two different aspects.

Couldn't you imagine making an exhibition with these two perspectives together? . . . When you always think of Germany as the country of the perpetrators, it also means that the people who were persecuted in the past are always seen as victims in this society.

FISCHER-DEFOY: I think they should be separated in space. This was one of the reasons why the provisory exhibition at the Topography of Terror had this emotional impact even though it was very abstract—the authentic place, these basements, and the concrete history presented about the basements. At this place there were of course victims. . . . The last rudiment of original traces . . . will be the place of mourning . . . on this symbolic and exemplary piece of floor that is still left [of the Gestapo house prison]. Of course, you cannot separate that completely. When you think about the crimes, you also think about the victims.

You think that there is a danger when it is seen as a place of victims . . .

FISCHER-DEFOY: The one thing covers the other. (Interview, 1998)

There are political and pedagogical reasons for representing Germany as a society of perpetrators. By designating Germans as perpetrators, educators, historians, politicians, and activists wanted to challenge neoconservative attempts at normalizing the German nation during the 1980s. While German normalization has been a central part of every German administration after 1945,[14] under the former chancellor Helmut Kohl, it was defined by two agendas. First was the goal of realizing the ideal of the *Kulturnation* (a unified cultural-political nation) through German-German unification, a goal that built on Willy Brandt's (SPD) idea of cooperation between the West and East Blocs but simultaneously promoted a neo-Adenauerian (CDU) notion of shared Western values (such as individual liberty and national self-determination). Second, Kohl sought an agenda of historical normalization in which the "German question" (the problem of a divided nation resulting from the history of National Socialism) would be disengaged from the "Jewish question" (the representation of the Holocaust as a unique event in German memory and international history). This second agenda, historical normalization, was first introduced by SPD chancellor Schmidt. But under Kohl it was pursued through international public ceremony and the establishment of national places of memory.

During the 1980s, the Kohl administration pursued a cultural political agenda that promoted a positive historical understanding of the German nation through the establishment of national history museums in Berlin (the German Historical Museum) and Bonn (the House of History), proposals to erect a national war memorial for all fallen soldiers in Bonn, and commemorative acts typical for other European nations, such as a visit with American president Ronald Reagan to a war cemetery in Bitburg (where infantry soliders as well as SS officers from World War II were buried) to celebrate the forty-year anniversary of the end of World War II. These places and performances were very controversial, however, for they intended to communicate to German citizens and to the Western world more generally that Germany had earned the status of a normal modern European nation-state and need no longer be haunted by its National Socialist past. Some critics came to describe Kohl's agenda, in terms of these performances, as producing "Bitburg history." For historian Charles Maier, Bitburg history represents the past in ways that intentionally confuse moral categories and historical agents and make it almost impossible to define social responsibility for past actions.[15] Bitburg history distorts the logical dependence of victim and victimizer to a common dialectic that results in shared responsibility for the wrong(s) committed. It also relativizes the past: Nazi crimes are represented as one of many mass murders committed in the twentieth century.

Not only were Kohl and neoconservative politicians accused of a "geopolitics of nostalgia," that is, the promotion of a positive national identity through selective images of pasts not tarnished by Nazi crimes (such as the imperial tradition); so too were well-respected historians.[16] Heated public discussions in the media about politically motivated representations of the Holocaust and German national history also occurred as a result of the so-called Historians' Debate.[17] Historians and cultural critics argued that well-known scholars, such as Ernst Nolte (Free University of Berlin) and Andreas Hillgruber (University of Cologne), represented the horrors of the Nazi regime in terms similar to genocides perpetrated by other regimes. Critics argued that inappropriate historical comparisons (across and through political space and time) confused the categories of victims and perpetrators and made it difficult to assign responsibility for the actions of Germans during that period. Jürgen Habermas in particular denounced the selective use of historical methods and interpretive frameworks, such as everyday history, for overt political purposes; according to Habermas, Hillgruber's "empathetic history" of the Wehrmacht justified the actions of Germans in defending their nation, and hence perpetrating the Holocaust.[18]

Within this cultural context in the 1980s, the Topography of Terror was seen by activists and historians as a critical political presence. A site of perpetrators demanded that Germans acknowledge responsibility for past crimes and come to terms with post-war denial, including the contemporary neoconservative "*Schlußstrich* mentality," or attempts to draw a final line under, or come to closure with, the National Socialist past. (After unification, many argued that Kohl's geopolitical agenda of normalization intensified, as evidenced by the establishment of a central memorial to all victims of war and tyranny, the Neue Wache, and the drastic budget cuts to national concentration camp memorial museums.)[19] A site of perpetrators required that Germans no longer see themselves as victims of the evil Nazi elite, a dominant myth in German society;[20] victim and perpetrator categories must be clearly defined.

The political agenda of representing Germany as a society of perpetrators also reflected a vision for the future based on the West German liberal to socialist ideal of postnationalism. The idea of a "postnational democracy among nation-states" was first coined by the Bonn political scientist Karl Dietrich Bracher in 1982; later it became associated with the Frankfurt social and political philosopher Jürgen Habermas's concept of "constitutional patriotism."[21] Habermas believed that culturally diverse Europeans could learn from the experience of Switzerland and the United States and find common rules for political participation without asking citizens to give up their various ethnic identities and cultural ties. By separating political from cultural spaces and identities, Habermas believed that Germans could move beyond traditional understandings of the nation—in particular, the cultural-political entity of the *Kulturnation*. This concept was viewed as a breakthrough—as both an improvement of, and step toward, overcoming traditional German nationalism. Postnationalism was an ideal that "transformed a German deficiency into a European virtue: because the [old] Federal Republic was not a nation-state she seemed particularly suited to promoting the supranational integration of Western Europe."[22] Not only was the German nation partitioned into occupied sectors after the war and then divided through the Cold War; West Germany emphasized a federal approach to cultural identity, as evidenced by the legal and financial framework that supported state-based or regional cultural institutions. Because the nation was considered a taboo category at the time, West Germans came to identify strongly with their regional and European attachments.

As I suggested in the previous chapter, activists, inspired by both the postnational ideal and locally based history workshop movements, established memorial museums at historic sites throughout Germany that questioned the ideal of the nation. They created what would later be referred to as a decentralized network of places of memory that confronted the past and promoted educational work about tolerance, human rights, and democratization. These places of memory were defined by the cultural discourse of reappraisal and confrontation with the past *(Aufarbeitung der Vergangenheit)* and an internationalist humanitarian Western agenda. At the same time, the distinction between victim and perpetrator identities would be narrated through site-specific historical representations of the past, of the history of National Socialism on the one hand and the history of the Holocaust on the other. The history of National Socialism would be documented through sites of perpetrators both to narrate a larger story about the emergence of a police state from a democracy and to pursue a pedagogical goal of accepting social responsibility for the past. At historic sites of suffering, the story of the Holocaust and persecution would be told, and the moral goal of bearing witness to this past would be realized through the harrowing stories of survivors and the places where people suffered and were murdered.

At the Gestapo Terrain, such an interpretation of postnationalism through place was defined in opposition to existing aesthetic and historical forms, such as the *Mahnmal* or *Gedenkstätte*. While the separation of victim and perpetrator sites implicit to the *Ort der Täter* was tied to both political and pedagogical ideals, Topography directors, citizen initiatives, and educators acknowledge that this strict division is imposed on the past. They point out that internal variations existed within those categories. Rürup, for example, responding to an earlier version of this chapter, noted that the Topography represents Germany not as a *nation* of perpetrators but rather as a *society* with "a lot of internal variation. When you say that Germany is a society of perpetrators, you have to differentiate. It is not a society of Himmlers or Heydrichs. But they belong to it, and others belong to it; those who tried to make things better were very few, but they also existed. Because of that we cannot say that this was a 'people' of perpetrators.... [In addition,] not all the victims were Jews, but also non-Jewish Germans, and the majority were non-Germans, residents of other European countries" (interview, 1998).[23] Similarly, the expert commission's report acknowledged the importance of commemorating those who were tortured and died at the Gestapo house prison. As the expert commission explained, "The memory and commemoration of those persecuted and murdered by the Nazis, especially those victims who have been 'forgotten,' should be commemorated at the terrain."[24] Indeed, their memory continues to haunt the terrain through the presence of the prison cell foundations and the very establishment of the Topography. It was their memory that motivated survivor groups to call for a memorial in the early 1980s.

To mourn for the dead, yet create a site of perpetrators, the expert commission proposed a spatial and temporal thinning-out of the terrain. To honor those who were unjustly killed, and to appropriately lay the dead to rest, three locations were designated as commemorative spaces. The first would be a permanent place of mourning at the ruins of the Gestapo in-house prison cell floors. The other two were temporary places of commemoration that would accommodate group activities on special occasions, one at the northeast section of the terrain (behind the smaller hill of rubble), and the other at the area in front of the Martin Gropius Bau. In this way, the dead would be honored, but the Topography's main social function would be defined by contemporary hauntings of German ancestors.

But how exactly did the expert commission propose to represent the history of National Socialism at a historic site of perpetrators? This is no simple question. Representing a violent national history is not a dilemma unique to Germany, although it is more heavily scrutinized by the international community because of the past to be remembered.

Citizen groups and human rights activists around the world face the same problem, for example, when they wish to create historical exhibits that confront the legacies of authoritarianism and state-perpetrated violence in their societies. At a different scale, in the 1970s and 1980s, museum curators also grappled with similar issues when they explored design options for exhibiting social and everyday histories: how does one present the history of domestic violence without condoning it? Live performances are particularly problematic representations of violent pasts, as the directors of the living history museum at Colonial Williamsburg found. When they staged a slave auction to help visitors imagine what the history of slavery meant in everyday life, contemporary people protested, arguing that the historical reenactment created an environment of approval rather than condemnation of the racism, inhumanity, and social relations portrayed.

Representation is always political and intertextual; it is a practice that refers to already existing cultural narratives. At the Topography, the political and pedagogical goal of distinguishing perpetrators from victims in space and time clearly defined the temporary exhibit, the concept for the proposed future center, and the Topography of Terror that evolved after 1990. In addition, the expert commission recommended particular representational strategies to narrate a difficult national past such that the individuals involved in creating, contributing to, and supporting systems of terror that led to xenophobia, anti-Semitism, racism, homophobia, and violence and genocide would not be easily demonized. Through preservation, topographical mapping, and a structural history of perpetrators, future generations of Germans would learn about their national past. As I describe in the next section, these approaches to the past indicate particular West German cultural and political understandings of the role of affect and historical narrative in public memory.

Preserving, Mapping, and Documenting a Violent Past

In 1989 and 1990, the expert commission recommended three culturally specific approaches to the past that were ultimately adopted at the Topography of Terror. I roughly label these as preservation, topography, and documentation.[25] Although these three approaches were interrelated, the idea of a documentation in particular was considered by academic staff to be distinctive and indeed influenced the aesthetics of memory at memorial centers throughout Germany in the late 1980s and 1990s. After 2000, this approach has begun to have a noticeable international influence as well.

Preserving the Ort der Täter

The first approach, historic preservation (Denkmalschutz), was pragmatic: securing the terrain in a real estate property system. Historic preservation is a typical response, according to David Lowenthal, to the fear and threat of enormous change.[26] In this case, it was a strategy that would ensure that the city-state could not sell or use that tract of land for other purposes.[27] As academic director Reinhard Rürup pointed out, after unification "Berlin became an important city again, a center, a capital city, and the area [of the

Topography of Terror] is 6.2 hectares at a prime location. There will be a lot of pressure to develop this area" (interview, 1998). Soon after the Wall fell, reports spread that the Topography of Terror might be closed due to bids made for the terrain's real estate, now valuable for its proximity to the future city center (near Potsdamer Platz). In this context, experts argued that the "terrain in its present character offers an unusual chance to lead people to confront the history of National Socialism" and "is the starting point of further considerations."[28]

As Yi-Fu Tuan points out, preservation often stems from the need to support a sense of identity through tangible objects.[29] What was the material object to be created? The expert commission recommended preserving the terrain in its 1987 form, including the deserted fields, piles of rubble, overgrown vegetation, and section of the Wall between the Martin Gropius Bau and Wilhelmstraße. They even recommended cutting back the vegetation that had grown since 1987 and stabilizing piles of rubble to preserve the character of the site. These landscape features, preserved as artifacts, were interpreted by the commission as embodying a deep psychological desire by Germans to forget their dark past: "a visible sign of the long-term effects of the National Socialist Regime."[30] In addition, the unearthed remnants of buildings used during the time of National Socialism were preserved in situ, which meant that the earth around those artifacts would also become part of the jurisdiction of Berlin's archaeological division as a *Bodendenkmal,* literally an "earth memorial." The one change they did recommend was to reorient the entrance of the terrain to the north, which was not possible when the Wall stood, to indicate the historical orientation of the no-longer-standing buildings.

Preservation is a process of creation *and* containment;[31] it stops the process of landscape as a continuously changing outcome of everyday life. A preserved landscape is understood as an "authentic" historical and located material object. Although safeguarding artifacts that reflect atrocities rather than the greatness of a group may seem odd, groups in many Western countries began in the 1970s to preserve local histories through "structures and scenes that would never qualify as 'aesthetic' or 'historic,' perhaps not even as pleasant or comfortable."[32] However, there is a difference between preserving a poorhouse and the remains and earth of the former Nazi headquarters. According to the city archaeologist Alfred Kernd'l, the idea of preserving the terrain as an archaeological site was quite unusual for the twentieth century, "certainly a paradox and a sign of German repression."[33] Kernd'l suggests that Germans had to preserve their profane past to confront it and in doing so have the opportunity to move toward a more humane future.

Because of the reasons motivating the establishment of a site of perpetrators, through preservation a preunification symbol—the Gestapo Terrain "discovered" in 1987—was also protected and contained. This once-abandoned landscape, according to the expert commission, would become an even more powerful physical disturbance in the midst of a new bustling city center with high-rise office buildings.

> From the West-Berlin periphery, [the terrain] was restored as a
> place in the center of Berlin. The Terrain will no longer be out of

the way, inviting the unexpected discovery beyond the reach of the
normal [everyday] path, but rather it will be located in the middle
of the pulsating inner city life, conspicuous also to those residents
and visitors of Berlin who are in no way looking for the National
Socialist past.[34]

Treating the landscape as a cultural artifact also stabilized the interpretation of the
terrain as an open wound, as part of Germany's heritage, as a site where visitors could
confront National Socialist and postwar histories.[35]

The city supported the request for preservation and legally protected the uncovered
ruins; sand was placed on the floors of the Gestapo prison cells, and wooden structures
were erected to protect other ruins. Although it was a successful strategy to protect the
property legally, by containing meaning in this way, historic preservation paradoxically undermined the activist approach to landscape as an ongoing process of embodied
memory, interpretation, and digging. As a preserved landscape, the Gestapo Terrain became a "window into the past" that also protected the activists' symbol of the problems
of the nation and of the crisis of Western modernity. Yet these multiple layers of history
(including the postwar histories of the site, the nation, of German modernity) would
be open to embodied experiences and reflection in an ever-changing present. When
recalling the preunification terrain in 1993, Topography managing director Andreas
Nachama described it as "the end of the world. The world did not continue there; it
was a rupture. It was not only the division of a city, but a whole world. This was the end
of the Western world, and at this end there was this area that did not stand out much.
But today it is very visible. In ten years, when all the construction sites are finished and
everything is beautiful, all of a sudden there will be that open wound in the city. I think
that this is better than any attempt to design it, because so far there is no adequate form
to translate the Holocaust in an artistic way. I think you can only do that by walking on
these traces, by reconstructing it for yourself" (interview, 1993). Through the process
of protecting the landscape as a symbolic open wound, Nachama emphasized the postnational ideal that was implicit to the establishment of a site of perpetrators.

Mapping Identity: A Postnational Topography

The expert committee stressed the international significance of the Gestapo Terrain
through its "topography." A topography represents a material and symbolic mapping
of the histories of National Socialism and the Holocaust according to sites of perpetrators and sites of victims. As the Topography of Terror academic staff member Frank
Dingel described in 1998, the topography represents both "the history of the terrain
[Geländekunde], that this was the Prinz Albrecht terrain," and the symbolic link "to the
name of the institution. We will have one map [at the future center] which will show the
crimes in Europe, and one that will show the administration in Berlin. It becomes very
clear that history is not only taking place in time, it is also linked to places. It is both—in

space and in time. This spatial aspect must be made clear . . . that this is a place where European history between 1933–34 and 1945 is presented."

Rürup explained in 1998 that the term "topography" was "intentionally developed," but "only hesitantly labeled." For the 1987 temporary exhibition, "there was an area that needed to be explained and presented. Because of that it was rather obvious to take the place as a starting point." But there was some hesitancy in using the term for the future center because "nobody knows what a topography is. . . . We kept it because it expressed some things that we wanted, but there was a long debate by the expert commission about whether we should give it a different name. Since there was no convincing alternative, we kept it." Other consultants also agreed that the term "topography" is a difficult one for politicians and the general public to understand.

The historians working on the temporary exhibition and the expert commission afterward may have adopted the term "topography" because it was a concept used in scholarly discussions about social memory at the time. Classic works by Maurice Halbwachs, Pierre Nora, Frances Yates, and Walter Benjamin are filled with spatial metaphors to describe the process of memory.[36] Halbwachs in particular used the word "topography" to refer to the mapping of sacred places to establish a group identity; Nora discussed sites, environments, and "topographical aspects" of memory in terms of material qualities, such as the specificity of location and traditions being rooted in place. Whereas Halbwachs discussed topography as the symbolic mapping of places through the narration of group stories that may or may not have existed, the term as deployed at the Gestapo Terrain is often used in Nora's sense, as the material qualities of a site that may also be symbolic. Topography at the terrain refers to a historical approach, a "scientific" mapping and inventory of the networks of National Socialist terror, as well as to a symbolic mapping of identity.

By the early 1990s, museum memorial experts and Holocaust studies scholars adopted this inventory approach to the past and associated it with a progressive political project. "Topography" was used as a kind of methodology, of physically mapping out a place—the spatial layout and artifacts of a historic concentration camp in the present day—to construct and interpret history through that spatial process. The present-day map, as a kind of objective, historical inventory of ruins and objects, would be compared with other historical documents to ascertain changes in land use through time. These historical comparisons, often part of exhibitions, would allow a broader public to see the past in the present-day landscape. Many graduate students in the early to mid-1990s worked on such projects for their degrees, mapping archaeological digs and their historical findings at different sites and comparing those material inventories with archival sources. Similarly, the expert commission recommended physically mapping the site for the future Topography of Terror; they argued that "knowledge about National Socialist criminality should not be abstract, but rather concrete."[37]

At the future Topography of Terror, maps of perpetrator space will offer visitors a way to visualize, or "see at a glance," all sites where National Socialist acts against humanity took place in Berlin, Germany, and Europe. Visitors can then search for related documents about particular locales in the center's databases. Giving a visual image to National Socialism by mapping past crimes is one way to document and confront the past, to make the unknowable seem tangible. Yet the topographical map is a model of the world, a symbolic approach to seeing and interpreting the physical environment. Through surveying and mapping the world at a moment in time, scientists produce and control space by classifying and ordering what and who belongs where.[38] At the Topography of Terror, such a mapping, according to the commission, would provide evidence of "the special German accountability and responsibility for the Holocaust" and demonstrate the international significance of this historic site. The Gestapo Terrain was thus represented as the zenith of a *European* National Socialist topography of terror. For this reason, the expert commission viewed the future center as having an "extraordinary value for humanity"; it was "a site not only of German, but rather also of European history, and in many respects of world history as well."[39] They recommended that the Federal Republic make a formal application to include the terrain as part of the UNESCO World Heritage List, a list that includes Auschwitz.[40] Being classified in the same inventory as Auschwitz not only reinforced the idea of separate spaces of victims and perpetrators but underscored the centrality of the Gestapo Terrain for a humanitarian future.

In addition to mapping, the expert committee emphasized the international location of the Topography of Terror through the memory-work of the proposed future international center. "No place in Germany is more appropriate . . . to accomplish this mourning work *[Trauerarbeit]* through an exchange of individuals from every country and religion, from every political position and social group, and, last but not least, from every academic discipline—a task that is a condition for a [more] humane future."[41] The center would allow a range of individuals to choose how to conduct their memory-work, as well as where and how to frame their collective and personal identities. It would provide opportunities for artists, academics, politicians, and educators of various countries to exchange their thoughts and ideas.[42] The commission also proposed building an international youth center *(internationale Begegnungsstätte),* as well as forming international working and discussion groups on various topics, such as basic human rights, the status of minority groups, the existence of radical right movements, and expressions of extreme nationalism.

At the same time that this international mapping of perpetrator space promoted the postnational ideal of moving toward a more humanitarian future, it was also strategically used to gain *national* recognition for this historic site of perpetrators. After calling for a public architectural competition for the Topography's permanent center in 1992, the Berlin Senate used the expert commission's report to pressure the federal government for financial support.[43] Although the Senate ultimately came to an informal compromise to share the costs of the future Topography with the federal government, the immediate response in Bonn to Berlin's request for funding was that the history of National Socialism would be exhibited in the planned German Historical Museum; it was Berlin's responsibility to deal with "local" history. Federal finance minister Theo Waigel (CSU) was not convinced of the national and international significance of the site. In response, SPD Berlin senator of cultural affairs Anke Martiny stated, "In my view, we also say that whoever wants a German History Museum cannot overlook the fact that there is also a Wannsee-Villa and the Gestapo Terrain in Berlin. Together, these are a national task and not simply a Berlin matter."[44]

By the late 1990s, the international significance of the Topography came to be recognized by federal officials, but some politicians nonetheless have difficulties with the idea of a national historic site of perpetrators. This remains a problem for the pedagogical goals of the center and its postnational political agenda. For Thomas Lutz, director of the national Memorial Museums Division of the Topography, "The Topography has to be part of Germany's historical image *[Geschichtsbild]*. Internationally the Holocaust is the 'bad' per se, and other countries like Israel use it for their political interests. For me it is interesting to ask, 'What does the history of National Socialism mean for the history of humans in general?'" (interview, 2000). Lutz describes the memory-work at the Topography of Terror as not only significant for Germans; confronting the history of National Socialism is also an important task for being a citizen in the world.

A Documentary Approach to the Past: Fear of Emotion

In addition to the topographical mapping of perpetrator space, historical documents provided material evidence of past crimes. This was the third approach to the past at the Topography—the documentation—and is considered by experts to be the major contribution made to German cultures of memory. According to Topography academic staff Klaus Hesse, "We were among the first who introduced this style, who did not use pathos. Now you find documentations in all the memorial centers, and they follow the same concept" (focus group interview, 1998).

A documentation represents the structural history of the rise of a fascist regime and its terror apparatus, or a state's legal and political institutions of repression and criminal oppression (such as the Gestapo, SS, Security Service, and Reich Security Main Office). It outlines the roles of key players in those institutions, the existing social support (or lack of resistance) for a regime, and other factors that created, supported, and made possible socially systematic networks of terror. It also exhibits the consequences of those networks.

The exhibit communicates information, according to the Topography academic staff member Andreas Sanders, in "a very plain, direct manner. . . . A documentation attempts to present the material as it is, leaving the viewers to draw their own conclusions" (interview, 1994). For former Topography managing director Gabriele Camphausen, a documentation "presents what are proven facts. It can be supplemented by memories, but it has to be made clear that those are memories only. . . . These two levels must be strictly separated from each other" (focus group interview, 1998). Topography academic staff member Frank Dingel described the documentation as a presentation of historical information accompanied by reproductions of authentic documents (legal orders, maps, photos, and other documents); there are no frills in the exhibit, no films, no reproductions, no flashy graphics.

Although Topography of Terror directors and academic staff acknowledge that every exhibit is an interpretation, they feel that a stark presentation of facts may result in a less subjective view of the historical material presented. According to Sanders, "I understand a documentation as a reconstruction of history that is very close to the sources: documents, photos, and reports by time witnesses. . . . These different sources have to be treated critically. . . . The documentation tries to reconstruct history from the material we have, and [we try] to stand in the background as the designer of the exhibition. But you cannot do this completely because you have to organize the material" (focus group interview, 1998). This particular narrative form of history is intended to reach a German audience, to make a social link to the heritage of perpetrators, but not in an emotional way. Sanders described "the factual approach of the exhibition" as a "counterweight—we don't intend to present the past in an emotional way. Of course we interpret, but we try to keep it down. We want to let visitors emotionally deal with the topic and interpret the exhibit. We try to confront them with facts—or rather, not *the* facts, but with facts in general—to get a person to draw his or her own conclusions. That is why many people . . . still find this type of exhibition convincing. It has something to do with the emotional nature of the topic" (interview, 1997). Similarly, Dingel described a documentation as the "most appropriate" way of representing National Socialist history. In a 1994 public lecture introducing a traveling exhibition in Chicago, he explained that

> staging historical events and facts could give visitors the impression that they are being manipulated, which is often indeed the case. In addition, regarding an exhibit such as this one, it is absolutely necessary to be as correct as possible. . . . If you consider all the debates over the exact number of persons murdered in Auschwitz, then you can see that emotions sometimes run so high that they shut out the possibility of rational arguments. Nevertheless, if educational work is to be successful in the long term there is no alternative to a critical and self-critical presentation of the facts, that is, one which continually contributes to a reevaluation of one's own level of information.[45]

The documentary approach to representing the history of perpetrators is considered to be a historically accurate, "rational," and "self-critical presentation of the facts." It is contrasted to other approaches to representing the past associated with exhibitions in the 1960s and 1970s, or associated with exhibitions about the history of victims, including staging historical events and facts or manipulating visitors by emphasizing emotion and pathos. These oppositional categories indicate at least three interrelated assumptions inherent to the documentary approach that are culturally specific to West Germany: concern about Holocaust denial and historical revisionism, negative reactions to popular representations of the Holocaust, and fear of emotions.

The mention by Dingel of Auschwitz and "exact numbers" is a direct reference to Holocaust denial. While political education was strongly influenced by Marxist structural approaches and the critical theories of the Frankfurt school in the 1960s and 1970s, which in part explains the emphasis on a "rational" approach to the topic, another reason why the Topography of Terror (and other *Gedenkstätten* more generally) stresses a systematic and structural presentation of facts is to challenge extremists. While Holocaust denial is not as strong after 2000 as it was in the 1980s and 1990s, there are people who argue that the Holocaust never happened and assert that concentration camps were not death camps but merely labor camps. Holocaust deniers go to great lengths to argue that the photos, documents, and artifacts at concentration camp memorials have been manufactured and use conspiracy theories to support their anti-Semitic and white supremacist agendas. Deniers assert that the current historical knowledge about death camps is a fabrication—what they call "Auschwitz lies"—and reject the fact that National Socialists and German citizens, aided by others, collectively murdered millions of Jews, Sinti and Roma, homosexuals, Jehovah's Witnesses, and other individuals. They use shock tactics to make their point and intimidate others, such as by going to places considered to be morally sacred, including Auschwitz, and harassing tour guides and visitors. As depicted in the film *Beruf Neonazi* (Occupation Neo-Nazi), for example, a neo-Nazi attends a tour at Auschwitz I.[46] In the gas chamber, he yells at the group and proceeds to tell the "real" truth about the ovens at Auschwitz. He takes advantage of the group's silence of shock, disbelief, and horror and continues speaking until one visitor confronts him. This example may be extreme, but confronting Holocaust denial and denial of German's social responsibility for the past is a common experience for educators and tour guides at memorial centers in Germany and elsewhere.

After the collapse of the East Bloc, Holocaust denial became more complex. The political uses of National Socialist sites by East Germany and other East Bloc states were, of necessity, publicly exposed. Photographs, places, and historical information at historic sites were a combination of historical fact and propaganda. Directors, guides, and educators at various memorial centers mentioned that school groups from the former GDR in particular were not interested in the topics presented. Some suggested they were angry and mistrustful because of the ways the GDR manipulated National Socialist history to promote a "national" identity based on antifascism. According to one Berlin memorial center educator in 1992, youth from the former GDR became quite cynical: "When the words 'resistance' or 'communist' are mentioned in tours or seminars, students' eyes glaze over." From my observations on numerous tours in the early to mid-1990s, that comment seemed pretty accurate.

Exposing the ways that history was used to promote socialist agendas has resulted in other problems. With new research, historians now agree, for example, that Auschwitz I was modified after the war; the small gas chamber there was originally built as a prototype, and after much larger and more efficient gas chambers were constructed at Auschwitz II, or Birkenau, it was remodeled as a bomb shelter. After the war, memorial center authorities changed the look of the structure to reflect what they thought the gas chamber should look like by adding the smokestack—an architectural feature that has become an iconic landscape symbol for the Holocaust.[47] Holocaust deniers use this evidence to argue that everything at Auschwitz is a fake.

In response to Holocaust denial before the collapse of the East Bloc, the strategy adopted at the Topography of Terror and elsewhere in the former Federal Republic was to overwhelm visitors with concrete, exact, factual information that cannot be repudiated. At the Topography, the documents and photos on exhibit are exact reproductions that have been enlarged but have not been tampered with, edited, or cropped. Although these are not "originals," academic staff take care that the exhibition's aesthetics do not offer evidence that the terrain, artifacts, or documents have been changed. Further, there are no historical re-creations of past scenes. The ruins at the Topography of Terror terrain may be mundane, but they are authentic. Directors have never considered reconstructing the Gestapo house prison cells because they feel such a re-creation would exploit a visitor's emotions and inappropriately encourage voyeurism at a historic site of perpetrators.

The emphasis on a low-tech, nonmanipulative approach at the Topography of Terror reflects a second cultural assumption: a rejection of what the Frankfurt school of critical theory labeled as "the colonization of consciousness by the culture industries." This reaction is largely a negative response to the American-dominated global Holocaust industry that emerged after the war. Many historians, educators, and memory experts clearly reject what they consider entertainment-based approaches to educating the public about the history of National Socialism and the Holocaust. Moreover, they reject a global process whereby few recognizable images and narratives are produced that fetishizes the Holocaust as a cultural product, even as kitsch that can be pleasurably consumed and from which profits are made. According to Gabrielle Kreutzner, intellectuals on the left inherited the Frankfurt school's hostility toward "popular" phenomena that have a broad appeal and tend to be partial toward "high culture."[48] Kreutzner traces the influence of the Frankfurt school in the 1968 student movements and argues that a particular set of assumptions and ideas about culture and society were carried over by this younger generation when they got jobs in the media, educational institutions, and other arenas of social life during the 1970s and 1980s. The result is that left intellectual circles positioned themselves as morally and politically "*outside* of the culture industries' ideological practices" and superficial "flood of images," especially those produced by Hollywood and other popular-culture industries.[49] The politically progressive subject, in this view, rejects products of the mass-production culture industries and turns toward more "authentic" objects of culture and history.

Animosity toward popular culture is evident in many areas of West German culture, including museum practices, the film industry, and historical research. Many German museum curators, for example, feel that American representations of the past are products for entertainment, for "having fun," which, in the views of some critics, gets in the way of education. Dramatized stories are emphasized, and high-tech and multimedia technologies are used to stage "lifelike" performances. The metaphor for this "emotional" and capitalist approach to history, associated with tourism and commodification of the past, is a popular-culture icon that also represents America: Disneyland. For example, the German press initially criticized the U.S. Holocaust Memorial Museum as a Disney approach to the Holocaust. While many of my consultants pointed out that this criticism was unwarranted, they pointed out some specific examples that would be inappropriate to educational work in Germany, such as giving each visitor an "identity pass." At the Gestapo Terrain, it would not have made political or pedagogical sense to encourage personal identification with perpetrators in the context of the neoconservative revisionism, Holocaust denial, and violence toward foreigners that was part of German society in the late 1980s and early 1990s.

The negative attitude toward entertainment-based, or Disney-like, approaches to the past is also related to postwar debates about who has the right to represent, exhibit, control, and produce German public memory. The criticism by the New German Cinema group of Hollywood films, for example, provides a good example of the reasons why American filmic productions of the Holocaust were rejected in West Germany among some progressive circles. The New German Cinema is a group of filmmakers that began as a radical organization in the early 1960s; they rejected Allied, and more specifically American, control over education and media. In their view, which still influences many discussions today, Americans are cultural imperialists who profit from the production of German history and popular culture—a political and economic trend they trace back to the history of the American-led denazification programs. Common to most of their films was a criticism of the policies of the Federal Republic and the materialism of German contemporary society.[50]

The films they produced, however, did not have the public impact that the American-produced films did, such as the 1979 miniseries *Holocaust,* which captured more than 20 million viewers and triggered numerous public debates about the ethics of representing the Holocaust as a family melodrama and thriller. For New German Film director Edgar Reitz, however, *Holocaust* was a "glaring example [of an] international aesthetics of commercialism [for which] the misery produced by the Nazis is nothing but a welcome background spectacle for a sentimental family story."[51] Although *Holocaust* was heavily criticized (also by Americans) for trivializing horror and for commercializing historical suffering, it did what no German film to date had done, namely, to "inform the Germans about crimes against Jews committed in their name so that millions were emotionally touched and moved."[52] Similar debates about the positive and negative aspects of popular, sentimental films emerged more recently after the blockbuster success of Steven Spielberg's *Schindler's List.*

The *Holocaust* miniseries was no doubt indicative of the larger booming Holocaust industry of the late 1970s and 1980s, in which images and traumatic survivors' stories that define popular knowledge about the Holocaust were produced, recirculated, and consumed globally by a mass viewing public. This American-dominated industry began shortly after the war through the various theatrical and commercialized representations of Anne Frank's story; since the 1990s, the proliferation of scholarly and popular books, memoirs, documentaries, oral histories, fiction, art, films, and places of memory has only increased.[53] Related Holocaust tourism economies have also developed, whereby individuals and organized groups visit places of memory and historic sites to learn about their familial and ethnic-cultural pasts. American Jewish tour groups, for example, often begin their trips at historic sites of suffering and pain in Eastern Europe (in particular Treblinka and Auschwitz), make a brief stop in Germany, and conclude in the redemptive spaces of the Yad Vashem Museum in Israel.[54] Many other individuals also visit Holocaust sites as part of their travels to a city or country.

German educators, historians, filmmakers, and others have moral concerns with making profits on Holocaust productions, or worse, turning the Holocaust into sentimental kitsch. They also comment negatively on the educational effects of this "globalization of the Holocaust." Despite the opening of more archives, museums, and research centers in numerous countries in recent years, which has made more than 2 million photos available, the scope and content of the images reproduced in scholarly and popular venues remain remarkably limited.[55] A few popular iconic images and words, and victims' stories of traumatic recall, have come to stand for complex historical processes of the rise of the National Socialist regime and the consequent institutionalized genocide of Jews, Sinti and Roma, homosexuals, the physically and mentally handicapped, and other groups. Some experts fear that the repetition of viewing and listening to the same images and stories—which have become familiar and recognizable icons of the Holocaust—will result in an uncritical acceptance of simplified historical knowledge about complex events and encourage an emotive overidentification with victims (symbolized by Jews).

The scholars Geoffrey Hartman and Barbie Zelizer also argue that the (re)circulation of Holocaust representations internationally has resulted in a "saturation" by the public; this surfeit of signification has "desensitized" and "dulled" viewers' responses to what Susan Sontag calls "the photographic inventory of ultimate horror."[56] Even the word "Holocaust" has been so overused that some argue it is no longer meaningful.[57] Leslie Morris, in summarizing these arguments, and noting the emphasis on visual forms of representation in Germany, argues that "the repetition and echo of the word 'Holocaust' in public discourse in Germany and the repetition of the 'unspeakability' of the event creates a similar effect of a dulling and numbing, ultimately taking the listener from these sites (and sounds) of remembrance."[58]

The West German liberal to left bias against the commercialization of the Holocaust, and its assumed related effects of dulling historical critical thinking and numbing human responses toward genocide, is also reflected within the historical profession. This is the third cultural bias in the documentary approach: representing a violent national history through a distanced, unemotional perspective. In academia, structural approaches to the history of National Socialism have been privileged over other historical methods and narratives, including *Alltagsgeschichte,* or the history of everyday life. Moreover, the National Socialist state is generally interpreted by structural scholars as modern, yet traditional; that is, the state used romanticized and emotive ways to gain power and popular support. Thus some historians adopted the most "rational" and "objective" approaches possible to studying this historical period (as defined by West German scholars) so as to be as "anti-Nazi" as possible and thereby gain scholarly legitimacy.[59] In contrast, *Alltagsgeschichte* has been criticized as trivializing German history, especially the history of the Third Reich, by privileging experiences of ordinary people without offering scientific analysis or scholarly interpretation. It is an approach that emerged from the discontent of historians in the 1960s and 1970s with the structural social history of the Bielefeld school.[60] Historians of everyday life draw from a range of theoretical approaches not often accepted by mainstream historians, including feminism and poststructuralism; they employ rigorous methods to challenge the underlying assumptions of structural history and question abstract concepts such as industrialization. They offer a different way of approaching the past, namely, through an attempt to understand the actions of individuals who produced history. Their sources include oral histories, diaries, and other archival sources. Yet their work—which has reached a popular audience through local history workshop movements in the 1970s and 1980s—has been derided as emotional and subjective.[61]

The Topography of Terror's documentary approach reflects this historical bias toward claims to rationality and objectivity. It represents a structural history of National Socialism based on "known facts" and is considered to be distanced from emotional approaches. Legal documents, maps, photographs, and other historical materials are presented as data supporting the historical narrative yet stand on their own to be interpreted by visitors. Although biographies of individuals imprisoned at the Gestapo prison or involved in resistance movements are presented, and some examples of written correspondence displayed, in general, those individuals are also treated as factual evidence.

While the pedagogical goals of confronting Holocaust denial and encouraging critical historical thinking at the Topography have been important and effective, the related claims to objectivity and rationality remain problematic. Because of the privileging of structural history and the use of a stark black-and-white documentary genre, an authoritative voice prevails at the Topography's temporary exhibit. It is a disembodied presentation of history that assumes that the scientist-historian and viewer can be distanced from the knowledge he produces. As feminist and poststructuralist scholars have argued, however, the assumption that an all-knowing, all-seeing scientist can distance himself from the objects he studies is a "god trick."[62] Historical facts are always produced in particular contexts of the present day; they cannot speak for themselves. A documentation too is defined by its social contexts, forms of production, and aesthetics of display, as well as by the imaginations that people bring to the exhibit and terrain.

Not only are there clear differences between legal documents, maps, landscape sketches, and photos of Gestapo prison inmates, for example, but the same "document" will acquire different meanings by virtue of its location within the terrain, situated above or below ground, inside or outside, near or at uncovered ruins. Take, for example, the photograph as document. Black-and-white photos function as signifiers in many Western societies as proof or evidence of reality, that the event depicted, and subject matter being viewed, happened. Such a reality effect may not encourage the visitors who look at these images to think about the reasons the photos were taken or how that image of reality was framed and produced. Although photos may signify a particular historical moment, they also depict a particular, and incredibly subjective, perspective—namely, that of the person taking the photo. One person chooses what is important: what to include and what to exclude from the photo, how to set up and compose the shot, or how many photos to take of the same event or place. The photographer often has a reason for taking the picture; he or she will definitely have an audience and function in mind for the final print. Furthermore, the technologies and production of the image and print may also be significant to understand the uses of the photographic image.

A different, but complementary, approach to the difficult nature of exhibiting a violent past while socially accepting responsibility for it would be to provide more information about the documents selected and, where possible, to discuss why this distanced aesthetic presentation was adopted. Giving visitors more information about the material exhibited would enhance the pedagogical and political work of a documentation, that is, encourage critical historical thinking and prompt visitors to interpret the presented material on their own.[63] It would also help visitors learn more about the National Socialist state regime. Civilians, SS officers, Nazi soldiers, or others may have taken photos for publicity, for use in their own photo albums, or for the more obvious use of police and identification purposes; some of these images may have been intentionally staged. Photography in the National Socialist police state, moreover, was used as a form of violence. Did individuals want to have their photos taken and be remembered by strangers in this way? If they were forced to have their photograph taken, how did they confront the camera?

This information, when available, would provide a more human(e)—and historically informative—perspective to the photographs on exhibit. It would ask the visitor to look differently at the subject(s) in the photograph. The politics of viewing violent images are no small matter. Yaffah Eliach, a historian, author of an exhibit at the U.S. Holocaust Memorial Museum, and Holocaust survivor, argues that photos taken by perpetrators have no place in a public exhibit, since they present a picture of individuals who have been robbed of their humanity.[64] These individuals, she emphasizes, were tortured, executed, imprisoned, and murdered. If they are represented in historical and educational institutions, they should be depicted and remembered as their friends and families knew them. While Eliach's view may be considered by some to be extreme, the contrast between images of the same individual, as photographed by a Nazi soldier, on the one hand, and as photographed by a family member, on the other, quite dramatically illustrates her point. The photographs of those interned at the Gestapo house prison as opposed to images of people involved in the resistance movement at the Topography exhibit offer such a striking difference.

Klaus Hesse, the Topography's academic staff responsible for photography, acknowledges the problems of using photographs as self-evident factual information. At the same time, he argues that when photos are selected and exhibited as historical documents, they can be a direct and powerful way of communicating information about the past. Hesse noted the pragmatic difficulties of using and researching photographs for an exhibit about the history of perpetrators as opposed to the history of victims. Few personal photos exist; most come from official sources, such as those taken by the SS or for propaganda uses. Finding information about the histories of production and publication of many of these photographs can in some instances be quite difficult, whereas for others "the information can be very detailed, and each photograph can become a research project" (in conversation, 2003).

Certainly more recent research by academic staff at the Topography since the late 1980s will have an influence on exhibitions at the future center. Academic staff have already created an extensive photo archive, published an impressive book with historical images and information about their production, and produced a CD-ROM of the main exhibition that offers additional information about the photographs. The new four-story building will provide space for permanent and temporary exhibits and offer visitors a research center, oral history and photographic archives, and other resources. Different databases, for example, will provide more information about the documents exhibited; audio tours have been made that will provide more flexibility and depth for the new permanent offerings. Visitors will also have access to enough information to create their own electronic "exhibition" on a particular topic at the future center.

Nonetheless, the future permanent exhibition will continue to emphasize the detached, rational documentary approach to the subject matter, what academic staff Andreas Sanders described as a "coolness" toward the emotional nature of the subject. He argued that when emotions are aroused, they could result in a "blurring of vision" that might lead to an inability to deal with the presented information in a rational way. In contrast, he suggested that an objective distance helps Germans confront the National Socialist past in the present. Yet, as I have argued here, this emphasis on objectivity and emotional distance is itself an emotional response to the history of representation in Germany and to the material being presented, one that should also be documented and added to histories exhibited at the Topography. As Hesse described, "The careful approach of the Topography is a reaction to the 'terror pedagogy' that existed before: piles of bodies were used, and sometimes without adequate explanation. It [the documentation] was the reaction to a realization that this [terror pedagogy] does not work. . . . It either moves those even more who already care about what happened, or makes those who had reason to start thinking [critically about the past] feel accused" (interview, 1998). The documentation, as a reaction to past terror pedagogies, however, is marked by a fear about the possible range of emotional responses to the topic. The documentation, described as an approach that limits those emotional responses through rational distance, is also an emotionally based response based on fear and control. As Sanders commented in 1997, "You mentioned that this type of exhibition has something to do with West German culture. I would underscore that. It has something to do with the culture of commemoration of National Socialism. It is still a very problematic topic, and emotionally charged."

The Future: The (National) International Topography of Terror

The political activism that initially sparked the discussions about the Gestapo Terrain in the late 1970s and early 1980s, and the subsequent opening of the Topography of Terror in 1987, marked a change in German postwar public cultures of memory. For Active

Museum managing director Christiana Hoss, the Topography was a very important step in confronting the National Socialist past through a new type of place, "especially when one considers that, as late as 1986, some individuals suggested simply putting flowers at the site or building a parking lot there and not dealing with the topic at all" (interview, 1997). Fifteen years after it opened, the documentary aesthetic and its associated post-national discourse of reappraisal have become prevalent at memorial museum centers throughout Germany. As Andreas Sanders noted, "People still think that this rational, plain style is appropriate for the topic. This is linked to the political and psychological charge of the topic. We have to be aware that Germany is the society of perpetrators.... For such a society, it is important to get the facts and not an emotionalizing interpretation—and not the perspective of the victims—because that allows the stereotypical German visitor to deal with guilt.... Identification with the victims impedes the perpetrators' dealing with the fact that they were involved. In this way you also become a victim.... We want to make it clear that there were people who made decisions and acted. There was an administration—they were not monsters; it could have just as well been one's neighbor" (interview, 1997).

The Topography fills a gap in commemorative culture nationally and internationally. The historical research presented about the rise to power of the National Socialist state through institutional structures is impressive, particularly in an age when the production of Holocaust documentaries and emotive feature films has dramatically increased, but when few films have been made that critically include the perspective of the perpetrators.[65] The rejection of stereotypical portrayals of the Holocaust as the work of "evil" Hitler elites will remain an important part of the moral charge of documentation; future databases at the Topography will also include information about a range of perpetrators. Moreover, the emphasis on working through a place, in this case a historic site, to imagine the past and future, pays attention to the particular cultural needs and pedagogical concerns in Germany.

While the idea of a site of perpetrators was a West German liberal to left response to existing places of memory in the 1980s and to productions of a global Holocaust industry, the Topography is beginning to have an impact internationally. This is related to its relatively new national role. According to Sanders, "While we all have different ideas about what a documentation center means, we have consensus that it should be a dynamic service center. We are not an archive, we are not a museum; we are a service institution. Visitors with different interests can come and ask questions" (interview, 2000). In recent years, directors and academic staff pointed to the numerous official tours organized by the German government that bring dignitaries, educators, and activists from nations around the world, such as South Africa and Chile, to the Gestapo Terrain. The Topography also organizes a number of seminars, lectures, and traveling exhibits abroad, working with and sponsoring foreign institutions and scholars. The Topography's Memorial Museums Department coordinates exchanges, seminars, research and pedagogical support, and hosts a Web page with an online Gedenkstätten Forum, which connects memorial museum centers in Europe and beyond.[66] Internationalization has become more of a possibility through new transnational networks, such as the International Committee of

Memorial Museum Centers for the Remembrance of Victims of Public Crimes, and the Internet.[67]

The institutionalization of the Topography as a state, and later national, center has resulted in some losses, however, such as the citizen initiative activists' archaeological approach to landscape and memory. As Active Museum director Christine Fischer-Defoy noted in 1998, "The idea of active work was already lost or only present to a very small degree [in 1987]—it [the Topography] was more like a museum. There were a few tables in the pavilion with documents where you could have worked with school classes." Part of the reason was practical: there was little space for such activities due to funding. The proposed international youth center and other similar parts of the future center, for example, were dropped because of Berlin's and Germany's postunification budget crisis. But another part was the emphasis on the documentation. Fischer-Defoy, who is part of the Topography's advisory board, also stated that "the active part [of the center] was pushed more toward the periphery. When the new building was planned—in the plans that said how many rooms would be used for what—we [the Active Museum] always asked where the rooms are for the workshop and the photo labs. . . . Where are all the things we thought should be part of the future Topography of Terror with its new building? And then that was cut, and there was no money for anything else. It is left out now, or almost completely left out." In addition, she mentioned that personal stories were also "rather marginal in the concept developed by the Topography of Terror Foundation, which prefers this structural, theoretical, abstract presentation."

> *The exhibition was very successful—why should it be changed? Does the foundation hold onto this concept because of institutionalization?*
> CHRISTINE FISCHER-DEFOY: (hesitates) It partly has something to do with people wanting to stick to things that have been successful. From my point of view we have to react more to how perceptions of people change, how the concepts of museums change. I think that a lot would have to change for the permanent exhibition. It is maybe partly being afraid of again opening something up that was finished—because it means questioning it to a certain extent. I think it is something like fear. It is the same concerning opening up toward feminist approaches. (laughter)
> *It also means a lot of work.*
> FISCHER-DEFOY: I would want to have more flexibility within the permanent exhibition—that we can react to parts [of the exhibit] becoming more important, by expanding a certain part and shortening another one. I would like the permanent exhibition to be like that—that you can experiment a lot more with it, that you can try out things. (Interview, 1998)

The success of the documentation, however, did not guarantee that the future center would be built, particularly in the rapidly changing political economic context of a unified city. Months after building finally began on the new permanent center in 1997, the CDU city government threatened to pull all funds for the Topography. Only after Ignatz

Bubis, then head of the international advisory board of the Topography and chair of the national Central Council of Jews in Germany, strongly spoke out against this threat in the media did the city back down. The Active Museum also formed a successful international lobby protesting the threat of closure. Construction finally got under way but was again put on hold various times due to the spiraling costs of the building—from DM 45 million to 70 million, and then from DM 70 million to 90 million between 1999 and 2000. While Zumthor's architectural team attributed these rising costs to the unusual conceptual design of the building, the situation was seen as scandalous politically. Additional delays occurred later because the construction firm for the project went bankrupt. These political, financial, and at times random problems took place in a city that had to deal with many financial crises due to unification, corruption, and misplanning. It also resulted in strong feelings of frustration, cynicism, and even paralysis expressed by some Topography staff and Active Museum members, who were disappointed that their work and political activism still hadn't resulted in a permanent center. Moreover, staff and foundation members who were critical of Zumthor's designs felt as though they had to hold back their opinions during the funding crises because they were afraid that any reason would be used to shut the Topography down.

The Topography's national role became more clearly delineated in relation to the Holocaust Memorial debates in the late 1990s. When Schröder's first appointee as cultural minister, Michael Naumann, proposed building a national Holocaust museum modeled after the U.S. museum that would accommodate Steven Spielberg's Shoah Foundation,

Topography of Terror construction site with Martin Gropius Bau in background, 1998. Photograph courtesy of Thomas Ernst/Stiftung Topographie des Terrors.

Topography Foundation directors had to explain why the documentation center would still be needed.[68] They knew that if a national museum was built, similar histories (albeit in a different way) would be displayed. In response, the foundation adopted a *national* strategy to support its internationalist agenda and guarantee its future. As I describe in chapter 6, they promoted the idea of a memory district, with three different types of places—the Jewish Museum, the Holocaust Memorial, and the Topography of Terror—as the most appropriate way for the new capital to represent the history and consequences of National Socialism. As former managing director Gabriele Camphausen described, while "nobody planned it, suddenly three famous architects are working here: Libeskind, Eisenman, Zumthor. If we stop working with Zumthor, it would be negative for the Topography. . . . It would disturb the aforementioned constellation [of the memory district] and place the Topography at a lower level. Now it's too late. . . . The coordinates have changed throughout Berlin, and a small solution is not possible anymore" (interview, 2000).

Such a move was possible only after Gerhard Schröder's SPD-Green coalition was voted into power in 1998. The new chancellor introduced a more central role for the federal government to fund and support cultural institutions, including places of memory. His approach marked a new direction in the cultural politics of postwar Germany because it "shifted the debate from whether or not to have a national cultural policy to how such a policy should be defined."[69] Schröder, and many members of his cabinet who are associated with the '68 generation, openly acknowledge that the Nazi past is part of contemporary Germany's responsibility. He set aside funds for nationally significant memorial centers and organized new national *Gedenkstätten* commissions. Unlike earlier SPD administrations, however, the politics of remembering National Socialism are no longer the central defining issue of German normalization. Like Kohl, Schröder makes clear that Germans need not feel ashamed of their identity. He defines cultural values as distinct from political ones—drawing on left to liberal traditions of postnationalism—at the same time that he embraces nontraditional German values, such as multiculturalism, for the new Germany and Berlin Republic. According to Thomas Lutz, head of the Memorial Museums Department of the Topography, who coordinates memorial museums nationwide and organizes international symposia and exchanges, "A certain anxiety has disappeared, but sometimes it seems like the political establishment uses these historical debates to find international acclaim" (interview, 2000).

While Schröder also supports the West German tradition of a regionally based European identity, his agenda of German normalization is defined by the themes of openness, multiculturalism, and cosmopolitanism. Under the banner of cosmopolitanism, his administration has promoted international cultural exchange, avant-garde art, and the establishment of cultural institutions, international architecture, and global corporate culture. A central memory district works within such a cosmopolitan agenda, as I suggest in chapter 6. Yet the concept of a site of perpetrators continues to be a difficult concept for politicians to understand; the name "Topography of Terror" still creates confusion. Thomas Lutz mentioned in 2002 that "the SPD do not know how to use the Topography of Terror. Politicians don't know how to deal with the idea of a 'site of perpetrators.' On the one hand there's the international success [of the Topography]; on the other hand, it's an ambiguous topic for [German] political officials."

Nonetheless, as a result of these public discussions, by 2000 the Topography began to be viewed differently by state and federal officials, perhaps because of its international recognition. As Sanders noted in 2000, "During the [1997] funding crisis, more politicians would have agreed to close the Topography than would do so today." The CDU parliamentary member Norbert Lammert suggested such a shift, noting in 2003 that through the work of the Topography, many CDU politicians now acknowledge that National Socialist history is an important part of German public commemoration.[70]

Because of its anticipated opening date of 2008, the future Topography of Terror will have an opportunity to modify aspects of its preunification approaches to the past, of preservation, topographical mapping, and documentation. It is unclear how future generations of Germans will respond to a documentation in the future, an approach that was a response to the "terror pedagogy" of the 1950s and 1960s and clearly tied to the '68 generation's political agendas. Will the emotional distance of a documentary approach create yet another distance for future generations to travel in trying to make sense of their postmemories? Will a documentation work when placed inside the new Zumthor building rather than through the experience of physically moving through the terrain? I pose these questions to interrogate critically the cultural biases of a documentary approach without rejecting it or supporting a "thin" exhibition in terms of scholarly historical research.[71] The cultural biases in the approach, as I have argued, include emotional responses—such as the fear of emotions and the fear of feeling haunted—despite claims to scientific, rational detachment. Perhaps future tours and temporary exhibitions might critically discuss different postwar German aesthetics and styles of representing the National Socialist past, as well as the emotional responses that visitors have to those aesthetics and that are implicit in those historical approaches. Such conversations would point not only to the social hauntings tied to representations of violent pasts but also to the personal expectations and feelings each individual brings to the site.

Although there are problems with representing German identity in terms of a society of perpetrators, a site that focuses on perpetrator history in the memory district will be an important complement to the Holocaust Memorial and the Jewish Museum. It might be important, nonetheless, to consider how third, fourth, and later generations will respond to such a classification (produced by second- and third-generation Germans). As Hanno Loewy, director of the Fritz Bauer Institute in Frankfurt, explained, "In the personal experiences of [German] people, in their consciousness, in what is handed down from generation to generation, the Holocaust is an outsider. The diffuse historical material only becomes what we call the Holocaust through the Jewish perspective. As soon as I take the German perspective there is no Holocaust—there is population policy, colonization of the East, war, militarism, exploitation, and so on. And there is also anti-Semitism. But anti-Semitism and Holocaust are not the same" (interview, 1993). Certainly Israel and America have used survivors' stories to support their national myths defined by heroic struggle and perseverance against all odds, narratives inappropriate to postwar Germany. But why represent the past in such a stark aesthetic form or through such a narrow historical theoretical approach? Loewy replied that a "close perspective often leads to revisionism. As soon as I start to reconstruct the perspective of a particular perpetrator, to explore his motivations—psychologically, politically, ideologically, economically—when I start to reconstruct this perspective *[pause]*, everybody is looking for his or her own continuities. The result is that it leads to revisionism, even if it happens unconsciously. As soon as I can follow the motivations, and when I go one step further to explain the crime with these motivations *[pause]*, I state that this was part of a chain of events—and with that I have made what happened less harsh. . . . For a German, it is impossible to take this close perspective."

Emotions are likely to be complex when, to quote Loewy, "Germans are permanently confronted by this problem—they have to take a perspective they cannot take." Yet as I have already suggested, the idea of "students' eyes glazing over" might hold true for younger Germans more generally. Compared to French or even American groups, I noticed a general lack of interest in the material discussed by many German student groups. Such responses may reflect differences in levels of knowledge about the topics presented, educational cultures, and attitudes toward foreign educators and places. But as a general trend, memorial center educators, and student surveys and reports seem to agree: younger people mention they are sick of hearing about National Socialism and the Holocaust, particularly because it doesn't affect them personally. It has become part of a "distant" (and therefore foreign) past.[72]

But there may be more. Youthful eyes glazing over may also have to do with the fears of denial and identification, namely, the anxiety evoked when one wants to connect personally with the past but cannot because of one's family history or because it is not acceptable socially. The tension of wanting to identify with and connect to one's ancestors, but not being allowed to morally, may explain, at least in part, why Holocaust denial, as well as the fear of it, is an ongoing political problem in Germany.[73] Yet it also gets to another underlying cultural tension: the fear of the complex emotions that accompany a national past with which one should not identify. These specters from the past are evoked through complex personal and social hauntings, and are tied to ambivalent feelings. At the Gestapo Terrain, some German visitors may experience shock about what one's ancestors perpetrated, confusion and anger about the intentional denial and forgetting in the postwar period, fear about emotionally connecting to perpetrators, and relief about their personal distance to the past, or may fantasize about having some other family's ghosts.

People need to be able to live with their ghosts at the same time they should critically interrogate why they feel the need to evoke them. Places of memory can create spaces for individuals to confront feelings of discomfort that accompany social hauntings. Sometimes through the process of making places, people may begin to work through cultural trauma and their inheritances of a violent national past.

> FISCHER-DEFOY: I think that the danger [of blurring victims and perpetrators] is still quite great, despite many things that have brought it into public awareness again. But on the political level there is a tendency to say that this is

enough. It is now fifty, sixty years ago, and it is enough now. This is where I see the role of the Active Museum: to say that there is no end.

About the future, the younger generations: I read a couple of articles where you say that the widespread opinion of many German youths is that "we have political education in school, we go to the Gedenkstätten, we do not want to hear more about that time."... How can you approach this history with the younger generation? I think the meaning of the National Socialist past to German society was very clear for the 1968 generation—and that generation was very important for the Active Museum. How can you build a bridge?

FISCHER-DEFOY: To the young people? It has something to do with the design and concept of an exhibition. Our experience is that the authentic things, the biographical approach works—even when we have fewer and fewer time witnesses. But what you can preserve with them is a bridge. And then there is the possibility of reaching young people through the media. I think the most important thing is still personal communication—and when it is not with the victim generation itself, then it is with the children of the victims. They are there to talk to young people. I think that this is still the most efficient way to interest young people in this topic.

To make an exhibition more accessible ...

FISCHER-DEFOY: To include them, and not to simply present something to them. To include them in discussions or activities, to create working groups at the memorial centers. I really like the concept for Ravensbrück [concentration camp memorial museum]—to "excavate" the area over a time period of ten years or so and design it with the help of school classes. I think that is how not all, but maybe two or three out of every class, may be won for that cause. And that is a lot. (Interview, 1998)

Note to Reader

As this book was being prepared for publication, new developments unexpectedly emerged that will influence the future of the Gestapo terrain. In 2004, after construction did not resume on the Zumthor building, the federal government announced that the special funds allocated for the future international center would be cut. Topography academic director Reinhard Rürup resigned in protest. In response, the federal government and city-state of Berlin rescinded the contract awarded to Zumthor, based on the investigations of an expert committee that noted problems with escalating costs and delays in the construction.

While the future of the Topography of Terror in Berlin remains to be seen, a new architectural competition will be announced in 2005, and, if all goes well, construction on a new building will begin.

"Jews in Berlin are only allowed to buy food between four and five o'clock in the afternoon. July 4, 1940." Berlin-Schöneberg, Bavarian Quarter, 1994. Photograph courtesy of Renata Stih and Frieder Schnock.

A Neighborhood

Berlin-Schöneberg, 1994, with Later Reflections

As I was walking to a doctor's appointment, distracted and lost in thought, I saw out of the corner of my eye a street sign that had an image of a hopscotch game with bold colors one might expect to see in a children's book. I kept walking, and a bit later I saw another sign, this time of a dog, again in a stylized form with inviting colors. As I walked toward the image of the German shepherd for a closer look, I noticed yet another sign across the street. On the other side of the image of the dog were words: "Jewish veterinarians may not open practices. April 3, 1936. General employment ban. January 17, 1939." Confused and curious, I began looking for more signs and went back to the hopscotch game sign. It was located next to a children's park, and on its back it stated: "Aryan and non-Aryan children are forbidden to play together. 1938." I looked for other signs and saw more, down the street, by a central park, across the way, next to the U-Bahn, near a bank. The signs were attached to lampposts facing alternate directions, so that you might first see an image and then a sign with a text (or vice versa). As I continued to walk around the neighborhood, I realized I had missed my doctor's appointment and went to a coffee shop to write down what I had found.

I had lived in this neighborhood for only a few weeks when I saw these signs. Usually I walk different routes for errands, such as to the weekly market or into town, to become more familiar with a neighborhood. This time I also began to walk home on unfamiliar streets and take different metros or buses just to find more signs.

The images and colors of these signs were so friendly and enjoyable to look at that when I read the words on the back—"laws" written in the present tense—they became especially disturbing. Some of the signs were connected to a place, such as the sign next to the children's playground or the loaf of bread by a grocery store that said,

"Jews in Berlin are only allowed to buy food between four and five o'clock in the after-noon. July 4, 1940." These signs seemed to comment directly on everyday life in this residential district and what might have happened to the social spaces of that place in the past. The texts on the back of the signs didn't always directly connect to the im-ages on the front, nor did the images always connect to their immediate contemporary settings. Some signs had dates on them, such as a picture of an ashtray that said, "Cigarettes and cigars are no longer sold to Jews. June 11, 1942." Others listed only a year: "At Bayerischer Platz, Jews may sit only on yellow park benches. Eyewitness reports 1939."

I wanted to know what these signs were, why they were here, and who put them here. But I couldn't connect them to a central place that would help me interpret them together. After a couple of days of looking for signs, I found two large billboards with maps that referred to the signs, one by the neighborhood's central metro station and park (Bayerisches Platz), and one by the Schöneberg town hall (I later found a third billboard at a school). On the billboards, two superimposed city maps, one from 1933 and one from 1993, depicted the changes from past to present, the destruction of the area during the war, and the contemporary spaces of the city. Around the edge of the maps were pictures of the signs, eighty in total, that depicted how everyday actions in the neighborhood had led to the social institutionalization of exclusion and ultimately genocide. Dots on the maps indicated specific locations of individual signs. This city map *(Stadtplan)* invited the viewer who was curious about these signs to make sense of his or her *Standort* (location) in the past and present.

Only later, while in Washington, DC, sitting in on tours at the U.S. Holocaust Memorial Museum, did I find out more about these signs. I was chatting with some-one who had lived in Berlin, who mentioned that the most powerful memorial she had ever seen in the city, or anywhere else, for that matter, was the Bavarian Quarter (Bayerisches Viertel) Holocaust Memorial. I had chanced upon this memorial as a short-term resident and spent time trying to see all the signs. When I found out that they were a memorial, I wanted to know more about the artists who made them.

I met conceptual artists Renata Stih and Frieder Schnock when I returned to Berlin in 1997. I was there doing research and also presented some of my work to a summer historic preservation seminar organized by a colleague at another American university; I happily tagged along when they went on a field excursion to the memorial. Renata, bubbling with energy, and Frieder, with a disarming sense of humor, gave us a walk-ing tour of their memorial and answered our questions. They described the memorial competition and their research about the neighborhood. Before Hitler's rise to power, this neighborhood was known as "Jewish Switzerland" because of the number of professional and well-to-do Jews who had settled there in the late 1800s and early 1900s. (A 1933 census counted 16,261 "Germans of Jewish faith" who lived in this residential district, mostly in the Bavarian Quarter.) A local neighborhood group had also researched the number of people whose homes and belongings had been confiscated, and who had been deported during the Third Reich; when the list grew to well over six thousand, the Schöneberg district council voted to erect a memorial to

Berufsverbot für jüdische
Zahnärzte, Zahntechniker,
Apotheker, Heilpraktiker
und Krankenpfleger.

17.1.1939

"Employment ban for Jewish dentists, dental technicians, pharmacists, homeopathic doctors, and nurses. January 17, 1939." Image on reverse side: peppermint plants.

the murdered Jews of the neighborhood.[1] Using historical documents and an outstanding archival collection from a Jewish historian from Breslau, Joseph Walk, Stih
and Schnock interpreted past laws through the contemporary aesthetics of advertisement.[2] Their concept unanimously won the competition (of ninety-six submissions),
and they installed the memorial in 1993.

Toward the end of our tour, I asked the artists why they called their work a *Denkmal*.
This memorial was obviously not of the traditional sort, with a monumental abstract
sculpture. (I was thinking about the history of the Gestapo Terrain and the groups
that responded negatively to traditional memorials and created new types of place
to confront the past.) As a geographer, I was especially curious about why the artists
had conceptually mapped the demise of the past neighborhood through everyday
practices. Stih and Schnock quite clearly stated that this was a *Denkmal*: it had an artistic form, was located at a historic site, and commemorated the Jews who, from this
neighborhood, had been persecuted, deported, and murdered.

Local residents didn't initially understand that the signs were a memorial, however: "It was a shock when it came," stated Stih in a 1998 interview. "When we installed it, the secret police *[Staatsschutz]* took it down again because people called;
the press was there, and they thought it was anti-Semitic propaganda—they did not
realize that this was a memorial. And later they all realized that it was the memorial
they were waiting for." Stih and Schnock intentionally wanted to present historical
documents in a way that would encourage passersby to take notice and confront the
past in the present. "If we had said that 'Jews were not allowed to buy milk,' everybody would say, 'Yes, that was terrible back then.' But when we said, 'Jews are not
allowed'—it created a scandal. People did not look at the date [on the signs] but said,
'This is incredible. How can someone post this?'" The artists also mentioned that
when people go looking for more signs, for more places, they may come to view the
city, their routes through the city, and their place in it differently. By looking at a sequence of signs, residents experience a progression of everyday exclusions that led to
the systematic persecution, social exclusion, and ultimately murder of social groups
in their own neighborhood and country.

The Bavarian Quarter memorial not only challenges the iconography, meaning, and
spatiality of the traditional *Denkmal*; it also uses an aesthetic considered taboo for
representing the Holocaust and interpreting historical documents in Germany: popular
images. The signs offer pleasurable forms that are familiar to consumers walking by:
advertisements, images in children's books, street signs. These seemingly innocent
pictures, when connected to past laws and situated in the spaces of a residential
neighborhood, communicate violent pasts that permeate the comfortable world of
the contemporary.

> FRIEDER SCHNOCK: We searched for sources and found this perfidious system of how
> the Nazis extended their power and segmented certain sectors to exclude
> Jews, marginalize them, see and represent them as a different group, and

finally exterminate them. . . . We used this historical collection in order to translate them into a contemporary language.

Renata Stih: This was the artistic form. The question was how to communicate that to people. It was clear to us that this has to be done in a modern press language: short. Drivers have to read the signs—the form has to be a kind of commercial. We accomplished that using advertising techniques . . . the pictograms. The pictures always have some connection with the text, but then again not.

The question was what object [to represent], of course. But the meaning of such an object, like a glass, changes when you have a memory of it, a special memory of something. This [memory] can be a kiss, but it can also be the murder of the father. These are strong extremes. We

[Photograph courtesy of Frieder Schnock and Renata Stih.] Take, for example, the sign with an image of the hat on Landshuter Straße. In German, there is a cultural expression commonly used when someone is fired from their job: "Nimmt deinen Hut"—roughly speaking, "Take your hat and go." These are pictograms, not just pictures. The multiple meanings inherent to these images, texts, and their immediate surroundings will reach people in many different ways.

—*Conversation with Frieder Schnock, Berlin conceptual artist, 2003* have objects that do not remind us of anything, but other images are very specific. And also places, moods, weather, wind, sun—all this we wanted to include. It was very sensually oriented and works psychologically—we influence people as soon as they see it. The size of the signs played a role—we observed exactly how we responded, how others reacted, and how it might have an impact on younger people, older people, and so on. It works.

FRIEDER SCHNOCK: It is quite subtle. The signs are not too large, but when you see one, all of a sudden you see the next one. (Interview, 1998)

Every time I go back to Berlin, I visit some of the neighborhoods where I used to live and go to my favorite places. In Schöneberg, I return to my former local hangouts, an Indian restaurant with cramped sidewalk seating at wooden tables and benches (next to many other restaurants and cafés with cramped tables), a favorite café across the street from my old apartment, and a couple of stalls at the open-air market (held on Wednesdays and Sundays). I walk by other places that I liked seeing or would occasionally visit to make sure they are still there, such as an oddly placed funeral parlor, an art supply store, a bad and dimly lit Mexican restaurant, a shoe store, and an Italian shop. Ritualistically, again and again, I walk through the streets of the Bavarian Quarter, looking for more signs.

5 | Aestheticizing the Rupture: Berlin's Holocaust Memorial

The competition in 1983 for the Gestapo area . . . was announced very quickly—the location was not understood. Similarly, the [Holocaust Memorial] competition guidelines did not make clear what the goal was. Immediately 228 artists, architects, and landscape planners made plans for this location with walls and artificial excavations, gigantic craters . . . that is what is in people's heads about National Socialism, horror, Auschwitz. . . . They should have realized [after the public competition for the Gestapo Terrain] that you cannot do this a second time on this level.

—*Interview with Stefanie Endlich, art historian, publicist, and expert juror on first Holocaust Memorial public art competition, 1998*

The artistic competition [for the Holocaust Memorial] makes clear . . . that today's Germany is assuming its obligation:
—not to avoid the truth, or to give in to forgetfulness
—to honor the murdered Jews of Europe
—to remember them in sorrow and shame
—to accept the burden of German history
—to give the signal for a new chapter of human cohabitation in which injustice to minorities will no longer be possible.

—*City of Berlin guidelines to first public art competition for the Memorial to Murdered Jews of Europe, 1994*[1]

The Holocaust is an unquestioned global symbol of the failure of the project of modernity. It stands for the "break in civilization" *(Zivilizationsbruch)*, a universal moral symbol used both to justify international geopolitical acts and national imaginaries within distinct cultural signifying systems.[2] During the Cold War, the Holocaust represented what was at stake for the future: the "civilized" world (the West) must protect the good and innocent and fight against "evil" (regimes that perpetrate crimes against humanity) to prevent such a rupture from happening again.[3]

In the Federal Republic of Germany, "the land of the perpetrators," the Holocaust signifies not only the Western metacategories of good and evil but also national guilt and accountability. German postwar cultural politics of memory have thus been defined by a basic tension: how can Germany represent the Holocaust and its responsibility yet still make claims to nationhood and belonging to the civilized world? This difficult question has haunted postwar German national imaginations and hopes for the future and has been given form through places of memory like Holocaust memorials. These places are established to commemorate, to acknowledge, and to belong.

Many of these memorials have been controversial, such as the Memorial to the Murdered Jews of Europe (Denkmal für die ermordeten Juden Europas, hereafter referred to as the Holocaust Memorial). Debates about the memorial began in the late 1980s with Perspective for Berlin's proposal for the Gestapo Terrain and were quite intense throughout the 1990s. Multiple understandings of how the Holocaust should be represented and remembered in German society were debated through public discussions, art competitions, expert colloquiums, media events, and other venues. Although construction on the memorial would not begin until 2002, during the late 1990s, citizens would argue that "the debate is a memorial!" as the graffiti on the memorial's temporary construction fence proclaimed in 1997. The memorial became understood as a defining site and aesthetic form through which Germany's postunification politics of memory were negotiated.

I begin this chapter with four distinct stories about the memorial by individuals who participated in these debates. Each person described what he or she felt was at stake by pointing to perceived societal needs in the present, narrating the past, and articulating hopes for the future. Through different ideals of the functions, forms, and spaces of this place of memory, they communicated their understandings of what contemporary Germany's relationship to a violent national past should be.

Memorial Stories

> I was in the middle of working on a four-part documentary for
> [the national television station] ARD with the historian Eberhard
> Jaeckel about the murder of Jews with the title *Death Is a Master
> from Germany* [*Der Tod is ein Meister aus Deutschland*, a title after
> Paul Celan's *Death March*]. . . . How was it all these other countries
> (seven in Europe) didn't participate in the hunt after their Jews?
> Why not? We wanted to understand that, and on the other hand,
> how the murder of Jews in other countries was organized. What
> was the experience like? Who did this?
>
> We traveled with their television team to Israel, to interview
> survivors, to get documents. . . .
>
> . . . Walking with Jaeckel along the "Path of the Just" (Allee der
> Gerechten) in Yad Vashem, a lane we had walked along before,

we were newly impressed. Anyone who helped Jews anywhere
in Europe from being deported and death was allowed to plant a
tree here. At the base of the trees, there is a mosaic wall with the
names of the people who saved individuals and what country they
came from. Germany is not often discovered under those trees.
Nor is Austria. Holland is often there. So is Italy. France. Belgium.
Norway. Sweden. Poland.

The weather was nice, the sun warmed us. It was lovely *(tröstlich)*
to read the many names of the saviors under which lay a wonder-
ful history. And in the middle of this [ambience of] feeling good,
Jaeckel said, "Look, we don't remember anything, in the land of
the perpetrators, about this fact. No memorial commemorates the
murdered Jews in Europe. In Germany there are only memorials for Germans, but not for the murdered European Jews. And
Germans are only 2 percent of the victims, 98 percent came from
other European countries."

I was surprised that after all my trips through Europe, the
numerous interviews with survivors, I myself had never had this
thought expressed by Jaeckel along this path, namely, that in
Germany a memorial must exist for the murdered Jews, a memorial to remember the facts and to honor the victims.

When back in Berlin, I made the memorial the theme of the
next citizen initiative meeting.

—*Lea Rosh, director, Association for the Memorial to the Murdered
Jews of Europe, 1999*[4]

How should the Holocaust be remembered in the land of the perpetrators? It is a question that haunted Lea Rosh personally, as well as members of Perspective for Berlin who
would form a working group called the Association Supporting the Memorial to Commemorate the Murdered Jews of Europe (Förderkreis zur Errichtung eines Denkmals
für die Ermordeten Juden Europas) in 1989.[5] Their story, as represented by various publications and media statements, such as the passage just quoted from Lea Rosh's book,
was defined by their discomfort at feeling haunted, by knowing that one belongs to "the
land of the perpetrators," yet desiring to be connected to the heroic land of the victims
(Israel) and to the rest of the "civilized" world.

Rosh experienced a crisis at Yad Vashem: she clearly felt that she belonged to a larger
international community of Holocaust scholars and documentary filmmakers, but experienced a sense of Germanness that shattered her feelings of contentment as she walked
through the gardenlike Path of the Just. That rupture turned to a sense of shame and
then anger when she realized that Germany did not have a place of public commemoration that socially acknowledged the suffering of European Jews. Once in Germany,
her moral indignation, and at times self-righteousness, resulted in a passionate sense of

duty. Rosh typified her mission to establish the memorial as a difficult battle and often took hard-line "fighting" positions to make sure the project would be realized, sometimes ostracizing people in the process.[6]

The national Holocaust Memorial embodies these personal and social hauntings. Clearly conceived as an international gesture and national task, a monumental memorial would communicate to the rest of the world the monstrosity of what had happened. It would represent German guilt and publicly acknowledge past crimes. For Rosh and the Association, the memorial would also communicate that Germany, like other Western nations, was committed to fighting injustice and contributing to a more humanitarian future.

> We have an organically grown federal landscape of memory with historic sites linked to specific places. [Federal cultural minister Naumann's proposal for] a Holocaust museum would undermine the relationship between history and space. Even with the best intentions, such a museum would be a reversal of what has developed over time. The old is not always better than the new, but I consider decentrality an advantage. A gigantic museum in the center [of Berlin, tied to a memorial] would distance history from the actual references and places. This has been a heated discussion.
> —*Interview with Gabriele Camphausen, former managing director of the Topography of Terror, 2000*

The same question, how to represent the Holocaust in Germany, also haunted memorial museum center experts and Berlin activists. For Camphausen, a centralized, monumental place of memory might have offered public space for national catharsis and identification with victims but would not help German citizens engage in memory-work in the future. Representing the break in civilization and remembering its consequences in the land of perpetrators demands more than a global act of repentance for memorial museum experts. It requires that Germans acknowledge and confront their past complicity through historic sites. To give the abstract category "the Holocaust" meaning in the land of the perpetrators, the history of National Socialism where criminal acts were organized, supported, and occurred must be documented. Through historic sites, Germans may begin to understand how their country became a fascist state and how an institutionalized system of terror grew out of a "civilized" land. Learning about this history in a concrete way may encourage citizens to accept responsibility for past national and international crimes. As Camphausen suggests, when that relationship between National Socialist history and site is severed, so are the possibilities for acknowledging social responsibility for the past, questioning the histories of the nation, and imagining humanitarian futures.

As instructive as the memorial debate had been, however, it had neither warned nor chastened a new generation of xenophobic neo-

Nazis—part of whose identity depends on forgetting the crimes of their forebears. And although the memorial debate has generated plenty of shame in Germans, it is largely the shame they feel for an unseemly argument—not for mass murder once committed in their name. . . .

. . . Speaker of the Berlin Senate Peter Radunski called to ask if I would join a Findungskommission [expert jury commission] of five members appointed to find a suitable design.[7] . . . I was the only true expert on Holocaust memorials [of the five], he said. And, as I then realized, I would be the only foreigner and Jew. . . . I asked myself: Was I invited as an academic authority on memorials or as a token American and foreigner? Is it my expertise they want, or are they looking for a Jewish blessing on whatever design is finally chosen? . . . Just where is the line between my role as an arbiter of German memory and my part in a fraught political process far beyond my own grasp?

And yet, I wondered, how is Germany to make momentous decisions like this *without* the Jewish sensibility so mercilessly expunged from its national consciousness? . . . Good, sensible Jewish leaders like Ignatz Bubis counsel wisdom and discretion. But even that is not a cure for this aphasia. A well-meaning German like Lea Rosh takes a Jewish name and initiates a monument. Neither is this a cure. No, the missing Jewish part of German culture remained a palpable and gaping wound in the German psyche—and it must appear as such in Berlin's otherwise reunified cityscape.

The problem was that in voiding itself of Jews, Germany had forever voided itself of the capacity for a normal, healthy response to Jews and their ideas. . . . Thus, I began to grasp just this need for a foreigner and a Jew on the Findungskommission. Without a Jewish eye to save it from egregiously misguided judgments (like the winner of the first competition), anything was possible. This might be as practical a matter as it was political.

> —*James E. Young, professor of English and Judaic studies, University of Massachusetts at Amherst, and expert juror for second memorial competition, 2000 and 2001*[8]

Is it possible for Germans to have a healthy relationship with Jews after the Holocaust? How do Americans, and American Jews in particular, have a role in the process of social memory in Germany?

In 1993, James Young, a respected literary scholar about Holocaust testimony and narrative, published a powerful and accessible book entitled *The Texture of Memory: Holocaust Memorials and Meaning in Europe, Israel, and America*.[9] It came out before the first public art competition for the Holocaust Memorial in Berlin was declared a failure. When he was later invited by the city to participate in three symposia about the future of the memorial in 1995, he felt that no material structure should be built, that the memorial should remain an ongoing public debate.[10] But something happened at the symposia. He became disillusioned with his role as scholar/spectator "whose primary interest was in perpetuating the process." In the public debates, some of the people he knew and respected through his research "called themselves 'the successionists.' That was hard for me to accept" (interview, 2001). This term, he explained, referred to the turn-of-the-century movement of artists, many of whom would become Jewish victims of the Nazis. The same people who stressed that victims and perpetrators must be distinguished located themselves in the space of the avant-garde, and worse, of the victims, by identifying themselves as successionists. "And here, I realized, my personal stake in the memorial had begun to change."

Young began to speak with a different voice.[11] His practical (and quite American) approach was to ensure that if a memorial would be built, it would be an aesthetically respectable Jewish presence in the New Berlin. While he acknowledged that he was used politically as a Jew and as an American to justify the memorial process, he felt that he could also use his new position by offering a "Jewish eye"—by his definition a foreign perspective in Germany—to help heal Germany's "wounded" psyche. "If they had grown up with certain symbols or stories, they would have known that the Jackob-Marks design [from the first competition] or the Burning Rachel design [from the second] would have offended people" (interview, 2001). Young, as an expert on Holocaust memorials, is also aware that the memorial will have a traditional role in the new capital: "Yes, it is in the center of the city, yes, it is a large site, but that is what they have to work with" (interview, 2001). Memory, he argued, shouldn't just be preserved—it had to be created. He argued that if Germans only preserve historic sites of National Socialism, then the process of remembering in the present is defined by the historic Nazi plan and structure only. A centrally located memorial at a symbolic site, in contrast, might offer a contemporary interpretation of the violent legacy of the German nation.

So much was torn down after the war. I went to the cemetery to visit the graves of my family, of my friends . . . and I realized that, of course, in Germany you tear everything down because . . . it is linked to the Nazi time. You tear the palace down because you do not want to have any memory at all because it is so horrible.

. . . And now, many years later, people learn to differentiate, that there are different kinds of pasts. Not just one. People are trying to approach the Nazi time in a more differentiated way. Because of that I think that the form of the [Peter] Eisenman [Holocaust] memorial is so wrong. It is a form of the 1970s, not of the 1990s. Germany has to rethink history now. Reunification is a new beginning. . . . Only documents and information can serve as the basis for a new common history. The Holocaust Memorial is not an independent memorial; it is the beginning of German-German history.

—*Interview with Renata Stih, conceptual artist, Berliner (of Croatian descent), and participant in first memorial public art competition with partner Frieder Schnock, 1998*

To create a national memorial that represents a violent history of state and social perpetration is a triple crisis: a crisis of memory, legitimation, and representation. Unification provided an opportunity to confront postwar national imaginaries that performed the myth of the nation through public monuments where, in both East and West Germany, citizens enacted state rituals of guilt and mourning and identified themselves as victims to silence the past.

Artists like Renata Stih and Frieder Schnock felt haunted by the description of the official task of the memorial because, like other repetitions before, it called for a traditional memorial that they felt masked disturbing absences and forgetful national histories. A traditional memorial tells the visitor how he or she should feel through monumental sculpture. It is a form that provides national catharsis. Instead, these artists wanted to question the expected performance of the memorial by encouraging visitors to question the national histories of remembering and forgetting inscribed in their contemporary landscapes. Through public art, the taken-for-granted meanings of places may be questioned when individuals unexpectedly feel out of place in familiar settings. For example, an individual may notice something strange or different in his or her daily routine, and through that experience be confronted with the presence of a repressed, violent past. The person may respond by taking notice, or by becoming curious, confused, or even angry. Creating such experiential moments through a memorial (*Denk-mal,* to think for a moment) encourages citizens to think about the past and to look at their lives and their social position in the world (as citizens) from a different perspective.

All four of these people were critical of Germany's postwar national histories of forgetting. Yet each described a different memorial, and a distinct (often personal) moment of crisis, to represent German identity. Lea Rosh, speaking for the Memorial Association, became upset at Yad Vashem because there was no such memorial space to walk through in Germany. Gabriele Camphausen was troubled about the effects a large museum might have on the organic network of historic sites, and by separating history from actual places. James Young unexpectedly became aware of his outsider status in the debates and chose to use that Americanness, expertise, and "Jewish eye" to give advice about the memorial. At a cemetery, conceptual artists Renata Stih and Frieder Schnock realized that all places are cemeteries; through the artistic process, they make connections with the past occupants of a place and question why people tear down old structures to forget.

These memorial stories localize emotions and define social relations to the past. They indicate different reactions to feeling haunted as Germans or as foreigners in Germany and describe personal attachments to belonging. In this chapter, I focus on two such memorial stories, the proposal by the Memorial Association and the artistic concept by artists Renata Stih and Frieder Schnock called *Bus Stop!* Before describing their distinct understandings, I first sketch the complex history of Berlin's Holocaust Memorial to highlight its controversial nature and to suggest other possible stories.

The Memorial to the Murdered Jews of Europe

Construction for the Denkmal für die ermordeten Juden Europas began in 2002 at a large area of land just east of the Tiergarten and at the western edge of the historic district, in the residential district of Berlin-Mitte in the former East.[12] Scheduled to open in 2005, the memorial is symbolically located between the federal district and the Potsdamer Platz business district in the New Berlin, just south of the new American Embassy. Designed by American architect Peter Eisenman, this undulating field of 2,700 concrete stelae of different heights (from about one and one-half feet to about ten feet tall) will be arranged on a grid pattern on a 19,000-square-meter lot. Individuals are asked to interpret a field that moves and changes in relation to the human body, rather than be told how to mourn for the past through a centrally placed sculptural form atop a pedestal. According to the Foundation of the Memorial to the Murdered Jews of Europe, established in 2000 as an independent organization, "passing through the rows of discreetly leaning pillars, which are standing on seemingly unstable ground, could cause a sensation of insecurity; however, since the dimensions of the pillars allow for a clear

Model of Memorial to the Murdered Jews of Europe. Design by Eisenman Architects. Photograph by Bernhard Schurian, 1998; copyright Foundation Memorial to the Murdered Jews of Europe.

overview, the individual visitor will not feel overawed or reduced to insignificance." Eisenman describes his design as presenting "a new idea of memory as distinct from nostalgia," one that radically confronts the traditional concept of a memorial.[13]

Beneath the southeast corner of the field of stelae, an information center of 800 square meters will "turn the abstract form of remembrance provided by the Memorial into concrete facts, to complement it with information about the victims."[14] Designed by Berlin-based Dagmar von Wilcken, a central feature of the information center will include a Room of Names, in which, through Yad Vashem's database, all known names of Jews murdered in the Holocaust will be accessible to the public. A Room of Fates will portray stories of around twelve Jewish families from across Europe through photographic material "to illustrate the contrast between life before and after persecution as well as the destruction of a culture and the loss arising therefrom." A Room of Sites will depict the geographic dimension "of the killing by the National Socialist regime as the genocide spread throughout Europe" and offer visitors information about the many memorial sites in Germany and Europe, including their locations, bus and train connections, and opening times. As such, the information center is considered a "portal" to the "authentic memorial sites both in Germany and abroad as well as to other victim groups."

Much will be written in months to come about how visitors respond to the site, what their experiences of moving through the field and information center are, and how their experiences will constitute their understandings of the past. Because no formal place of

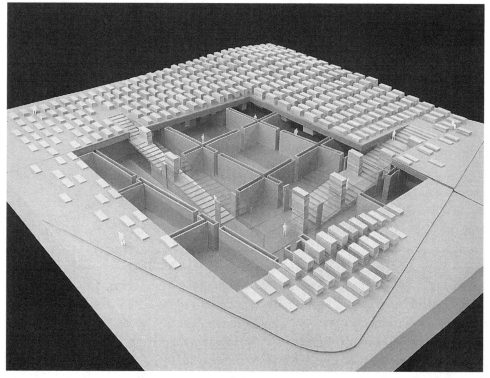

Model of Memorial to the Murdered Jews of Europe, with view of underground information center. Design by Eisenman Architects. Photograph copyright 2001 Eisenman Architects.

entrance or exit exists, visitors must find their own way in and out of the field. James Young speculated that visitors will become physically disoriented, making them rethink the memory of past events. Visitors' relationship to the memorial space, according to Young, will neither reassure nor reconcile the history of the mass murder of millions.[15] At the same time, because of the memorial's central location and function, visitors will enter this commemorative space knowing that they should feel sad and moved. When the Bundestag finally decided in favor of such a memorial in 1999, the stated goal was to "maintain the memory of this unthinkable occurrence in German history." The work of the memorial should also "admonish all future generations to never again violate human rights, to defend the democratic constitutional state at all times, to secure equality before the law for all people and to resist all forms of dictatorship and regimes based on violence."[16]

Of all of Germany's places of post-Holocaust memory, this memorial will be the most visible and accessible, and for that reason it will most likely continue to be interpreted and discussed by scholars, politicians, and tourists for years to come. But even before it was built, it was among the most contentious places of memory in postwar Berlin. It was heavily debated since the late 1980s in different venues by many individuals of different generations and with a range of political and social affiliations. The memorial was discussed (and hence also defined) in relation to the Topography of Terror, the Jewish Museum, and the decentralized landscape of memorial museums. After the first controversial public art competition, for example, many argued that Daniel Libeskind's recently constructed building for the Jewish Museum would be a far more moving memorial than the two first-prize winners. Other alternatives to a built memorial were proposed, including spending the memorial funds on existing historic sites, or establishing a university, or supporting survivors. Some suggested leaving the plot of land in the center of the city empty, save a simple sign stating: "Germany's Holocaust Memorial. We debated it for twelve years and couldn't find a solution." The memorial was also defined in relation to other international projects, in particular Yad Vashem and the U.S. Holocaust Memorial Museum, even though local memory experts emphasized that the memorial should be situated within Germany's existing public cultures of memory.

The process of establishing this memorial was unusual, resulting in unexpected results and reactions; parts of the process also took place outside the typical public realms one would normally expect for a public art project. For example, the three official sponsors were the Memorial Association, the city-state *(Land)* Berlin, and the Federal Republic—the first time ever, perhaps, that a private citizen initiative was an official sponsor of a state or federally funded cultural project. A number of local experts complained that international opinion (institutions and individuals) played too large a role in this process; state and federal public figures used their power and influence more directly in this process than is normally the case.[17] It was also the first time in the history of the FRG that the German Parliament made a decision for a public art project to be realized.[18] Public debates were especially well covered in the media. The two public art competitions were also unusual in process and outcome for a number of reasons.

The first competition was announced by the city in 1994, and 1,078 Germans requested competition guidelines; proposals were also commissioned by twelve internationally known artists, including Richard Serra, Christian Boltanski, and Rebecca Horn. In total 528 proposals were submitted, and one newspaper proclaimed that the competition was, quantitatively speaking, one of the largest ever in art history.[19] The expert jury was unusually large, with fifteen jurors, to accommodate demands by the three sponsors, but of those people few were art or architecture experts, Jews, former East Germans, or memorial center experts. As the jury deliberated over the proposals, sharp disagreements became apparent between the art experts and historians; debates about whether the memorial should be for Jewish victims only also ensued.[20] After a week, the jury announced two first-prize winners, another odd outcome.[21] Usually if the jury is split, two second-prize awards are awarded, and a limited number of finalists are asked to revise and resubmit their proposals for a final jury deliberation and vote.[22]

For this competition, the two winning designs included one by Simon Ungers, Christian Moss, and Christina Alt from Cologne, who proposed an 85-by-85-meter steel frame structure with names of concentration and extermination camps cut out of the frame; the rectangular structure would enclose a 2.5-meter interior plateau. The second winning design was by Berlin-based Christine Jackob-Marks, Hella Rolfes, Hans Scheib, and Reinhard Stangl. They proposed an enormous tilted metal plate (the size of two football fields, and seven meters thick) with eighteen broken stones from Massada National Park (representing the eighteen European countries from which Jews were persecuted and murdered) and on which 4.5 million known names of murdered Jews would be engraved.[23] This project was the favorite of the Memorial Association but was heavily criticized in public debates—derided as the *Grabplatte* (tombstone), which referred to its Christian aesthetic (of Christ's rising from the tomb at the resurrection). It was also criticized for its monstrous size and for not being well integrated into the urban fabric, with its massive stone plate tilting at an incline of eleven meters. Perhaps most troubling was the proposal to name people. Whose names should be included (who were the "real" victims to be commemorated?), those who died between 1933 and 1945, or those who were persecuted (and should survivors' names be included)? How would people's real names be found? How would small engravings of millions of people lift them from their anonymity? Because funding for the memorial was also a concern, a shocking proposal was introduced to realize the project: as German citizens donated funds for the project, additional names would be engraved. Some argued that this idea was akin to the Christian tradition of donating money to purge guilt; Germans would be able to "sponsor" a dead Jew.[24] Kohl ultimately rejected the Jackob-Marks proposal, calling it a bad copy of the Vietnam War Memorial.[25]

After this controversial and internationally embarrassing outcome, the memorial process continued to take an unusual course. The competition was declared a failure, and Berlin's Senate of Building and Construction handed over the project to the Berlin Senate of Cultural Affairs. After a break of more than a year, three colloquiums were organized at which seventy Berlin, German, and international experts discussed the future of the memorial. From these discussions, five people were selected as jurors (including James Young) for a second, invitation-only competition. The top nine finalists from the first competition were invited to resubmit their proposals, and ten international artists were asked to submit new ones. In 1997 the jurors chose four finalists: Richard Serra and Peter Eisenman, Daniel Libeskind, Jochen Gerz, and Gesine Weinmiller. In public and media discussions, the Serra/Eisenman proposal received the most attention. Kohl was also interested in the project but asked the team to reduce the number and height of the stelae (originally four thousand, ranging from just above ground level to sixteen feet high) to make the dense and somewhat disorienting field more open and accessible to tourist buses. Serra dropped out of the competition, stating that any change would compromise what he was trying to accomplish with his art. Later, another finalist, Jochen Gerz, also withdrew his proposal. Weinmiller, a Berlin architect, felt that the 1999 Bundestag decision negated the purpose and spirit of the artistic competition. She noted in a 2001 interview that federally elected politicians weren't qualified to be expert jurors for competitions; moreover, only one (Eisenman's), not all four, of the finalists' proposals were considered by the Bundestag.

The Memorial Association pushed for the German Parliament to make a final decision because the memorial process was put on hold during the 1998 federal elections. Because Chancellor Kohl and SPD candidate Gerhard Schröder had such different opinions about the controversial project, they chose to delay the decision for the second competition until after elections. With a new federal government in place, additional ideas were proposed, such as by cultural senator Michael Naumann, who wanted to establish a Holocaust museum with support from Yad Vashem and the U.S. Holocaust Memorial Museum. Naumann argued that memorials obscure commemoration and stated that Eisenman's proposal was too "Speerish" and abstract to be meaningful for younger generations. Eisenman again redesigned his proposal to include a House of Remembrance to address critics' concerns (including Schröder's) about the entirely symbolic, rather than also educational, function of the memorial.[26] With continued pressure and controversy, the Bundestag was called on to make a decision and chose Eisenman's first modification to the original design.[27] But they added two stipulations: that the memorial be meaningfully integrated "into the ensemble of memorial sites in Berlin" and include an information center, and that an independent memorial foundation administer and oversee the project.

Because so much has already been written about the Holocaust Memorial, I highlight only two, very distinct, concepts for the memorial: the Memorial Association's idea for the memorial and a proposal submitted in the first public art competition that opposed the association's vision. These memorial concepts demonstrate how ghosts are evoked through place making, revenants that haunt the German nation in an ongoing present and future.

The Memorial Association

In 1989, the Memorial Association was established by the citizen initiative Perspective for Berlin.[28] The association had three goals: to convince the public that a memorial was necessary, to finance it, and to convince the state of Berlin to support the project.[29] The first goal was the most important. Association members stated that the establishment of such a memorial should be the task of German society, not the state. For Jochen Schulze-Rohr, Memorial Association founding member and cochair, "It doesn't really matter what people from other countries say. What is more important is that we as Germans need this. It belongs to our cultural history just as much as Bertolt Brecht, or Goethe, or Bach. It should not even be a question. When we don't realize this, and don't make it part of our everyday culture, then something is wrong" (interview, 1998). It was also important to association members for German citizens, not victims (Jews), to establish the memorial. Lea Rosh relates this view through a story she described in one of Perspective for Berlin's publications.

> I asked Heinz Galinski, then chair of the Jewish Community in
> Berlin but also chair of the Central Council of Jews in Germany,
> for a meeting. I informed him about our project. I didn't ask for
> an approval or rejection, I just offered information. He listened
> silently. He immediately understood. That it shouldn't be a task of
> Jews, not the victims. That it should be the task of non-Jews. He
> didn't want to get involved. "But if you are asked," I then wanted to
> know, "what will you say then?" "Then," he said, and looked at me
> with his honest, strong, and sad eyes, "then I would of course be
> supportive of it. How could I be against it!"[30]

In other publications, the association claimed to organize "a broad-based civic movement" for the memorial,[31] as evidenced by letters and petitions with thousands of signatures.[32] They also sought the support of well-respected people from "the fields of culture, academia and industry," such as Edzard Reuter of Daimler-Benz, Marcus Bierich of Bosch, the author Siegfried Lenz, and the musician Kurt Masur, using their media attention to encourage donations not just "from a few big sponsors, but from the German people as a whole"; they consciously decided not to ask leaders of political parties to join the initiative.[33]

For the association, the memorial should educate Germans about the international dimensions of the Holocaust, a historical understanding that they felt was missing in Germany, despite the existence of other memorials. To quote Schulze-Rohr: "Through artistic means you cannot bring an accidental bystander to break out in tears about the Holocaust. That is totally clear. But what is more important is that something will be represented about the European dimension of the Holocaust. That is very often forgotten. That doesn't yet exist [in Germany]. If you find a *Denkmal* here in Berlin, it is usually for local [commemorative] purposes . . . for example, for the Jews who lived on Bayerischer Platz, or the [memorials at the] deportation train stations. And that is important. But only 2 percent of the Holocaust victims were German Jews. Ninety-eight percent were predominantly Polish and Russian Jews. These stories are not clear to the people. So when Mayor Eberhard Diepgen says, 'We have enough Holocaust memorials in Berlin,' that is simply not true" (interview, 1998). This understanding of the social function of the memorial in Germany was also clearly defined through international comparisons, as the following 1994 public art competition guidelines indicate.

> The loss of Jewish life and Jewish culture in Europe is irreversible. . . .
>
> Where, apart from books, is that documented in our country, the country of the perpetrators?
>
> Where is our memorial?
>
> . . . In Germany there is nothing comparable [to the U.S. Holocaust Memorial Museum or Yad Vashem]. . . .
>
> We Germans must place a symbol that will be visible from afar to show to the world that we have accepted the burden of our history, that we intend writing a new chapter in our history. . . .
>
> It is a question of predominantly non-Jewish Germans erecting a memorial to the Jews who were murdered by the Germans, a memorial to the dead, but also a memorial to remind us that a whole nation allowed a section of itself to be singled out and annihilated.[34]

The association felt that the location of the memorial should reflect these goals. When it became clear that the memorial would not be built at the Gestapo Terrain, Lea Rosh discussed other possible locations with German organizations, federal and state officials, and GDR groups.[35] The association wanted a central historic location and pushed for the former site of Hitler's bunker. The Memorial Association member and historian Eberhard Jaeckel made a plea to the first unified German Parliament to establish the memorial at a location of "great symbolic value," specifically the area around the former Reich Chancellery building. Yet shortly before and after unification, other discussions were held about future land uses at the large stretch of the former buffer zone, or death strip, between the two Berlin Walls. Because the Kohl administration supported the project, in 1992 the federal government donated a large tract of land in a central location for the memorial,[36] not at Hitler's bunker but rather at an area known as the Ministry Gardens, where eighteenth-century gardens had originally been designed to complement the newly built palaces by the royal court's elite. The gardens were included in the designs for the governmental ministry buildings of the Prussian and later German Reich and in 1938 became part of the designs to complement Hitler's New Reich Chancellery designed by Albert Speer.[37]

The association's arguments for locating the memorial at Hitler's bunker or a central historic place in Nazi Berlin were linked to their conception of history. Association members believed that the memorial should represent the Holocaust as a unique event defined by the systematic mass murder of European Jews. They argued that Jewish genocide was a defining feature of National Socialism and Hitler's vision for Germany and Europe. Not only did the association argue in public debates that, numerically speaking, Jewish suffering and loss was unique (compared to those of other groups), but they also pointed out that the dimensions of persecution were well planned and far-reaching:

victims came from seventeen different European countries.[38] In addition, they argued that the Holocaust was the climax of two thousand years of anti-Semitism in Europe and Germany. Margherita von Bretano, a philosopher and association member, stated that

> the Jews [were] the exemplary victims, the victims of the "final solution." Anti-Semitism was not only one element of National Socialism; it was its very core. In and on the Jews it saw the whole: the whole damage, the whole evil, the distorted view of human life and human society which determined its whole view of the world.[39]

Such an understanding of the Holocaust is an "intentionalist" reading of history, one that views the systematic annihilation of European Jews as central to the ideology of National Socialism before or at the beginning of the Nazis' reign of power.[40] From an intentionalist perspective, the Holocaust is a unique event that cannot be compared to other modern genocides. The association also argued that the Nazi state was responsible for ending an ancient tradition through the systematic murder of more than one-third of the entire Jewish world population. Finally, Rosh argued that Hitler and a close-knit group of officials and officers were responsible for perpetrating the Holocaust.[41] In competition guidelines, Germans as a people were not classified as "evil" perpetrators but as silent bystanders to the crimes.

It was Hitler's ghost that the association evoked in the competition guidelines to haunt the site and define their understanding of German responsibility for past actions. They wanted the memorial to be located at a site personally touched by Hitler, a site that would represent the metaphysical category of evil. At numerous points in the competition guidelines, Hitler's presence was raised. For example, the place where Hitler's political testament was written, "in his bunker behind the Chancellery of the Reich on Voss-Strasse" during his defeat on April 29, 1945, defined the memorial's location. Later on in the guidelines, the memorial was specified by its "proximity to the Reich Chancellery, Hitler's headquarters, [which] alludes to the perpetrators but also to their defeat and disarming."[42] Elsewhere, the memorial was again located

> only a few meters away from Hitler's official headquarters, where he wrote the words which led to the deeds that changed the fate of Jewish citizens throughout Europe, through suffering, exile and death. . . . This site symbolizes in a quite particular way the fact that the remembrance of the millions of Jews who were murdered is an obligation of all Germans.[43]

At such a historic location, the establishment of the memorial would purge Hitler's ghost, the lingering presence of evil, from the German body politic. His touch would be replaced through the presence of the memorial and the act of honoring the memory of the innocent Jews who suffered under the National Socialist regime. As Rosh described in the 1994 artistic competition guidelines, "placing a memorial to the murdered Jews on the rubble of what was the center of Nazi power means elevating the murder victims above their murderers, the victims above the perpetrators."[44] Further, to "honor the murdered Jews of Europe," Rosh specifically recommended in the guidelines that the names of the individuals who died be made known through the memorial, evoking the memory of millions to replace that of the few evil Nazi elite. Finally, to cleanse the underground caverns from lingering evil and properly lay the memory of the innocent victims to rest, the guidelines recommended creating a memorial that had both a sub-terranean and an above-ground form. The memorial would remind future generations to "never forget" and would communicate that Germans "have accepted the burden of our history, that we intend writing a new chapter in our history."[45]

Images of Hitler in competition guidelines were located as subterranean evil pres-ences and given an aesthetic form through designs of Swiss exhibition artist Harald Szeemann. Szeemann was commissioned by the association to develop a concept for the memorial in 1991, when they were still pushing to get the tract of land at the site of Hitler's bunker. An abbreviated version of his concept was included in the first competi-tion guidelines.[46] Szeemann described his work as a new kind of memorial that integrated accusation and commemoration, emotion and reflection. This "synthetic memorial" repre-sented the uniqueness of historical events through a "living structure" (Ereignisstrucktur): visitors would walk through an underground landscape of memory.[47] As they moved through different rooms, visitors would confront the past through both artistic forms and a dispassionate presentation of the facts of mass murder. In this way the scale of Jewish genocide would be made clear, as well as the fact that the millions who were mur-dered were individuals, not just numbers.[48]

Szeemann cited Hitler as bearing ultimate responsibility for these crimes but also noted that "any place that accuses the perpetrators must be a warning to everyone who enables such deeds to happen."[49] He proposed to rid the site of Hitler's presence by trans-forming the spaces of his former underground chamber into a series of rooms following a path of redemption. Describing the location of the memorial at the Reich Chancellery, Szeemann stated that "buried deep in the earth were bunkers in which the perpetrators hid in the final hour before the destruction they had wreaked on others struck back at them and in which Hitler's mania ended in suicide. Reference should be made to this combination of hubris, destruction and self-destruction."[50] In the longer version of his concept, which was informally circulated during the competition period, Szeemann stated that the memorial should "violate the earth," "sink into it like memory," like the heaviness of Richard Serra's art.[51] Beneath this sinking sculptural form, Szeemann en-visioned an underground structure shaped in the Star of David that would admonish, inform, and mourn.

Visitors would enter and exit this "living structure" of memory through reconstructed concentration camp gates bearing the words "Place of Commemoration for the Mur-dered Jews" (instead of "Arbeit Macht Frei") and ornamented by a "violated" Star of David. Once in the memorial, visitors would move through a scripted narrative through a series of underground rooms. They would walk from the room of the perpetrators (an empty room that would include nineteenth-century anti-Semitic sayings as well as passages from Hitler's diary) to the room of the victims (an empty room with a historical chronology and statistics representing the extent of the crimes). Another room would represent individual destinies of Jews and their families; another would be a room of documents. At the center of the structure would be the room of speechlessness. Along the walls of these underground rooms and passages inscriptions from Paul Celan's poem *Todesfuge* (Death March) would be inscribed. Szeemann specifically mentioned that well-known Holocaust artists, including Christian Boltanski, Bruce Naumann, Rebecca Horn, and Ulrich Rückreim, should ideally design the subterranean rooms. The proposed budget for his memorial was DM 10 million, a figure close to the DM 15 million proposed in the 1994 public competition.

The Memorial Association's interpretation of the Holocaust through the competition guidelines and the concept designed by Szeemann reflected both the West German, Christian public culture of dismay *(Betroffenheit)*, typical of the *Mahnmal* (described in chapter 3), and dominant Western international symbols and narratives representing the Holocaust. Visitors were to go to Hitler's lair to confront evil and bear witness to suffering and death as a result of Germany's monstrous crimes. The experience would leave visitors *betroffen* (emotionally moved) and speechless; only as they walked up a redemptive path to a new humanitarian society in the future would they reemerge above ground, cleansed of collective guilt. By replacing Hitler's underground bunkers with a redemptive memorial, Germans could atone for past crimes by lifting the memory of the victims victoriously above Hitler. Through the memorial, Germans might begin a new chapter of history located in the spaces of the civilized world. It embodied a public act of atonement and communicated membership in the global North. According to competition guidelines, the memorial symbolized Germany's "obligation" to "accept the burden of German history" and thus enacted "the signal for a new chapter of cohabitation in which injuries to minorities will no longer be possible." The memorial would represent the exclusive guilt of a Nazi elite and the collective responsibility for past crimes.

Yet there are a number of ways to represent guilt and responsibility, as Aleida Assmann and Ute Frevert note.[52] Hannah Arendt, for example, argues that the term "German people" does not distinguish between Germans and Nazis. She suggests the term "organized guilt" to denote degrees of responsibility for perpetrators, sympathizers, and people who knew what was happening. Such an understanding avoids the problematic categories of both "exclusive guilt," in which responsibility for past crimes is ascribed to Hitler and a Nazi elite only, and "collective guilt," ascribed to all Germans. Karl Jaspers, in *The Question of German Guilt (Die Schuldfrage: Ein Beitrag zur deutschen Frage)*, also describes different approaches to representing guilt: criminal (individual), political (crimes committed in the name of the state), moral (defined by one's own conscience), and metaphysical (with reference to god).[53] According to Assmann and Frevert, Jaspers's introduction of the notion of political guilt replaces the category of collective guilt with that of collective responsibility. Contemporary citizens may think of the actions by Germans living in the past as far removed from their personal lives but may nonetheless as German citizens be willing to accept social responsibility for past state-perpetrated crimes.

One reason why the association's vision was so controversial—and problematic— was because they defined German guilt through metaphysical categories of good and evil. The proposal for the memorial—that German visitors should walk through a hall of horrors, enter in guilt and darkness, and reemerge redeemed—did not necessarily encourage citizens to accept social responsibility for the past. It displaced guilt and responsibility for past crimes onto the evoked icon of Hitler, a phantom raised not to haunt this project in the present but to symbolize the metacategory of evil and to locate that object in the past. In the view of museum memorial experts, Szeemann's proposed memorial may also have encouraged Germans to identify with the unjust suffering of victims.

In addition to the problems of representing guilt, and hence responsibility, for past actions, the intentionalist understanding of history that was implicit to the Memorial Association's vision similarly delineated clear-cut categories for past actions. Actors' intentions were interpreted as directly leading to historical processes and outcomes. In contrast, a functionalist understanding to National Socialist history and the history of the Holocaust—one I find more convincing—treats the systematic mass murder of Jews and Sinti and Roma, the policies of eugenics, and the exclusionary persecution of particular social groups during the regime as evolving over a number of years rather than as executed by a Nazi elite according to a premeditated plan.[54] A functionalist approach examines all forms of state-perpetrated violence, against Sinti and Roma, homosexuals, mentally and physically handicapped individuals, Jehovah's Witnesses, political opponents, and so on, even though it acknowledges the particular role of anti-Semitism in Nazi ideology. It examines the ways that German society supported and contributed to the management and evolution of an institutional system of industrial mass murder and exclusion. Unlike intentionalists, functionalists argue that historical comparisons of modern genocides should be made to further understandings of the particular nature of the systematic persecution of particular groups, such as Jews under National Socialism, or the formation of the Nazi terror state.

I suspect that many people, including those who supported the idea of a national Holocaust memorial in general, were critical of the Memorial Association's original aesthetic vision because of their understandings of history, and of German guilt and responsibility. Because the Memorial Association's interpretations of past actions were at once dichotomous and vague, the proposed memorial's social functions were not clearly specified in competition guidelines. As Günter Schlusche of the Holocaust Memorial Foundation, who is currently responsible for engineering and planning aspects of the memorial that was built, noted, "I think that mistakes were made during the first competition that were not related to the creativity of the artists. Mistakes were made in the description of the task. Before one asks architects and artists to develop ideas, one should describe the problem" (interview, 2001). Stefanie Endlich, an art historian and expert juror for the first public competition, also argued that the memorial's task description was short and ill-defined. Jan-Holger Kirsch, a scholar at the Center for Contemporary History in Potsdam, noted that the stated goal that the memorial should "mourn" (trauer) was vaguely defined both in competition guidelines and in public discussions. It is a term that functions in German society as both moral category and expectation (people "should" mourn at a memorial) and has come to replace the more critical understanding of a social process that, when tied to memory-work, produces and questions understandings of Self and Other.[55] Endlich similarly noted that "it is not even stated precisely who erects the memorial for whom. There is also that difficult discussion: Is it a memorial for the Jews, or is it for commemoration by the descendants of the perpetrators? . . . What is the goal of the memorial? Can we commemorate with large sculptures?" (interview, 1998).

Many individuals noted the negative influence of Szeemann's proposal in the artistic process. Endlich explained that in a public competition, "Artists read the application, they look who is in the jury, and they talk among themselves and see signals. I think that this prehistory and Szeemann's project with the Star of David and the experiential path [Ereignisweg] had a very negative impact on the work of the artists. . . . There were at least a hundred Stars of David in the competition!" (interview, 1997). Anecdotal evidence supports her interpretation. At the open information session for the competition, numerous artists asked about Szeemann's proposal, Hitler's bunker, and the expected underground dimensions of the memorial.[56] Frieder Schnock, an artist who submitted a proposal in the first competition with artistic partner Renata Stih, stated that "Szeemann was in the jury, and when you look at the history of the competition, you will come across a proposal by him to build subterranean bunkers. This was not officially part of the defined task of the memorial, but the proposal indicated that some sort of memory trail was expected. He had already planned to include art by Serra and Boltanski in this subterranean exhibition room in the shape of the Star of David. Because of his Dokumenta 5, I highly respect him, but he completely failed in this competition. He addressed the topic with this formalism, with this emphasis on memorial art. . . . He built a subterranean museum. He used architecture to create a museum in which you would walk through memory rooms" (interview, 1998).

Finally there was the problematic goal of representing German guilt. According to Endlich, "the sum of 15 million marks, . . . [together with] this enormous lot motivated artists to create gigantic monuments and sculptures that have nothing to do with their normal artistic language [Formensprache]. When you look at the list of the artists, here is the list of all five hundred or so people, you see that there are a lot of interesting artists in the list who usually work in a different way than what they presented in this competition" (interview, 1997). Despite the large number of proposals and the significant public interest in the competition, there was a notable lack of creativity by the artists: most used Jewish symbols (Stars of David, the menorah, the twelve tribes of Israel), created large graves or gashes in the earth, or used concentration camp icons (barracks, train tracks, cattle cars, concentration camp gates, ovens).[57]

The outcomes of the first public competition suggest some reasons why dominant international understandings and icons of the Holocaust, particularly when used in memorial form, are problematic ways of interpreting the past and representing social responsibility in postunification Germany. But what, then, should the function of a Holocaust memorial be in Germany? Is it even possible for German society to represent the Holocaust and still make claims to Western nationhood? To explore these questions further, I look at a different proposal for the memorial, one that highlighted the inherent contradictions of establishing such a memorial in Germany. The proposal submitted by conceptual artists Renata Stih and Frieder Schnock questioned the premises of the competition, namely, that a centrally located memorial could represent understandings of the past and national belonging in the present and future.

Conceptual Art as Public Memorial: *Bus Stop!*

Renata Stih and Frieder Schnock submitted a concept for the first public art competition called *Bus Stop!* Their idea was simple: build a central station where red buses would depart hourly to take visitors to historical places of persecution in and beyond Berlin. On a daily basis, buses would depart to well-known places like Auschwitz and Sobibor, as well as to lesser-known places like Hessisch Lichtenau. Like city buses, the red memorial buses would declare their destinations in large white letters above their front windows: Sachsenhausen. Their noticeable presence, coming and going from the center of the city, would communicate to locals and visitors the historical extent of the National Socialist system in a contemporary modern form. At the same time, visitors could access information and documents about these places through an information and educational center at the main bus terminal. The database would provide contemporary information about the points of destination and historical documents about the people who went to these places (forcibly and by assignment). Stih and Schnock's proposal questioned the assumption that Germany's violent legacy of National Socialism could be spatially and temporally located—and hence contained—through the crypt of Hitler's underground headquarters. They also challenged the premise that the memorial should commemorate Jews only. The bus stops and database information included numerous different sites of National Socialist persecution, as well as deportation information about Sinti and Roma and other groups.

Bus Stop! was awarded eleventh place in the first artistic competition, just short of the ninth rank needed to be invited in the second invited competition. It was a controversial proposal for some of the expert jurors. According to Endlich, "Conceptual artists were discouraged to participate [in the first public competition]. People like Renata Stih and Frieder Schnock—they participated, but the way their project was discussed in the jury shows that they were on a different wavelength. They were not understood at all" (interview, 1998). Nonetheless the project found broad public support and international attention in the media and by public spokespersons such as Amnon Barzel, former chair of the Council of Jews in Germany, who mentioned that regardless of the memorial competition outcome, *Bus Stop!* should be built in Berlin. Many individuals who came to look at the 528 models proposed for the first competition and displayed for public viewing in 1995 and 1996 wrote a number of positive comments about Stih and Schnock's proposal. National conservative newspaper *Die Welt* declared that *Bus Stop!* was clearly the popular favorite.[58]

Bus Stop! model design and concept. Copyright Renata Stih and Frieder Schnock. Courtesy of Renata Stih and Frieder Schnock.

For Stih and Schnock, all places in Germany are haunted by the National Socialist past. They do not understand the history of the Holocaust as originating from one central location or resulting from the actions of a small group of men. Rather, this history *took place* through people's actions and movements through homes, parks, city streets, public squares and train stations, surrounding greenbelts, forests, and networks of concentration and extermination camps and sites of persecution. According to Stih, "You have to be aware that Germany's wealth is based on dead people—what was stolen from people. As a result they had a better starting position. People inherit, and travel, and know many languages, but that's not all. They also inherit the Holocaust" (interview, 1998). Schnock also mentioned that every German family has objects at home that they "inherited" from other families during the war, including the letters, food, and material objects they received from traveling German soldiers in different occupied countries (in conversation, 2003).[59]

For a Holocaust memorial to make sense, it had to represent those complex everyday histories and spatialities of past and present in Berlin, Germany, and Europe. It had to communicate the movements of those routines, routes, and networks, the fluid interconnections between places and people, in an aesthetic form that was accessible, yet capable of subtly transforming the contemporary lived geographies of the city. To make people aware of the interconnected web of places that helped create National Socialist society and power structures, Stih and Schnock combined the authority of historical documents with the immediacy of everyday experience to encourage memory-work.

"These mobile monuments traversing the streets of everyday life . . . refocus attention on the authentic sites of the systematic mass murder of various victimized groups" and "provoke discussion among the people who are collectively visiting these places."[60]

As a memorial, *Bus Stop!* encourages personal memory-work through bodies moving through multiple space-times. But the individual visitor must take the responsibility to remember, to confront the past. As Schnock explained, "the visitor alone decides to go to a historic site, to get on the bus, to go to the research center and search for documents . . . or not" (interview, 1999). When people make this decision, they confront a difficult past with others. They go on the bus, move through the city, traverse streets and the Autobahn, and cross political boundaries as they travel to, and return home to, places touched by the history of National Socialism. In those social settings, individuals may travel silently, but they are not alone. They will most likely overhear conversations on the bus and at the historic sites. The everyday spaces of the city, the moving buses, and the people moving through those spaces in the buses, the conversations on the buses—these movements, these becomings, are the memorial.

In addition to moving through social space, the individual moves through time by accessing historical documents that detail stories about these places. Stih and Schnock's use of documents in the process of making their art, while inspired by the history of citizen group activism and decentralized approaches, is different from the understanding of a documentation at the Topography of Terror or at memorial museum centers. The artists use documents to represent history but make the information accessible through the use of popular culture to reach a wide audience.

> FRIEDER SCHNOCK: A document is never the whole truth. There are
>   always layers. You always have to look at why that document exists
>   and where the other corresponding documents are, because only
>   that [intertextuality] reveals the complete history. It cannot be only
>   one document in iron, which is taken as a monument . . .
> RENATA STIH: I want to put it this way: We are doing the splits. We take
>   these documents, but we bring them into a popular form. This is
>   the process. You can only communicate when it works psychologi-
>   cally. (Interview, 1998)

Bus Stop! is a process rather than an object of art. For Stih and Schnock, memorials are social spaces that should bring people from the present into contact with the people from the past through the documents, words, institutions, and unseen presences and structures that always haunt every place. Their approach to public memorial art changed after creating and installing their Bavarian Quarter memorial; they thought about their art and the role of place in that process in a different way. According to Stih, "Earlier we both made art separately, and we always first had the external form. We made sketches and installations, and photos. Now the process is completely different. We look at the place, and all of a sudden it is there—exactly what we need. It [the art, the place] opens up through the [creative] process alone. And we know that we can address and include people directly" (interview, 1998).

Their approach to art, public space, and place reflects a larger trend in the international art community that began in the late 1980s and 1990s. Conceptual artists in particular began to reject public art as traditional sculpture. According to Richard Serra, putting sculpture on a pedestal in a public square meant that the object of art was separated from the lived world of the onlooker.[61] Sculpture on a pedestal transmits "the effect of power without distinction"; it requires a subdued, even invented, audience to accept an idealized topic defined by the art community as worthy of commemoration. As Suzanne Lacy describes, while the idea of exhibiting art in public areas was progressive in the 1980s, most artists continued to accommodate the existing museum system, with its art critics and connoisseurs, because public art was nurtured by various museum institutions and the art market.[62] So artists, according to Jeff Kelley, parachuted into a place and displaced it with art. "Site specificity was really more like the imposition of a kind of disembodied museum zone onto what already had been very meaningful and present before that, which was the place."[63]

Place-based art, argues Serra, must refer to its contexts and scale-specific boundaries. Even when one simply takes a sculpture from the art gallery and places it in an urban setting, the meaning of the art changes, just as the art redefines the locale by changing its architectonic spatial relations. Public art, including sculpture, must work within and through the limits of a place to question the context, to simultaneously recognize and undermine boundaries, textures, and everyday uses. For place-based public art, what is important, according to Serra, is the "how" of the art process, a process that defines the work and is also defined by its content and place. Site-specific art and architecture are therefore not the same as place-based art. One cannot design place. According to Kelley, it feels different to be "on site" than in a place. "This sense of the human particularity of places—as distinct from the art-like specificity of sites—has informed and even become the contents of the best 'public' art."[64]

For Stih and Schnock, the artistic process begins with place.

> RENATA STIH: Places are important because they exist; they do not have to be artificially created. Crimes took place in certain places, and we have to say how many people, which people, and how, who watched. . . . It works psychologically only when you start with yourself and you think, "That is what would have happened to me." People do not understand it in any other way . . .
>
> FRIEDER SCHNOCK: We want to show the reality that still exists. And for that, you have to go to places. Or you have to make a trip in connection with the deportation. You take some of your own time and give it in order to remember something.
>
> RENATA STIH: This is where people are the most tight-fisted in our society— with time. They have time for tennis, golf, TV, traveling, and their

work, but for something like that, people have no time. People watch
a video about it [National Socialism and the Holocaust] and quickly
run through an exhibition, but that is what we wanted to avoid.
(Interview, 1998)

The artists' idea for *Bus Stop!* resulted from the simple realization that it is difficult to
travel to the historic sites of the National Socialist persecution from Berlin. They wanted
to find a way to make it easier for people to get to the historic sites, yet also to make that
history accessible as part of the lived spaces of the New Berlin. Rather than propose a
centrally located memorial, they instead offered visitors a starting point for their travels
within and beyond the new capital. They did research about the history of past places,
movements, and networks for the bus timetables and information databases. Through
this artistic process, they came to realize how tightly meshed, yet extensive, the National
Socialist system of extermination was, with lengthy distances "between the centers of
the terror apparatus and the other sites of violence and horror."[65] Stih and Schnock remapped parts of this National Socialist network through documents and moving buses,
the latter of which defined the aesthetic concept of the memorial. But there is no memorial without the people who engage in the artistic process, looking up information at the
main terminal or bus timetables, mapping this network by moving through the space-
times of the historic sites, listening to tour guides, and discussing their experiences on
the bus with others.

Stih and Schnock's *Bus Stop!* memorial pushes the possibilities of place-based art in
another way, namely, to question existing German political, economic, and social structures and spaces that too are haunted by the legacies of the past. The buses would not
work without contemporary tourism economies, consumption patterns, and transportation networks. The memorial thus is simultaneously emplaced in and moves through
contemporary Germany's political economies, a capitalist system based on the artifacts,
institutions, and other inheritances of World War II and National Socialism, including
one of Germany's most valued symbols of identity: the Autobahn. The Neue Gesellschaft
für bildende Kunst in Berlin (New Society for the Arts) recognized this implicit social
critique in Stih and Schnock's proposal and, with the support of numerous individuals,
city districts, and organizations, attempted to make *Bus Stop!* a reality for a limited period of time. The society was able to get a small grant from the Berlin Cultural Senate and
donations from private individuals for the project. While it wasn't enough to rent a bus
for a short period of time, it was enough to publish a *Bus Stop!* timetable, what Schnock
described as a "portable memorial you carry around in your pocket" (interview, 1999).

The timetable was about the same size as an ordinary German train schedule and
used the same basic layout inside. The outside cover was similar to that of an art activities
quarterly pamphlet that circulates in Berlin. The New Society for the Arts, working with
Stih and Schnock, published historical information about twenty-nine sites in Berlin and
fifty-nine sites in Germany and Europe. For each place there was a page or two of information about opening times, bus information about how to get there, distances from
major cities, and specific historical information about how the place functioned within

Bus Stop → Maly Trostenez

1145 km   Fahrtdauer ca. 17 Std.

ab	Bus	über	an
18.00	Hinfahrt	Brzesc, Baranowicze	11.00
8.00	Rückfahrt		1.00

Maly Trostenez und Blagowschtschina liegen 12 km südöstlich von Minsk an der Straße nach Mogilov.

Berlin Hbf → Minsk

Fahrtdauer 16 Std. 24 Min.

ab	Zug	umsteigen	an	ab	Zug	an
8.19	EC 41	Warszawa Centralna	14.30	14.52	D 11001	00.43

Übernachtung in Minsk

Minsk → Berlin-Lichtenberg

Fahrtdauer 19 Std. 37 Min.

ab	Zug		an
10.11	D 13		5.48

Zwischen November 1941 und Oktober 1943 wurde von dem "Befehlshaber der Sicherheitspolizei und des SD-Weißruthenien", SS-Obersturmbannführer Ehrlinger, südöstlich von Minsk das Vernichtungslager Maly Trostenez und der zentrale Exekutionsort Blagowschtschina eingerichtet. Ab dem Sommer 1942 trafen auf dem inzwischen bei Blagowschtschina eingerichteten Gleisanschluß zweimal wöchentlich Deportationszüge aus dem Deutschen Reich und besetzten europäischen Ländern ein. Mehr als 35.000 Juden aus Deutschland, Böhmen und Mähren, insgesamt etwa 150.000 Deportierte und Juden aus dem Ghetto in Minsk wurden hier erschossen oder in Gaswagen umgebracht und in 34 Massengräbern verscharrt. Das SS "Sonderkommando 1005" ließ ab dem Herbst 1943 und bis zum Juni 1944 die Massengräber öffnen und die Leichen bei Schaschkowka verbrennen; die russischen Arbeitskommandos wurden danach ebenfalls getötet.
Im "Stalag 352" bei Minsk ließ die deutsche Wehrmacht 120.000 sowjetische Kriegsgefangene hinter Stacheldraht sterben.

Bus Stop → Mauthausen

650 km   Fahrtdauer ca. 9 Std.

ab	Bus	über	an
9.00	Hinfahrt	Terezin, Linz, Gusen	18.00
15.00	Rückfahrt		24.00

Halt in Theresienstadt und Gusen; Übernachtung in Linz

Berlin Hbf → Linz → Mauthausen

Fahrtdauer 9 Std. 54 Min.

ab	Zug	umsteigen	an	ab	Zug	an
8.30	IR 2203	Nürnberg Hbf	14.13	14.25	EC 27	17.54
8.00	E 1809	St. Valentin	8.19	8.22	R 6107	8.30

Übernachtung in Linz

Mauthausen/Linz → Bln.-Lichtenberg

Fahrtdauer 9 Std. 47 Min.

ab	Zug	umsteigen	an	ab	Zug	an
15.26	R 6108	St. Valentin	15.34	15.38	E 1904	15.57
12.04	EC 26	Regensburg	14.30	14.35	IR 2602	21.20

Öffentliches Denkmal und Museum Mauthausen (Leitung: Bundesministerium für Inneres, Abteilung IV/7) Marbach 38, A-4310 Mauthausen, Tel. 07238-2269/3696 geöffnet April-Sept 8-18 Uhr (Einlaß bis 17 Uhr) Feb-März und Okt-Dez tägl. 8-16 Uhr (Einlaß bis 15 Uhr) geschlossen ab 16. Dezember bis Ende Januar
Am 29. März 1938, wenige Tage nach dem "Anschluß" verkündete Gauleiter Eigruber, daß nun auch Österreich endlich ein eigenes KZ bekäme, als "Auszeichnung für unsere Leistungen während der Kampfzeit". Im Jahr 1941 starben im KZ Mauthausen und dem seit Mai 1940 bestehenden Zweiglager Gusen 8000 Häftlinge. Einweisungen nach Mauthausen und dessen Nebenlager waren als Todesurteil aufzufassen, denn diese Lager hatten die höchsten Todesraten. Neben dem Prinzip "Vernichtung durch Arbeit", der Vorenthaltung jeder medizinischen Versorgung und von Nahrung, wurden mehrere Mordarten praktiziert: durch Gaswagen, mit einer Gaskammer im Lager und im benachbarten Schloß Hartheim und in einer getarnten Genickschußanlage. Einer der größten Abnehmer für die Häftlingsarbeit war die Steyr Daimler Puch AG mit Produktionsanlagen in Steyr-Münichholz, für Panzer in St. Valentin, für Kugellager in Melk und für Maschinengewehre im KZ Gusen. (s.S. 53 u. 66)

Bus Stop ist ein Projekt Die Bus Stop - Verbindung besteht noch nicht

Bus Stop! Fahrplan: sample pages from the timetable/memorial. Copyright Renata Stih and Frieder Schnock.

the National Socialist network. For each bus trip, the artists pointed out other sites nearby or along the way, forests, towns, cemeteries. At the end of the book, they included a brief description of the memorial proposal, visitor comments about the Holocaust Memorial competition, and a bibliographic reference guide for additional readings—historical sources that interested individuals can find at the library at Berlin's Haus der Wannsee Konference (House of the Wannsee Conference) memorial museum. Stih described the *Bus Stop!* timetable as a "social structure" rather than an object of art (interview, 1999). It worked. The New Society for the Arts produced five thousand books in 1995 that sold out in the first month; the Foundation for Brandenburg Memorial Centers ordered an additional two thousand copies, available at the Sachsenhausen Memorial Museum bookstore and the ifa-Galerie Berlin issued a new edition of the timetable in 2005.

While Stih and Schnock's artwork includes more than their Holocaust memorial projects, both the Bayerisches Viertel memorial and *Bus Stop!* helped redefine the meanings and functions of memorials and public art in Germany during the 1990s. According to Stefanie Endlich, until the 1960s, postwar memorials were "always 'for the victims,' and there is a person with chains on his hands, mourning. That says everything and nothing at the same time, since everybody can mourn about something. The Germans always like to see themselves as victims of the war. . . . I think that the development in the 1980s went away from this way of centrality and generality and instead tried to mark sites and structures, to change places and spaces" (interview, 1997).[66] Conceptual artists in particular played an important role in the politics of memory in Germany. They changed memorial art, commented Endlich, "from something material, touchable, and durable [to something] in the direction of thought processes. . . . The goal is to make a sign at a certain place, a relatively simple one, which also has to be aesthetic, but not [communicate] that the artist is important. There is a very important trend away from the central to the decentralized [approach]—making a web between what is already there and new things. That also changes the role of the art because the artwork is no longer at the center, but rather just a piece of the overall picture."

When Stih and Schnock realized that the 1994 public art competition guidelines outlined a traditional social function for the memorial, of mourning and guilt, and a site-based aesthetic form of public art, they entered the competition knowing that their proposal might not be understood or even considered. According to Schnock, *Bus Stop!* met the requirements of the guidelines but also "fought against the idea of a memorial on a fixed site, the form of the competition" (interview, 2000). For Stih, "The memorial question [*Denkmalsfrage*] is a psychological one. It is one of how to reach people so that they will understand in the following generation what happened, and that it does not happen again. And that is the largest problem. . . . How can we reach a twelve-year-old student so that he or she remembers? . . . You reach the youth by making it obvious to them that in every house there are places where things happened. . . . There are places of deportation—in Berlin, in every single small town. That is the reason why we have included other places in our *Bus Stop!* timetable, not just concentration camps but also places were people were buried in the forest—that is not known anymore" (interview, 1998).

Aestheticizing the Past

In the attempt to represent Germany as a "normal" nation after 1945, and again after 1990, officials and citizens have had to confront past violences that accompany the existence of their modern democratic nation-state. The Holocaust Memorial reflects those tensions, namely, between claims to uphold ostensibly universal values associated with democracy and human rights on the one hand, and to accept responsibility for the legacies and social consequences of past state-perpetrated violence on the other. To build a Holocaust memorial in Germany is to recognize the absence of groups of people in contemporary German and European society, a loss of life resulting from the historic actions of its citizenry and state leaders.

Through the memorial debates, seemingly irreconcilable differences in understandings of the past and future, of guilt and responsibility, were negotiated and ultimately given a location, form, and function. Originally, the Memorial Association wanted the memorial at a historical location that would symbolize Hitler's ghost in an abstract way, as evil incarnate. The memorial was to purge the evil impurities from the national body politic, making space for honoring the memory of murdered Jews and allowing Germans to declare that their democracy was based on tolerance and humanitarian agendas. Later, after the first failed competition, the memorial's location was represented as a symbolic public presence in the center of the New Berlin. According to Günter Schlusche of the Holocaust Memorial Foundation, the *civic* status of the project became clear with the public discussions and the results of an informal investigation of fifteen different possible locations for the memorial in 1995. The examination team felt that the memorial "should stand in the middle of society, with as much publicity as possible. It should stand at an especially important point of the city's public space. The chosen location has exactly these qualities" (interview, 2000).

The emphasis on publicity and centrality indicates the memorial's national role as a symbol of Western democracy. It will be accessible to dignitaries and tourists coming to the capital. Unlike the Topography of Terror—a new type of place defined in opposition to existing Holocaust places of memory that criticized understandings of the nation—the Holocaust Memorial was conceived as a place of memory that performs the nation to an international audience. As Endlich noted, "The growing public consensus that a [Holocaust] memorial should be built has probably more to do with concerns about Germany's image in other countries than the conviction that it is really needed."[67] Critics note that the memorial mimics the aesthetic forms and functions of places of memory in lands of the survivors, in particular the United States and Israel, and therefore is inappropriate to the land of the perpetrators.

Despite these criticisms, others supported the international agenda of the Holocaust Memorial. One journalist argued that most European Jews were murdered in concentration camps in Poland; "pointing to Sachsenhausen or Buchenwald when talking about the extermination of European Jews is historically wrong" because camps in Germany were erected mainly for political prisoners.[68] Because German memorial centers, according to this journalist, were not at the "authentic" historical sites of Jewish persecution, building a symbolic memorial commemorating Jewish memory made sense. Some American groups also felt that the central location in the new capital was appropriate. The American Jewish Community, for example, argued in 1998 that historic sites cannot replace a central memorial in the government quarter. James Young, who initially was critical of the memorial, also came to support it because he felt that there was space in Berlin for a number of different kinds of memorials, including this more traditional, centralized one.[69]

The Holocaust Memorial, of course, is not just a replica of memorials elsewhere. It was an outcome of negotiated German and international cultures of memory, each defined by distinct hauntings, political perspectives, social relations, and histories. As a cultural artifact, the memorial is part *Mahnmal,* working within a monumental memorial culture of admonishment located in a highly visible public space. Its mandate that Germans show guilt and mourning reflects the culture of dismay and consternation *(Betroffenheit),* which are in turn defined by universal Western metaphysical categories of good and evil, and Christian discourses of suffering, repentance, and redemption. The call for a large, central sculptural form in a symbolic location reflects site-specific approaches to public art. At the same time, Eisenman's abstract field of stelae is more subtle than the memorial forms of the 1980s, which were typically designed with heavy, modern sculptures representing pain and suffering through stylized anguished bodies or abstract art. Schlusche commented that Eisenman's art offers a radical confrontation with the traditional concept of a memorial in public space (in conversation, 2003). The undulating field of stelae, representing loss and encouraging reflection, will no doubt invite curiosity. Finally, the small information center, while no documentation, at least gestures to the decentralized culture of commemoration in Germany and is considered to be a portal to this memorial landscape by providing maps and information about memorial museums located at historic sites of suffering and persecution. It will also name people and provide information about the life histories of individuals, using Yad Vashem's database.[70]

Yet the social function of this national place of memory in Berlin ultimately remains problematic, for, to use Habermas's words, the "superior image of the Jews for us Germans" was considered to be more important than "the moral necessity to honor and commemorate all victim groups."[71] As Andreas Nachama of the Topography of Terror pointed out: "Where is the information center for Sinti and Roma and other groups?" (interview, 2003). Even with the addition of an information center, the form and function of the memorial still represent what Heidegger describes as a monumental past. Such a historiography represents inspirational examples from the past, in this case of victims overcoming evil perpetrators or of a nation overcoming its forgetful tendencies, to evoke utopian imaginations for the future.[72] It will do what is expected by tourists and visitors rather than create a space through which they can confront how they think about a memorial, the nation, and the past. Moreover, by separating Jews from other victims of Nazi genocide and violent acts, thereby creating a meta-Holocaust victim category, Germany will continue to define Jews as Other in the nation's contemporary society through the memorial and the culture of dismay and mourning. It remains unclear how the memory of other social groups will be represented and remembered in the New Berlin.

A Newspaper Article

O f the hundreds of articles I read about the Holocaust Memorial debates, the most memorable was Rudolf Kraft's 1992 depiction in *Die Zeit* of a memory landscape in the (future) new capital city. Kraft begins his article, "In trennendem Gedenken," with a guided tour:

> It is the year 2001. The German capital city has in the interim also become the seat of the government. Our tourist bus turns from the Street of Tolerance, formerly Wilhelmstraße and later Grotewohlstraße, onto Leipziger Straße, squeezes through the narrow passage of Potsdamer Platz under the Mercedes Benz Star that sits atop a massive skyscraper, and turns right onto the Street of Memory. It used to be named Ebertstraße, before that Göringstraße, and before that Königgrätzer Straße. Slowly the bus drives by the former Ministry Gardens. The foreign tour guide speaks relatively quickly into the microphone because he has a lot to explain here:
>
> > We find ourselves here, beloved Berlin visitors, at the National Memorial Park for the Victims of National Socialism. It stretches across the entire area between Potsdamer and Pariser Platz. As the tallest building in the park, you can immediately make

189

out the Holocaust Memorial to Murdered Jews in the middle.
The memorial stands atop underground "Rooms of Experience
and Memory" through which the public can walk, where the
memorial's educational and media offices are also located. . . . No
madam, not in Hitler's Bunker, that was ten meters deeper and
stood further to the right . . . On the left side you can now see the
Holocaust Memorial II for the Murdered Sinti and Roma. On
the right side, right above the bunker of Hitler's driver, with the
original SS paintings, stands the Reich Chancellery memorial
center. A tunnel leads from there to the nearby memorial center
"Topography of Terror" located at the former Gestapo Terrain.
Over there, diagonally to the right, the thirty-meter-tall triangle
of rose granite, is the Memorial for Murdered Homosexuals . . .
The somewhat larger star of red granite—no, I don't mean the Star
of David, that belongs to the Holocaust Memorial—also not the
six-pointed star, but rather the five-pointed star, commemorates
the murdered communist resistance fighters. And if you look very
closely, between the red star and the Star of David, you will see the
Brandenburg Gate, a 1792 classical structure by Langhans . . .

Kraft's fictive bus tour, a dystopian depiction of a Disney-like Holocaust tourism
landscape, represented the fears and cynicism articulated by a number of people I had
interviewed. When the article was first published in the national newspaper *Die Zeit*
on July 24, 1992, debates about the Holocaust Memorial were quite intense. Critics
feared that building an exclusive memorial to Jews would result in a social hierarchy of
victims and would be expressed through numerous Holocaust memorials competing
for the best location, artist, funding, and public visibility.

The article reminded me of the arguments made by conservatives in the early
1980s about Germany's supposed "hysteria" with the Nazi past. Then the "German
neurosis"—a term conservatives used to indicate what they perceived as a social crisis
caused by an obsessive preoccupation with National Socialism—was represented as
a cancer-like growth of thousands of *Mahnmäler* and history workshop movement
projects dotting small towns and cities throughout the country. Their solution: build
a centrally located history museum in Berlin to promote a positive understanding of
national identity. Ten years later in a newly unified city and country, liberal to left-
wing commentators characterized the German identity crisis in terms of an artificial
landscape of centrally located Holocaust memorials staged for the tourist gaze. In the
1990s, their solution was to bring future generations to the authentic historic sites of
suffering and perpetration located throughout Germany and Europe.

Berlin, 2002.

6 | Memory in the New Berlin

Journal name: The New Berlin
Guide pen name: travel2000
Type of trip: Pleasure
Date created: 10/31/2000
Description: Prior to my visit, I had no strong impres-
                   sion of Berlin, except for images of Berlin
                   Wall and its fall ten years ago. My sister, an
                   architecture graduate, was excited about
                   Berlin. "There's lots to see—it's a brand
                   new Berlin!" She was 100 percent right.
—http://www.igougo.com/planning/journal.asp?JournalID=3010

The New Berlin, described by city marketers as a large architectural exhibition, is a city (again) reborn. Berlin is the chronotope, or space-time formation, through which contemporary dreams of national futures are imagined. Celebrated by its engineering feats, architectural designs, and youthful energy, the city, as Germany's reunified capital, represents a new millennium in a new Europe and is advertised to be cosmopolitan, world class, and open. As one virtual tourist guide proclaimed, "When the wall came crashing down in the late 1990s, even Berliners would never have guessed that a city plagued by war could become a global destination sought after by the uber hip."[1]

The grand spectacle of Berlin's performance, of becoming new again, demands attention, asking locals and visitors "to keep your eyes open," to watch closely so as to remember the progress of the new. According to one marketing spokesperson who described summer tours to the construction sites, "Berlin is a large architectural exhibition. Each and every year things change. Normal tours might show you similar things, but they do not go into depth. We [Partners for Berlin] tell you who is constructing what and what lies behind it. Other sightseeing tours in cities are always superficial. I don't have to do a tour a second time in Munich, but in Berlin I have to do it again and again because things change so fast" (interview, 2000). The cover of a 1997 brochure for these summer tours and events, called Schaustelle Berlin, or Showcase Berlin, depicted young people (Germany's future?) watching the spectacle of construction, a landscape somewhere between Berlin's imagined dusk and sunrise. The object of their collective gaze was not the contemporary city but a moving spectacle of past and future landmarks. They watched from the vantage point of the future, remembering a dreamscape in transition, awaiting the next scene. This New Berlin reframed the city by detaching existing places from their known, everyday experienced spaces and times and relocating them as icons of the new Germany in an always becoming, always deferred future.

Such portrayals of "the new" create temporal categories—the historic, old, new, future—as well as the locations of their meaning. In the optic of the new, past and contemporary social problems are removed from the spectacle of the city, which for Berlin include corruption, the lack of affordable housing, an increase in poverty, racism, and xenophobia, and the disenfranchisement of the public. The New Berlin, as the object of desire, is distanced from the gray Cold War and dark National Socialist cities by mapping the "old" city as consumable objects, as tourist attractions. Places such as Checkpoint Charlie or the Berlin Wall become exhibitions, even museums, of themselves.[2] At the same time, the historic, or royal, Berlin is given material form through urban design, architecture, aesthetics, and advertising images. City planners self-consciously reclaim a nineteenth-century Berlin in the spaces of the contemporary/future city through land use and building code restrictions.

Contemporary architectural re-creations of hip, cosmopolitan Weimar Berlin are also present in the mappings of the new, such as through glass display cultures of department stores that, according to Janet Ward, include the "Stilwerk building of furniture and interior design stores on the Kantstraße in Charlottenburg, with its rounded glass corner eye-catchingly reminiscent of Mendelsohnian consumerist architecture." This contemporary interpretation of early-nineteenth-century Berlin not only indicates the postmodern reconstitution of the flaneur in "spaces of streetwise consumption." For Ward, these architectural elements

> also signify the most interesting underbelly of post-Wall Berlin's reconstruction craze, amidst its obvious ongoing need to recreate itself as the metaphorical extension of a new nationhood. These new city windows reflect an impossible wish: the desire to recapture the Berlin of the 1920s. It is an eternal return that can seek but never arrive at a continually reminisced Weimar identity.[3]

These material performances of the New Berlin assume that urban space is transparent, that the city can be visually known. Yet any representation of national pasts and desired futures through urban icons is haunted by past structures of meaning as well as personal memories of residents and visitors. The city is not merely an exhibition for the drama of utopian visions of national history, some of which were materialized and others that were not. As Steve Pile suggests, "Cities haunt . . . at least in the sense that they force us to recognize the lives of those who have gone (before). In this sense, the physicality of the city itself shimmers as it becomes a flexible and durable place of memory."[4]

"Take a close look or you might miss something. That's the odd thing about Berlin. One day you notice something new and yet you have the feeling it's always been there. So the best thing is to keep your eyes open. Then you will be able to remember later on how things used to be" (Schaustelle Berlin [Showcase Berlin] summer tours brochure, 1997).

The places and people described in this book reveal how Berlin's materiality is haunted by past visions for the future and contemporary desires for the past. It is a city where temporalities collide in unexpected ways through the actions of individuals and groups—living, deceased, and not yet born—as they make places in their search for what it means to be German. In the process, people evoke ghosts, bump into past remnants of other Berlins, dig through social and material landscapes, and debate how the past should be remembered, for whom, where, and in what form. At the same time, precisely because Berlin is haunted by past and contemporary desires for the future, it will always be a city created, in part, by how it has been and will be staged for its citizens and visitors. Modern Berlin, as a concept and a place, is simultaneously haunted by past and future lives and presences, and shaped by the tourist gaze—an all-consuming scopic regime that circulates and judges, plays and performs.

In capital cities, tourism landscapes are material and symbolic expressions of the nation in a phase of late consumer capitalism.[5] They commodify the fears and fantasies of national hauntings by imposing order on time (often to discipline ghosts) and package a palatable and profitable identity through place. What is distinctive about contemporary Berlin's tourism productions is that these stagings of the (remembered) new cosmopolitan city include the public acknowledgment of past national crimes. At the intersection of tourism, government, and business districts, three places will form a memory district in the center of the city. The Jewish Museum, opened in 2002, celebrates Jewish contributions to Germany and Europe through family-oriented museum exhibitions in a dramatic new building designed by Daniel Libeskind. The centrally located Holocaust Memorial, completed in 2005, commemorates the memory of persecuted Jews through a large field of rising and falling stelae designed by Peter Eisenman and its underground information center. The new four-story building for the International Documentation Center Topography of Terror, designed by Peter Zumthor and projected to open in 2008, will educate the public about the National Socialist terror system at a historic site of perpetrators. This memory district, as a hypervisible performance of Holocaust memory in the New Berlin, acknowledges a violent national past at the same time that it locates Germany as central to an emerging global moral community.

For some, this staging of the new is troubling. Günter Morsch, director of Sachsenhausen Memorial Museum and Brandenburg Concentration Camp Memorial Museums Foundation,[6] argued that "the discussions about the Jewish Museum, the Topography of Terror, and the Holocaust Memorial result[ed] in a turning away from the authentic sites of terror and destruction.... The spectacular architecture [of these three places] finds more attention among *feuilletonists* [art and cultural critics in the media] than we could have ever won for our [memorial museum] projects" (interview, 2000). Morsch, like other memorial museum experts, is concerned about the public attention these places receive for their world-famous architect-stars rather than their social functions of critically coming to terms with the past. He believes that the "spectacular" memory district signifies a troubling direction in German public commemoration, a centralization of memory that may undermine the existing national, decentralized network of memorial museums. His concerns thus raise a significant question: what does it mean to highlight

National Socialist and Holocaust memory at a centrally located tourist destination in the new German capital?

While Morsch's criticisms about consumerist representations of a violent past are significant, the underlying dichotomy he presents to make his argument—between architectural surface, symbolic space, and consumption on the one hand and historical depth, authentic sites, and critical reflection on the other—is problematic. Such a dichotomy contains and constructs place and morality through materiality. The "authentic" or real place is defined according to its artifacts and historic location; it is understood as historical evidence (Zeugnis) of crimes against humanity and as a material trace (Spur), even sacred relic, that embodies a past that by definition is understood as unknowable and unrepresentable. When place is constructed as having an authentic aura, as being an eyewitness to past atrocities, it is also situated in social space, acquiring a special status in relationship to other places through international moral hierarchies and tourism economies.

Although authentic places are represented by survivors, their families, and memory experts (historians, educators, and others) as important moral moments and sites in the history of humanity that warn about possible futures, they do not exist outside these capitalist systems of value. No less than the centrally located Holocaust Memorial, the authentic place is created by and constitutes tourism spaces, geopolitical relations, and transnational commemorative practices. These inherent contradictions belong to the politics of place making and memory in postunification Berlin. Because places of memory are always located in international, moral, and economic spaces, they are also defined by the tensions and structural hauntings that accompany their classification and related mappings. In this chapter, I explore those tensions by describing the New Berlin's emerging memory district and its relationship to authentic historic sites, including Sachsenhausen, just north of the city, historically built as part of Hitler's vision for a new Berlin and now a national memorial museum.

The Nascent Memory District

With the completion of the future center for the Topography of Terror, Berlin will be different from the other cultural centers in Europe that are marketed as "new." Berlin's memory district will be the first cultural space internationally that publicly acknowledges national guilt, commemorates the suffering of victims, and represents the history of the perpetrators in a national capital. It will attract tourists who, in planning their travels, will include a visit to at least one, if not all, of these places of memory.

Tourists will come to the memory district for a number of reasons, drawn to the center of the city by their curiosity about Berlin's and Germany's unusual history or their knowledge or familiarity with images and narratives of the Holocaust and the Cold War. They might visit the Holocaust Memorial, for example, because of its location, near the Reichstag, Brandenburg Gate, and federal district, or because they are moved by the sea of blank concrete slabs with no names, sites, times, or faces. They may decide to go to the Topography of Terror because it is adjacent to one of the last remaining fragments

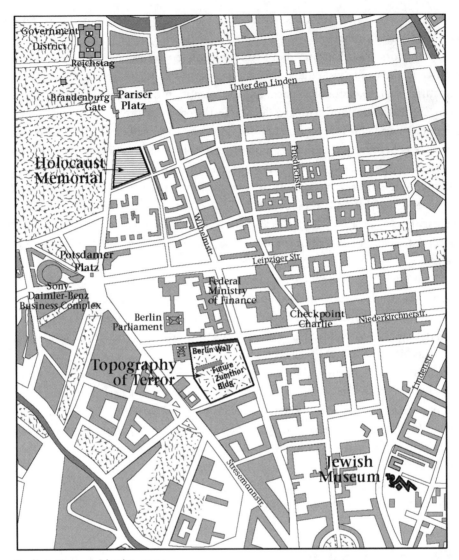

Berlin's Memory District, 2004.

of the Wall or because they wish to learn more about the history of Berlin during National Socialism. Even though the new international center is not yet finished, the Topography's central location has resulted in tourist groups coming all the time. For the academic staff member Andreas Sanders, these groups "have maybe twenty minutes [to] look at the excavations and then rush to their next site. This is a new development that we must anticipate when the new building opens" (interview, 2000).

Tourists will probably continue to spend part of a day at the Jewish Museum, already one of Germany's most visited museums.[7] Because of the powerful presence of Daniel Libeskind's design, what was originally envisioned as an extension of the Berlin Museum *became* the museum. Visitors must first go through the old Berlin museum, housed in an eighteenth-century yellow baroque building that is the last standing structure of its time in historic southern Friedrichstadt, to enter Libeskind's silver bolted structure.

Memorial to the Murdered Jews of Europe, 2004. Design by Eisenman Architects. Photograph courtesy of Iguana Photo.

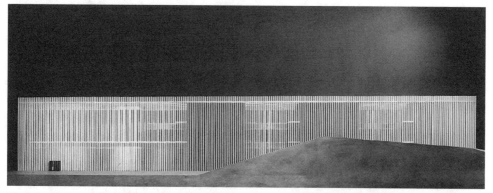

Model of Topography of Terror International Center. Design by Peter Zumthor. Courtesy of Stiftung Topographie des Terrors.

Organized around three intersecting axes—of exile, the Holocaust, and continuity—the Jewish Museum is created of voids and voided voids (empty spaces that can be seen but not physically accessed). At the end of the Axis of Exile, there is also an outdoor memorial, a concrete "garden" of forty-nine, closely spaced and tilted stelae in a compact courtyard space. While the physical space of the museum communicates rupture and loss, the historical content of the exhibitions indicates continuity, dating from medieval times to the present day.

These three very different types of place (memorial, documentation center, and museum), each with its own discrete history and aesthetic form, embody the contentious postwar history and inherent contradictions of representing the German nation after the Holocaust. Each will be exhausting to experience emotionally and, at least for the Topography of Terror and Jewish Museum, overwhelming in terms of the historical material presented. Tourists visiting the Topography of Terror in recent years, for instance, described their experiences using words such as "unsettling," "chilling," "grim," and "somber." At the Jewish Museum, some called the building "complicated and confusing" and described the museum's exhibit about the Nazi period as "disturbing."[8] While the memory district will soon become a tourism attraction in its own right, visitors will probably go to only one of these three places in their travels, including it as part of an existing tourism route, such as "Nazi Berlin," "Jewish Berlin," or "Retracing the Path of the Berlin Wall."

The memory district as a distinctive cultural space in the city, however, was never planned or marketed: it evolved to become a coherent tourism concept. Discussions for all three places began in the preunification city independently. In 1971, for example, when Berlin's Jewish community celebrated its 300th anniversary through an exhibition at the Berlin Museum, there was a great deal of interest in establishing a Jewish Museum.[9] An association was founded in 1975 with the goal of reviving the historic museum at Oranienburgerstrasse, near the city's main synagogue. (The original museum opened shortly before the National Socialist rise to power and displayed Berlin's

The Jewish Museum, 2002. Design by Daniel Libeskind.

Jewish community's collection of art and Judaica. It was closed in 1938 by the Gestapo, and its collections were confiscated.) In addition to reviving the historical museum, the Association for a Jewish Museum wanted to emphasize the history of Berlin's Jewish community, including the diversity of Jewish life before and after the period of National Socialism, and the role played by important Jewish figures in German society. From the late 1970s to the 1990s, a newly organized Jewish Department in the Berlin Museum began to produce exhibitions in new galleries in the city, and Heinz Galinski, the former chair of Berlin's Jewish Community, pushed for an independent museum. Shortly before unification, an architectural competition was held for an extension to the Berlin Museum; 165 architects submitted proposals, and Daniel Libeskind's concept was chosen as the winning design.

Far from a tightly conceived plan, the memory district emerged as an effect of local and national discussions about German identity in the 1990s. Public awareness about representing National Socialist and Holocaust histories was at a peak after unification due to commemorative anniversary events for the end of World War II in 1995 and a number of heated controversies, including debates about a traveling exhibition by the Hamburg Institute for Social Research (War of Extermination: Crimes of the Wehrmacht [German Infantry], 1941–1944); Daniel Goldhagen's contentious book *Hitler's Willing Executioners*; the extent of German corporate and state responsibility for compensating forced and slave laborers; and the so-called Walser-Bubis affair, a public debate between the German author Martin Walser and former head of the Council of German Jews Ignatz Bubis about the political uses of the Holocaust in Germany.[10]

During this time, Berlin faced a number of local funding difficulties. In response, the directors of the Topography of Terror Foundation introduced the idea of a memory district.[11] Academic director Reinhard Rürup emphasized the reasons why three, rather than one, places of memory were needed in the new capital.

> The Foundation has tried to convince parliamentary members, government officials, and journalists that the Topography of Terror is a site where National Socialist crimes and the society of perpetrators are represented and explained, a central and indisputable part of the memory culture of the capital. In retrospect, the Jewish Museum in Berlin and the Holocaust Memorial have important architectural designs from Daniel Libeskind and Peter Eisenman; the Foundation reminds people that the architecture of Peter Zumthor is also appropriate and compelling. In view of the complementary character of the three institutions, the Topography of Terror cannot be left behind these other two impressive buildings in terms of the aesthetic quality of the building.[12]

To claim national status and gain financial support, directors located the Topography squarely in the center of the symbolic map of the New Berlin. As Andreas Sanders commented, the "'trio' [of places] is important: the [Holocaust] Memorial, Topography, and

Jewish Museum. . . . The three places will create an interesting tension. There are certain points where we overlap and would reasonably compete with each other, but the three institutions could create a very interesting whole" (interview, 2000).

Thus, although the memory district was not designed explicitly, it signaled the emergence of a new centralized public culture of commemoration. At the same time, however, the presence of the Topography of Terror, as a site of perpetrators, will question the spatial logic of performing history as an architectural exhibition and object to be consumed through the tourist gaze.

A Hypervisible Cosmopolitan Holocaust Memory

The symbolic commemorative space of the memory district, while unique in terms of historical content and social responsibility, will function in ways similar to other Western national theaters of memory. It will be centrally located, highly visible in the media, and highlighted in tourism guidebooks. Because of its proximity to the federal district and embassies, it will be visited by national politicians and foreign dignitaries, functioning much like Washington, DC's, mall of memorials. To borrow Caroline Widmer's description for the Holocaust Memorial, the memory district will be both a "self-effacing and self-aggrandizing gesture of public memorialization."[13]

This new dramaturgic space of national commemoration will stage a hypervisible cosmopolitan Holocaust memory for citizens, politicians, foreigners, and a Western moral community of democratic nations. Through these three places of memory, the Holocaust—the metacategory of the unknowable, the unrepresentable, the break in civilization and rupture in modernity—will be represented through international narratives and images based on metaphysical categories of good and evil, as described in the previous chapter. Berlin's spectacular public acts of atonement, mourning, and healing—of publicly demonstrating how "we the descendants of the perpetrators show shame and mourning"[14]—will be given material form through internationally respected architecture and symbolic spaces.[15] The Jewish Museum emphasizes the gaping holes left in German and European society in the wake of the Holocaust, yet offers redemption to visitors as they move from the depths of Holocaust hell/death to the above-ground exhibitions that display Jewish contributions to global society. The Holocaust Memorial's information center will represent the names, stories of trauma, and memories of victims and survivors and through its sculptural form will offer a space for transforming horror into hope. Even the Topography of Terror is interpreted as a Holocaust museum by public officials. As Thomas Lutz, head of the national Memorial Museum Department, described in 1997, "Foreign pressure results in this recent social interest in the Topography. When other countries ask about a Holocaust Museum in Germany, the federal government argues that the Topography—because it deals with the [National Socialist] crimes and German structures—could be a special form of a Holocaust museum, even if it does not have such a central position as do the museums in Washington and Jerusalem."

The memory district's location, access to the public, and visibility will also communicate an understanding of the nation: that the new Germany is open and has nothing to hide. In this symbolic space, nothing will appear to be hidden from view. Information about the past will be clearly accessible through databases, tours, guides, and artistic forms. Yet through the establishment of these places of memory, the nation will not only repent for past crimes; through tourism and ceremonial performance, it will also be recognized by other nations as belonging to a Western global moral order. The memory district, in other words, materializes Schröder's cultural political agenda of normalization by representing Germany as a cosmopolitan, moral, and open society.

Schröder's neoliberal agenda is similar to those of other Western world leaders, including former president Bill Clinton, prime minister Tony Blair, and president Jacques Chirac, global figures who have apologized for past national crimes perpetrated by the state against its own citizens and other peoples. According to Elazar Barkan, within this post–Cold War order,

> moral issues came to dominate public attention and political issues
> and displayed the willingness of nations to embrace their own
> guilt. This national self-reflexivity is the new guilt of nations. . . .
> It is the growth of both identities—the victims and the perpetra-
> tor, both as subjective identities—that informs this new space in
> international and national politics.[16]

Although world leaders continue to deploy the Holocaust to organize the past and contemporary geopolitical relations according to the universal categories of good and evil, and according to victims (symbolized by Jews) and perpetrators (symbolized by Hitler),[17] as I suggested in chapter 5, claims to moral status and belonging to the "civilized world" are now accomplished through the recognition of, and compensation for, past national acts of injustice. In Germany, politicians present the Topography to foreigners "as an example for Germany's dealing with its own history. Although some people think it's not the best part of the new Berlin, nobody has dared so far to suggest getting rid of the Topography" (Andreas Sanders, interview, 2000). Through public apologies, financial compensation, and commemorative displays, national leaders in other countries have similarly acknowledged the inhumane treatment of citizens and social groups in internment camps, reservations, or sex slavery networks.

European debates in the late 1990s about war reparations for survivors and their families, for example, focused on the profits made by German corporations as well as Swiss banks.[18] American law firms, the U.S. Senate, the American Jewish Committee, and the Jewish Claims Conference pressured Germany to compensate individuals who worked for large German corporations during World War II and were living in Eastern European countries without pensions. Most of the powerful German corporations, who saved an estimated 16 billion Reichsmark in wages (about DM 95 billion in 1999 standards), balked at demands for compensation; foreign pressure and later intercessions by Schröder resulted in a 1999 agreement to pay DM 10 billion (by German industry and the state) to survivors still living.[19] Around the same time, international pressure was exerted on Swiss banks to divulge information about what happened to the so-called

Nazi gold (stolen and laundered money, gold, artwork, and other treasures) and bank accounts of Jewish clients. The neutral Swiss had to explore their past complicity with Nazi Germany and the institution of postwar banking policies that legally denied restitution claims by survivors and the families of those who died.

Although Schröder's administration cannot be criticized for a nostalgic geopolitics of normalizing the past, as was the case under the former Kohl administration, there are problems with using Berlin to stage the nation as a moral and open society. Acknowledging national crimes and representing a cosmopolitan understanding of the Holocaust in a central location of the national capital equates visibility with clear-sightedness as well as moral foresight. It also represents the Holocaust as knowable through highly visible places of memory that are located in symbolic, yet assumedly transparent, spaces. Avery Gordon argues that such an emphasis on knowing about the past through vision, or hypervisibility, renders the hauntings that accompany any representation of difference and social injustice, and in this case of a violent national past, spatially invisible. Hypervisible spaces are temporally flat. They have

> no shadows, no ghosts. In a culture seemingly ruled by technologies of hypervisibility, we are led to believe not only that everything can be seen, but also that everything is available and accessible for our consumption. In a culture seemingly ruled by technologies of hypervisibility, we are led to believe that neither repression nor the return of the repressed, in the form of either improperly buried bodies or countervailing systems of value or difference, occurs with any meaningful result.[20]

Each performance of the city, each spectacular display, has both spatial and temporal effects. Because place making and memory as social processes cannot be contained in space or time, the creation of a new symbolic space in the national capital will have specific impacts on other places situated in other contexts and settings. As I explore in the following sections, the emergence of a memory district in the new capital has sent ripples through the decentralized network of memorial museums that were established in West Germany in the 1980s and expanded into the former East after unification. Those ripples, in turn, evoke yet other specters and possibilities in and through the space-times of the contemporary city.

Centralizing National Memory: A New Public Culture of Commemoration
Memorial museum experts expressed concerns about the emergent politics and symbols of the nation, of representing memory through large, architectonic, centrally located places. From their perspective, the nascent memory district of the New Berlin allows for no vantage point from which to engage in critical memory-work.

Critics of a centralized national memory suggest that it is an American approach to representing the Holocaust. According to Klaus Hesse, a Topography of Terror academic staff member, "Until 1990, the memorial landscape in West Germany was regionally based, an integral part of the federal system. After reunification another trend developed: centralized places are now demanded. It's like a prayer wheel: they always say that something exists in Washington and we do not have it. . . . The trio of places [in the memory district] includes institutions that fulfill national demands and functions. It is a very new development, and the Topography will have to deal with that as well" (focus group interview, 1998). As I have suggested in previous chapters, some experts and educators argue that Germans must not only bear witness to victims' suffering and pain at historic sites; unlike other citizens, they must confront their heritage as a society of perpetrators. For this reason, the representational strategies used in the United States and Israel are considered to be inappropriate by these German memorial museum experts. For Hanno Loewy, the director of the Fritz Bauer Institute in Frankfurt, "The problem is that here in Germany—as opposed to the United States or Israel—we have historic places [of National Socialist perpetration] everywhere. . . . There are hundreds or thousands of places, all of which are linked to [particular] histories. This despite the fact that in Germany there is no single place which can work as a symbol for the Holocaust—even the Topography of Terror is no symbol for the Holocaust" (interview, 1993). As Loewy suggests, a centralized memory district cannot represent the history of National Socialism at the sites where criminal acts took place (except, of course, at the Topography of Terror). At the very least, such a district is a problematic response to international norms that represent the Holocaust from the perspective of the victims.

The trend toward centralization is also interpreted as undermining the national network of locally based historic sites and memorial museums.[21] When commenting on the Holocaust Memorial, Stefanie Endlich, an art historian and expert juror for public art competitions, pointed out that "when you declare that you want to create the central, the national monument, that means that—like a magnet in a magnetic field—you are in the center, and everything else that is already there has to adapt, to change direction. This is a fatal claim. In reality the opposite was true [in Germany]: in the course of several decades, a landscape of memorials has developed with cooperation, communication, exchange of experiences, and so on, which is very positive and productive" (interview, 1998). Even Topography staff acknowledged the challenges of the centralization of memory after 1990. According to director Reinhard Rürup, "The Topography will be a big building in a central location that deals with the National Socialist era in a comprehensive way. Because of that, no matter how the development [of Berlin] continues, the Topography will have to take on some functions of a national Holocaust museum. . . . Second is the question of how the Topography relates to the historical development of a decentralized landscape of commemoration in Berlin, Brandenburg, and Germany. We think of the Topography as opening up this landscape, not replacing it. . . . We will also offer certain services for this landscape through the national Memorial Museums Department" (interview, 1998).

Although the Topography will function as a service center for the existing network of historic sites, centralizing memory has already had negative fiscal consequences on the decentralized landscape. Because there is one pot of federal money designated for memorial museums, the establishment of new centralized places necessarily results in increased competition for limited funds, resources, and public attention with existing places. When projects such as the Neue Wache memorial or the Holocaust Memorial were approved after unification, Sachsenhausen director Günter Morsch argued that they "took money away from the *Gedenkstätten*" (interview, 1993). Others similarly argued that existing concentration camp memorial museums should continue to be the highest national funding priority, particularly in face of large budget cuts that accompanied unification and economic recession. The historian Arno Lustiger demanded that the DM 15 million budgeted for the Holocaust Memorial be allocated to existing national *Gedenkstätten* that, together, only had a total annual total budget of DM 8.8 million in 1995—down from DM 15 million in 1993.[22]

To stress the importance of existing memorial museums, a new Working Group for Concentration Camp Memorial Museum Centers in Germany was established in 1997.[23] Under the Schröder administration, moreover, funding for national concentration camp memorial museums did increase in 1999. But the overall negative effects of centralization continue to be felt by existing memorial museums. Shortly after the decision was made by the federal government to provide DM 30 million for the Holocaust Memorial's information center, Sachsenhausen director Morsch commented in 2000 that "I have to listen to politicians who tell me that money must not be the measure of commemoration. I'm starting to question their attitude, because we [at Sachsenhausen] are not important enough [to get financial support]. If they [at the Holocaust Memorial] get whatever they want, but we have to live with whatever they throw at us, then we are on the margins."

Sachsenhausen provides a good example of the concerns expressed by memorial museum experts about centralization. It also demonstrates the problems with staging the nation through hypervisible spaces. Like other concentration camp memorial museums in the former East, Sachsenhausen's buildings had to be preserved and restored; new research had to be conducted; existing archival materials, artifacts, and collections had to be properly protected; exhibitions reflecting contemporary historical research had to be created; and new pedagogical concepts had to be developed.[24] As Morsch described shortly after unification: "I cannot express it adequately. Behind the facade of the *Gedenkstätte* there is decay, an academic disaster, chaotic collections. . . . The walls are disintegrating, the barracks are in bad condition—we estimate we will need to invest 20 to 30 million marks [for preservation alone]" (interview, 1993).[25] Yet between 1993 and 1999, Sachsenhausen and Ravensbrück received only a total of DM 25.7 million between them from state and federal agencies, private investors, and public foundations.

The situation at Sachsenhausen is particularly troubling when one considers its national significance.[26] Unlike the places of Berlin's memory district—all of which were defined by Western cultures of memory—the postunification debates about Sachsenhausen demanded a working through of Eastern and Western histories and memory cultures by planners, politicians, historic preservationists, artists and architects, international and national survivor groups, and local residents from both Germanys. These public discussions were particularly intense because of the pasts to be confronted. Originally created in 1936 as the "model" modern concentration camp, Sachsenhausen was also an SS concentration commando training camp. These camps, with the neighboring labor and satellite camps, served the political economy of Berlin during the Third Reich. After the war, Sachsenhausen functioned briefly as a postwar Soviet internment camp; later it was transformed into a GDR *Mahnmal* and *Gedenkstätte,* where GDR youth learned about the heroic struggle and suffering of communist resistance fighters. Unification resulted in historical research that emphasized these complex histories and different understandings of a concentration camp—as a place of perpetrators and criminal acts, and as a place of victims. Further, shortly after unification, mass graves from the postwar internment camp were discovered, resulting in the creation of a new category of victim at Sachsenhausen.

Yet Sachsenhausen has received far less international and media attention than the three central places of the memory district during the 1990s. Located in the realm of the Eastern "Other," media representations of Sachsenhausen were largely negative and sensationalized, reporting on neo-Nazi activities in Brandenburg and "Ossis" (former East Germans) who supposedly did not deal with their National Socialist pasts, rather than on the new concepts and debates about the memorial museum. Rather ironically, after unification, Sachsenhausen was displaced as a central, highly visible GDR place of memory and became a less visible national place of memory. Offstage of the performance of the New Berlin, Germany's haunted house was stained by decay and debris, confusion and anger, and desires to be rid of its violent heritage.[27]

Sachsenhausen, 2002.

Spuren and *Zeugnisse*: Traces, Evidence, Eyewitnesses

Concentration camp memorial museums are understood by most people as morally significant places because of their historic and authentic aura—a spiritual field resulting from the suffering of those who no longer live, which can be sensed by people in the present through memories, artifacts, history, and the moral obligation to remember past atrocities and acts of injustice.[28] These historic sites are defined by their horrific imprints of death. They are political forums where, according to Morsch, "Everybody who wants to have an influence on the future development of Germany can exert influence. This is the ground on which you can stand because it is—as brutal as this sounds—a ground which contains bones and blood" (interview, 1993).

To communicate the value of these authentic places for humanity, historians, experts, and survivors classify them in terms of their materiality.[29] Authentic historic sites are understood as material evidence, as traces or *Spuren,* and as testimonies or objective proof *(Zeugnisse)* of the horrors that transpired.[30] They are sites of criminal acts and traces of violent acts against humanity. At the same time, these places are understood in very personal ways, defined by the touch of humans; they are where people left their last footprints, tears, and even hopes. For some of the living, these places are cemeteries, where their loved ones lie buried. These are places of cultural trauma, "the wound that cries out, that addresses us in the attempt to tell us of a reality or truth that is not otherwise available. This truth . . . cannot be linked only to what is known, but also to what remains unknown in our own very actions and language."[31] Yet the wound that cries out speaks a different story about the "reality or truth that is not otherwise available" depending on the listener and his or her relationship to the lives that went before, and the silences left in their wake. How place is constructed as trace, evidence, and testimony embodies those generational and personal relationships to the past, as well as the different desires that people in the present have to make these places speak.

The word *Spur* (literally trace) refers to what is left behind by humans. *Spur* denotes the physical and spiritual imprint of the human touch, and the connection of that touch across time and through space. For people in the present, the *Spur* is a marking that indicates past actions, (then) present movements, and future intentions of someone or some creature that lived in the past or occupied a particular space. Only people who arrive at a scene or search out a place find *Spuren*: the act of discovery constitutes their meaning as material traces. Detectives, historians, archaeologists, and forensic specialists and other experts who work with archives, fragments, and sites, for example, reconstruct past actions, such as criminal acts, through traces. *Spuren* may also imply secrecy: people may try to cover up their tracks to get rid of what they did or witnessed, or may leave fake evidence to confuse those who come later and want to know what happened.

It is through this sense of trace, as evidence of past crimes, that the '68 and '79 generations of Germans understand concentration camp memorials. They have assumed the role of detective in their search for the truth because the state and their parents—witnesses, bystanders, and later accomplices—silenced and covered up the evidence of past violence.

*When you say that Germany is a society of perpetrators, you have
to differentiate. It is not a society of Himmlers or Heydrichs. But
they belong to it, and others belong to it; those who tried to make
things better were very few, but they existed also.*
    —Interview with Reinhard Rürup, 1998

Yet the trace can be interpreted in a number of ways, not only as evidence left behind at the crime scene but also as a special message for a loved one or for those who come later. *Spur,* when used in a more positive spiritual sense, can be understood as symbolic footprints left for a future generation (as when used in the expression "to follow in some-one else's footprints") or can suggest a path or trail left in a scary place and time that can help others find their way later on. In this second sense, the human imprint left behind is understood by those living as a compassionate touch. These *Spuren* acquire a special spiritual status and may be interpreted as sacred relics. Such an understanding, together with the first meaning, is a more common interpretation of second generations and rela-tives of survivors and those who died as a result of Nazi persecution.

*I saw an old lady who was a survivor from the United States. She
herself was not in Auschwitz, but lost most of her family there.
I saw this woman standing in front of the crematorium and approaching the oven. You could literally see how something formed
in her throat, how she couldn't breathe anymore. She gasped for
air and then started crying. After she had cried she came closer to
the ovens, touched them, looked through this hole, put her head
in. She was no longer touching this oven as an instrument for
murder, but touching it like a shroud, like a thing that touched the
dead in their last minutes of living.*
    —Interview with Hanno Loewy, director of the Fritz Bauer
    Holocaust Institute, 1993

The word *Zeugnis* (evidence) refers to the material proof of past crimes. The detec-tive in a court of law uses this evidence, including traces, to reconstruct what happened objectively: "Exhibit A." But *Zeugnis* also refers to a testimony or firsthand account, and specifically to the act of bearing witness to past events. Only the witness *(Zeuge)* can utter the truth, the narrative form of evidence *(Zeugnis),* about what took place based on what he or she saw and experienced. Thus the term *Zeugnis* signifies both the material evidence and spoken testimony. It is associated with the moral demand by society to bear witness, to tell the truth, to reveal what actually happened through the act of testi-mony and judgment. The *Zeugnis,* in other words, is also created in the present through specific social roles, legal contracts, and institutional spaces. The witness, bystander, victim, and survivor must swear to tell the truth; the expert prosecutor and defense present a case; the jury and judge observe and adjudicate in an impartial court of law designed to find the truth.

> *I understand a documentation as a reconstruction of history that*
> *is very close to the sources: documents, photos, and reports by*
> *time witnesses. . . . These different sources have to be treated*
> *critically. . . . The documentation tries to reconstruct history from*
> *the material we have, and [we try] to stand in the background.*
> —Interview with Andreas Sanders, 2000

For survivors, authentic places are sites to return to without having to speak, to relive their traumatic recall of that which they can never fully know. According to Robert Jay Lifton, the survivor comes into contact with death in a bodily or psychic fashion, yet remains alive.[32] These places know of their near experience of death and of the death of others. This special emotive connection is so intensely personal for survivors that for them, historic sites have become "a sort of home, however perverse that sounds. They have spent part of their lives there, and even though it may only have been a short period, it was one which they will never forget, one that is very important to them" (Morsch, interview, 1993). Just as some Holocaust survivors who write memoirs and diaries about their experiences "see themselves as traces of experiences, and their words as extensions of themselves,"[33] so historic sites as *Spuren* and *Zeugnisse* are similarly understood as embodying belated encounters with death.

Yet the *Spuren* left by those who died and survived were quickly covered up and destroyed during and immediately following the war. Survivors pressured local authorities not only to establish memorials at these historic sites of suffering, persecution, and death to honor the dead; in many cases, they wanted to preserve the camps as material evidence that would corroborate their firsthand accounts and speak to future generations. Their encounter with death is embodied through place as material proof and testimony *(Zeugnis)* that can be seen and experienced by those who would come later. The visitor who comes to this historic site, although removed from the firsthand experience of what happened, can bear witness to past atrocities and understand calls of "Never Again!"

In the 1960s and 1970s, liberal- to left-leaning second and third post-Holocaust German generations of survivors, perpetrators, and bystanders began to interpret these sites, as well as their everyday settings, as tombs: "We stand upon graves." They dug for the past and their relationship to the past. They tended to affiliate with antifascists, resistance fighters, and survivors, took seriously their demands to bear witness, and adopted the call of "Never Again!" For the children of perpetrators and bystanders, these places were *Spuren* of the crime scene. They acted as detectives, tracing the evidence, but also felt the moral duty to prosecute, to use the *Spuren* as *Zeugnisse,* as material proof for the past crimes committed by their parents, their relatives, their nation-state. Yet this was a difficult role to play, for while they looked for the trace of their ancestors, they were horrified by the possibility of finding a past message. Because their parents did not testify and kept silent about what had happened, the new generations had to find material objects, documents, and sites that would speak the truth.

*I remember when I decided to become an educator in this field the
fear I had when I began to look through archival materials. I kept
searching through the documents, and especially the photos. It
is an awful feeling not knowing whom you might find. I remember
studying each photo, looking for the image of my father or uncle.*
—Interview with German seminar leader and tour guide for the
German Resistance Memorial Center in Berlin, 1992

The children and relatives of those who perished treated these places as sites of
horror, the crying wound of trauma, and sacred relics. This was where their beloved
relatives last left their human imprint. For them, these places stood for the silence that
accompanied the loss of a loved one, or the inability to speak about the unknown, the
violent events, by the survivor. The place was the location of a last possible message. It
speaks to them through their imaginations, telling them what would have been said had
their loved ones been allowed to live.

As human survivors began to pass away in the late 1970s, 1980s, and 1990s, the meaning of these places as *Spuren* and *Zeugnisse* shifted. There was an anxiety that the "real"
past, defined by firsthand experience, would become replaced by the fake, the fictional,
and the ephemeral. The fear of loss stimulated the production of films, memorial sites,
and images. In recent years, the memoir and oral testimony have become especially
important Holocaust representational forms as the children and relatives of survivors,
scholars, filmmakers, and others feel an urgent need to chronicle and record stories
about incomprehensible events that continue to haunt a larger public. Yet these contemporary Holocaust productions also created other anxieties: that representation, the
fake, would replace firsthand knowledge, the truth. As Geoffrey Hartman explains, by
the mid-1980s, most Americans and Europeans were born after the beginning of World
War II, and for them,

> knowledge about the war and the Holocaust comes primarily from
> history books and the media rather than from personal recall or
> contact with individual survivors. This is a turning point, then,
> and a crucial one. Education and ritual must supplement personal
> experience; and these, *in less than one more generation,* may have
> to carry the entire burden of sustaining the collective memory.[34]

In such a context, authentic places have become even more important and valuable.
While they are still understood as *Spuren* (evidence, material relics, footprints from the
past) and *Zeugnisse* (proof and testimony of past crimes), they are now also constructed
as eyewitnesses *(Zeuge)* that will be left for future generations. Place, as metaphysical
subject—the last survivor—and as the "real" and authentic material site, is a trace defined by the future. It is defined by the mourning for that which no longer is present and
through the knowledge that places will remain to bear witness after human survivors

have passed away. Places, as *Spuren, Zeugnisse,* and *Zeuge,* are understood as belonging to humanity's cultural heritage and for that reason are funded, preserved, and protected by local, federal, and international institutions and private donors. Accredited historians and other experts list these historic sites as landmarks in international or national registries, and international groups claim them as religious or sacred icons of their past.[35]

The meaning and materiality of authentic historic sites therefore are specific to the social and affective relationships people have to the past and the ways those pasts are located in the spaces of the present and desired future. Place as eyewitness or survivor materializes the capacity to survive human mortality by offering continuity between generations to bear witness to the past. Yet as Andrea Liss argues, the demand to bear witness to criminal acts becomes complicated with third, fourth, and subsequent generations because of the increased distance to these representations of the past.[36] Yet third and fourth generations bear witness through their imaginations as well as through their bodies. They come to these places to understand the past through historical and artistic representations, but they also come to walk the same paths as inmates, to see the preserved and reconstructed artifacts, to experience the silence.

Rethinking Claims to Authenticity

For German educators, historic sites provide evidence of the past through existing material artifacts and their unique locations in historic networks of power. Morsch notes, for

Jewish barracks, Sachsenhausen, 2002.

Interior of Jewish barracks, Sachsenhausen, 2002.

example, that unlike other concentration camp memorials, Sachsenhausen has a rela-tively large number of original buildings that were built during the National Socialist period, which makes it an important historic site in Germany and Europe. So while "the impact the place has depends on the visitor—he or she brings expectations with him or her . . . visitors orient themselves to certain relics [*Spuren*] trying to integrate them into an overall picture and become impressed by the aura of these relics. The relics are the real exhibits" (interview, 1998). Moreover, Morsch describes how educators "use this authenticity to tell what has happened. . . . In Station Z [where the crematoriums are], the history of the concentration camp and extermination is told. We begin with what happened at Station Z and then come to the more general questions of concentration camps and extermination. . . . In addition you also come to understand the different phases of the history of the camp and realize that in the different phases extermination varied" (interview, 1997).[37]

Memorial museum educators point out that *Spuren* confront the limited understand-ings visitors have of how concentration camps historically functioned, and that through these relics the complex histories and geographies of the rise of fascism, the structures and functioning of dictatorships, the use of subtle techniques to realize terror, vio-lence, and genocide, and other historical processes can be explained. Morsch attributes visitors' lack of historical knowledge to the so-called globalization of the Holocaust. American visitors in particular "criticize us for our silence about the Jewish catastrophe [at Sachsenhausen]. This is an absurd argument, because we have [the exhibitions in] the Jewish barracks here. Their comments indicate how the murder of the Jews has become synonymous with the history of National Socialism. If we point out that only 15 percent of the inmates at Sachsenhausen were Jews, then people call us revisionists. . . . Visitors complain that we try to hide something" (interview, 2000). These biases are troubling, argues Morsch, if part of the reason to come to these places is to learn from the past and prevent such a system from being realized again.

One of the most significant German contributions to the international politics of memory has been an insistence on confronting the past through local places and the documentation and historical mapping of spatial networks of terror and genocide. Yet Sachsenhausen, too, is a place of memory defined through the global Holocaust tourism industry. By classifying a place as an authentic historic site, experts locate it in a moral hierarchy that is, in part, also defined by tourism economies. They also claim the expert status and social role of detectives who uncover the traces of the crime scene and represent it as evidence to a larger international public. In the process, experts fix authentic places in Cartesian space and historical time and classify them as objective, material evidence. As I have suggested, however, there are multiple, nuanced, and ever shifting social relations, temporalities, and emotional relationships people have (and will continue to have) to these places, which result in a number of ways that their materiality is constituted as *Spuren, Zeugnisse,* and *Zeugen.*

When experts state that they are concerned about the impacts of the centralization of memory and the globalization of the Holocaust, they articulate more than educational concerns, even though these concerns are valid. They also assert authority over how these places should be defined in contemporary Germany. Authenticity is a relational and normative concept that acquires meaning through specific contexts, sites, and users.[38] When people make places as stable material traces of the past, they give form to their search for a timeless identity, for a mythic sense of self. These sites are understood as subjects and relics that are socially valuable in a moral sense because they provide a material means to mourn and remember; they house traumatic memories. Understandably, these places are considered special; their unique and historic aura, their human imprint, offers contemporary and future generations educational and research possibilities. However, when classified as authentic and contrasted to artificial places, these sites become flattened out temporally and affectively. Rejecting global capitalism, tourism, and popular culture as a means of constituting the morality or reality of these memorial museums is a rather limited way to think about place. It denies simultaneous locations and interconnections to other people and places in multiple times and spaces.

Haunting Presences: Places of Memory

In the summer of 2002, I ran into a school group of American university students who were studying in Berlin and had chosen to make a day trip to Sachsenhausen. I asked some of them what they thought about the new exhibit close to where we were standing, known as the Jewish barracks. They didn't have much to say about this specific exhibition; they hadn't realized that the barracks had been reconstructed in 1961 by the GDR (with original materials) or that in 1992 two male arsonists burned down part of

Main exhibition hall, Sachsenhausen, 2002.

the building. They assumed that it all was original from the Nazi period, including the damaged area of the building from the recent fire, which was incorporated as part of the new exhibition. Three women stated that they were going to spend time going through the exhibition because they wanted to see as much of the prisoner camp as possible. They were using the new audio tour to learn about Sachsenhausen and about everyday life in the camp.[39] One woman, with tears in her eyes, said that the books, information from school, and films could in no way come close to the experience of being at a historic camp. Another said she hadn't known that Sachsenhausen was so close to Berlin because one of her school instructors had stated that there were no concentration camps in Germany. She said she was going to learn all about Sachsenhausen, go back home, and tell her instructor he was wrong.

Ultimately, it is the visitors who assess, create, and validate the authenticity of places of memory.[40] As Topography academic staff member Andreas Sanders mentioned in 2000, "Every visitor brings the present with him, his individual experiences and perceptions. The visitor has to answer the question why this [place] is important himself—I do not have to tell him why—because he was the one who decided to visit the exhibition." Tourists visiting places of memory in Berlin describe them in terms of their expectations and prior knowledge, highlighting what they did not expect to see or what was frustrating. Some Internet "tour guides" for Igougo.com (who are mostly North Americans), for example, were surprised, perhaps disappointed, that the Jewish Museum was not a Holocaust museum, a response that indicates the influence of the global, largely American-based Holocaust industry. But what they highlighted, what they seemed to see and remember, were the spaces they couldn't figure out (a complicated building) or

Guide pen name:	becks
Category:	Activity
Date of Entry:	10/3/2002
Name:	Jüdisches/Jewish Museum
Address:	Lindenstrasse 14
City:	Berlin
Type of Museum:	Cultural Museum

What it's like:

The Jewish Museum was designed by Daniel Libeskind and is a very modern and complicated construction. The passages zig-zag and represent a torn Star of David. The layout is full of symbolism and represents complicated philosophical ideas related to the loss of Jewish culture through the holocaust. Frankly speaking this worked better in a video program on this very interesting building that I saw prior to visiting the museum. In reality I found the layout at first a bit complicated and confusing, although very friendly and abundant multilingual staff are willing to point you in the right direction.

The museum surprisingly doesn't focus on the holocaust but rather on the history of Jews in Germany. The first exhibition area is on Jewish life in medieval Germany, especially in the city of Worms with interesting multimedia displays. From there displays are progressively more recent and trace the role of German Jews in public life as well as major contributions to arts, literature, music, science, commerce, and law.

A large section focuses on various Jewish customs and their development from ancient times into modern practices. I found this section particularly interesting in explaining some of the finer details of concepts that a non-Jew is only vaguely familiar with from films and television programs.

The section on the Nazi era was somewhat smaller than I expected but still comprehensive. Unfortunately circumstances forced us to spend less time here than we were planning to, but still had time to see some interesting displays of the harrowing times.

Visiting the Jewish Museum can in no way be described as an enjoyable experience—the subject matter is simply too disturbing. However, I'm very happy that I did go. Beforehand I had my doubts, but in the end I found the presentation excellent and the information well balanced as far as I could see. I didn't see anything that looked like propaganda, denial, or blame.It is wise to travel light when visiting this museum, as you have to go through airport style security. Bags and coats must be checked in. In addition it is a fair walk from the subway station but well worth it.

http://www.igougo.com/planning/journalEntryActivity.asp?journalID=13059&EntryID=21726
&n=J%FCdisches+%wF+Jewish+Museum

the narratives they didn't anticipate they would read (exhibits about Jewish culture). What becomes for them striking about this place, then, also offers an opportunity to rethink what they thought they already knew about the past, about the city, about Germany, and even about the Holocaust.

North American tourism companies, not surprisingly, emphasize a cosmopolitan Holocaust memory, such as the metaphysical category of evil as represented by Nazis. The Topography of Terror, for example, is highlighted by the presence of the SS and Gestapo through partially correct historical information about underground bunkers, torture cells, and horror. "Tripadvisor" states: "Free tours are offered of these old Nazi bunkers, which house exhibits on the torture the SS often inflicted on prisoners."[41] The American Automobile Association (AAA) listing: "The grim Topographie des Terrors (Topography of Terror) occupies the site of the former Nazi secret police headquarters, where prisoners were interrogated and tortured. Photographs trace the emergence of Nazism, and a nearby viewing platform overlooks the enormous Regierungsviertel (Government Quarter), where the Third Reich had its administrative offices."[42] Canadian "travelcanoe" writes: "A short walk east [of Checkpoint Charlie] and you will discover one of the few remaining sections of the Wall. Behind it, one should take a free walk through Topography of Terror, located in the ruined bunkers where people were tortured by the SS. Photos and displays recount some of the Nazi horror, but the text is only in German. Tours are available."[43]

These sensationalistic ways of classifying the Topography of Terror, however, may collide with visitors' experiences of confronting the historical information and docu-

---

Guide pen name:	travel2000
Category:	Activity
Date of Entry:	10/31/2000
Name:	Topography of Terror Foundation
Address:	Budapester Strasse 40
City:	Berlin

What it's like:
Website: www.topographie.de. This is an outdoor exhibit, trailing the terrors of the Nazi's and the happenings in the Gestapo (the headquarters being the building next to this exhibit). Look out for parts of the Berlin Wall at the back of the exhibit. It is on the site of the Gestapo Prison, where reports of mass murders were sent and compiled. This is ground zero. Don't make the mistake we made—start at the right entrance, and stop by the information trailer to purchase a history brochure. Everything is in German so you need some information to understand it. Though it's in chronological order, I wish I could understand the captions.

http://www.igougo.com/planning/journalEntryActivity.asp?journalID=3010&EntryID=4889

ments on display, shattering (and perhaps making them rethink) the voyeuristic reason for coming—the desire and pleasure of experiencing that which is disturbing and horrific within the safe and predictable spaces of tourism. The narratives of some Igougo.com guides, for example, tell other (virtual) tourists to go to the Topography not to "have fun" but to learn about the past. As guide "Tyguy" wrote in 2001:

> This is one of the most unusual museums that I've been to. It's actually an outdoor history lesson built on the location of a former Nazi bunker/HQ and gives the history of the rise and fall of the Nazi party through text, photos, and maps. It's written in German, so if Sie sprech kein Deutsch, you should buy the guidebook in your language from the information trailer (they're available in English. As for other languages, you will have to ask yourself). It is a somber experience, especially when you consider you are standing in the area of Berlin that was the center of the Nazi command. As for content of the information, the guidebook wasn't as comprehensive as what is written on the displays.
>
> If you are in Berlin only to party and have a good time, this site might not be for you. I give it a high recommendation, not as a site to seek out like you would the Eiffel Tower or a famous dance club, but because if you are in Berlin and visiting the other historic sites, it will add to your travel experiences. Also note—the Berlin Wall is directly behind the Topography of Terror.[44]

These post-Holocaust generations of visitors interpret Berlin's places of memory intertextually, in relation to representations that circulate globally and through their repetitive consumption. Andreas Huyssen argues that "no matter how much representations of the Holocaust may be fractured by geography of subject position, ultimately it all comes down to unimaginable, unspeakable and unrepresentable horror."[45] Yet it is not only representation, and the tension between knowing and not knowing, that explain the post-Holocaust generations' repetitive attempts to understand (and re-represent and consume) the past. Rather, they also attempt to understand affectively—through their bodies and places—the inability of survivors and eyewitnesses to speak about past events, for, as Michael Perlman writes, part of being human "is the capacity to know, to imagine, death as physical reality and as metaphor."[46]

Places of memory can thus provide transgenerational representational and experiential spaces through which visitors can intersubjectively identify with past lives and with living survivors, as well as confront their understandings of what they think they know of that trauma.[47] This is another reason why the dichotomy between the "real" (material, located site) and artificial place is problematic. For post-Holocaust generations, the past can only be known through postmemorial and personal relationships to the "unrepresentable." Places of memory haunt because they cannot be easily classified in time and space. People come to these places because they may wish to bridge past, present, and future lives. Sometimes the collision of imaginations, representations, bodies, and experiences in these places may encourage post-Holocaust generations to think differently about their personal and social hauntings.

Fieldnotes

"Extension to the Berlin Museum" (later known as the Jewish Museum),
Berlin Kreuzberg, August 1997 [with later reflections]

Another construction fence in the center of Berlin. A small crowd of people in their twenties to forties has gathered outside it. A thin, stylish woman wearing trendy glasses emerges from behind the fence, and a dense line quickly appears at the barrier. The air buzzes with chatter. I am looking, taking notes, trying to take in who is here. People start offering to buy tickets, asking for extras, but no one responds. (Tickets were sold out at the INFOBOX almost as soon as they became available earlier this summer.) Some grab their bikes angrily and ride away. Others aggressively ask the woman to be let in. She follows the rules, only lets in those with the tickets.

After we are inside, she closes the temporary opening to the fence, and we hear the collective moan of those left outside. Behind the fence I feel secretly happy to be part of this group, one of the lucky few that had a ticket for the Showcase Berlin (Schaustelle Berlin) tour of Daniel Libeskind's unfinished building. I read a lot about this building and its conceptual design in architectural journals, scholarly articles, and newspapers and wanted to see how the ideas took material form.[48] Before unification, Libeskind's design, the first of his to be commissioned, was quite controversial; some critics argued that the jagged layout and metallic materials evoked SS lightning bolts. As soon as the building was completed, however, local residents came to understand this place as one of the most powerful statements about social memory in the city. People began going on tours of the empty building and were so moved they felt it should be left empty as the Holocaust Memorial.

We follow our guide into the baroque pale yellow Berlin Museum and walk through a hallway where we find a set of recently built stairs descending into darkness. As we walk down the stairs, we are not sure where we are or where we are going; we just know that we have entered the space of a building that has already become a Berlin landmark even though it is not yet open. At the bottom of the stairs, our guide introduces herself and systematically describes the complex ground floor of the museum and spatial layout of the building. Her matter-of-fact tone matches the cool, damp floor of the untreated concrete we are standing on. Only later, after moving to the floors above ground, does she engage visitors' questions and attempt informal conversation. At some point in the tour, a national television news camera crew joins us, and we all become quite aware of our presence as "behind-the-scenes tourists" through the media's cameras, through our collective gaze of the staging of the city.

As we walk over planks and wires jutting out of the floors, we notice the angular walls and ceilings, and the irregularly shaped bands carved low into the walls to be used for exhibition space. We listen to our guide describe the conceptual design for the underground level. Libeskind developed his concept by creating imaginary lines of connection between the homes of prominent Berliners, historic sites of Jewish culture, and important events in the city, a geography that connected past and future. "Between the lines" of this zigzagging ground plan, he organized the interior spaces and volumes of the building around five spatial voids, empty rooms that signify the disappearance of Jewish culture in the city and the contemporary legacies of the "presence of absence" in the city and the nation. These conceptual ideas are expressed through the movements and tensions of interior/exterior spaces and intentionally violate traditional architectural ideals of rooms, windows, spatial layout, and functional design.

The fluorescent lights overhead cast a bluish glow onto our bodies. We come to the end of one corridor and quietly enter a room that is completely dark, standing behind an extremely heavy door. I feel an instinctive need to crouch to protect myself from the heavy weight of an unknown volume of darkness rapidly collapsing on me from above. We have entered a void. As my eyes adjust to narrow bands of light coming from a couple of slitted windows five or six stories overhead, the darkness

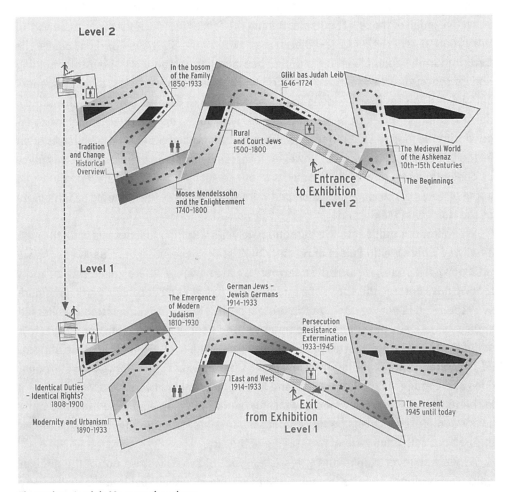

Floor plan, Jewish Museum brochure.

changes its motion. Now moving upward, the darkness dissipates somewhat, and I look at the shape of the room with its angled walls of different heights and widths; I tentatively begin to stand upright.

After coming out, our guide tells us that this space was the end point of the Axis of

Jewish Museum, interior stairwell, 1997.

Darkness [later renamed Axis of Holocaust]. Next we find the Axis of Continuity (and Hope), which brings us to a stairway. As we walk up two floors, we learn more about the conceptual design and the difficulties the building has posed for museum experts. I become fascinated by the irregular geometric gashes that punctuate the walls, providing uneven lighting through angled slats of glass, and walk away from the group. As I look out of these "windows" I note that the view of the city is always partial. I find "internal windows," thin bands of glass in narrow corridors that ask me to look inward, to catch a glimpse of the darkness of the voided voids, those empty rooms that can never be physically entered, can never be known.

I notice others walking on their own, traversing the motion of the building underfoot and around them. No two walls or floors come together at a ninety-degree angle. The slanting floors remind me of articles about the temporary use of these rooms by groups such as the Batshiva Dance Company. Until directors figure out a way to create spaces that house exhibitions of artifacts, bodily displays interact with the movement of these spaces as part of their performance. Wandering through these empty rooms, people began discussing what kind of exhibitions could be created given the unusual sculptural nature of the building's interior space. They also raised the question—current then in the media—about exactly what history should be presented there: the history of Jews in Berlin, or of Jews in all of Germany, or of Jews in German history, or of Jews in a larger European history. By being in the very spaces where those questions would be materially resolved, we gained a sense of authority, an imagined sense of expert knowledge whereby one could say, "I was there while the building was being built and these questions being debated." Through the experience of being in a place yet to be finished, the time of this transitional period (of "Berlin-being-built") was located in our bodily and sensory memories of this building.

The camera crew and news journalists pull me away from my observations and note taking and ask me and my fellow researcher, Rhodri Williams, why we were taking such detailed notes, and of what. Were we also journalists? "No," we said, and explained that we were scholars conducting preliminary research about the Schaustelle Berlin tours. They took notes of us taking notes of the tourists, the guide, and the tour. And we took notes of their taking notes of us.

We walked back down to the basement level and along the Axis of Exile, which took us outside to the museum's Holocaust Memorial. After touching and wandering through the tilted stelae, the Garden of Exile, people stepped back to look again at the tall, zinc-paneled and riveted building and began to chat in small groups about what history the museum should represent. The journalists selected a few of them to interview as others watched them being filmed. Still others asked our guide technical questions about the building or personal questions about what it was like to work with Libeskind. Through the tour, the empty building became a historical trace of the present-past city defined by the spaces of a present-future city, or New Berlin.

[2002: Even now, this tour remains one of the most vivid and striking memories of the city for me. I was disappointed when I revisited the museum after it opened. The interior spaces were painted, bright, polished, and overly interpreted with directional signs,

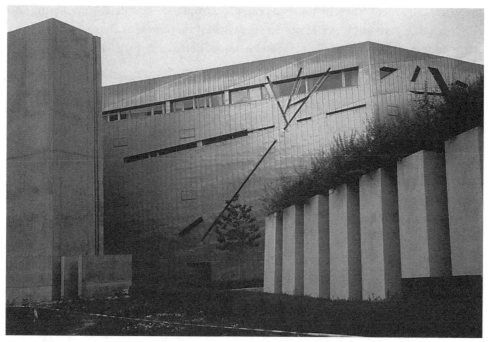

Jewish Museum, exterior view of Holocaust Tower/void and Garden of Exile, 2002.

maps, and museum assistants. Temporary walls covered up some of the irregularly shaped walls, windows, and uneven floors to create (false) "normal" rooms for exhibition.[49] But then again, my expectations were quite high: I wanted the unfinished building to be there for me when I returned to Berlin so that I could speculate about the city's future and watch others do the same. I was disappointed because the new material form of the museum covered the powerful social hauntings evoked through my bodily experiences of being in this building and navigating these unmarked spaces. By folding empty spaces into the interiors of a building—by making empty crypts—Libeskind powerfully represented the futility of trying to represent the unknown in space and time from the position of post-Holocaust generations.]

Places of memory, even when they work as tourist attractions, can challenge traditional understandings of their social performances and in the process create new kinds of social spaces and relationships to the past. Stih and Schnock's proposal for *Bus Stop!* for example, engages tourism practices to create a mobile, living memorial through which past, present, and future inform the experience of visiting a historic site. The social and personal hauntings that went into the making of places like the Topography of Terror are still powerfully experienced even when (re)located in the tourism spaces of the nascent memory district. As former managing director Gabriele Camphausen reflected in 2000, "We did not expect such an increase in the number of visitors. The location has become very attractive, and I think the open-air exhibition has a lot to do with that. Especially because we are so close to the new center of Berlin. We have more visitors from foreign countries. We benefit from the tourism boom and from the 'New Berlin' marketing and vice versa. The marketing would not be successful if there weren't more than the [new urban centers at] Potsdamer Platz. Wilhelmstraße, Potsdamer Platz, Topography—this has become 'the' tourism route."

Despite the stagings of a hypervisible Holocaust memory in the center of the city, the emergence of such a cultural district draws attention to the inherent problems of celebrating the mythic construct of the nation in the "land of the perpetrators." The ways that the three places of the memory district will shape the city and understandings of the nation in the future will be defined not only by their perceived social and international presence but also by the ways their meanings will continue to be contested and interpreted by locals and tourists. The Topography's presence in the center of the city, at the site of past and contemporary imagined new Berlins, works to question the dominant discourse of German national identity embodied in the corporate and consumer landscape spectacles nearby. It, too, is part of the New Berlin. While academic staff of the Topography point to the contradictions that accompany their new centrality (including being "used" by politicians, trying to maintain respectability for other smaller memorial centers, and trying to use their visibility to pursue memory-work), they also note that politicians and even the general public have begun to realize that Germany can no longer suppress its history of National Socialism. The haunting presence of the past lives at places like the Topography create ripples and fissures in the smooth surfaces of the cosmopolitan and tourist city. "Ghosts . . . haunt the places where cities are out of joint; out of joint in terms of both time and space."[50]

> In ten years, when all the construction sites are finished and every
> thing is beautiful, all of a sudden there will be that open wound
> in the city. I think that this is better than any attempt to design it,
> because so far there is no adequate form to translate the Holocaust
> in an artistic way. I think you can only do that by walking on these
> traces, by reconstructing it for yourself.
> —Interview with Andreas Nachama, managing director of the
> Topography, 1993

Places of memory are made to evoke ghosts, localize emotions associated with hauntings, and establish cultural practices that delimit social relations to the past. Yet the ghost that returns to haunt is not the dead, according to Nicolas Abraham and Maria Torok, but rather a phantom that "bears witness to the existence of the dead buried within the other."[51] What haunt and return to speak are the silences of those who went before us, their shameful secrets, their undisclosed sufferings, and their unspoken knowledge of violent events. Ghosts work transgenerationally to signify the losses and hopes entombed in others, even though the presence of those secrets, and desires defies our ability to know about them and may lead to yet other traumas.[52] Ghosts make us aware of the losses resulting from violent events, yet they also remind us of our inability to really "know" about those past losses.

Ghosts are "radically hetereogeneous," to use Abraham and Torok's words. While the unconscious may be relieved by "placing the effects of the phantom in the social realm," the ghost will continue to haunt until the unspoken yet powerfully present tombs of the parents, loved ones, or even the state—the shameful secrets, unfinished business, unspoken deaths—are laid bare. So we make places to house these ghosts, to try to understand our inheritance of cultural loss and trauma. We return to these places to feel haunted. We make places of memory to get near those gaps and in this way become closer to those who went before us and to those who may come in the future.

Fieldnotes

The New Berlin, June 17, 2002

I decided to walk to the Topography of Terror from Unter den Linden along one of the new tourism routes. I headed south on Wilhelmstraße, taking photos for this book, and noticed (again) how this stretch had changed since the last time I was here: the sleek British Embassy, new shops and restaurants, and clear Plexiglas signs about the history of the "Wilhelmstraße Mile"—the National Socialist government quarter—had been added to the existing postwar landscapes of GDR high-rise apartment buildings in the area. Further south and to the west, a series of foreign embassies and federal ministries were under construction or newly built. Beyond them were the new business centers and skyscrapers at Potsdamer Platz.

A new memorial caught my eye; it was dedicated to the GDR workers who protested the construction of Stalinallee in 1953. The memorial is in front of a historic building in Berlin, the former National Socialist Air Ministry (Luftwaffe) building, which, after the war, became the GDR House of Ministry. After unification, it housed the East German privatization company, Treuhandanstadt, for a number of years, after which it became the new federal Finance Ministry. This building was "reused," like some of the other older buildings in the city, because of the enormous unanticipated expenses of unification, moving the capital to Berlin, and the economic recession in general. Otherwise, the politicians in Bonn wanted to build all new buildings, perhaps in an attempt to ignore the historical presence of Berlin.

I continued to walk to the corner of Niederkirchner Straße, formerly Prinz-Albrecht-Straße. Five red tour buses drove by in less than five minutes on a Sunday summer afternoon. In this short stretch between Wilhelmstraße and Stresemannstraße, tourists can see the Berlin Parliamentary Building, the Wall, the Topography of Terror, and the former Nazi Luftwaffe building.

I turned east onto Niederkirchner Straße, walked along the Wall, and turned south into the Topography of Terror just before the Martin Gropius Bau. A vendor loudly offered his wares—water, ice cream, pictures—and yet I had come to know this area as quiet and rather empty, a feeling I still have when I am in the terrain, looking at the temporary exhibit, or watching other people walk across this area. But maybe that is part of my attachment to (and nostalgia for?) this place, a place that I always return to

Topography of Terror, temporary exhibition, 2002.

when I'm in the city, a place that I tell my friends to visit if they come to Berlin. I watched people read the information sign about the Topography of Terror and joined them in the unearthed foundations and historical exhibition below, leaving the vendor behind.

It is still hard for me to imagine what the Topography of Terror will be like in the future, after the Zumthor building is finally finished. I looked in the temporary trailer that serves as an information center, and noticed tourists—many of whom were Americans—asking questions and picking up the audio tour (which is free, in multiple languages, and available until 8 p.m. in the summer). I stayed in the trailer for a while, looking at the new CD-ROM. I leafed through the visitor book, filled mostly with signatures of visitors from various countries. Most comments were very positive. One stated: "The Topography of Terror is too important a place for this to be its current state." Another declared: "Germany can do better than this!" (Were these visitors responding to the last part of the exhibition about the funding crisis in 1997?) I took special interest in entries written by several Americans about September 11, 2001.

5/11/02: What goes around comes around.
Watch out Arab World—the Americans are awake.

6/14/02: To any Americans passing through this exhibit—think about the early days of the Reich, as they took away the rights of *all* German people. Then think about what is going on at home in the name of counter terrorism. Insert the word "Arab" for "Jew"—or any group or nationality. Please understand that this was written by

a New Yorker—but one who believes that people who want power
will use *any* situation, *any* excuse to grab it. We are *so* fortunate to
have our freedom. Do NOT give it up.

I went back outside and noticed another wooden construction fence in the middle
of Berlin. Instead of protecting an empty lot, this fence surrounded two large looming
cement walls that will become the Zumthor building. Like the fence at the Holocaust
Memorial lot in 1997, this barrier was effectively used as a public space. It was made into
a transitional protest site by the Active Museum in 1997. Today it was an exhibition space
for the collaborative work of seven students from the Department of Communication
Design at the Art College Berlin-Weissensee "who developed statements, comments
and visual interventions" about racism, exclusion, and right-wing radicalism in contemporary Germany. "The debate on right-wing radicalism and xenophobia which we see
as societal problems needs to take place in public. The project wants to raise people's
attention for this topic at a much-visited place, the historical center of Nazi-terror. We
want to contribute to the beginning of a (re)thought-process."[53]

Their project was called "Anschläge," a word that has two meanings in German:
attacks against someone, or putting posters on a wall.[54] Running parallel to the Topography's open-air exhibition, yet located above ground, on top of the grass, parts
of the exhibition focused on the legal definitions of refugees and foreigners in Berlin's
Social Security Offices, or words used in everyday German language to signify "strangers": *Auslander, Fremde, Aussiedler, Asylbewerber*. Adjacent collages of words and images from the Internet, newspapers, and legal documents questioned the role of media
in reproducing intolerance. What would "propaganda" look like today? How does the

Anschläge exhibition on construction fence, 2002.

Opfer/Täter/Zuschauer? (Victim/Perpetrator/Bystander?). The new Berlin, 2002.

media contribute to a lack of tolerance in society? One section took advertising and political language phrases from the Third Reich and juxtaposed them with present-day equivalents. Images and texts from radical right-wing Internet sites were interspersed with phrases from Internet lingo, such as "cookie."

In another part of the exhibit, a series of biographies and pictures were posted on the fence that represented the more than one hundred victims of right-wing violence in Germany since 1990. A leftist skinhead beaten to death by a right-wing skinhead group. A homeless person pummeled. A Turkish person harassed. Life-size portraits were accompanied by the person's name, age, occupation, and the circumstances of his or her death. Some people were not identified; these victims without a face were represented by blank spaces. Postcards from several German cities were interspersed to confront the image of a "cosmopolitan Germany." Mirrors printed with the words for perpetrator (Täter), victim (Opfer), and bystander (Zuschauer) punctuated these pictures and biographies so that the tourist would see his or her reflection and shifting identity in them. Visitors became spectators of themselves, a somewhat clichéd but effective approach that encouraged people to read the posted biographies (both at this exhibit and at the Topography exhibit below) differently.

This was a different new Berlin from the spectacle advertised by city marketers. Walking through this space, citizens and visitors were asked to look critically at their performances in the staging of a Weltstadt, to relate their everyday urban experiences to those of others living in the past, present, and future. In doing so, some individuals may have experienced a momentary shock of recognition, an awakening to the not yet conscious knowledge of the "what has been" in the now.[55]

Notes

A Fence

1. The full text reads: "Memorial for the Murdered Jews of Europe. Here is the place! When the German Bundestag can decide, after ten years of discussion the memorial will be built at this site in 1999/2000.—By the Federal Republic of Germany, the Association Supporting the Establishment of a Memorial for the Murdered Jews of Europe, and the city of Berlin." The Förderkreis zur Errichtung eines Denkmals für die ermordeten Juden Europas e.V. was the organization responsible for this and other posters. See chapter 5.

2. Under the equation, the text continues: "Since 1989 there has been public discussion about the construction, location, and design of a memorial for murdered Jews in this country of perpetrators. In 1999 the decision will be made [by the German Bundestag] concerning whether and how it should be built. Compensation payments and the construction of the memorial shall be the end of the discussion about responsibility for National Socialist crimes. We are opposed to this." The Initiativkreis gegen den Schlußstrich was responsible for this and other posters.

1. Hauntings, Memory, Place

1. Manuela Hoelterhoff, "The Art of Renewal," *Condé Nast Traveler,* May 2002, 170–79, 253–54, www.cntraveler.com. The quote is from Boris Grésillon, "Berlin, Cultural Metropolis: Changes in the Cultural Geography of Berlin since Reunification," *Ecumene* 6, no. 3 (1999): 285. Grésillon counted nine symphonic orchestras, three opera houses, 880 choirs, 350 galleries, more than one hundred museums, and 140 theaters in 1999. See also Alan Riding, "Seeking a New Identity, Berlin Shakes Up Its Art Legacy," *New York Times,* March 12, 2002, nytimes.com.

2. Rudy Koshar, *Germany's Transient Pasts: Preservation and National Memory in the Twentieth Century* (Chapel Hill: University of North Carolina Press, 1998).

3. Berlin was the capital of the first unified German nation-state (including Weimar

Germany), National Socialist Germany, the German Democratic Republic (East Germany), and now reunified Germany (Federal Republic).

4. In the discourse about the postunification city, the "new" is a contested term that I explore in chapter 2.

5. Michel de Certeau and Luce Giard, "Ghosts in the City," in *The Practice of Everyday Life*, vol. 2, *Living and Cooking*, ed. Michel de Certeau, Luce Giard, and Pierre Mayol, trans. Timothy Tomasik, rev. ed. (Minneapolis: University of Minnesota Press, 1998), 133.

6. Women's bodies have often represented the city. See Elizabeth Wilson, *Sphinx in the City* (London: Virgo Press, 1991); Amy Bingaman, Lise Sanders, and Rebecca Zorach, *Embodied Utopias: Gender, Social Change, and the Modern Metropolis* (New York: Routledge, 2002); and Linda McDowell, *Capital Culture: Gender at Work in the City* (Malden, Mass.: Blackwell, 1977).

7. Walter Benjamin, *Berliner Chronik: Gesammelte Schriften* (Frankfurt am Main: Suhrkamp, 1972).

8. Much has been written about the politics of normalization in the Federal Republic. See Timothy Garten Ash, *In Europe's Name* (New York: Vintage Books, 1993); Peter Baldwin, ed., *Reworking the Past: Hitler, the Holocaust, and the Historians' Debate* (Boston: Beacon Press, 1990); Peter Bender, *Das Ende des ideologischen Zeitalters: Die Europäisierung Europas* (Berlin: Severin and Siedler, 1981); Stefan Berger, *The Search for Normality: National Identity and Historical Consciousness in Germany since 1800* (Providence: Berghahn Books, 1997); Mary Fulbrook, *The Divided Nation: A History of Germany, 1918–1990* (New York: Oxford University Press, 1992); Jürgen Habermas, *The New Conservatism: Cultural Criticism and the Historians' Debate*, trans. Shierry Weber Nicholsen (Cambridge: MIT Press, 1989); Heinrich August Winkler, "Rebuilding of a Nation," *Daedalus* 123, no. 1 (1994): 107-27.

9. For a discussion of the political and economic contexts of urban development, see Elizabeth Strom, *Building the New Berlin: The Politics of Urban Development in Germany's Capital City* (Lanham and Boulder: Lexington Books, 2001).

10. For a delightful discussion of the City Palace debates, see Svetlana Boym, *The Future of Nostalgia* (New York: Basic Books, 2001). See also Wilhelm von Boddien and Helmut Engel, *Die Berliner Schlossdebatte—Pro und Contra* (Berlin: Berlin Verlag, 2000).

11. For a discussion of the German Historical Museum, see Charles Maier, *The Unmasterable Past: History, Holocaust, and German National Identity* (Cambridge: Harvard University Press, 1988); and Karen Till, "Verortung des Museums: Ein geo-ethnographischer Ansatz zum Verständnis der sozialen Erinnerung," in *Geschichtskultur in der Zweiten Moderne*, ed. Rosmarie Beier (Frankfurt: Campus, 2000), 183–206.

12. For a selection on *Vergangenheitsbewältigung*, see Aleida Assmann and Ute Frevert, *Geschichtsvergessenheit—Geschichtsversessenheit: Vom Umgang mit deutschen Vergangenheiten nach 1945* (Stuttgart: Deutsche Verlags-Anstalt, 1999); Ralph Giordano, *Die zweite Schuld oder von der Last Deutscher zu sein* (München: Knaur, 1990); Manfred Kittel, *Die Legende von der zweiten Schuld: Vergangenheitsbewältigung in der Ära Adenauer* (Berlin, 1993). See also note 8. The problem of confronting the past after the GDR resulted in discussions of a second *Vergangenheitsbewältigung*. See the special issue on this topic guest edited by William Donahue, Rachel Freudenburg, and Daniel Reynolds in *German Politics and Society* 27 (1992). On Berlin, see John Borneman, *After the Wall: East Meets West in the New Berlin* (New York: Basic Books, 1991); Hermine G. De Soto, "(Re)inventing Berlin: Dialectics of Power, Symbols and Pasts, 1990–1995," *City and Society* 1 (1996): 29–49; Jürgen Habermas, *A Berlin Republic: Writings on Germany*, trans. Steven Rendall (Lincoln: University of Nebraska Press, 1997);

Jane Kramer, *The Politics of Memory: Looking for Germany in the New Germany* (New York: Random House, 1996); Brian Ladd, *The Ghosts of Berlin: Confronting German History in the Urban Landscape* (Chicago: University of Chicago Press, 1997); and Alexandra Richie, *Faust's Metropolis: A History of Berlin* (New York: Carroll and Graf, 1998).

13. For exceptions see Andreas Huyssen, "The Voids of Berlin," *Critical Inquiry* 24 (Autumn 1997): 57–81; Jennifer Jordan, "Collective Memory and Locality in Global Cities," in *Global Cities: Cinema, Architecture, and Urbanism in a Digital Age,* ed. Patrice Petro and Linda Krause (New Brunswick: Rutgers University Press, 2003); Rudy Koshar, *From Monuments to Traces: Artifacts of German Memory* (Berkeley: University of California Press, 2000); and Karen Till, "Place and the Politics of Memory: A Geo-ethnography of Museums and Memorials in Berlin," Ph.D. diss. (Department of Geography, University of Wisconsin–Madison, 1996).

14. The literature on place is enormous. See Paul Adams, Steven Hoelscher, and Karen Till, eds., *The Textures of Place: Exploring Humanist Geographies* (Minneapolis: University of Minnesota Press, 2001); Tim Cresswell, *In Place/Out of Place: Geography, Ideology, and Transgression* (Minneapolis: University of Minnesota Press, 1996); James Duncan and David Ley, eds., *Place/Culture/Representation* (New York: Routledge, 1993); J. Nicholas Entrikin, *The Betweenness of Place: Towards a Geography of Modernity* (Baltimore: Johns Hopkins University Press, 1991); Michael Keith and Steve Pile, *Place and the Politics of Identity* (New York: Routledge, 1993); Doreen Massey, *Space, Place, and Gender* (Minneapolis: University of Minnesota Press, 1994); Steve Pile, *The Body and the City: Psychoanalysis, Space, and Subjectivity* (New York: Routledge, 1996); Jani Scandura, *Down in the Dumps: Place, Modernity, and America's Depression* (Durham, N.C.: Duke University Press, forthcoming); and Yi-Fu Tuan, *Space and Place: The Perspective of Experience* (Minneapolis: University of Minnesota Press, 1977).

15. Compare Andreas Huyssen, "The Voids of Berlin."

16. Andreas Huyssen, *Twilight Memories* (New York: Routledge, 1995), 251.

17. Avery Gordon, *Ghostly Matters: Haunting and the Sociological Imagination* (Minneapolis: University of Minnesota Press, 1997).

18. Little work has explicitly connected hauntings, ghosts, and place theoretically, but see Michael Bell, "The Ghosts of Place," *Theory and Society* 26 (1997): 813–36; Monica Degan and Kevin Hetherington, eds., "Spatial Hauntings," special issue, *Space and Culture* 11–12 (2001); Tim Edensor, *Industrial Ruins: Aesthetics, Materiality, and Memory* (London: Berg, 2005); Sonja Kuftinec, "[Walking through a] Ghost Town: Cultural Hauntology in Mostar, Bosnia-Herzegovina, or Mostar: A Performance Review," *Text and Performance Quarterly* 18, no. 2 (1998): 81–95; Steve Pile, "Spectral Cities: Where the Repressed Returns and Other Short Stories," in *Habitus: A Sense of Place,* ed. Jean Hillier and Emma Rooksby (Aldershot: Ashgate, 2002), 219–39; Steve Pile, *Real Cities: Modernity, Space, and the Phantasmagorias of City Life* (London: Sage, 2005).

19. Steve Pile, "Ghosts and the City of Hope," in *The Emancipatory City?* ed. Loretta Lees (London: Sage, 2004), 210–28.

20. After Jacques Derrida, *Specters of Marx: The State of the Debt, the Work of Mourning, and the New International,* trans. Peggy Kamuf (New York: Routledge, 1994).

21. M. Christine Boyer, *The City of Collective Memory: Its Historical Imagery and Architectural Entertainments* (Cambridge: MIT Press, 1994); Nuala Johnson, *Ireland, the Great War, and the Geography of Remembrance* (Cambridge: Cambridge University Press, 2003); Karen E. Till, "Places of Memory," in *A Companion to Political Geography,* ed. John Agnew, Katharyne Mitchell, and Gerard Toal (Oxford: Blackwell, 2003), 289–301.

22. For a discussion about the meanings of crypts within the subject and within the history of "America" that hide repressed national traumas, see Nicolas Abraham and Maria Torok, *The Shell and the Kernel: Renewals of Psychoanalysis*, ed. and trans. Nicholas Rand (Chicago: University of Chicago Press, 1994); Jani Scandura and Michael Thurston, *Modernism, Inc.: Body, Memory, Capital* (New York: New York University Press, 2001).

23. Compared to other European nation-states, Rudy Koshar suggests that Germany's relationship to historic locales and landscapes as a site through which to imagine the nation has been particularly intense. Koshar, *Germany's Transient Pasts.*

24. Simon Schama, *Landscape and Memory* (London: Harper Collins, 1995), 16–17.

25. Homi Bhabha, *Nation and Narration* (London: Routledge, 1990).

26. As geographer Doreen Massey argues, social relations always have a spatial form and content; they exist *in* and *through* place as well as *across* space (*Space, Place, and Gender* [Minneapolis: University of Minnesota Press, 1994], 168).

27. Walter Benjamin, *Berliner Chronik*, 486–87. I adopt Gerhard Richter's translation of Benjamin. My readings of Benjamin owe much to discussions with Gerhard Richter, Rudy Koshar, Rick McCormick, and the graduate students in our fall 1999 memory seminar at the University of Minnesota and University of Wisconsin.

28. Jaques Derrida, *Writing and Difference,* trans. Alan Bass (Chicago: University of Chicago Press, 1978).

29. See Josef Beuys's discussion of open wounds in *Josef Beuys: Zeige deine Wunde* (München: Schellmann und Klüser, Städtische Galerie im Lenbachhaus, 1980) and Cathy Caruth's discussion of the "weeping wound" in Cathy Caruth, ed., *Trauma: Explorations in Memory* (Baltimore: Johns Hopkins University Press, 1995).

30. Jacques Derrida, *Memoires for Paul de Man* (New York: Columbia University Press, 1989), 59; compare Louis Marin, *Utopics: Spatial Play,* trans. Robert Vollrath (Atlantic Highlands, NJ: Humanities Press, 1984).

31. De Certeau and Giard, "Ghosts in the City," 142.

32. See the section titled "Hauntings: Of Places and Returns" hereafter.

33. See Paul Adams, Steven Hoelscher, and Karen Till, "Place in Context: Rethinking Humanist Geographies," in *Textures of Place* (Minneapolis: University of Minnesota Press, 2001), xiii–xxxiii; Norman Denzin and Yvonna Lincoln, "Introduction: The Discipline and Practice of Qualitative Research," in *Handbook of Qualitative Research*, ed. Norman Denzin and Yvonna Lincoln, 2nd ed. (Thousand Oaks: Sage, 2000), 1–28; Steve Herbert, "For Ethnography," *Progress in Human Geography* 24, no. 4 (2000): 550–68; Richa Nagar, "Exploring Methodological Borderlands through Oral Narratives," in *Thresholds in Feminist Geography: Difference, Methodology, Representation,* ed. John Paul Jones III, Heidi Nast, and Susan Roberts (New York: Rowman and Littlefield, 1997), 203–24; Gillian Rose, *Visual Methodologies: An Introduction to the Interpretation of Visual Materials* (London: Sage, 2001); Diane Wolf, ed., *Feminist Dilemmas in Fieldwork* (Boulder, CO: Westview, 1996).

34. Linda McDowell, *Gender, Identity, and Place: Understanding Feminist Geographies* (Minneapolis: University of Minnesota Press, 1999).

35. Compare with Avery Gordon's discussion of haunting in *Ghostly Matters.*

36. Derrida introduces the term "hauntology" in *Specters of Marx* to describe how contemporary social discourses, institutions, and cultural meanings are always already haunted by past structures of meaning. These presences, while not considered experientially part of

present-day "reality," nonetheless define the very possibility for that reality to exist. For a discussion of hauntology in Mostar, see Kuftinec, "[Walking through a] Ghost Town."

37. Gordon, *Ghostly Matters*.

38. Michael Perlman, *Imaginal Memory and the Place of Hiroshima* (Albany: State University of New York Press, 1988).

39. Compare Benjamin, *Berliner Chronik*.

40. Compare Michel de Certeau, "Walking in the City," in *The Practice of Everyday Life*, trans. Steven Rendall (Berkeley and Los Angeles: University of California Press, 1984), 91–110; Gordon, *Ghostly Matters*; Pile, "Spectral Cities."

41. De Certeau, "Walking in the City," 108.

42. T. S. Eliot, "Burnt Norton," in *Four Quartets* (San Diego: Harvest/Harcourt Brace Jovanovich, 1943), 14.

43. Dydia DeLyser, "When Less Is More: Absence and Social Memory in a California Ghost Town," in *Textures of Place: Exploring Humanist Geographies*, ed. Paul Adams, Steven Hoelscher, and Karen Till (Minneapolis: University of Minnesota Press, 2001), 24–40.

44. Pierre Nora, *Realms of Memory: Rethinking the French Past*, English language edition, ed. Lawrence D. Kritzman, trans. Arthur Goldhammer (New York: Columbia University Press, 1996–1998).

45. Marita Sturken, *Tangled Memories: The Vietnam War, the AIDS Epidemic, and the Politics of Remembering* (Berkeley: University of California Press, 1997).

46. David Lowenthal, *The Past Is a Foreign Country* (Cambridge: Cambridge University Press, 1985), 191.

47. Derrida, *Memoires for Paul de Man*.

48. Entrikin, *The Betweenness of Place*; Yi-Fu Tuan, "Space and Place: Humanistic Perspective," *Progress in Human Geography* 6 (1974): 213–52.

49. After Maurice Halbwachs, *On Collective Memory*, ed. and trans. Lewis Coser (1941; 1952; Chicago: University of Chicago Press, 1992). Although Halbwachs's work has been criticized for his implicit assumption of a Durkheimian collective consciousness, his work is important in contemporary scholarly discussions about memory because he explored how individual memory is socially and spatially constructed. For critiques, see J. Fentress and C. Wickham, *Social Memory* (Oxford and Cambridge: Blackwell, 1992); Sturken, *Tangled Memories*; Charlie Withers, "Place, Memory, Monument: Memorializing the Past in Contemporary Highland Scotland," *Ecumene* 3 (1996): 325–44.

50. Steve Pile, "Memory and the City," in *Temporalities: Autobiography in a Postmodern Age*, ed. Jan Campbell and Janet Harbord (Manchester: Manchester University Press, 2002), 111–27.

51. Elizabeth Wilson, "The Rhetoric of Urban Space," *New Left Review* 209 (1995): 151.

52. Elizabeth Wilson, "Looking Backward: Nostalgia and the City," in *Imagining Cities*, ed. Sallie Westwood and John Williams (New York: Routledge, 1997), 127–39.

53. Nostalgia is not always reactionary or politically regressive. With sentimentality, argues Elizabeth Wilson, nostalgia can bring an awareness and perhaps acceptance of change. Wilson, "Rhetoric of Urban Space"; see also Boym, *The Future of Nostalgia*.

54. Marianne Hirsch, *Family Frames: Photography, Narrative, and Postmemory* (Cambridge: Harvard University Press, 1997); Andrea Liss, *Trespassing through Shadows: Memory, Photography, and the Holocaust* (Minneapolis: University of Minnesota Press, 1998).

55. See also Sturken, *Tangled Memories*.

56. *Peace of Mind: Coexistence through the Eyes of Palestinian and Israeli Teens,* a documentary film produced and directed by Mark Landsman; coproduced by Yaron Avni, Reut Elkouby, Bushra Jawabri, Amer Kamal, Sivan Ranon, Hazem El Zanoun, and Yossi Zilberman; and edited by George O'Donnell (New York: Global Action Project, June 1999). See http://www .global-action.org/html/videos/peaceom/pom.html and http://www.seedsofpeace.org/index.cfm. The teens videotaped their everyday lives to tell the story of conflict and their hopes for the future.

57. See Mieke Bal, Jonathan Crewe, and Leo Spitzer, eds., *Acts of Memory: Cultural Recall in the Present* (Hanover, NH: University Press of New England, 1999).

58. Dominick LaCapra, *Representing the Holocaust: History, Theory, Trauma* (Ithaca: Cornell University Press, 1994).

59. Compare Perlman, *Imaginal Memory.*

60. Edward Casey, *Remembering: A Phenomenological Study,* ed. James Edie, Studies in Phenomenology and Existential Philosophy (Bloomington: Indiana University Press, 1987), 182, italics in original. Casey distinguishes site (as a point in Cartesian space as well as relative location) from place but then uses a more traditional (and problematic) understanding of place: "It is the stabilizing persistence of place as a container of experiences that contributes so powerfully to its intrinsic memorability" (186).

61. Kuftinec, "[Walking through a] Ghost Town."

62. Judith Butler, *Gender Trouble: Feminism and the Subversion of Identity* (New York: Routledge, 1999).

63. See also Nancy Duncan, ed., *Body Space* (New York: Routledge, 1996); Heidi Nast and Steve Pile, eds., *Places through the Body* (London: Routledge, 1998).

64. Karen Till, "Staging the Past: Landscape Designs, Cultural Identity, and Erinnerungspolitik at Berlin's Neue Wache," *Ecumene* 6, no. 3 (1999): 251–83.

65. Quoted in *taz,* "Mahnmal für 'Political Correctness,'" June 26, 1999.

66. Normally a jury of five or more individuals is created with two categories of expert jurors: *Fachjuroren,* who are experts in public art, art history, and architecture or are practicing artists and architects, and *Sachjuroren,* experts and representatives responsible for the project, such as city officials or citizen groups. For more about competitions in Berlin, see Strom, *Building the New Berlin.* For an interesting cultural commentary and critique of this process for the Holocaust Memorial, see Jochen Spielmann, "Der Prozeß ist genauso wichtig wie das Ergebnis: Fußnoten[1] zu Kunst-Wettbewerben als Kommunikationsformen der Auseinandersetzung: London 1953—Oświęcim 1959—Berlin 1995," in Neue Gesellschaft für bildende Kunst, *Der Wettbewerb für das 'Denkmal für die ermordeten Juden Europas: Eine Streitschrift* (Berlin: Verlag der Kunst, NGbK, 1995), 128–45.

67. Such was the case with the establishment of the Neue Wache memorial. See Till, "Staging the Past."

68. Interview with Stephanie Endlich, art historian and Berlin memory expert, 1998.

69. Gordon, *Ghostly Matters,* 25.

70. See Daphne Berdahl, *Where the World Ended: Re-unification and Identity in the German Borderland* (Berkeley: University of California Press, 1999); John Borneman, *Belonging in the Two Berlins: Kin, State, Nation* (New York: Cambridge University Press, 1992); Borneman, *After the Wall*; Dinah Dodds and Pam Allen-Thompson, eds., *The Wall in My Backyard: East German Women in Transition* (Amherst: University of Massachusetts Press, 1994).

71. Jeffrey Herf, *Divided Memory: The Nazi Past in the Two Germanies* (Cambridge: Harvard University Press, 1997).

72. There was much debate, for example, about proposals to build a national history museum in Berlin. See Maier, *The Unmasterable Past*; Christoph Stölzl, ed., *Deutsches Historisches Museum: Ideen-Kontroversen-Perspektiven* (Berlin: Popyläen, 1988); Till, *Place and Politics*.

73. Herf, *Divided Memory*.

74. Notable exceptions include Bruno Flierl and Wolfgang Thierse. See chapter 5.

75. On feminist debates about positionality and reflexivity, see Liz Bondi et al., *Subjectivities, Knowledges, and Feminist Geographies* (Lanham, MD, and Boulder, CO: Rowman and Littlefield, 2002); Richa Nagar and Susan Geiger, "Reflexivity, Positionality, and Identity in Feminist Fieldwork: Beyond the Impasse," paper presented at the annual national Women's Studies Association conference, Albuquerque, N.Mex., June 1999; Heidi Nast, "The Body as 'Place': Reflexivity and Fieldwork in Kano, Nigeria," in *Places through the Body*, 93–116; Gillian Rose, "Situating Knowledges: Positionality, Reflexivity, and Other Tactics," *Progress in Human Geography* 21, no. 3 (1997): 305–20. About my shifting positions "at home and in the field," see Karen Till, "Returning Home and to the Field," *Geographical Review* 91, nos. 1–2 (2001): 46–56.

76. Gordon, *Ghostly Matters*.

77. As a result of my conversations with people in interviews and informal settings, the ideas and feedback of particular people helped me focus my questions. Because I wrote and revised during a lengthy period of research, I often returned to my interview transcripts only to rediscover and interpret them again. I found myself drawn to familiar passages and words, to the insights of these consultants. In some instances, when I reread what people had to say, I remembered not only our conversations but also other interviews, other experiences, and other moments when I gained a better understanding of the processes of memory and place making in Berlin.

78. Pile, "Spectral Cities," 235.

79. Otherwise, to use Jani Scandura's and Michel Thurston's words, "one brings the lost object into the self and encrypts it—buries it alive—refusing to mourn the loss, denying that anything ever was lost, that the self might ever have to transform as a result" (*Modernism, Inc.*, 7). The authors are referring to Nicholas Abraham and Maria Torok's work on melancholia.

A Metro Stop

1. Open from 1995 to 2000, the INFOBOX housed exhibitions, gift shops, and views of the Potsdamer Platz area under construction. It displayed information about "man's" technological feats: state-of-the-art transportation technologies, groundwater management techniques, and engineering feats in which "nature" was mastered, such as changing the direction of the Spree River. Investors in the new city center sponsored the exhibitions, including Daimler, Sony/ Tishman Speyer/Kajima, ABB + Terreno, Bewag, Deutsche Telekom, Deutsche Bahn, the Berlin Senate for Building, Housing, and Transportation, Mercedes, and A + T Investment Group. *INFO BOX: The Catalogue* (Berlin: Dirk Nishen, 1996).

2. After Gaston Bachelard, *Poetics of Space*, trans. Maria Jolas, with a foreword by Étienne Gilson (New York: Orion, 1964); Henri Lefebvre, *The Production of Space*, trans. D. Nicholson-Smith (Cambridge: Blackwell, 1991).

2. The New Berlin

1. Elizabeth Wilson, "Looking Backward: Nostalgia and the City," in *Imagining Cities*, ed. Sallie Westwood and John Williams (New York: Routledge, 1997), 127–139; David Frisby, *Fragments of Modernity: Theories of Modernity in the Work of Simmel, Kracauer, and Benjamin* (Cambridge: Polity Press, 1985).

2. Models and architectural proposals were displayed at the former GDR Staatsratgebäude (Executive Council of State Building). For information see the Berlin Senate Department of Urban Development's Web page, http://www.stadtentwicklung.berlin.de/planen/stadtmodelle/de/ausstellung.shtml. Information about the places described in this chapter can be accessed online at this site.

3. Fiona Henderson, "The Guidebook and the European City: Tourist Geographies of London, Paris, and Berlin, 1945–2002" (Ph.D. diss., Department of Geography, University of London, Royal Holloway, 2003); Karen Till, "Construction Sites and Showcases: Tourism, Maps, and Spatial Practices of the New Berlin," in *Mapping Tourism*, ed. Stephen Hanna and Vincent Del Casino (Minneapolis: University of Minnesota Press, 2003), 51–78.

4. Quoted in Partners for Berlin, *Schaustelle Berlin Program-Journal,* June 25–August 25, 1996, 3.

5. See Vittorio Magnago Lampugnani, ed., *Berlin Tomorrow,* special issue of *Architectural Design* 92 (1991).

6. In 1990 this area was sectioned off and sold by the Berlin Senate to four international corporations: Sony (headquartered in Japan), DaimlerChrysler (Germany's Daimler-Benz and the United States' Chrysler), Hertie (Germany), and Asea Brown Boveri (Switzerland). In 1991 the Munich firm Hilmer and Sattler won the public competition to design the master plan. They maintained the historic octagonal shape of neighboring Leipziger Platz and retraced many streets from the original Potsdamer Platz. Private architectural competitions were held by the four corporations for their respective sites.

7. Wim Wenders, director, *Wings of Desire/Der Himmel über Berlin* (Berlin: Road Movies, Paris: Argos Films, 1987), 128 minutes.

8. http://berlinge.ags.myareaguide.com/detail.html?detailID=252726, accessed August 2003.

9. Alan Riding, "Seeking a New Identity, Berlin Shakes Up Its Art Legacy," *New York Times,* March 12, 2002). According to the Berlin Senate Department of Urban Development, Prussian king Friedrich Wilhelm IV wished to continue the urban development plan proposed by the court architect Karl Friedrich Schinkel (who designed the Altes Museum [1822–1830]) "to turn the entire Spree Island behind the museum into a sanctuary for art and learning." "Berlin's Museumsinsel, an architectural ensemble of individual, harmoniously constructed museums of outstanding historical and artistic importance located in the center of the city, fulfills the criteria of a cultural monument in accordance with the Cultural and Natural Heritage of Humankind Convention." See http://www.stadtentwicklung.berlin.de/denkmal/denkmale_in_berlin/en/weltkulturerbe/.

10. Boris Grésillon, "Berlin, Cultural Metropolis: Changes in the Cultural Geography of Berlin since Reunification," *Ecumene* 6, no. 3 (1999): 284–94.

11. See Senate Department of Urban Development in Berlin's Web page, http://www.stadtentwicklung.berlin.de/bauen/grosse_projekte/en/tacheles.shtml, accessed August 2003.

12. Hans Stimmann, "The Texture of the City," *Foyer: Journal for Urban Development* (2000): 10–11.

13. Michael Perlman, "Sources of Memory," in *Imaginal Memory and the Place of Hiroshima* (Albany: State University of New York Press, 1988), 37.

14. Amy Bingaman, Lise Sanders, and Rebecca Zorach, *Embodied Utopias: Gender, Social Change, and the Modern Metropolis* (New York: Routledge, 2002).

15. Adolf Hitler, quoted in Alan Balfour, *Berlin: The Politics of Order, 1737–1989* (New York: Rizzoli, 1990), 83.

16. Ibid., 79.

17. Ibid., 72.

18. Goodsell, quoted in Michael Wise, *Capital Dilemma: Germany's Search for a New Architecture of Democracy* (New York: Princeton Architectural Press, 1998), 16.

19. John Agnew, "The Impossible Capital: Monumental Rome under Liberal and Fascist Regimes, 1870–1943," *Geografiska Annaler* 80B (1989): 229–40. Compare with Leonardo Benevolo, "Political Compromise and the Struggle with the Authoritarian Regimes," in *History of Modern Architecture* (Cambridge: MIT Press, 1971), esp. 540–85.

20. Robert Jan van Pelt and Deborah Dwork, *Auschwitz: 1270 to the Present* (New Haven: Yale University Press, 1996). The contrast between "classical" and "modernist" architecture and urban design is especially problematic when considering the history, politics, and structure of the National Socialist state. According to Jeffrey Herf, Nazis were "reactionary modernists"; they combined traditional romanticist ideas and forms with modernist ones in their imaginings and productions of the German nation-state. See Jeffrey Herf, *Reactionary Modernism: Technology, Culture, and Politics in Weimar and the Third Reich* (Cambridge: Cambridge University Press, 1986); and Gavriel Rosenfeld, *Munich and Memory: Architecture, Monuments, and the Legacy of the Third Reich* (Berkeley: University of California Press, 2000).

21. Deborah Howell-Ardila, "Berlin's Search for a 'Democratic' Architecture: Post–World War II and Post-unification," *German Politics and Society* 16, no. 3 (1998): 62–85; Wise, *Capital Dilemma.*

22. Giuseppe Terragni, speaking about his 1932 design for the Casa del Fascio, quoted in Wise, *Capital Dilemma,* 16.

23. Much of the information in this and the following paragraphs comes from Balfour, *Berlin*; Howell-Ardila, "Berlin's Search"; Gavriel Rosenfeld, "Architecture and the Memory of Nazism in Postwar Munich," *German Politics and Society* 16, no. 4 (1998): 140–59; and Wise, *Capital Dilemma.*

24. Quoted in Howell-Ardila, "Berlin's Search," 62.

25. Mary Fulbrook, *The Divided Nation: A History of Germany, 1918–1990* (New York: Oxford University Press, 1992); Detlev Heikamp, "Demolition in Berlin," in *Postwar Berlin 25: Architectural Design Profile,* ed. Doug Clelland (New York, 1982), 52–57; Howell-Ardila, "Berlin's Search."

26. Howell-Ardila, "Berlin's Search," 64.

27. See also Rainer Autzen et al., *Stadterneuerung in Berlin: Sanierung und Zerstörung vor und neben der IBA,* vol. 2, *Berliner Topografien* (Berlin: Ästhetik und Kommunikation, 1984).

28. Howell-Ardila, "Berlin's Search," 69.

29. Speech delivered at the 1950 SED Party Congress, quoted in Howell-Ardila, "Berlin's Search," 69.

30. Howell-Ardila, "Berlin's Search," 73. This is not to deny that state claims to the future based on the past weren't questioned, as evidenced by the Stalinallee workers' rebellion whose protests about the increasing demands placed on them initiated the larger June 1953 uprising in the GDR.

31. Architects associated with the Bauhaus, including Walter Gropius and Mies van der Rohe, played important roles in shaping the FRG's "democratic" architecture. FRG planners and officials claimed that some of these architects were persecuted under the Nazi regime. Some also participated in Nazi architectural competitions and constructed buildings during the Third Reich, although they became increasingly marginalized. Mies van der Rohe went

to Cuba, for example, and after the 1959 revolution returned to Berlin. See Balfour, *Berlin*; Howell-Ardila, "Berlin's Search"; and Katheleen James, "Ludwig Mies van der Rohe in Chicago," in *Exiles and Emigres: The Flight of European Artists from Hitler* (Los Angeles: Los Angeles County Museum of Art, 1997), 236–41.

32. Rosenfeld, "Architecture and the Memory of Nazism."

33. Howell-Ardila, "Berlin's Search," 72.

34. Quoted in Autzen, *Stadterneuerung in Berlin,* 12.

35. Ibid.

36. While such a statement is propaganda, so too were Western representations. Howell-Ardila and Rosenfeld point out that FRG planners and officials ignored the National Socialist activities of some of their important postwar architects, excusing their past as an "unfortunate mistake." They also argued that architecture was "high culture" and "above politics." Howell-Ardila, "Berlin's Search"; Rosenfeld, "Architecture and the Memory of Nazism"; and Rosenfeld, *Munich and Memory.* See also note 31.

37. Berliner Festspiele and Architektenkammer Berlin, *Berlin: Open City; The City on Exhibition; The Guide* (Berlin: Nicolai, 1999). The Philharmonic Hall is used today to market the New Berlin.

38. Scharoun, quoted in Balfour, *Berlin,* 214.

39. Berliner Festspiele and Architektenkammer Berlin, *Berlin*.

40. Balfour, *Berlin,* 215. For a history of the Kulturforum, see the Berlin Senate Department of Urban Development's Web page, http://www.stadtentwicklung.berlin.de/planen/ staedtebau-projekte/kulturforum/index.shtml.

41. Jan Fischer, quoted in Jane Kramer, "Living with Berlin," *New Yorker,* July 5, 1999, 53.

42. Balfour, *Berlin*.

43. For further examples see Balfour, *Berlin: The Politics of Order*.

44. Linda McDowell, *Capital Culture: Gender at Work in the City* (Malden, MA: Blackwell, 1997). See also M. Christine Boyer, *The City of Collective Memory: Its Historical Imagery and Architectural Entertainments* (Cambridge: MIT Press, 1994); Sharon Zukin, *The Cultures of Cities* (Cambridge: Blackwell, 1995).

45. Elizabeth Strom and Margit Mayer, "The New Berlin," *German Politics and Society* 16, no. 4 (1998): 122–39.

46. Interview with author, 2000. Debis is the Daimler Benz real estate and investment company.

47. Quoted in P. R. Range, "Reinventing Berlin," *National Geographic,* December 1996, 104.

48. Much has been written about architecture and real estate development in Berlin during the past ten years. For a selection see Rick Atkinson, "Building a Better Berlin? Critics See Too Much of Its Past in Its Future," *Washington Post,* January 9, 1995, G1, G4, G5; Annegret Burg and Hans Stimmann, eds., *Berlin Mitte: Die Entstehung einer urbanen Architektur* [Downtown Berlin: Building the Metropolitan Mix] (Berlin: Birhäuser Verlag, 1995); Christian Caryl, "Reinventing Berlin: The Once and Future German Capital Rebuilds Itself," *U.S. News and World Report,* September 1, 1997, 37–39; and Elizabeth Strom, *Building the New Berlin: The Politics of Urban Development in Germany's Capital City* (Lanham, MD: Lexington Books, 2001).

49. Strom and Mayer, "The New Berlin." Strom and Mayer, as well as other authors, described West Berlin economies as corrupt, a system that many argue carried over into the postunification city. For example, the Committee for the Coordination of Inner-City Investment (Koordinierungsauschuß für innerstädtische Investitionen, or KOAI) operated outside public

and parliamentary scrutiny and disbanded after the committee finished its task. In addition to the rapid level of privatization and development, the financial crises and scandals in the late 1990s and afterward are cited as further evidence of corruption. See Jane Kramer, "Living with Berlin," *New Yorker,* July 5, 1999, 20–64; K. Lehnhart, "'Bubble Politics' in Berlin: Das Beispiel Koordinierungsauschuß für innerstädtische Investitionen—eine 'black box' als Macht und Entscheidungszentrale," *Prokla,* March 1, 1998, 41–66; Strom, *Building the New Berlin.*

50. Linda McDowell, *Capital Culture.* Large international developers make profits largely on speculation. They build for prospective tenants rather than for a corporate client, a practice common in the United States and the United Kingdom, but not Germany.

51. Stimmann was appointed by the Berlin Senate as the director of Building Affairs from 1991 to 1996 and was later appointed secretary for Urban Development, Environmental Protection, and Transportation.

52. Other prominent spokespersons for critical reconstruction include Peter Strieder (SPD), Berlin senator of Building and Transportation, 1999–2002; Vittorio Magnago Lampugnani, an Italian architectural historian and former director of Frankfurt's Museum of Architecture; the architectural theorist Detleff Hoffmann-Axthelm; and the architect Hans Kollhoff.

53. Josef Paul Kleihues, "New Building Areas, Buildings, and Projects," in *Internationale Bauausstellung Berlin: 1987 Project Report,* 3rd English edition (Berlin: Internationale Bauausstellung Berlin, 1990), 6–9.

54. Ibid. The IBA had two programs, "careful urban renewal" for existing buildings and districts, and "critical reconstruction" for new projects.

55. Hans Stimmann, "The Texture of the City," *Foyer: Journal for Urban Development* (2000): 10–11.

56. Ibid.

57. Ibid. See also Elizabeth Strom, *Building the New Berlin.*

58. Hans Stimmann, "Neue Berliner Büro- und Geschäftshäuser" [New Berlin Office and Commercial Buildings], in Burg and Stimmann, *Berlin Mitte,* 11. Stimmann argued that deconstruction and postmodern architecture were appropriate in America, not Europe.

59. Ibid., 17.

60. Ibid.

61. Stimmann, "Texture of the City," 13. According to a planning spokesperson for the City of Berlin, it wasn't until 1994 that the first citywide land-use plan was passed (interview, 2000).

62. Stimmann, "Texture of the City," 10.

63. Ibid., 10–11. This urban planning analysis and drawing technique is now also being promoted within Europe. Berlin's black plans were part of the German contribution at the 2001 Architecture Biennial in Venice and have been reproduced in architectural books and magazines as well. Burg and Stimmann, *Berlin Mitte*; Stimmann, "Texture of the City."

64. Kleihues, "New Building Areas," 6.

65. Stimmann, "Texture of the City," 11.

66. Ibid.

67. M. Christine Boyer, *Dreaming the Rational City: The Myth of American City Planning* (Cambridge: MIT Press, 1983).

68. See Candice Slater, "Amazonia as Edenic Narrative," in *Uncommon Ground: Rethinking the Human Place in Nature,* ed. William Cronon (New York: W. W. Norton, 1996), 114–31; Carolyn Merchant, *The Death of Nature: Women, Ecology, and the Scientific Revolution* (San Francisco: Harper and Row, 1980).

69. As espoused through New Urbanism in the United States and the Urban Villages movement in the United Kingdom, neotraditionalism is an international urban development movement. See Nan Ellin, *Postmodern Urbanism* (Cambridge, MA: Blackwell, 1996); Karen Falconer Al-Hindi and Karen Till, "(Re)Placing the New Urbanism Debates: Towards an Interdisciplinary Research Agenda," *Urban Geography* 22, no. 3 (2001): 189–201; Michelle Thompson-Fawcett, "Leon Krier and the Organic Revival within Urban Policy and Practice," *Planning Perspectives* 13 (1998): 167–94.

70. Robin Dowling, "Neotraditionalism in the Suburban Landscape: Cultural Geographies of Exclusion in Vancouver, Canada," *Urban Geography* 19 (1998): 105–22; Deborah Leslie, "Femininity, Post-Fordism, and the 'New Traditionalism,'" *Environment and Planning D: Society and Space* 11 (1993): 689–708.

71. Atkinson, "Building a Better Berlin?" Stimmann in particular was considered inflexible enough that he was fired as the Berlin Senate building manager in 1996 under a conservative CDU government. They immediately rehired him, however, as the secretary for urban development, environmental protection, and transportation.

72. Lampugnani's comments, as well as his commentaries thereafter, were first published in the popular magazine *Der Spiegel*. See Howell-Ardila, "Berlin's Search."

73. Cited in Howell-Ardila, "Berlin's Search," 77.

74. Ibid.

75. M. Christine Boyer, *The City of Collective Memory: Its Historical Imagery and Architectural Entertainments* (Cambridge: MIT Press, 1994), 1–2.

76. Cengiz Bektas, "42 Years Later," *StadtBauwelt* 154 (2002): 39.

77. M. Christine Boyer, *The City of Collective Memory*, 1–2.

78. Howell-Ardila, "Berlin's Search"; and Daniel Libeskind, "Interview with *Die Welt*," *Die Welt*, April 26, 2000. Libeskind was the only famous architect to argue for preserving the GDR past through architecture.

79. Libeskind, "Interview."

80. State of Berlin, Public Relations Department, *Berlin*, trans. Sabine Dorn, 3rd ed. (Berlin: Jaron Verlag, 2000).

81. Ibid., 15 (in unpaginated brochure).

82. Stimmann, "Neue Berliner Büro."

83. The banner greets the new Philharmonie conductor, Sir Simon Rattle from England.

84. Partners for Berlin, New Berlin postcard "Kulturmetropole," n.d.

85. See http://www.berlin.de/partner-fuer-berlin/english/newberlin/index1.html.

86. Partners for Berlin, New Berlin postcard "Hauptstadt," n.d.

87. Partners is the successor organization of Olympia 2000, the entity that promoted the city during the (failed) Berlin 2000 Olympic campaign. Drawing from this experience and the model in the United States, Diepgen endorsed the idea of a private-public partnership to promote a positive image of the city. In addition to Partners, the private-public agency Berlin Economic Development Corporation was also hired by city officials to sell Berlin to international businesses.

88. Partners for Berlin spokesperson, interview, 2000. Unless otherwise cited, quotes in this section come from this interview. Partners for Berlin started with twenty-eight corporate sponsors and now has over one hundred. Companies can be shareholders (four-year contracts) or licensees (two-year contracts) and can contribute anywhere from DM 35,000 to 300,000 annu-

ally (as of 2000). Depending on the capital shares contributed, companies have different rights, including voting rights on marketing concepts, using the Partners and "New Berlin" logo in their public relations and advertisements, and being mentioned in the New Berlin advertisements, posters, brochures, and promotional events organized by Partners.

89. On feminized representations of the city, see chapter 1, note 6.

90. Partners for Berlin, "Perfect Place to Live" postcard, n.d. See http://www.berlin.de/partner-fuer-berlin/english/newberlin/leben.html.

91. Briavel Holcomb, "Revisioning Place: De- and Re-constructing the Image of the Industrial City," in *Selling Places: The City as Cultural Capital, Past and Present,* ed. Gerry Kearns and Chris Philo (New York: Pergamon Press, 1993), 133–43; McDowell, *Capital Culture.*

92. Deborah Smail and Corey Ross, "New Berlins and New Germanies: History, Myth, and the German Capital in the 1920s and 1990s," in *Representing the German Nation: History and Identity in Twentieth-Century Germany,* ed. Mary Fulbrook and Martin Swales (New York: Manchester University Press, 2000), 63–76. In 1927 the Berlin Tourist Office launched a promotion called "Everyone Should Be in Berlin at Least Once" (Jeder Einmal in Berlin) and used the Brandenburg Gate as its main symbol. See Rudy Koshar, *German Travel Cultures* (Oxford: Berg, 2000).

93. Adolf Schick, director of the Berlin Tourist Office (1928), quoted in Smail and Ross, "New Berlins," 66.

94. Koshar, *German Travel Cultures*; Smail and Ross, "New Berlins."

95. On Weimar Berlin, see Alex Vasudevan, "Metropolitan Theatrics: Performing the Modern in Weimar Berlin" (Ph.D. diss., Department of Geography, University of British Columbia, Vancouver, 2005); and Janet Ward, *Weimar Surfaces: Urban Visual Culture in 1920s Germany* (Berkeley and Los Angeles: University of California Press, 2001).

96. Herbert Muschamp, "Berlin's Brief Dawn, before the Darkness," *New York Times,* November 12, 1999, E39.

97. Strom and Mayer, "New Berlins," 124.

98. Peter Marcuse, "Reflections on Berlin: The Meaning of Construction and the Construction of Meaning," *International Journal of Urban and Regional Research (IJURR)* 22 (1998): 331–38; Scott Campbell, "Capital Reconstruction and Capital Accumulation in Berlin: A Reply to Peter Marcuse," *IJURR* 23 (1999): 173–79. See also Hartmut Häussermann, "Economic and Political Power in the New Berlin: A Response to Peter Marcuse," *IJURR* 23 (1999): 180–84; Peter Marcuse, "Reply to Campbell and Häussermann," *IJURR* 23 (1999): 185–87.

99. Boyer, *City of Collective Memory*; Michel de Certeau, *The Writing of History*, trans. Tom Conley (New York: Columbia University Press, 1988).

100. Quoted in Smail and Ross, "New Berlins."

101. Former East Germans may share some of these emotions but may also experience shame about the GDR as well as anger about Western depictions of—and intentional forgetting of—East German history.

102. Roger Cohen, "To Be German and Proud: Patriotism versus the Past," *New York Times,* January 10, 2001, A8.

103. Barbara Jakubeit, cited in Wise, *Capital Dilemma,* 16.

104. Oscar Schnieder, cited in Wise, *Capital Dilemma,* 17.

105. Mathias Scheiber, cultural editor of *Der Speigel*, quoted in Wise, *Capital Dilemma,* 17–18.

106. Kramer, "Living with Berlin," 54.

107. Cohen, "To Be German and Proud"; and Roger Cohen, "Schröder Affirms National Pride in Patriotism Debate," *International Herald Tribune,* March 20, 2001.

108. Cohen, "Schröder Affirms National Pride."

109. Svetlana Boym, *The Future of Nostalgia* (New York: Basic Books, 2001); Stephen Legg, "Contesting and Surviving Memory: Space, Nation and Nostalgia in *Les lieux de mémoire*," *Environment and Planning D: Society and Space* (forthcoming); Wilson, "Looking Backward."

110. Wilson, "Looking Backward." See also Elizabeth Wilson, "The Rhetoric of Urban Space," *New Left Review* 209 (1995): 146–60.

111. Rudy Koshar, *Germany's Transient Pasts: Preservation and National Memory in the Twentieth Century* (Chapel Hill: University of North Carolina Press, 1998), 331.

112. Jeff Kelley, "Common Work," in *Mapping the Terrain: New Genre Public Art,* ed. Suzanne Lacy (Seattle: Bay Press, 1995), 143.

A Flyer

1. Stadtbild Berlin eV, undated flyer, "Wie soll der Lustgarten aussehen?" and "Der Lustgarten: Seine bewegte Geschichte—Die heutige Situation—Perspektive für die Zukunkft," Stadtbild Berlin eV, Stresemannstr. 27, 10963 Berlin, Germany. Stadtbild protested the winning designs of two public architectural competitions (in 1994 and 1996).

2. The first winning design was awarded to artist Gerhard Merz, who proposed a concrete garden with a long pavilion separating the plaza from Karl-Liebknecht-Straße. The second winning design was awarded to Gustav Lange, with two water basins, rows of trees, and tubs of plants set along a central axis, but it "did not have public resonance." In 1997 the Berlin Senate voted to reconstruct the plaza according to Schinkel's nineteenth-century "desired vision" for the Lustgarten, based on the geometric proportions of the Altes Museum. The city-state of Berlin and the Allianz Foundation for the Environment funded the project; Professor Hans Loidl and Grün Berlin Park und Garten GmbH oversaw it. See http://www.stadtentwicklung.berlin.de/aktuell/wettbewerbe/ergebnisse/1999/lustgarten/index2.shtml.

3. Berliner Festspiele and Architektenkammer Berlin, ed., Berlin: *Open City/Berlin: offene Stadt: The City on Exhibition* (Berlin: Nicolai, 1999), 136. The guidebook was part of a project commissioned by the Berlin Senate and Partners for Berlin.

3. The Gestapo Terrain

1. See David Lowenthal, *Possessed by the Past: The Heritage Crusade and the Spoils of History* (New York: Free Press, 1996).

2. John Berger, *Ways of Seeing* (London: British Broadcasting Corporation and Pelican Books, 1972), 11.

3. Nachama is currently the managing director of the Topography of Terror and was formerly the chair of the Berlin Council of Jews. He is also a practicing rabbi in Berlin. See http://www.nachama.com/an1_frames.htm.

4. Lore Ditzen, "Ein Ort deutscher Geschichte," *Süddeutsche Zeitung,* May 26, 1983.

5. Walter Benjamin, *Berliner Chronik: Gesammelte Schriften* (Frankfurt am Main: Suhrkamp, 1972), 486–87; English translation of passage by Gerhard Richter. Compare with Edmund Jephcott's translation of "A Berlin Chronicle," in *Reflections: Essays, Aphorisms, Autobiographical Writings,* by Walter Benjamin (New York: Harcourt Brace Jovanovich, 1978), 25–26; and Rodney Livingstone's translation (based on Jephcott's) of "A Berlin Chronicle" and

"Excavation and Memory," in *Selected Writings, Volume 2, 1927–1934,* by Walter Benjamin (Cambridge: Belknap, 1999), 611, 576.

6. For classics in geography on landscape, see Denis Cosgrove, *Social Formation and Symbolic Landscape* (Totawa, NJ: Barnes and Noble, 1984); Denis Cosgrove and Stephen Daniels, eds., *The Iconography of Landscape* (New York: Cambridge University Press, 1987); James Duncan and Nancy Duncan, "(Re)reading the Landscape," *Environment and Planning D* 6 (1988): 117–26; Gillian Rose, "Looking at Landscape: The Uneasy Pleasures of Power," in *Feminism and Geography* (Minneapolis: University of Minnesota Press, 1993), 86–112.

7. Rich Schein discusses the metaphor of landscape as palimpsest in "The Place of Landscape: A Conceptual Framework for an American Scene," *Annals of the Association of American Geographers* 87, no. 4 (1997): 660–80.

8. In this chapter, I do not follow a precise chronology and generalize opinions held by individuals and groups. Key sources on which I draw (that detail sequences and dates of events) include Akademie der Künste, *Diskussion zum Umgang mit dem "Gestapo-Gelände": Dokumentation, Diskussionsbeiträge anläßlich des Hearings zum Umgang mit dem "Gestapo-Gelände" am 27. Februar 1986 in der Akademie der Künste,* (Berlin, 1986), 49 pp.; Akademie der Künste, *Zum Umgang mit dem Gestapo-Gelände, Gutachten im Auftrag der Akademie der Künste Berlin* (December 1988), 73 pp.; Leonie Baumann, "Erinnern für die Zukunft: Das 'Gestapo-Gelände' in Berlin—Zur Geshichte eines Denk-Ortes," in *Das Kunstwerk als Geschichtsdokument,* ed. Annette Tietenberg (München: Klinkhardt and Biermann, 1999), 174–91; Stefanie Endlich, *Denkort Gestapogelände,* Shriftenreihe Aktives Museum, Band 2 (Berlin: Aktives Museum Faschismus und Widerstand in Berlin, 1990); Reinhard Rürup, ed., *Topography of Terror: Gestapo, SS, and Reichssicherheitshauptamt on the 'Prinz-Albrecht-Terrain': A Documentation,* trans. Werner Angress (Berlin: Willmuth Arenhövel, 1989); and Florian von Buttlar and Stephanie Endlich, *Synopse zum Umgang mit dem Gestapo Gelände* (Berlin: Aktives Museum, 1986).

9. "Green" Greens (largely ecologists), "brown Greens" (right-wing defenders of the German homeland), and "red" Greens (supporting the "small is beautiful" ideal associated with socialist political agendas) were part of the environmental movement. See Mary Fulbrook, *The Divided Nation: A History of Germans, 1918–1990* (New York: Oxford University Press, 1992), 214.

10. West Berlin emigration became a concern after 1961. Chancellor Adenauer paid DM 100 of "jitters money" to each West Berliner to encourage them to stay. On the basis of out-migration rates from the late 1970s and early 1980s, population estimates for 2000 were projected to be below 1.7 million. Investors and businesses, including Siemens and AEG, relocated because transportation was unreliable, making production in Berlin too expensive. Traditional industries such as machine, electrical equipment, and garment manufacturing declined, and so did high-tech industries because of West Berlin's location. No products of military significance could be made because of the city's proximity to East Germany. See Joachim Mawrocki, "Berliner Wirtschaft: Waschstum auf begrenztem Raum," in *Berlin Fibel: Berichte zur Lage der Stadt,* ed. Dieter Baumeister (Berlin, 1975), 269–71; Alexandra Richie, *Faust's Metropolis: A History of Berlin* (New York: Carroll and Graf, 1998); Klaus Schütz, "The Wall and West Berlin's Development," in *Living with the Wall: West Berlin, 1961–1985,* ed. Richard Merritt and Anna Merritt (Durham, NC: Duke University Press, 1985), 37, 225; and Wolfgang Watter, "The West Berlin Economy," in Merritt, *Living with the Wall,* 138.

11. In September 1939, the Prinz-Albrecht-Palais was the headquarters of the head of the Reich Security Main Office, first run by Heydrich, and later by Kaltenbrunner (after 1943). The

Reich Security Main Office also had administrative offices throughout the city. Helmut Engel and Wolfgang Ribbe, eds., *Geschichtsmeile Wilhelmstraße* (Berlin: Akademie Verlag, 1997); Rürup, *Topography of Terror.*

12. While the people who worked at these offices are known as "desktop perpetrators" *(Schreibtischtäter),* some of the Reich Security Office staff and directors also participated in the extermination policy of Einsatzgruppen in the occupied countries.

13. Quoted in Rürup, *Topography of Terror,* 210.

14. For a compilation of recorded stories, reflections, documents, and historical photos of former prisoners in the house prison see Evangelische Akademie Berlin, *In der Gestapo-Zentrale Prinz-Albrecht-Straße 8: Berichte ehemaliger Häftlinge; Eine Dokumetation der Evangelischen Akademie Berlin (West) im Evangelischen Bildungswerk* (Berlin, 1989), 247 pp.

15. Rürup, *Topography of Terror,* 211.

16. For a documentation of the debates about a Berlin history museum and later debates about the German Historical Museum, see Christoph Stölzl, ed., *Deutsches Historisches Museum: Ideen-Kontroversen-Perspektiven* (Berlin: Popyläen, 1988).

17. Hartmut Boockmann et al., "Denkschrift von Hartmut Boockmann, Eberhard Jäckel, Hagen Schulze und Michael Stürmer für den Senator für Wissenschaft und Kulturelle Angelegenheiten des Landes Berlin" (January 1982), reprinted in Stölzl, *Deutsches Historisches Museum,* 61–66.

18. *Berliner Morgenpost,* "Es gibt keine Alternative für den Standort Berlin: Interview mit dem Regierenden Bürgermeister von Berlin, Richard von Weizsäcker," May 1–2, 1982, in Stölzl, *Deutsches Historisches Museum,* 82–84.

19. While most of these individuals were political conservatives, this group was diverse. Richard von Weizsäcker, for example, was born in 1920 and was part of the generation whose positive experiences of prewar Nazi years were overshadowed by the hopelessness of the situation after 1943. He "overcame his incipient Nazi complicity" to become "one of West Germany's most honest, open, and respected democrats." Through a critical public speech he later delivered in 1985 as the president of the FRG, he directly acknowledged the suffering and persecution of various victim groups, an important event in the public process of coming to terms with Nazism. See Harald Marcuse, *Legacies of Dachau* (Cambridge: Cambridge Univeristy Press, 2001), 294.

20. Much of the historical information for this section comes from Rürup, *Topography of Terror.*

21. Goerd Peschken, *Berlin: Eine Residenz wird errichtet,* Berliner Topograpfien 1, Museumspädagogischer Dienst Berlin (Berlin: Ästhetik und Kommunikation, 1987).

22. The train station was originally built in 1841.

23. Studios on the top floor were still rented out to artists until 1933.

24. Akademie der Künste, "Niederschrift einer Diskussionsveranstaltung der Akademie der Künste" (September 14, 1983), reprinted in Stölzl, *Deutsches Historisches Museum,* 63.

25. The historical information for this section stems from Rürup, *Topography of Terror,* and is displayed in a small section at the end of the Topography's permanent exhibition.

26. In 1951, in the new Eastern district of Mitte, Prinz-Albrecht-Straße became Niederkirchner-Straße to honor the communist fighter Käthe Niederkirchner, killed in Ravensbrück concentration camp.

27. Fulbrook, *Divided Nation*; Deborah Howell-Ardila, "Berlin's Search for a 'Democratic' Architecture: Post–World War II and Post-unification," *German Politics and Society* 16, no. 3

(1998): 62–85; Marcuse, *Legacies of Dachau*; Rürup, *Topography of Terror*; Dariuš Zifonun, "Symbol und Mythos im Erinnerungsdiskurs: Zur Konstruktion kollektiver Identitäten am Beispiel der KZ-Gedenkstätte Dachau," in *Der Sinn der Politik: Kulturwissenschaftliche Politikanalysen,* ed. Michael Müller, Thilo Raufer, and Dariuš Zifonun (Konstanz: UVK Verlagsgesellschaft, 2002), 123–58. Some concentration camps, such as Dachau and Buchenwald, were used by Americans and Soviets as internment camps for Nazi functionaries, and for temporary housing for German refugees from the eastern territories of the German Reich (before 1945) in current-day Poland.

28. The demolition of the former Gestapo headquarters (Prinz-Albrecht-Straße 8) occurred in 1953 and 1954; remaining walls were blown up in 1956. In 1958 and 1959 the buildings on Wilhelmstraße that were used as administrative offices by the SS and SD beginning in 1935 were leveled and cleared. It is unclear why the relatively well-preserved Museum of Ethnology (constructed between 1881 and 1886 by Hermann Ende and Wilhelm Böckmann) was blown up in 1962 and 1963. The building was partially renovated in the early 1950s and used after 1955 as the Museum for Prehistory and Ancient History. The demolition of this museum occurred at the same time the buildings on Niederkirchner-Straße and Wilhelmstraße were razed.

29. See Rürup, *Topography of Terror,* 197–207.

30. Ibid., 199.

31. Not every person in Berlin wanted to forget the atrocities of the Nazi regime. Immediately following the war, commemorative ceremonies were widely attended by Berlin residents, such as the "Commemorative Rally for Victims of Fascist Terror" in the residential district of Neukölln (adjacent to Kreuzberg) on September 9, 1945, attended by 35,000 people.

32. Quoted in Rürup, *Topography of Terror,* 198.

33. In addition, a significant amount of public attention surrounded the destruction of the New Reich Chancellery in 1949.

34. Western indignation over the so-called narrow-minded destruction of the "historic heart" of the city for political reasons (i.e., according to the SED Marxist-Leninist view of history) remains part of Berlin's cultural politics today. See chapter 2.

35. Fulbrook, *Divided Nation,* 1992.

36. Fulbrook, *Divided Nation*; Marcuse, *Legacies of Dachau.*

37. Michael Kammen, *The Mystic Chords of Memory: The Transformation of Tradition in American Culture* (New York: Vintage Books, 1991).

38. See Anton Kaes, *From Hitler to Heimat: The Return of History as Film* (Cambridge: Harvard University Press, 1989); Susan Linville, *Feminism, Film, Fascism* (Austin: University of Texas Press, 1998); Peter Märthesheimer and Ivo Frenzel, eds., *Im Kreuzfeuer: Der Fernsehfilm 'Holocaust': Eine Nation ist betroffen* (Frankfurt am Main: Fischer, 1979); Margarete Mitscherlich-Nielsen, "Die Notwendigkeit zu trauern," in Märthesheimer and Franzl, *Im Kreuzfeuer,* 207–18; and David Morley and Kevin Robins, "No Place like Heimat: Images of Home(land) in European Culture," *New Formations* 12 (1990): 1–23.

39. Richard von Weizsäcker, quoted in Rürup, *Topography of Terror,* 211. Unless otherwise cited, additional information about the public competition here and in the following section comes from Baumann, "Erinnern für die Zukunft"; von Buttlar and Endlich, *Synopse zum Umgang*; and Rürup, *Topography of Terror.*

40. See Christoph Heinrich, *Strategien des Erinnerns: Der veränderte Denkmalbegriff in der Kunst der achtziger Jahre* (München, 1993); Brigitte Hausmann, *Duell mit der Verdrängung? Denkmäler für die Opfer des Nationalsozialismus in der Bundesrepublik Deutschland 1980 bis*

1990, Theorie der Gegenwartskunst Band 11 (Münster, 1997); Jan-Holger Kirsch, "Trauer und historische Erinnerung in der Berliner Republik: Überlegungen aus Anlaß der Mahnmalsdebatte," in *Trauer und Geschichte,* ed. Burkhard Liebsch and Jörn Rüsen (Köln, Weimar, and Vienna: Böhlau Verlag, 2001), 339–74; Ries Roowaan, *Herdenken in Duitsland: De centrale monumenten van de Bondsrepubliek, 1949–1993* (Amsterdam: Boom, 1999).

41. Some of these acknowledged heroic or moral figures, like resistance fighters, through plaques or street sign names, particularly in the GDR.

42. In an impressive edited two-volume collection, Ulrike Puvogel describes most of the memorials dedicated to the memory of victims of National Socialism in Germany. In her 1987 map, I counted over two hundred sites in West Germany that in some way addressed the National Socialist period and the Holocaust. The classification scheme included memorial centers *(Gedenkstätten)*; large cemeteries *(Friedhöfe)*; small cemeteries; smaller memorial centers; sites of admonition *(Mahnmäler)*; memorial plaques *(Gedenktafeln)*; memorial stones *(Gedenksteine)*; and memorial plaques and stones at former locations of synagogues. See Ulrike Puvogel, ed., *Gedenkstätten für die Opfer des Nationalsozialismus: Eine Dokumentation,* Schriftenreihe der Bundeszentrale für politische Bildung 245, 2nd ed. (Bonn: Franz Spiegel Buch, 1995).

43. The *Ehrenmal* is a monumental memorial of honor, usually dedicated to soldiers and heroes; because of its association with the Nazi cult of the soldier after 1933, it was no longer used in the FRG.

44. Cornelia Brink, "Visualisierte Geschichte: Zu Austellungen an Orten Nationalsozialistischer Konzentrationslager" (thesis, Department of Philosophy, Albert-Ludwigs University, Frieberg, 1989). See also Puvogel, *Gedenkstätten für die Opfer des Nationalsozialismus.*

45. Dariuš Zifonun, "Symbol und Mythos."

46. The sculpture was designed by Nandor Glid and dedicated in 1968.

47. James Young, *The Texture of Memory: Holocaust Memorials and Meaning* (New Haven: Yale University Press, 1993).

48. GDR educational institutions were reevaluated in the 1960s to focus on training skilled workers. In the West, the educational system was also reevaluated, but in terms of content taught and pedagogy; during the 1980s there was an expanded acknowledgment of the suffering of other groups, including Sinti and Roma gypsies, homosexuals, the handicapped, Jehovah's Witnesses, among others. It wasn't until the mid-1980s that the specific racist and anti-Semitic nature of Jewish persecution under National Socialism was discussed in the GDR, and even then there were problems with those representations. See Fulbrook, *Divided Nation,* chapter 9; Marcuse, *Legacies of Dachau.*

49. Ian Buruma, *The Wages of Guilt: Memories of War in Germany and Japan* (New York: Farrar, Straus, and Giroux, 1994), 203. See also Elizabeth Domansky, "Die gespaltene Erinnerung," in *Kunst und Literatur nach Auschwitz,* ed. Manuel Köppen (Berlin: Erich Schmidt Verlag, 1993).

50. "Der Erfolg der Preußen-Ausstellung hat gezeigt, wie stark Interesse an der Aufarbeitung der deutschen Geschichte in der Bevölkerung ist: Interview mit dem Berliner Senator für Wissenschaft und Kulturelle Angelegenheiten, Wilhelm Kewenig," *Berliner Morgenpost,* February 21, 1982, in Stölzl, *Deutsches Historisches Museum,* 69–71; Rudolf Stiege, "In Berlin zeigen, was deutsche Geschichte ist," *Berliner Morgenpost,* February 14, 1982, in Stölzl, *Deutsches Historisches Museum,* 67–69; "Es gibt keine Alternative," *Berliner Morgenpost,* n.d.

51. Miles Richardson, "The Gift of Presence: The Act of Leaving Artifacts at Shrines, Memo-

rials, and Other Tragedies," in *Textures of Place,* ed. Paul Adams, Steven Hoelscher, and Karen Till (Minneapolis: University of Minnesota Press, 2001), 257–72.

52. On memorials in the geographic literature, see Owen Dwyer, "Memory on the Margins: Alabama's Civil Rights Journey as a Memorial Text," in *Mapping Tourism,* ed. Stephen Hanna and Vincent Del Casino Jr. (Minnepolis: University of Minnesota Press, 2003), 28–50; Ben Forest and Juliet Johnson, "Unraveling the Threads of History: Soviet-Era Monuments and Post-Soviet National Identity in Moscow," *Annals of the Association of American Geographers* 92 (2002): 524–47; Nuala Johnson, "Cast in Stone: Monuments, Geography, and Nationalism," *Environment and Planning D: Society and Space* 13 (1995): 51–65; David Lowenthal, *The Past Is a Foreign Country* (Cambridge: Cambridge University Press, 1985).

53. Much has been written about museums in recent years. For a selection, see Benedict Anderson, *Imagined Communities: Reflections on the Origin and Spread of Nationalism,* rev. and extended ed. (New York: Verso, 1991); James Clifford, *The Predicament of Culture: Twentieth Century Ethnography, Literature, and Art* (Cambridge: Harvard University Press, 1988); Johannes Fabian, *Time and the Other: How Anthropology Makes Its Object* (New York: Columbia University Press, 1983); Paula Findlen, "The Museum: Its Classical Etymology and Renaissance Genealogy," *Journal of the History of Collections* 1:59–78; Richard Handler, *Nationalism and the Politics of Culture in Quebec* (Madison: University of Wisconsin Press, 1988); Donna Haraway, *Primate Visions: Gender, Race, and Nature in the World of Modern Science* (New York: Routledge, 1989); Ivan Karp and Steven Lavine, eds., *Exhibiting Cultures: The Poetics and Politics of Museum Display* (Washington, DC: Smithsonian Institution Press, 1991).

54. For a discussion of the political uses of history in the FRG, see Mary Fulbrook, "Representing the Nation: History and Identity in East and West Germany," in *Representing the German Nation: History and Identity in Twentieth-Century Germany,* ed. Mary Fulbrook and Martin Swales (New York: Manchester University Press, 2000), 172–92.

55. Quoted in Stölzl, *Deutsches Historisches Museum,* 131. See also Stiege, "In Berlin zeigen, was deutsche Geschichte ist."

56. "Protokoll der Anhörung des Senators für Kulturelle Angelegenheiten zum Forum für Geschichte und Gegenwart," November 18, 1983, reprinted in Stölzl, *Deutsches Historisches Museum,* 63.

57. See Peter Baldwin, ed., *Reworking the Past: Hitler, the Holocaust, and the Historians' Debate* (Boston: Beacon Press, 1990).

58. Quoted in Stölzl, *Deutsches Historisches Museum,* 110.

59. Akademie der Künste, "Niederschrift."

60. Ibid.

61. Information about political education in this and the following paragraphs comes from Gotthar Breit and Peter Massing, eds., *Grundfagen und Praxisprobleme der politischen Bildung,* Schriftenreihe 305 (Bonn: Bundeszentrale für politische Bildung, 1992); Fulbook, *Divided Nation*; and Günter Renner and Wolfgang Sander, "Bundesrepublik Deutschland," in *Politische Bildung für Europa,* Schriftenreihe 306 (Bonn: Bundeszentrale für politische Bildung, 1991), 107–38.

62. Allied denazification and reeducation programs varied between Soviet, American, British, and French forces, but also among and between them. The American reeducation policy was heavily influenced by the pedagogy of John Dewey, in particular the thesis that democracy is not just a form of government but rather a way of life.

63. Fulbrook, *Divided Nation*; Jeffrey Herf, *Divided Memory: The Nazi Past in the Two Germanies* (Cambridge, MA: Harvard University Press, 1997).

64. Fulbrook, *Divided Nation*; Marcuse, *Legacies of Dachau.*

65. Quoted in Ackermann, G. Niemetz, "Arbeit vor Ort: Univerzichtbarer Bestandteil geographischen Unterrichts," *Geographie und Schule* 6, no. 2 (1980): 2–10, 3; italics mine.

66. Hans Werner Kuhn and Peter Massing, "Politische Bildung seit 1945: Konzeptionen, Kontroversen, Perspektiven," in *Grundfragen und Praxisprobleme,* ed. Breit and Massing, 32.

67. Marcuse, *Legacies of Dachau.* Marcuse also argued that it wasn't until the 1990s that the pedagogical rigidity associated with the 1968 generation and their abstract ideals was actively confronted.

68. The actual balance between rational and emotional approaches to political education, however, has been and continues to be an area of intense debate. See Siegfried Schiele and Herbert Schneider, eds., *Rationalität und Emotionalität in der politischen Bildung,* Sonderauflage für die Landeszentrale für politisches Bildungsarbeit Berlin (Stuttgart: J. B. Metzler, 1991).

69. Dariuš Zifonun, "Elements of a Cultural Politics of Memory: Holocaust Memorial Sites and Political Discourse in Germany," paper presented at the Canadian Centre for German and European Studies, York University, Toronto, September 9, 1999, MS available from author, University of Konstanz, Department of Public Policy and Management, P.O. Box 5560, D 89; D-78434 Konstanz, Germany, Darius.Zifonun@uni-konstanz.de; Zifonun, "Symbol und Mythos."

70. Zifonun suggests that the discourse of reappraisal situates the National Socialist past as an opportunity rather than a "burden" or "thorn in the flesh of German identity," as has been commonly interpreted. He argues that this discourse is tied to a new construction of national identity. See Dariuš Zifonun, "Heilsame Wunden: Holocaust-Gedenkstätten also Orte nationaler Identitätsbildung—Das Beispiel der 'Topographie des Terrors' in Berlin," in *Figurative Politik: Zur Performanz der Macht in der modernen Gesellschaft,* ed. Hans-Georg Soeffner and Dirk Tänzler (Opladen: Leske and Budrich, 2002), 193–210. I similarly interpret this change but suggest that this shift is informed by a liberal to socialist understanding of "postnationalism" that imagines belonging in terms beyond the frame of the nation-state (see chapter 4).

71. *Internationale Begegnungstätten* developed out of the programs of the evangelical Aktion Sühnezeichen Friedensdienste (Signs of Atonement and Peace Service) that organized programs for German youth. Participants often had no immediate personal links to the history of 1933 to 1945 (they were too young) and forged such links through work at various centers in Israel and Central Europe. Some programs included youth exchanges. These social and educational outreach programs were intended to heal damaged relationships resulting from past injuries inflicted by Germans on peoples of other countries.

72. Young, *Texture of Memory,* 86.

73. Quoted in Rürup, *Topography of Terror.*

74. Leonie Baumann, former director of the Active Museum and current director of the New Society for Fine Arts in Berlin (NGBK), argues that this proposal remains impressive today, even in comparison to proposals submitted for the two public art competitions for the Holocaust Memorial in the 1990s. See Baumann, "Erinnern für die Zukunft."

75. Jury members who awarded the first prize added the concept of an active museum to the proposed memorial site and later decided against the entry. Gerhard Schoenberner, "Plädoyer für enge Zusammenarbeit mit der 'Initiative,'" Aktives Museum Faschismus und Widerstand in Berlin, *Mitgliederrundbrief* 1 (December 1987): 2.

76. Such sentiments may have been intensified because of other related top-down decisions made by officials. At about the same time that criticisms were leveled at the memorial competi-

tion, Berlin mayor Eberhard Diepgen, after consulting with Chancellor Kohl, decided to establish the Forum for History and Contemporary Affairs at the Martin Gropius Bau as a temporary stepping-stone for the German Historical Museum.

77. Baumann, "Erinnern für die Zukunft."

78. According to the first Active Museum member newsletter, dated December 1987, the member groups included the Association of Persecuted Social Democrats (Arbeitsgemeinschaft verfolgter Sozialdemokraten), Signs of Atonement and Peace Service (Aktion Sühnezeichen Friedensdienste), General Homosexual Action Group (Allgemeine Homosexuelle Aktion), Berlin Cultural Advisory Board (Berliner Kulturrat), Berlin History Workshop (Berliner Geschichtswerkstatt), Professional Association of the Fine Arts (Berufsverband Bildender Künstler), Democratic Organization of Women (Demokratischer Frauenbund), German Association of Free Thinkers (Deutscher Freidenker Verband), Elephant Press Gallery (Elefanten Press Galerie), Evangelical Academy (Evangelische Akademie), Evangelical Youth Group of Berlin (Evangelische Jugend Berlin), Friends of German Cinema (Freunde der Deutschen Kinemathek), Society for German-Soviet Friendship (Gesellschaft für Deutsch-Sowjetische Freundschaft), Magnus Hirschfeld Society (Magnus-Hirschfeld-Gesellschaft), Dutch Ecumenical Parish (Niederländisch-ökumenische Gemeinde), New Society for the Fine Arts (Neue Gesellschaft für bildende Kunst), Neukölln Cultural Organization (Neuköllner Kulturverein), Association of Antifascists (VVN—Verband der Antifaschisten), and Werkbund Archive (Werkbund Archiv). In June 1988, three groups joined: Socialist Youth of Germany "The Falcons" (Sozialistische Jugend Deutschlands Die Falken), Artist Colony of Berlin (Künstler Kolonie Berlin eV), and the Regional Office for Economics and Antiracism (Regionalbüro für Wirtschaft und Antirassismus).

79. West Germany's multiparty system was organized around two main parties, the CDU/CSU and the SPD. These parties compete for a majority of the popular vote and usually enter into coalitions with smaller parties, like the liberal FDP. The Green party, a new coalition partner at the national level (and at the state level in some instances a majority party), has had the highest rate of female participation, after which comes the SPD. The Greens were often viewed as emblematic of a crisis within West Germany's political party system: their presence in the Bundestag marked the first time since 1961 that there were four parliamentary groups represented in the German Parliament, and the first time since 1953 that a fourth party successfully broke into the established party system. By the late 1980s and 1990s, the Greens have had internal divisions, particularly between the "realists" *(Realos)* and "fundamentalists" *(Fundis),* and between green, brown, and red Greens, resulting in instabilities. See Fullbrook, *Divided Nation;* Thomas Scharf, *The German Greens: Challenging the Consensus* (Oxford: Berg, 1994).

80. Jane Kramer, *Europeans* (New York: Farrar, Straus, and Giroux, 1988).

81. The Active Museum began receiving roughly DM 200,000 in 1990, but as a result of the financial crisis after unification received only DM 170,000 in 1998 and €90,700 in 2004.

82. Marcuse, *Legacies of Dachau.*

83. As early as the late 1940s, artists attempted to confront the problems posed by the Nazi past in German society, as demonstrated by the Gruppe 47; later writers, film directors, and investigative reporters continued to be critical of Germany's uneasy relationship with its past. Fulbrook suggests that West German writers played a more critical role in public debate than was the case in Britain (see *Divided Nation*).

84. Christine Fischer-Defoy, personal correspondence, 2003, and Sabine Weißler, personal conversation, 2003. See also the Active Museum newsletter celebrating twenty years of the group's organization, with a special focus on the history and "construction site Gestapo Terrain." Verein Aktives Museum Faschismus und Widerstand in Berlin, *Mitgliederrundbrief* 49

(July 2003), available through the Active Museum, Stauffenbergstr. 13–14, 10785 Berlin, Germany; http://www.aktives-museum.de.

85. Michel Foucault, *The Archaeology of Knowledge and the Discourse on Language,* trans. A. M. Sheridan Smith (New York: Pantheon, 1972), 7.

86. Jani Scandura, *Down in the Dumps: Place, Modernity, the American Depression* (Durham, NC: Duke University Press, forthcoming).

87. Duncan and Duncan, "(Re)reading the Landscape," 120.

88. Benjamin, *Berliner Chronik.*

89. "Gestapoakten als Altmaterial verramscht," *Aufbau* (New York), December 30, 1955, n.p. *Aufbau* was a German immigrant newspaper in the United States. Article courtesy of the Active Museum archives.

90. After the Kohl administration selected a site for the national history museum across from the Reichstag, the Martin Gropius Bau continued to function as exhibition space in the city. Conservatives began voicing other suggestions for the Gestapo Terrain, including historic reconstruction.

91. Rürup, *Topography of Terror,* 218.

92. Ibid.

93. Josef Beuys, *Josef Beuys: Zeige deine Wunde* (München: Schellmann und Klüser, Städtische Galerie im Lenbachhaus, 1980). On Beuys, see Gene Ray, ed., *Joseph Beuys: Mapping the Legacy* (New York: John and Mable Ringling Museum, 2001).

94. Magistrat der Stadt Kassel Kulturamt, *Aschrott Brunnen: Offene Wunde der Stadtgeschichte* (Kassel, 1989), unpaginated brochure; personal conversation with the artist, 1993; see also Young, *Textures of Memory.*

95. *Denk-mal* literally means "think once" and plays on the traditional term for memorial, *Denkmal.*

96. Quoted in Magistrat der Stadt Kassel Kulturamt, *Aschrott Brunnen.*

97. Walter Benjamin, *The Arcades Project,* trans. Howard Eiland and Kevin McLaughlin (Cambridge: Belknap, 1999); Burkhardt Lindner, "The Passagen-Werk: The Berliner Kindheit, and the Archaeology of the 'Recent Past,'" *New German Critique* 39 (1986): 45–53.

98. Although this number may not seem large to American readers, by German standards, it was considered a high rate of attendance.

99. Stephen Daniels, "Marxism, Culture, and the Duplicity of Landscape," in *New Models in Geography,* ed. Richard Peet and Nigel Thrift (London: Unwin Hyman, 1989), 206.

100. Aktives Museum, *Mitgliederrundbrief* 5 (September 1988); Harald Martenstein, "Das tägliche Gewurstel: Grass, Hassemer, Lea Rosh und andere Stritten über Kulturpolitik," *Der Tagesspiegel,* November 2, 1988, 4.

101. The eight-person commission was led by Reinhard Rürup and included three historians, an architect (director of the IBA and president of the Academy of Arts), the head of the Berliner Festspiele (the organization responsible for the 750th anniversary events), an exhibition consultant/publicist, a journalist, and a priest (who cofounded Aktion Sühnezeichen Friedensdienste and was a concentration camp survivor). Half of these experts were also involved in local groups, such as the Active Museum and Concerned Citizens Initiatives.

102. According to Endlich, the participants of the first hearing (June 1–2, 1989) included representatives from the Central Council of Jews in Germany, the Jewish Community of Berlin, the Central Council of German Sinti and Roma, the International League for Human

Rights, the Society for Repressed Peoples, the Ecumenical Work Group for Homosexuals and Churches, the Working Society of Persecuted Social Democrats, the Alliance of Those Persecuted under the Nazi Regime (Berlin chapter), the Organization of Those Persecuted under the Nazi Regime, the Citizens Concerned about the Future of the Gestapo Terrain Initiative, the Active Museum, Signs of Atonement and Peace Service, the Evangelical Academy of Berlin (West), the research team for the exhibit "Topography of Terror," the Kreuzberg District City Council, the SPD and CDU fractions of the Parliament, and the DGB. Eight groups were invited but did not participate, including Perspective for Berlin and the Berlin History Workshop. The themes of the first roundtable were the importance of the authentic ruins; the relevance of the documentary exhibit; the possibility of research at the site; the idea of a site of explanation and learning *(Ort des Aufklärens und Lernens)*; the idea of a site of thinking and contemplation *(Ort des Gedenkens)*; the establishment of a memorial at the terrain, specifically a *Denkmal* or a *Mahnmal*; and other possible functions for the site.

103. The second hearing (August 10–11) in Berlin included representatives from the National Memorial Yad Vashem, Israel; the Concentration Camp Memorial Dachau, FRG; the Concentration Camp Memorial Neuengamme, FRG; the Memorial Center Mauthausen, Austria; the Institute for National Memorials, Warsaw, Poland; the Anne-Frank Foundation, Amsterdam, Holland; and the National Memorial Brandenburg, GDR. An expert from the U.S. Holocaust Memorial Museum submitted her responses in writing. Members of the first hearing were invited, as were representatives from the Kreuzberg-District City Council. At this roundtable, experts discussed the international significance of a site of thinking and contemplation *(Denkort)*, and existing models and legal and organizational possibilities for such a place.

104. The expert commission also referred to two large public events held at the terrain in 1989 to support their recommendations: the German Evangelical Church Day, under the theme of "Time of Memory" *(Erinnerungszeit),* and a German History Workshop rally. The interim report was approved by the commission in a meeting on September 29, 1989, and formally submitted to the Berlin Senate on October 23. After November 1989, the expert commission discussed their ideas with representatives from East Germany before submitting a final report in March 1990 to the West Berlin Senate. This was a time when the future of the GDR was unclear, but unification was becoming more certain. See Fachkommission, appendix 2, "Zwischenbericht der Fachkommission zur Erarbeitung von Vorschlägen für die künftige Nutzung des 'Prinz-Albrecht-Geländes' ('Gestapo-Geländes'): Vorgelegt zur Sitzung des Kulturausschusses des Berliner Abgeordnetenhauses am 23.10.1989" (Berlin, 1990).

105. Berlin Senatsverwaltung für Bau- und Wohnungswesen, *Beschränkter, kooperativer Realiserungs- und Ideenwettbewerb: Austellungshalle, Besucher- und Dokumentationszentrum und Internationales Begegnungszentrum Topographie des Terrors: Ausschreibung* (Berlin, 1993).

106. See Berlin Senatsverwaltung für Bau- und Wohnungswesen, *Beschränkter, kooperativer Realiserungs- und Ideenwettbewerb: Austellungshalle, Besucher- und Dokumentationszentrum und Internationales Begegnungszentrum Topographie des Terrors: Ergebnisprotokoll* (Berlin, 1993), for a description of the award-winning submissions. The proposed compact, seven-story building for the international place of encounter for youth, planned to be located in front of the Martin Gropius Bau on Stresemannstraße, was eliminated later in the process by the Berlin Senate because of budgetary problems. See also note 71.

107. Quoted in Berlin Senatsverwaltung für Bau- und Wohnungswesen, *Beschränkter . . . Ergebnisprotokoll,* 25.

Fieldnotes

1. My original intention in writing these field notes was to provide the reader with a feeling for the "sense of place" at the Topography and the kinds of experiences a visitor might have. Cultural geographers often use this term to indicate what an "insider's" perspective of a place might be. Through careful observation and descriptive ("transparent") writing (often heavily biased toward the visual), it is assumed that the geographer can communicate a feeling of what a place is like. I have since become more critical of the concept of "sense of place" because it suggests a kind of underlying "essence" or truth for a place. My 1994 notes are edited from Karen Till, "Place and the Politics of Memory: A Geo-ethnography of Museums and Memorials in Berlin" (Ph.D. diss., Department of Geography, University of Wisconsin–Madison, 1996).

2. Reinhard Rürup, ed., *Topography of Terror: Gestapo, SS, Reichssicherheitshauptamt on the "Prinz-Albrecht-Terrain"—a Documentation,* 11th English edition (Berlin: Verlag Willmuth Arenhövel, 2001), 218.

3. Roger Shattuck, quoted in David Lowenthal, *The Past Is a Foreign Country* (Cambridge: Cambridge University Press, 1985), 203.

4. James Young, *Writing and Rewriting the Holocaust: Narrative and the Consequences of Interpretation* (Bloomington: Indiana University Press, 1988), 174–75.

5. At the end of the exhibit, tomes of information are arranged thematically for visitors who want to learn more about a certain topic, such as gas-cars designed to murder humans.

6. In 1991 the outdoor signboards were revised to include English translations when the temporary exhibit War against the Soviet Union was on display in the exhibit hall.

7. For a description of Hitler's drivers' bunker in relation to other National Socialist sites in Berlin, see Karl Meyer, "Digging Berlin's Chamber of Horrors," *Archaeology* 45, no. 4 (1992): 24–249. The rather eclectic "House at Checkpoint Charlie" Museum has existed in the Western part of Berlin on Friedrichstraße since 1983 and displays the history of peaceful revolutions, as well as exhibits of the various (often bizarre and ingenious) means used by individuals to escape from East Germany.

8. James Young, *The Texture of Memory: Holocaust Memorials and Meaning* (New Haven: Yale University Press, 1993).

9. Hazelton, *New York Times* (1992), 33.

10. Somewhat off to the side of the larger hill of rubble, where the former speedway used to be in the 1970s, is a small jungle of weeds, bushes, and trees, what directors call the "little forest" *(Robinienwäldchen)*. As far as I could tell, most people don't go into this part of the terrain, located behind the exhibit and off the main oval path that circumscribes the terrain's open area.

4. Berlin's Ort der Täter

1. Quoted in Hugh Eakin, "Schröder's *Kulturkampf,*" *The Nation,* November 11, 2002, 30.

2. The German word *Ort* is often translated into English as "place"; however, it does not have the richness of meaning that place has as a geographical concept in English. *Ort* is strongly related to the locational qualities of place, as in the sense of a meeting place. Other German words for site include *Stelle* and *Stätte* and are specifically used for a building site, archaeological site, or institution.

3. In addition to interviews, unless otherwise cited, the information in this section comes from Stefanie Endlich, ed., *Denkort Gestapogelände,* Schriftenreihe Aktives Museum 2 (Berlin: Aktives Museum, 1990), 10; and Fachkommission zur Erarbeitung von Vorschlägen für die

künftige Nutzung des "Prinz-Albrecht-Geländes" (Gestapo- Geländes) in Berlin-Kreuzberg, *Abschlussbericht* (Berlin: Senatsverwaltung für Bau- und Wohnungswesen, March 1990).

4. See chapter 5. Despite numerous attempts, I was unable to interview Rosh about Perspective for Berlin's history.

5. Perspective for Berlin was established in 1988 to promote public discussions about difficult contemporary topics, including "Film Censorship in Berlin Schools," "Capitalism, Our Best Export Product," and "Berlin Perspectives on Common East-West Projects," and to support "the traditions of social democracy, European education *[Aufklärung]* and the utopia of freedom." Bürgerinitiative Perspektive Berlin eV, ed., *Ein Denkmal für die Ermordeten Juden Europas, Dokumentation, 1988–1995* (Berlin: Bürgerinitiative Perspektive Berlin, 1995), inside cover.

6. Jane Kramer, "The Politics of Memory," *New Yorker,* August 14, 1995, 48–65; see 49. See also Harald Martenstein, "Das tägliche Gewurstel: Grass, Hassemer, Lea Rosh und andere stritten über Kulturpolitik," *Der Tagesspiegel,* November 2, 1988, 4.

7. See Peter Baldwin, ed., *Reworking the Past: Hitler, the Holocaust, and the Historians' Debate* (Boston: Beacon Press, 1990); Jürgen Habermas, *The New Conservatism: Cultural Criticism and the Historians' Debate,* trans. Shierry Weber Nicholsen (Cambridge: MIT Press, 1989); Charles Maier, *The Unmasterable Past: History, Holocaust, and German National Identity* (Cambridge: Harvard University Press, 1988).

8. The four artists Perspective for Berlin invited for the competition were Horst Hoheisel from Kassel, and Ruth Gindhardt, Paul Pfarr, and Georg Seibert, all from Berlin. See Bürgerinitiative Perspektive Berlin, *Ein Denkmal,* 38–43; Martenstein, "Das tägliche Gewurstel."

9. Jeff Kelley, "Common Work," in *Mapping the Terrain: New Genre Public Art,* ed. Suzanne Lacy (Seattle, WA: Bay Press, 1995), 145.

10. In chapter 6, I discuss these international and transnational contexts in terms of a Cold War, Western cosmopolitan Holocaust memory and the emergence of an American-dominated Holocaust memory industry.

11. Advertisement reprinted in Bürgerinitiative Perspektive Berlin, *Ein Denkmal,* 64. By June 1989, Berlin Cultural Senator Martiny declared that the memorial should be established for all victim groups. In response, Perspective for Berlin organized a discussion that included Active Museum members about the "hierarchization of victims" in September, a theme that continued to haunt postunification discussions about the Holocaust Memorial.

12. Andreas Nachama, managing director of the Topography of Terror, mentioned in 2003, however, that construction on the memorial was delayed and was concerned if it would actually be realized.

13. "Dabei kommen belanglose Gedenkstätten heraus," *taz,* April 13, 1989; "Perspektive Berlin würdigt Holocaust Opfer herab," *taz,* April 15, 1989; Aktives Museum Faschismus und Widerstand Berlin, eV, "Stellungnahme des Aktiven Museums zur Forderung nach einem Holocaust-Mahnmal auf dem Gestapo-Gelände," April 28, 1989, letter reprinted in Bürgerinitiative Perspektive Berlin, *Ein Denkmal,* 55; Lea Rosh, "Ein Mahnmal gehört in das Zentrum der Stadt," *taz,* May 9, 1989; "Kein monumentales Denkmal," *taz,* June 5, 1989. In the debate, old Nazi documents were cited as evidence by Perspective for Berlin members for determining what extermination campaign was more extreme. See "Inzwischen wird bereits mit 'Viertel-Juden' und 'Achtel-Zigeunern' argumentiert," *taz,* July 31, 1991; Bürgerinitiative Perspektive Berlin, *Ein Denkmal,* 55, 72–75, 105, 114–18.

14. Normalization was first introduced by Konrad Adenauer's CDU administration in the

1950s, when he described the partition of Germany as "abnormal" during a trip to Moscow. This "artificial construction of German division constitutes the basis for normalization in a divided Europe." While Adenauer indicated that the status of a single German nation-state should be returned, German unification was not his immediate strategic goal; rather, normalization was more explicitly linked to his agenda of establishing national sovereignty as inextricably bound to the West (in particular as defined by NATO and the European Community). Under Willy Brandt's SPD administration during the early 1970s, normalization meant a peaceful Europe defined by "Ostpolitik"—an initiative that coincided with a period of détente between the two superpowers—and the establishment of good working relations between the FRG and the East (in particular the Soviet Union, Poland, and the GDR). Conservatives who opposed Brandt's politics argued that normalization was an unconstitutional acceptance of the permanent division of Germany. By 1981, the SPD shifted normalization politics as indicated by chancellor Helmut Schmidt's public statement on a return flight from Israel "German foreign policy can and will no longer be overshadowed by Auschwitz." Schmidt's comment articulated the first call for historical normalization. Through this statement and subsequent geopolitical acts, later officials continued to create a political space to represent and imagine the German nation in positive terms and to reclaim temporal continuity between past Germanys and the postwar democratic achievements of the FRG. Under Kohl, a unified German cultural nation would function as a "normal" (Western) European political state, giving up some sovereign rights to transnational organizations like NATO and the EU. It meant that Germany would not be viewed with suspicion by other Western countries but have the freedom to define its national sovereignty and have normal working relations with Western and Eastern European nations. The Schröder administration builds on these traditions but embraces values seen as not typically German, including multicultural cosmopolitanism. Quotes: Peter Bender, *Das Ende des ideologischen Zeitalters: Die Europäisierung Europas* (Berlin: Severin and Siedler, 1981), 229; Anson Rabinbach, "The Jewish Question in the German Question," in *Reworking the Past,* ed. Baldwin, 59. See also Timothy Garten Ash, *In Europe's Name* (London: Vintage, 1994); Simon Dalby, *Creating the Second Cold War: The Discourse of Politics* (London: Pinter, 1990); Stefan Berger, *The Search for Normality: National Identity and Historical Consciousness in Germany since 1800* (Providence: Berghahn Books, 1997); Mary Fulbrook, *The Divided Nation: Germany, 1918–1990* (New York: Oxford University Press, 1991); Habermas, *The New Conservatism*; Mertes, "Germany's Social and Political Culture"; and Steven Muller, "Democracy in Germany," *Daedalus* 123, no. 1 (1994): 33–56.

15. Maier, *The Unmasterable Past.*

16. Maier, *The Unmasterable Past,* and Habermas, *New Conservatism.*

17. Ibid.; see also Baldwin, *Reworking the Past.* Martin Broszat promotes what Maier calls vertical historical normalization, that is, comparisons across time (rather than space) to understand continuities and differences between past and present economic, political, and social structures. Some historians argued that "within the [then] current ideological context," any form of historical normalization could be used to promote revisionist interpretations of German history. See Saul Friedländer and Adam P. Seligman, "The Israeli Memory of the Shoah: On Symbols, Rituals, and Ideological Polarizations," in *NowHere: Space, Time, and Modernity,* ed. Roger Friedland and Deirdre Boden (Berkeley: University of California Press, 1994), 89; Dan Diner, "Between Aporia and Apology: On the Limits of Historicizing National Socialism,"

in *Reworking the Past,* ed. Peter Baldwin, 133–45. These liberal to left historians argue that the Holocaust must be viewed as a unique historical event to ensure that the categories of victim and perpetrator are not blurred, and to protect the memory of the millions who were murdered and persecuted during the Third Reich.

18. Similarly, but argued much later, Fulbrook analyzed the interpretive frameworks of key historians, like Hillgruber, as being influenced by a historical consciousness derived from personal political sympathies (and perhaps also family experience). "How else are we to understand the 'empathy' Hillgruber promotes for soldiers and civilians battling to sustain Western civilization against the Bolshevik hordes on the eastern front, even if such an interpretation meant that the further murders in the concentration camps were to go unacknowledged?" Such a perspective, for Fulbrook, was an "extraordinary throwback to the Nazi version of heroes and villains" (*Interpretations of the Two Germanies,* 2nd ed. [London: Macmillan, 2000], 180–81).

19. For a discussion about the Neue Wache memorial, see Karen Till, "Staging the Past: Landscape Designs, Cultural Identity and Erinnerungspolitik at Berlin's Neue Wache," *Ecumene* 6, no. 3 (1999): 251–83; Jane Kramer, *The Politics of Memory: Looking for Germany in the New Germany* (New York: Random House, 1996); Brian Ladd, *The Ghosts of Berlin: Confronting German History in the Urban Landscape* (Chicago: University of Chicago Press, 1997); Carolyn Widmer, *The Claims of Memory: Representations of the Holocaust in Contemporary Germany and France* (Ithaca, N.Y.: Cornell University Press, 1999); James Young, *The Texture of Memory: Holocaust Memorials and Meaning* (New Haven: Yale University Press, 1993).

20. German myths of victimization can be dated back at least to the post–World War I period. The literature about Germans as victims is enormous. See Aleida Assmann and Ute Frevert, *Geschichtsvergessenheit, Geschichtsversessenheit* (Stuttgart: Deutsche Verlags-Anstalt, 1999); and Harold Marcuse, *Legacies of Dachau: The Uses and Abuses of a Concentration Camp, 1933–2001* (Cambridge: Cambridge University Press, 2001).

21. The conservative publicist and political scientist Dolf Sternberger coined the phrase "constitutional patriotism" in 1982, and Habermas used the term as part of the Historians' Debate in 1986. Heinrich August Winkler, "Rebuilding of a Nation," *Daedalus* 123 (1994, 107–27). See also Habermas, *The New Conservatism.*

22. Winkler, "Rebuilding," 107.

23. Only recently, however, and in relation to the popular success of the Topography, has perpetrator history begun to examine those variations.

24. Fachkommission, appendix 2, p. 4.

25. In the sections hereafter, I unpack culturally specific ways of representing a violent national past through a close reading of the expert commission reports written in 1989 and 1990, and through my observations and interviews after unification, especially in 1993 and 1994. Translations of reports are my own.

26. David Lowenthal, *The Past Is a Foreign Country* (New York: Cambridge University Press, 1985).

27. Karl Meyer, "Digging Berlin's Chamber of Horrors," *Archaeology* 45, no. 4 (1992): 24–29.

28. Fachkommission, *Abschlussbericht,* 14, 15.

29. Yi-Fu Tuan, *Space and Place: The Perspective of Experience* (Minneapolis: University of Minnesota Press, 1977), and "Landscape's Affective Domain: Raw Emotion to Intellectual Delight," *Landscape Architecture,* March 1978, 132–34. See also Rudy Koshar, *Germany's Transient*

Pasts: Preservation and National Memory in the Twentieth Century (Chapel Hill: University of North Carolina Press, 1998), and *From Monuments to Traces: Artifacts of German Memory, 1870–1990* (Berkeley: University of California Press, 2000).

30. Fachkommission, *Abschlussbericht,* 28.

31. Koshar, *Germany's Transient Pasts.*

32. Lowenthal, *The Past Is a Foreign Country,* 388. See also Ken Foote, *Shadowed Ground: America's Landscapes of Violence and Tragedy* (Austin: University of Texas Press, 1997); John Urry, *The Tourist Gaze: Leisure and Travel in Contemporary Societies* (London: Sage, 1990).

33. "Denkmalschutz für die Gestapozellen auf dem Prinz-Albrecht-Gelände," *Der Tagesspiegel,* November 3, 1998, 14. See also Archäologisches Landesamt Berlin, "Eintragung von Bodendenkmäler," *Amtsblatt für Berlin* 38, no. 52 (October 28, 1988): 1686.

34. Fachkommission, *Abschlussbericht,* 27.

35. Treating the landscape as a cultural artifact to stabilize specific meanings associated with it is a typical approach of preservationists. J. Nicholas Entrikin, *The Betweenness of Place: Towards a Geography of Modernity* (Baltimore: Johns Hopkins University Press, 1991); Joan Hackeling, "Authenticity in Preservation Thought: The Reconstruction of Mission La Purisima Conception" (thesis, Department of Geography, University of California, Los Angeles, 1989).

36. Maurice Halbwachs, *On Collective Memory* (Chicago: University of Chicago Press, 1992); Pierre Nora, *Realms of Memory: Rethinking the French Past,* vol. 1, *Conflicts and Divisions* (New York: Columbia University Press, 1996); Francis Yates, *The Art of Memory* (Chicago: University of Chicago Press, 1966). See also Karen Till, "Places of Memory," in *Companion to Political Geography,* ed. John Agnew, Kathryne Mitchell, and Gerard Toal (Oxford: Blackwell, 2003), 289–301.

37. Fachkommission, *Abschlussbericht,* 41.

38. Topographical surveys developed around the sixteenth century, about the same time that perspective became established as a form of representation in the visual arts. The product of the survey was the map, which is still understood as an objective and truthful representation of reality in Western society. See Trevor Barnes and Derek Gregory, eds., *Readings in Human Geography* (New York: Routledge, 1997); Denis Cosgrove, *Social Formation and Symbolic Landscape* (Totowa, NJ: Barnes and Noble, 1984); James Duncan and David Ley, eds., *Place/Culture/Representation* (New York: Routledge, 1993); Brian Harley, "Maps, Knowledge, and Power," in *The Iconography of Landscape,* ed. Denis Cosgrove and Steven Daniels (Cambridge: Cambridge University Press, 1988), 277–312.

39. Fachkommission, *Abschlussbericht,* 13.

40. Ibid., 60.

41. Ibid., 17. The original text reads: "Kein Ort in Deutschland ist besser geeignet für eine ständige Einrichtung, in der im Austausch von Menschen aus allen Nationen und Religionen, aus allen politischen Lagern und gesellschaftlichen Gruppierungen, nicht zuletzt auch aus allen wissenschaftlichen Disziplinen die Trauerarbeit geleistet wird, die eine Bedingung für eine menschenwürdige Zukunft ist." In this context, *Trauerarbeit* would also mean memory-work, or a working through of a painful past.

42. The visitor center, documentation center, and international youth center, moreover, were also related to the functions of the two other large memorial centers in Berlin, the German Resistance Center and the House at Wannsee-Villa. See note 44.

43. Gerd Nowakowski, "Gestapo-Gelände: Bonn blockiert Neugestaltung," *taz,* Decem-

ber 12, 1992, 31. This strategy was also a way for Berlin officials to absolve themselves of responsibility for the site. Reinhard Rürup criticized the Berlin Senate for handing over the responsibility of the terrain to the federal levels (at the time both FRG and GDR) and for not establishing dates to carry out the expert commission's recommendations. See "Die Spuren bleiben," *Der Tagesspiegel*, June 7, 1991; Sibylle Wirsing, "Wer soll des Ortes Hüter sein?" *Frankfurter Allgemeine Zeitung*, July 2, 1990.

44. Quoted in "Kontroverse um Gestaltung des Prinz-Albrecht Geländes," *Berliner Morgenpost*, June 30, 1990. See also Endlich, *Denkort Gestapogelände*. The Berlin Senate also requested that the proposed Wannsee-Villa memorial center should be a federally sponsored institution. The Wannsee-Villa is where the formal plans for the Final Solution were drafted. The establishment of a memorial center devoted to the history of the site and the history of the persecution of Jews was discussed at the same time that plans for the Topography of Terror were being considered. Many of the citizen initiatives and individuals involved in the establishment of the Topography of Terror were also quite active in the establishment of the Wannsee-Villa memorial center, which officially opened in 1992.

45. Public lecture delivered at opening of traveling Topography of Terror exhibit, Chicago, 1994. Manuscript made available to me courtesy of author.

46. *Beruf Neonazi,* documentary film written by Günter H. Jekubzik; Regie Winfried Bonengel, 83 minutes (Germany, 1993).

47. Jonathan Webber, *The Future of Auschwitz: Some Personal Reflections* (Oxford: Centre for Postgraduate Hebrew Studies, 1992); Robert Jan van Pelt and Deborah Dwork, *Auschwitz: 1270 to the Present* (New Haven: Yale University Press, 1996).

48. Gabriele Kreutzner, "On Doing Cultural Studies in West Germany," *Cultural Studies* 3 (1989): 240–49.

49. Ibid., 245, 246.

50. This postwar generation of filmmakers represented the first coherent effort to come to terms with what fascism meant at the private level. They made films that were banned following the war, such as producing politicized versions of traditional Heimat films in which they replaced bucolic, pastoral landscape images with settings of violence and chaos. See Thomas Elsaesser, *New German Cinema: A History* (New Brunswick, NJ: Rutgers University Press, 1989); James Franklin, *New German Cinema: From Oberhausen to Hamburg* (Boston: Twayne, 1983); Anton Kaes, *From Hitler to Heimat: The Return of History as Film* (Cambridge: Harvard University Press, 1989).

51. Quoted in Morley and Robins, "No Place like Heimat: Images of Homeland in European Culture," *New Formations* 12 (1990): 8. According to Reitz, "The most serious act of expropriation occurs when people are deprived of their history. With *Holocaust,* the Americans have taken away our history" (quoted in Elsaesser, *New German Cinema,* 272; see also Eric Santner, *Stranded Objects: Mourning, Memory, and Film in Postwar Germany* [Ithaca, NY: Cornell University Press, 1990], 75). In response to *Holocaust,* Reitz produced and directed his own film, *Heimat,* which depicted the history of one family in a fictional village in southern Germany from World War I to the postwar period. Ironically he was criticized for historical revisionism and for creating a sentimental story that ignored the Holocaust. According to Ian Burums, "It's difficult not to marvel at the blatant tokenism with which the film handles the more problematic aspects of German history" ("From Hirohito to Heimat," *New York Review of Books,* October 26, 1989, 43; see also M. Hansen, "Dossier on *Heimat,*" *New German Critique* [Fall

1985]: 3–24). Despite Reitz's outspoken criticism of commercialism, his film was turned into a successful television series that resulted in the creation of his own film production firm and two more *Heimat* television miniseries.

52. Hone, quoted in Morley and Robins, "No Place like Heimat," 8.

53. Barry Gewen, "Holocaust Documentaries: Too Much of a Bad Thing?" *New York Times,* June 15, 2003, sec. 2, p. 1; Hilene Flanzbaum, ed., *The Americanization of the Holocaust* (Baltimore: Johns Hopkins University Press, 1999); Annette Insdorf, *Indelible Shadows: Film and the Holocaust,* 3rd ed. (New York: Cambridge University Press, 2003); Michael Kammen, *The Mystic Chords of Memory: The Transformation of Tradition in American Culture* (New York: Vintage Books, 1991). Hilene Flanzbaum argues that the dominance of American-produced Holocaust productions was only possible once a younger generation of Jews became an accepted part of mainstream America. Their representations of the Holocaust "bear the imprint of a multicultural but predominantly Gentile America," including such malleable national myths as the Protestant work ethic, the American Dream (of working hard, suffering, yet persevering and "making it"), and good conquering evil. See *Americanization of the Holocaust.*

54. Jack Kugelmass, "The Rites of the Tribe: American Jewish Tourism in Poland," in *Museums and Communities: The Politics of Public Culture,* ed. Ivan Karp, Christine Mullen, and Steven Lavine (Washington, DC: Smithsonian Institution Press, 1992), 382–427.

55. Mirianne Hirsch, *Family Frames.* For a discussion of the limited reproductions of images of concentration and death camps in Germany, see Cornelia Brink, *Ikonen der Vernichtung: Öffentlicher Gebrauch von Fotografien aus nationalsozialistischen Konzentrationslagern nach 1945* (Berlin: Akademie Verlag, 1998).

56. Geoffrey Hartman, *The Longest Shadow: In the Aftermath of the Holocaust* (Bloomington: Indiana University Press, 1996); Susan Sontag, *On Photography* (New York: Anchor Doubleday, 1989), 20–21; Barbie Zelizer, *Remembering to Forget: Holocaust Memory through the Camera's Lens* (Chicago: University of Chicago Press, 1998). See Mirianne Hirsch's discussion of these tensions in "Surviving Images: Holocaust Photographs and the Work of Postmemory," *Yale Journal of Criticism* 14, no. 1 (2001): 5–37.

57. Numerous writers have addressed the problems of using "Holocaust," "genocide," "Shoah," and other words to represent particular historical processes, events, pasts, and traumas. See Giorgio Agamben, *Remnants of Auschwitz: The Witness and the Archive* (New York: Zone Books, 1999); Berel Lang, *Act and Idea in the Nazi Genocide* (Chicago: University of Chicago Press, 1990); Hayden White, "Historical Emplotment and the Problem of Truth," in *Probing the Limits of Representation: Nazism and the "Final Solution,"* ed. Saul Friedländer (Cambridge: Harvard University Press, 1992); and Zelizer, *Remembering to Forget.*

58. Leslie Morris, "The Sound of Memory," in "Sites of Memory," ed. Leslie Morris, special issue, *German Quarterly* 74, no. 4 (2001): 371. Morris discusses sound and sites of artistic and linguistic indeterminacy, rather than join "the repeated compulsive chorus of the trope of unspeakability (and incommensurability or incomprehensibility of the Holocaust."

59. I would like to thank Elizabeth Domansky for including this point in her comments as a discussant on an earlier version of this argument I presented at the German Studies Association conference in Washington, DC, April 1997.

60. David Crew, "Alltagesgeschichte: A New Social History 'from Below'?" *Central European History* 22 (1989): 394–407.

61. The critique of the history of everyday life was also part of the Historians' Debate. Some practitioners of *Alltagsgeschichte* questioned the appropriation of this method by conservatives

to write revisionist histories, asking if this historical approach was intrinsically subjective in nature. This internal critique, along with the larger media debates about *Heimat,* meant that everyday history has not been able to gain recognition by more established social structuralist historians in the Federal Republic. To a certain degree, this is surprising, since *Alltagsgeschichte* was ultimately meant to complement, not replace, structuralist histories. See Mary Nolan, "The Historkerstreit and Social History," in *Reworking the Past: Hitler, the Holocaust, and the Historians' Debate,* ed. Peter Baldwin (Boston: Beacon Press, 1990), 224–28.

62. Donna Haraway, *Simians, Cyborgs, and Women: The Reinvention of Nature* (New York: Routledge, 1991), esp. 183–201. The "normalizing gaze" associated with vision as a system of knowledge has been described by Foucault as a kind of surveillance that makes it possible to classify, judge, and punish individuals.

63. Databases and other resources in the new research center will provide additional information about these sources.

64. Personal conversation, August 1993, Auschwitz Memorial Center, Poland. See also Andrea Liss, *Trespassing through Shadows: Memory, Photography, and the Holocaust* (Minneapolis: University of Minnesota Press, 1998).

65. After Joseph Dorman, documentary filmmaker, cited in Gewen, "Holocaust Documentaries." See also Christopher Browning, *Ordinary Men: Reserve Police Battalion 101 and the Final Solution in Poland* (New York: Harper Collins, 1992); Insdorf, *Indelible Shadows*; Samantha Power, *A Problem from Hell: America and the Age of Genocide* (New York: Basic Books, 2002).

66. See http://212.68.78.12/Gedenkstaettenforum/index.htm

67. See International Committee of Memorial Museum Centers for the Remembrance of Victims of Public Crimes (ICMEMO) Web page, http://www.xs4all.nl/~kmlink/icmemo.htm. Another network established around the same time, based in New York, is the International Coalition of Historic Site Museums Web page, http://www.sitesofconscience.org/map.html.

68. "Naumann will Shoah-Stiftung als Holocaust-Mahnmal," *Der Tagesspiegel,* October 22, 1998; "Das hat nichts mehr mit einem Mahnmal zu tun," *Der Tagesspiegel,* December 12, 1998; "Berlin Rethinks Memorial Plan: Holocaust Center Proposed instead of Monumental Park," *Washington Post Foreign Service,* December 15, 1998; see also "Holocaust-Museum in Berlin: Eine 'verwirrende Initiative,'" *Berliner Morgenpost,* June 25, 1996.

69. Hugh Eakin "Schröder's Kulturkampf," *The Nation,* November 11, 2002, 34.

70. Jan-Hologer Kirsch, "Vom 'Gestapogelaende' zur 'Topographie des Terrors': Rückblick und Positionsbestimmung," report about May 21, 2003, conference in Berlin, working paper posted on H-Soz-u-Kult, June 1, 2003, http://hsozkult.geschichte.hu-berlin.de/tagungsberichte/id=225.

71. Some of my consultants, in response to my criticisms, expressed concerns about "dumbing down" the historical content of the exhibition or encouraging a mixing of "facts" with personal memories. I see a critical interpretation not as a replacement of the exhibition but rather as part of the ongoing process of place making. The Topography should provide space for critical interpretation of its form of representing the past (as well as other approaches in Germany) at the new center. For international audiences, such a dialogue would be of interest and may result in a critical self-reflection on dominant cultural forms of representing the past in the visitor's own society and country.

72. See Peter Schneider, "The Sins of the Grandfathers: How German Teen-Agers Confront the Holocaust and How They Don't," *New York Times Magazine,* December 3, 1995, 74–80; Marcuse, *Legacies of Dachau.*

73. While radical right and white supremacist movements are notable elsewhere, and often organized in the United States, the "shock effect" that Holocaust denial has politically on understandings of the nation-state are different in Germany given its National Socialist past and because existing laws prevent certain icons, expressions, and parties from being expressed in the public sphere.

A Neighborhood

1. For more information about the history of this neighborhood and of the memorial competition, see Renata Stih and Frieder Schnock, *Orte des Erinnerns: Ausgrenzung und Entrechtung, Vertreibung, Deportation und Ermordung von Berliner Juden in den Jahren 1933 bis 1945* [Places of Remembrance: Isolation and Deprivation of Rights, Explusion, Deportation, and Murder of Berlin Jews in the Years 1933 to 1945] *Denkmal/Memorial in Berlin-Schöneberg*, 1993 (Berlin: Haude and Spenersche Verlagsbuchhandlung, 2002); Carolyn Widmer, *The Claims of Memory: Representations of the Holocaust in Contemporary Germany and France* (Ithaca, NY: Cornell University Press, 1999), 103–15.

2. Joseph Walk, ed., *Das Sonderrecht für die Juden im NS-Staat: Eine Sammlung der gesetzlichen Maßnahmen und Richtlinien: Inhalt und Bedeutung* (1889; Heidelberg: Uni-Taschenbücher 1996).

5. Aestheticizing the Rupture

1. Quoted in Jane Kramer, *The Politics of Memory: Looking for Germany in the New Germany* (New York: Random House, 1996), 98.

2. The literature on Holocaust representation and iconography is enormous. See, for example, Geoffrey Hartman, ed., *Holocaust Remembrance: The Shapes of Memory* (Cambridge: Blackwell, 1993); Berel Lang, *Holocaust Representation: Art within the Limits of History and Ethics* (Baltimore: Johns Hopkins University Press, 2000); and references in this volume, chap. 4, n. 57.

3. See Daniel Levy and Natan Sznaider, *Erinnerung im globalen Zeitalter: Der Holocaust* (Frankfurt: Suhrkamp, 2001).

4. Lea Rosh, *"Die Juden, das sind doch die anderen": Der Streit um ein deutsches Denkmal* (Berlin: Philo, 1999), 15–19.

5. The Förderkreis zur Errichtung eines Mahnmals für die Ermordeten Juden Europas is difficult to translate in English. It literally means the Supporting or Sponsor Circle for the Erection of a Memorial for the Murdered Jews of Europe. In this chapter I use the abbreviated form "Memorial Association." For information about the history and goals of the Memorial Assocation, see Bürgerinitiative Perspektive Berlin, ed., *Ein Denkmal für die ermordeten Juden Europas: Dokumentation, 1988–1999* (Berlin, March 1995).

6. Critics described Rosh using extreme terms, describing her as a manipulative philo-Semite with "totalitarian charm." In commenting on the fact that Rosh adopted the name Lea (to replace her given name Annette), for example, one consultant stated that she took on a Jewish identity, a "sick way of not dealing with one's Germanness, [reflecting] a desire to identify with the victims" (interview, 1998). Consultants mentioned that the debates would have been more productive had Rosh demanded less power in the process of establishing the memorial.

7. The others were the directors of the German Historical Museum (Berlin), Christoph Stölzl, and the Museum of Contemporary Art (Bonn), Dieter Ronte; a preeminent German

twentieth-century art historian, Werner Hoffmann; and a widely respected and experienced Berlin postwar architecture critic, Josef Paul Kleihues.

8. Cited from James Young, *At Memory's Edge: After-images of the Holocaust in Contemporary Art and Architecture* (New Haven: Yale University Press, 2000), 195–96. Ethnographic texts are from a 2001 interview.

9. James Young, *The Texture of Memory* (New Haven: Yale University Press, 1993).

10. James Young, "Gegen das Denkmal, für Erinnerung," in *Der Wettbewerb für das Denkmal für die ermordeten Juden Europas: Eine Streitschrift,* ed. Neue Gesellschaft für bildende Kunst (Berlin: Verlag der Kunst, NGbK, 1995), 174–78.

11. When I asked Young how he changed as a result of this process, he noted that an academic voice as "public intellectual" is an important aspect of an open discussion in German society. In contrast, he noted that "we don't have that anymore in the U.S.; we only speak to each other." We spoke before the (unusual) public discussions in New York about the public competition for the World Trade Center urban redevelopment project (won by Daniel Libeskind) and related September 11 public memorial competition. Young would become one of the expert judges for the New York memorial competition.

12. The memorial is located between Ebertstrasse, Wilhelmstrasse, and Berhrenstrasse. The information in the following paragraphs comes from publications and discussions with the Foundation Memorial to the Murdered Jews of Europe, Stiftung Denkmal für die ermordeten Juden Europas, an independent public organization established in April 2000 to realize the construction, planning, and running of the memorial. See Sibylle Quack, ed., *Auf dem Weg zur Realisierung* (Stuttgart and München: Deutsche Verlag Anstalt, 2002); "The Memorial to the Murdered Jews of Europe," unpaginated color brochure (October, 2000), available from Foundation Memorial, Stresemannstrasse 90, 10963 Berlin, Germany; Stiftung Denkmal, http://www.holocaust-mahnmal.de/.

13. Both quotes in Stiftung Denkmal, memorial brochure.

14. Stiftung Denkmal, Web page.

15. James Young, *At Memory's Edge,* 211.

16. German Bundestag, "Resolution concerning the Memorial to the Murdered Jews of Europe," June 25, 1999, cited in Stiftung Denkmal, memorial brochure.

17. A number of politicians and public figures played important roles in these debates. Berlin's former CDU mayor Eberhard Diepgen opposed the memorial, whereas former chancellor Helmut Kohl (CDU) supported it. Kohl had more power than Diepgen to intervene and did so twice in the artistic competitions. While running for office, Gerhard Schröder opposed the memorial, causing one 1998 *Die Zeit* article to state that Schröder broke with the SPD tradition of placing the commemoration of murdered Jews at the center of their political agenda ("Traditionsbruch," August 13, 1998). Ignatz Bubis, at the time chair of the Council of Jews in Germany, was a staunch defender of the memorial but was at times critical of different artistic proposals. Not as powerful was Romani Rose, the chair of the Council of Sinti and Roma, who opposed a memorial because it would be dedicated to the memory of only Jews. Two former East Germans were also influential; in the early 1990s, Bruno Flierl argued that the memorial should be located near the Reichstag, and since 1998, SPD Wolfgang Thierse, German parliamentary president, has been supportive of the project.

18. Instead of voting on the four finalists, the Parliament considered proposals by Eisenman and another proposal that emerged through the public discussions, a piece by the German

theologian Richard Schroder that would simply have a sign saying "Thou Shalt Not Kill" in multiple languages in the empty field.

19. "Holocaust-Denkmal," *Tagesspiegel*, May 8, 1994. More people may have submitted proposals had there been no requirement to include a model of the concept. Such a requirement is typical for architecture, but not art, competitions.

20. Stefanie Endlich, interviews, 1997 and 1998; City of Berlin Senate for Cultural Affairs officials, focus group interview, 2000; Katharina von Ankum, "Ein Monument-beschädigt, ehe es steht," *Süddeutsche Zeitung*, July 7, 1995; Frank Böttcher, "Die Erinnerungsströme auf dem Todesstreifen," *Tagesspiegel*, June 2, 1994. As a result of the debates, the jury suggested establishing a memorial for Sinti and Roma between the Reichstag and Brandenburg Gate (which is now being realized). The Memorial Association had a lot of authority in this process, even demanding the power of veto for the competition (usually given only to state or federal authorities). Stefanie Endlich, who was named a juror by the city of Berlin because of her fifteen years of experience on such competitions, was asked to step down by Lea Rosh because of Endlich's allegedly critical views about memorials.

21. Berlin Senatsverwaltung für Bau- und Wohnungswesen, Abteilung Städtebau und Architektur (Berlin Senate Department of Building and Housing), *Art Competition: Memorial to the Murdered Jews of Europe, Invitation to Compete,* trans. Chris Charlesworth (Berlin, April 1994).

22. According to one of the expert jurors, Stefanie Endlich, this was a problem. "A good jury does not give away the decision. A good jury works until the project is realized; they accompany the process and help out when conflicts come up. But in this case the majority decided that the jury should leave the rest of the procedure to the sponsors. . . . It is a very complicated story" (interview, 1998).

23. A space would be saved for the remaining 1.5 million individuals whose names were unknown, mostly from the Soviet Union.

24. See Klaus Hartung, "Gedenken—aber wie?" *Die Zeit,* March 24, 1995, 24; Kramer, *The Politics of Memory,* 286–87; Reinhart Kosseleck, "Vier Minuten für die Ewigkeit," *Frankfurter Allgemeine Zeitung,* January 9, 1997; Jens Jessen, "Die Bewältungsprofis," *Frankfurter Allgemeine Zeitung,* March 20, 1995; see also Carolyn Widmer, *The Claims of Memory: Representations of the Holocaust in Contemporary Germany and France* (Ithaca, NY: Cornell University Press, 1999), 233; and Young, *At Memory's Edge.*

25. "Grabplatte über Deutschland," *Tagesspiegel,* July 9, 1995; "Eine platte Platte," *Der Spiegel,* July 10, 1995; "Holocaust-Mahnmal-ein 'Unsinnsprojekt,'" *taz,* July 11, 1995. For later criticisms see "Bubis erneuert Kritik an Entwurf zum Holocaust-Denkmal," *Tagesspiegel,* July 7, 1995; "Kritik an Mahnmal wächst," *Frankfurter Rundschau,* July 7, 1995; "Zuflucht zu sauberen Symbolen," *Märkische Allgemeine,* June 30, 1995. One of my consultants mentioned that this was the only good decision Kohl made with respect to the politics of memory during his time as chancellor (interview, 2000).

26. "Naumann will Shoah-Stiftung als Holocaust-Mahnmal," *Tagesspiegel,* October 22, 1998; "Das hat nichts mehr mit einem Mahnmal zu tun," *Tagesspiegel,* December 12, 1998; "Berlin Rethinks Memorial Plan: Holocaust Center Proposed instead of Monumental Park," *Washington Post Foreign Service,* December 15, 1998; "Ein Museum kann auch Mahnmal sein" *Tagesspiegel,* December 20, 1998; "Schröder Backs Design for a Vast Berlin Holocaust Memorial," *New York Times,* January 18, 1999. For criticisms of Naumann's proposal, see "Bubis hält nichts von der Alternative Museum," *Frankfurter Rundschau,* December 16, 1998; "Für die Idee

vom Holocaust-Museum erntet Naumann massive Kritik," *Frankfurter Rundschau,* December 15, 1998.

27. Part of the original plot of land is set off by trees (as a transition to the Tiergarten to the west). Space is also provided for tourism buses (to the south) and to the American Embassy for a security buffer (to the north).

28. The information in this section stems largely from Bürgerinitiative Perspektive Berlin, *Ein Denkmal*; Rosh, *Die Juden, das sind doch die anderen*; conversations and informal interviews with Jochen Schulze-Rohr (1995, 1998); Berlin Senate, *Memorial Competition Guidelines* (1994, 1995); and numerous German newspaper articles published between 1998 and 2002.

29. For the association's early history, see Bürgerinitiative Perspektive Berlin, *Ein Denkmal,* 103, 105.

30. Lea Rosh, in Bürgerinitiative Perspektive Berlin, *Ein Denkmal,* 4.

31. Joachim Braun, "The Association," in Berlin Senatsverwaltung, *Art Competition,* 65.

32. See Bürgerinitiative Perspektive Berlin, *Ein Denkmal,* 17–35. In this collection, the group also documented opposition to the proposal by the Active Museum and the Council of Sinti and Roma. Another section documents the hate mail the group received, some from radical right organizations and some from individuals. See pp. 44–46, 76–102.

33. Braun, "The Association"; "Ein Denkmal," *Die Welt,* May 6, 1994. Part of the reason for obtaining donations and corporate sponsors was that, in 1994 and 1995, the association was responsible for raising roughly half of the projected DM 15 million (the other half would come from Berlin and the federal government). When in 1998 they had only collected roughly DM 300,000, it soon became clear that the federal government would have to fund most of the project. One association member mentioned that the reparations payments made by large companies meant that the association would face difficulties gaining corporate sponsors.

34. Berlin Senatsverwaltung, *Art Competition,* 61, 62, 63 (English translation in guidelines).

35. See "Ein Denkmal für die ermordeten Juden Europas," *Die Welt,* May 6, 1994. The plot of land for the memorial was donated by the federal government and legally administered by the Berlin Building Authority (Bauverwaltung) which is linked to the Division for Public Art in Urban Spaces (Referat Kunst im Stadtraum). Hence a public competition was necessary. As described later, the Memorial Association had already commissioned an artistic concept in 1991 that influenced the outcome of the first public competition.

36. One reason Kohl supported the project was the discussions he had with Ignatz Bubis, chair of the Central Council of German Jews. Bubis felt it was inappropriate to commemorate Jews at the Central Memorial to Victims of War and Tyranny, locally known as the Neue Wache, a controversial national memorial established largely through the efforts of the Kohl administration to commemorate *all* victims of militarism, war, and tyranny. In addition to the moral problems of mourning for Holocaust victims and fallen German soldiers at the same place of memory, the central sculptural form was that of a Christian Pietà.

37. Berlin Senatsverwaltung, *Art Competition,* 57; see also 34–36.

38. See Rosh, in Berlin Senatsverwaltung, *Art Competition,* 61.

39. Bürgerinitiative Perspektive Berlin, *Ein Denkmal,* 62. See Rosh, *Die Juden, das sind doch die anderen.*

40. For an overview of the debate between intentionalists and functionalists during the West German Historians' Debate in the 1980s, see Charles Maier, *The Unmasterable Past: History, Holocaust, and German National Identity* (Cambridge: Harvard University Press, 1988).

41. See various articles in Bürgerinitiative Perspektive Berlin, *Ein Denkmal*; Rosh, *Die Juden, das sind doch die anderen.*

42. Berlin Senatsverwaltung, *Art Competition,* 57.

43. Ibid., 7.

44. Ibid.

45. Rosh, in Berlin Senatsverwaltung, *Art Competition,* 62–63.

46. Braun, "The Association." See also Harald Szeemann, "Ein Denkmal für die ermordeten Juden Europas," in Förderkreis zur Errichtung eines Denkmals für die ermordeten Juden Europas, *Errichtung eines Denkmals in Berlin für die ermordeten Juden Europas: Ausschreibung für die Einholung von Gestalutungsvorschlägen: Entwurf, April 1992* (Berlin), unpublished manuscript, 21 pp., Szeemann's contribution on pp. 12–18, written in April 1991; Harald Szeemann, "Description of the Concept," in Berlin Senatsverwaltung, *Art Competition,* 67; Bürgerinitiative Perspektive Berlin, *Ein Denkmal,* 123–30.

47. Berlin Senatsverwaltung, *Art Competition* (English and German versions), 67.

48. Ibid., German version, 67.

49. Ibid., English version, 67.

50. Ibid.

51. Quoted in Förderkreis zur Errichtung eines Denkmals für die ermordeten Juden Europas, *Errichtung eines Denkmals.*

52. Aleida Assmann and Ute Frevert, *Geschichtsvergessenheit, Geschichtsversessenheit* (Stuttgart: Deutsche Verlags-Anstalt, 1999).

53. Karl Jaspers, *The Question of German Guilt,* trans. E. B. Ashton (New York: Capricorn Books, 1961).

54. For support of a functionalist approach see, Martin Broszat, "A Plea for the Historicization of National Socialism," in *Reworking the Past,* ed. Peter Baldwin (Boston: Beacon Press, 1990), 77–87.

55. Jan-Holger Kirsch, "Trauer und historische Erinnerung in der Berliner Republik: Überlegungen aus Anlaß der Mahnmalsdebatte," in *Trauer und Geschichte,* ed. Burkhard Liebsch and Jörn Rüsen (Köln, Weimar, and Vienna: Böhlau Verlag, 2001), 339–74.

56. Berlin Senatsverwaltung, "Protokoll des Einführungskolloquiums am 11.05.1994," in *Art Competition,* 20–27.

57. Widmer, *Claims of Memory.* See also Henryk Broder, "Deutschmeister des Trauens," *Der Spiegel* 16 (1995), 222.

58. See, for example, Rainer Höynck, "Man konnte dagegen sein . . . ," in *Der Wettbewerb,* ed. Neue Gesellschaft für bildende Kunst (Berlin: NGBK, n.d.), 72–74; Stephen Kinzer, "Berlin Gives Unusual Idea for a Holocaust Memorial," *New York Times,* January 28, 1996, 4.

59. See also Götz Aly, "Hitlers zufriedene Räuber," *Die Zeit,* August 5, 2003, n.p.

60. Neue Gesellschaft für Bildende Kunst, Renata Stih, Frieder Schnock, Leonie Baumann, Eberthard Elfert, and Bernd Nicolai, *Bus Stop: Fahrplan* (Berlin: Oktoberdruck, 1995), 7.

61. Peter Eisenman and Richard Serra, "Interview of Richard Serra with Peter Eisenman," *Skyline: The Architecure and Design Review* (New York) (April 1983); reprinted in *Richard Serra: Schriften; Interviews, 1970–1989* (Bern: Bendeli, 1990), 170–81.

62. Suzanne Lacy, "Cultural Pilgrimages and Metaphoric Journeys," in *Mapping the Terrain: New Genre Public Art,* ed. Suzanne Lacy (Seattle, WA: Bay Press, 1995), 19–47.

63. Quoted in Lacy, "Cultural Pilgrimages," 24.

64. Jeff Kelley, "Common Work," in *Mapping the Terrain: New Genre Public Art,* ed. Suzanne Lacy (Seattle, WA: Bay Press, 1995), 141.

65. Neue Gesellschaft für bildende Kunst, et al., *Bus Stop,* 6.

66. See also Stefanie Endlich and Thomas Lutz, eds., *Gedenken und lernen an historischen Orten: Ein Wegweiser zu Gedenkstätten für die Opfer des Nationalsozialismus in Berlin,* 2nd ed. (Berlin: Landeszentrale für politische Bildungsarbeit, 1998); Young, *At Memory's Edge.*

67. Stefanie Endlich, "Less Is More: Zur Diskussion um das Denkmal für die ermordeten Juden Europas," *Kunststadt-Stadtkunst* 42 (Summer 1997).

68. "Was ist gültig?" *Berliner Zeitung,* August 24, 1998.

69. "Die Debatte kann nicht ewig weitergehen," *Der Tagesspiegel,* September 9, 1998; James Young, personal interview, 2001; Young, *At Memory's Edge.*

70. Stefanie Endlich, however, argues that the concept for the information center has become more like a mini-Holocaust museum than a portal, a serious criticism pointing to the still-tentative status of the completion of the Topography of Terror International Center. See Stefanie Endlich, "Die Stele als Design-Prinzip: 7. Beitragsfolge zum Denkmal für die ermordeten Juden Europas," *stadtkunst* 48 (Summer 2001): 11; Stefanie Endlich, "'Face to Face with History?': 8. Beitragsfolge zum Denkmal für die ermordeten Juden Europas," *stadtkunst* 49 (Spring 2002): 19.

71. Jürgen Habermas, "Der Zeigefinger: Die Deutschen und ihr Denkmal," *Die Zeit,* March 31, 1999.

72. Heidegger drew from Nietzsche's typology of monumental, antiquarian, and critical historiography to argue that the current state of being would make one view of the future more meaningful than others. See Pamela Shurmer-Smith and Kevin Hannam, *Worlds of Desire, Realms of Power* (London: Edward Arnold, 1994), chap. 3.

6. Memory in the New Berlin

1. Guide pen name: sunnydlite, "Berlin: Old City, Young Energy," Type of Trip: I Often Visit This Place, Date Created: 6/10/02; http://www.igougo.com/planning/journal .asp?JournalID=10740.

2. See Barbara Kirschenblatt-Gimblett, *Destination Culture: Tourism, Museums, and Heritage* (Berkeley and Los Angeles: University of California Press, 1998).

3. Janet Ward, *Weimar Surfaces: Urban Visual Culture in 1920s Germany* (Berkeley and Los Angeles: University of California Press, 2001), 240. See also Alex Vasudevan's brilliant discussion of postwar scholarly performances of Weimar theatricality, "Metropolitan Theatrics: Performing the Modern in Weimar Berlin" (Ph.D. diss., Department of Geography, University of British Columbia, Vancouver, 2005).

4. Steve Pile, "Spectral Cities: Where the Repressed Returns and Other Short Stories," in *Habitus: A Sense of Place,* ed. Jean Hillier and Emma Rooksby (Aldershot: Ashgate, 2002), 226–27.

5. Gundolf Graml, "Austrian National Identity: A Utopia of the Tourist Industry?" (PhD diss., Department of German: University of Minnesota, 2004). See also Kirschenblatt-Gimblett, *Destination Culture*; Vincent del Casino and Stephen Hannah, eds., *Mapping Tourism* (Minneapolis: University of Minnesota Press, 2003).

6. The Brandenburg Concentration Camp Memorial Museums Foundation oversees the work for Buchenwald, Ravensbrück, and Sachsenhausen memorial museums, all of which are located in the state of Brandenburg in the former GDR.

7. In 2002 the Jewish Museum had 650,000 guests.

8. In addition to visitor books, there are numerous Web page descriptions. See, for example, http://www.tripadvisor.com/Attraction_Review-g187323-d190535-Reviews-Topography_of_Terror-Berlin.html; http://www.igougo.com/home.html.

9. For general information about the Jewish Museum, see http://www.jmberlin.de/.

10. These debates were well covered in the German national press. See "Vom Wahnmal zum Mahnmal," *Der Spiegel* 35 (1998): 170–78; and "Die Vergangenheit holt uns noch mal ein," *Die Welt,* November 23, 1999, 3. For a summary in German, see Jan-Holger Kirsch, "'Die Zukunft hat eine lange Vergangenheit': Gedenkdebatten um den Nationalsozialismus im ersten Jahrzehnt der Berliner Republik," in *Kulturelle Identität,* ed. Steffen Bruendell and Nicole Grochowina (Berlin, 2000), 136–62; in English, see Bill Niven, *Facing the Nazi Past: United Germany and the Legacy of the Third Reich* (New York, 2002). On the Wehrmacht exhibit and the Goldhagen debate, see Hamburg Institute for Social Research, ed., *The German Army and Genocide: Crimes against War Prisoners, Jews, and Other Civilians, 1939–1945,* trans. Scott Abbot (New York: New Press, 1999); Daniel Goldhagen, *Hitler's Willing Executioners: Ordinary Germans and the Holocaust* (New York: Alfred Knopf, 1996); Norman Finkelstein and Ruth Bettina Birn, *A Nation on Trial: The Goldhagen Thesis and Historical Truth* (New York: Henry Holt, 1998); Johannes Heil and Rainer Erb, eds., *Geschichtswissenschaft und Öffentlichkeit: Der Streit um Daniel J. Goldhagen* (Frankfurt a.M, 1998). About restitutions, see Elazar Barkan, *The Guilt of Nations: Restitution and Negotiating Historical Injustices* (New York: W. W. Norton, 2000); Jeffrey Herf, *Divided Memory: The Nazi Past in the Two Germanys* (Cambridge: Harvard University Press, 1997).

11. As I described in chapter 4, the idea for a memory district was also a response both to suggestions by Chancellor Schröder's cultural minister Michael Naumann to establish a Holocaust museum, which threatened the future existence of the Topography, and to the increased projected costs of the Zumthor building.

12. Topography of Terror Foundation Annual Report, April 1999–March 2001, 6.

13. Carolyn Widmer, *The Claims of Memory: Representations of the Holocaust in Contemporary Germany and France* (Ithaca, NY: Cornell University Press, 1999), 141.

14. Rosh, in Bürgerinitiative Perspektive Berlin, *Ein Denkmal für die ermordeten Juden Europas: Dokumentation, 1988–1999* (Berlin, March 1995), 6.

15. Marita Sturken makes a similar point when scholars, war veterans, and others describe the Vietnam War Memorial in Washington, DC, as a "healing wound." See her *Tangled Memories: The Vietnam War, the AIDS Epidemic, and the Politics of Remembering* (Berkeley: University of California Press, 1997), 72–74.

16. Barkan, *The Guilt of Nations,* xvii–xviii.

17. Daniel Levy and Natan Sznaider, *Erinnerung im globalen Zeitalter: Der Holocaust* (Frankfurt: Suhrkamp, 2001).

18. For an overview of restitutions for historical injustices around the world (including Germany), see Barkan, *Guilt of Nations.* For a discussion of reparations in postwar Germany, see Herf, *Divided Memory.*

19. Between DM 5,000 and 15,000 per survivor was paid, mostly to families in Russia, the Ukraine, Poland, and the Czech Republic, in exchange for legal closure on future compensation claims.

20. Avery Gordon, *Ghostly Matters: Haunting and the Sociological Imagination* (Minneapolis: University of Minnesota Press, 1997), 16.

21. For a discussion of the network of memorial museums in Germany, see Reinhard Rürup, ed., *Netzwerk der Erinnerung: 10 Jahre Gedenkstättenreferat der Stiftung Topographie des Terrors* (Berlin: Stiftung Topograhie des Terrors, 2003).

22. "Holocaust-Mahnmal-ein 'Unsinnsprojekt,'" *taz*, July 11, 1995.

23. "Sorge um Tendenzen zur Zentralisierung des Gedenkens," *Märkische Allgemeine Zeitung*, April 13–14, 1997.

24. Stefanie Endlich, ed., *Brandenburgische Gedenkstätten für die Verfolgten des NS-Regimes: Perspektive, Kontroversen und internationale Vergleiche*, "Beiträge des internationale Gedenkstätten-Colloquiums in Potsdam am 8. und 9. März 1992" and "Empfehlungen der Expertenkommission zur Neukonzeption der brandenburgischen Gedenkstätten vom Januar 1992" (Oranienburg: Ministerium für Wissenschaft, Forschung und Kultur des Landes Brandenburg and Edition Hentrich, 1992); Günter Morsch, "Concentration Camp Memorials in Eastern Germany since 1989," in *Remembering for the Future: The Holocaust in an Age of Genocides*, ed. John Roth and Elisabeth Maxine (Basingstoke: Palgrave, 2001), 367–82; Günter Morsch, ed., *Von der Erinnerung zum Monument: Die Entstehungsgeschichte der Nationalen Mahn- und Gedenkstätte Sachsenhausen*, Schriftenreihe der Brandenburgische Gedenkstätten, Band 8 (Oranienburg: Stiftung Brandenburgische Gedenkstätten and Edition Hentrich, 1996); Christine Schoefer, "The Politics of Commemoration: Concentration Camp Memorial Sites in the Former GDR," European Society and Culture Research Group, Working Paper 3.9 (Center for German and European Studies: University of California–Berkeley, May 1993).

25. When Morsch explained this funding situation to me, he emphasized that other cultural institutions, such as the German Historical Museum, had an *annual* budget of DM 25 million and that local *Heimat* museums had higher budgets than did Sachsenhausen.

26. Sachsenhausen's significance in creating new postunification cultures of German memory is one topic of my future research. See also Benjamin Forest, Juliet Johnson, and Karen Till, "Post-totalitarian National Identity: Public Memory in Germany and Russia," *Social and Cultural Geography* 5, no. 3 (2004): 357–80.

27. Mark Wigley explores the term "haunted house" in *The Architecture of Deconstruction: Derrida's Haunt* (Cambridge: MIT Press, 1993).

28. Based on personal interviews with numerous consultants, the term "aura" was explicitly used in association with the category of "the authentic." See Walter Benjamin, "The Work of Art in the Age of Mechanical Reproduction," in *Illuminations* (New York: Schocken, 1969).

29. Morsch has tried to open out the category of "authentic" to include the multiple layered pasts of concentration camp memorials (including their National Socialist and Cold War periods) but has been met with harsh criticisms by other historians.

30. On testimony, see Giorgio Agamben, *Remnants of Auschwitz: The Witness and the Archive*, trans. Daniel Heller-Roazen (New York: Zone Books, 1999).

31. Cathy Caruth, *Unclaimed Experience: Trauma, Narrative, and History* (Baltimore: Johns Hopkins University Press, 1996), 4. See also Mieke Bal, Jonathan Crewe, and Leo Spitzer, eds., *Acts of Memory: Cultural Recall in the Present* (Hanover, NH: University Press of New England, 1999).

32. Quoted in Michael Perlman, *Imaginal Memory and the Place of Hiroshima* (Albany: State University of New York Press, 1988), 19. See Robert Jay Lifton, *Death in Life: Survivors of Hiroshima* (New York: Random House, 1967).

33. James Young, *Writing and Rewriting the Holocaust: Narrative and the Consequences of Interpretation* (Bloomington and Indianapolis: Indiana University Press, 1990), 24. For

a discussion of survivors' (in)ability to witness the deaths experienced in the camps, see Agamben, *Remnants of Auschwitz*.

34. Geoffrey Hartman, "Introduction: 1985," in *Bitburg in Moral and Political Perspective,* ed. Geoffrey Hartman (Bloomington: Indiana University Press, 1986).

35. When more than one group is interested in claiming those places, they may become contested symbols of memory, as the recent contested histories of Auschwitz, Dachau, and Sachsenhausen well demonstrate. See Andrew Charlesworth, "Contesting Places of Memory: The Case of Auschwitz," *Environment and Planning D: Society and Space* 12 (1994): 579–93.

36. Andrea Liss, *Trespassing through Shadows: Memory, Photography, and the Holocaust* (Minneapolis: University of Minnesota Press, 1998).

37. In the future, visitors will also learn about the national SS school at Sachsenhausen where officers were trained to become concentration camp commandos throughout Germany and Europe. At the stone quarry labor camp, an archaeological history park is being developed. Prisoners who worked there and at the nearby tile factory helped produce the stones that would build Hitler's new Berlin.

38. Dydia DeLyser, "Authenticity on the Ground: Engaging the Past in a California Ghost Town," *Annals of the Association of American Geographers* 89, no. 4: 602–32; Steven Hoelscher, *Heritage on Stage: The Invention of Ethnic Place in America's Little Switzerland* (Madison: University of Wisconsin Press, 1998); Karen Till, "Authenticity," in *A Feminist Glossary of Human Geography,* ed. Linda McDowell and Joanne Sharp (London: Arnold, 1999), 8–9.

39. The women explained their strategy to work through the camp; each took a turn listening to an audio station and then would explain to the other two what she heard. They also took notes on what they saw; one woman said when she saw me taking notes earlier that day, she began to do the same so she wouldn't forget all the information she was learning.

40. DeLyser, "Authenticity on the Ground." See also Edward Bruner, "Abraham Lincoln as Authentic Reproduction: A Critique of Postmodernism," *American Anthropologist* 96 (1994): 397–415.

41. http://www.tripadvisor.com/Attraction_Review-g187323-d190535-Reviews-Topography_of_Terror-Berlin.html.

42. http://www.aaa.com/eurotourbook/Berlys11.html.

43. Shelly Decker, "Touring Berlin," *Edmonton Sun Media,* June 22, 2000, reprinted at http://www.canoe.ca.

44. http://www.igougo.com/planning/journalEntryActivity.asp?JournalID=5175&EntryID=21957.

45. Andreas Huyssen, "Monument and Memory in a Postmodern Age," *Yale Journal of Criticism* 6, no. 2 (1993): 259.

46. Perlman, *Imaginal Memory,* 19.

47. See also Marianne Hirsch, *Family Frames: Photography, Narrative, and Postmemory* (Cambridge: Harvard University Press, 1997).

48. For a selection, see Andrew Benjamin, "The Architecture of Hope: Daniel Libeskind's Jewish Museum," in *Present Hope: Philosophy, Architecture, Judaism* (London: Routledge, 1997), 103–18; Michal Kobialka, "Of the Memory of a Human Unhoused in Being," *Performance Research* 5, no. 3 (2000): 41–55; Daniel Libeskind, *Daniel Libeskind: Countersign* (New York: Rizzoli, 1991); Bernhard Schneider, *Daniel Libeskind: Jewish Museum Berlin* (Munich: Prestle, 1999).

49. Museum directors tried to commission a number of conceptual artists to design the

museum's interior exhibition spaces, but they felt that those artistic interpretations would confuse visitors by adding another layer to an already densely textured space. The primary target audiences for the museum include families with children, international tour groups, and local residents. Directors decided to create more traditional exhibition spaces until they figure out ways to integrate the spaces of the building with their exhibition designs. The spaces of voids are nonetheless central to the museum exhibition design (Berlin artists, personal interviews, 1998; Ken Gorby, former assistant managing director, Jewish Museum, interview, 2000).

50. Steve Pile, "Ghosts and the City of Hope," in *The Emancipatory City?* ed. Loretta Lees (London: Sage, 2004), 210–28.

51. Nicolas Abraham and Maria Torok, *The Shell and the Kernel: Renewals of Psychoanalysis,* ed. and trans. Nicholas Rand (Chicago: University of Chicago Press, 1994), 175; italics in original.

52. After Jacques Derrida, *Specters of Marx: The State of the Debt, the Work of Mourning, and the New International,* trans. Peggy Kamuf (New York: Routledge, 1994).

53. Project team *Anschläge,* English exhibition flyer.

54. The exhibit was sponsored by the Berlin Senate for Urban Development, the Topography of Terror Foundation, and the Student Council of the Art College Berlin-Weissensee. For information, contact bauzaun@anschlaege.de. Information about the exhibition was available in a one-page flyer (in English and German) at the Topography's information trailer. According to the flyer, the exhibit was open from May 8 to June 23, 2002.

55. Walter Benjamin, *The Arcades Project,* ed. and trans. Howard Eiland and Kevin McLaughlin (based on the German volume edited by Rolf Tiedemann) (Cambridge: Belknap, 1999).

Index

Abraham, Nicolas, 224–25, 232n22, 235n79

absence: presence of, 1–3, 8, 9, 10

Academy of Arts, 36

action groups. *See* citizen initiatives

Active Museum of Resistance against Facism in Berlin (Aktives Museum Faschismus und Widerstand Berlin, eV), 65–66, 92–94, 124, 127, 147, 148

Adenauer, Konrad, 42, 84, 253–54n14

Adorno, Theodor, 1, 19

Agnew, John, 40–41

Alltagsgeschichte (history of everyday life), 90, 142–43, 258–59n61

Alternative List (AL), 88, 93

Altes Museum, 60, 236n9

American-German relations: history as popular culture, 140–42, 258n53; Jewish, 141–42, 165–66, 187; tourism, 25–26, 214–19, 226–27

Anhalter Bahnhof, 74, 107–8

Anschläge exhibition, 227–28, 269n54

archaeology: as history (metaphor of), 9–10; and landscape, 80; and memory, 94–96, 100–101. *See also* digging

architecture: Architects' Debate, 48–51; as art, 103, 183; black plans, 46–47, 239n60; Cold War, 41–43, 237–38n31, 238n36; competitions, 59–60, 242n2; deconstructionist, 46, 50, 220; fragments, 33, 39, 49, 107–8; modern, 41; National Socialism, 40–41, 48–49, 237n20; postmodern, 36, 48–51, 194, 239n58; postunification, 43–45. *See also* art; critical reconstruction; IBA; neotraditionalism

Arendt, Hannah, 111, 177

art: competitions for memorials, 18, 81–83, 90–92, 103, 125, 161, 170–72, 180, 234n66, 253n8, 260n1; conceptual, 104, 125, 148, 155–60, 167–68, 180–86, 219–22, 268–69n49; Neue Gessellschaft für bildende Kunst, 184; public, 36–37, 125, 180–86; site-specific vs. place-based, 125, 182–84

Aschrott-Brunnen memorial: Kassel, 99–102
Assmann, Aleida, 177, 230n12, 255n20
Association of Persecuted Social Democrats
    (AVS), 72–73
Association Supporting the Memorial to
    Commemorate the Murdered Jews of
    Europe (Förderkreis zur Errichtung eines
    Denkmals für die Ermordeten Juden
    Europas). See Memorial Association
Aufarbeitung der Vergangenheit (working
    through the past), 22, 88, 130; discourse of
    reappraisal, 90, 248n70. See also *Gedenk-
    stätten*; generational relations; memory:
    public cultures of
aura, 208, 213, 267n28. See also authenticity
Auschwitz, 22–23, 79, 136, 139
authenticity: as historic site, 212–14; and
    place, 208, 267n29

Balfour, Alan, 43
Barkan, Elazar, 203
Barzel, Amnon, 180
Baumann, Leonie, 93, 248n74
Bavarian Quarter (Bayerisches Viertel):
    Holocaust memorial, 9, 154–60
Begegnungsstätte (international youth cen-
    ters of encounter). See *internationale
    Begegnungsstätte*
Behrendt, Walter, 55–56
Bektas, Cengiz, 49
Benjamin, Walter, 10–11, 66, 96, 102, 135,
    230n7, 232n27, 233n39, 242–43n5, 250n88,
    250n97, 267n28, 269n55
Berger, John, 64
Berlin History Workshop, 65, 250–51n102.
    See also *Geschichtswerkstätten*
Berlin-Mitte, 36, 59, 75, 168
Berlin Museum, 198–201
Berlin Wall, 21, 25–26, 72, 75, 77, 116–17, 194
Beruf Neonazi (Occupation Neo-Nazi), 139,
    257n46
Betroffenheit (culture of dismay): as emotion-
    al encounter, 21–22, 125, 177, 187–88. *See
    also Gedenkstätten*; generational relations;
    memory: public cultures of
Beuys, Josef, 36, 99

Bitburg history, 129
black plans, 46–47, 239n60
Boltanski, Christian, 171, 177
Boyer, M. Christine, 49
Bracher, Karl Dietrich, 130
Brandenburg Gate, 35
Brandt, Willy, 89, 129, 253–54n14
Bretano, Margherita von, 175
Broszat, Martin, 254–55n17
Bubis, Ignatz, 147–48, 261n17, 263n36
Buchenwald, 85
Bundestag (German Parliament), 41, 261n16,
    261–62n18
Buruma, Ian, 86
Bus Stop!, 9, 180–86, 223. *See also* Holocaust
    Memorial

Campbell, Scott, 55
Camphausen, Gabriele, 137, 149, 164, 167, 223
Capital Berlin competition, 71–72
Caruth, Cathy, 208, 232n29
Casey, Edward, 16, 234n60
CDU. *See* Christian Democratic Union
Chamber Music Concert Hall, 34, 43
Checkpoint Charlie, 6, 26, 116–17, 194
Chipperfield, David, 36
Christian Democratic Union (CDU), 20, 150
chronotope, 10, 193
citizen initiatives, 18, 72–73, 79–81, 88, 92–94
city marketing. *See* marketing
City Palace (Stadtschloss), 7, 36, 37, 59, 75, 77
city planning: black plans, 46–47, 239n60;
    Capital Berlin competition, 71–72; Cold
    War, 41–43, 237–38n31, 238n36; New
    Urbanism, 37, 240n69; planners, 37–51;
    recovery myths, 47–48; Sixteen Prin-
    ciples of Town Planning (anti-Charter of
    Athens), 42. *See also* architecture; critical
    reconstruction; IBA
concentration camps: aura, 208; destruction
    of, 76, 244–45n27; memorial museums,
    206–7; memorials, 85; *Spuren* and *Zeug-
    nisse* (traces and evidence), 208–14. *See
    also* Sachsenhausen Concentration Camp
constitutional patriotism, 130, 255n21
construction sites, 30; Potsdamer Platz,

26–28, 235n1; Schaustelle Berlin tours, 31–33, 193–94, 219–23
cosmopolitanism, 36–37, 51–55, 149
critical reconstruction, 37–38, 45–51, 239n52
crypts: encryptment, 9, 57, 210, 223, 232n22, 235n79
Cultural Forum (Kulturforum), 34, 43

Dachau, 76, 84
Daimler Benz/Debis, 30, 34
Daniels, Stephen, 103
death, 218. *See also* violence
de Certeau, Michel, 11, 13
DeLyser, Dydia, 13
Denkmal für die ermordeten Juden Europas. *See* Holocaust Memorial
Denkmal (memorial), 82–83, 158, 167, 245–46n40
Denkstätte, 81, 88–90, 103
Derrida, Jacques, 11, 12, 232–33n36
desktop perpetrators (*Schreibtischtäter*), 63–64, 111–12, 123, 244n12
Diepgen, Eberhard, 33, 91, 96, 173, 261n17
digging, 10, 21, 66, 94–97. *See also* Benjamin, Walter
Dingel, Frank, 134, 137, 138
Disney approach, 140–41
documentation: Topography of Terror, 137–45, 147
documents: as antiterrain, 91; and artistic process, 158–60, 166, 182; historical, 59–60, 137–38, 140, 143. *See also* historic site
Domansky, Elizabeth, 258n59

East Germany. *See* German Democratic Republic
economy: postunification, 44, 53, 238–39n49; West Berlin, 68–69
education: political (FRG), 89–90
Ehrenmal (memorial of honor), 82, 246n43
Eisenman, Peter, 7, 22, 168–69, 172, 188, 196
Eliach, Yaffah, 144
emigration: West Berlin, 68–69, 243n10
Endlich, Stefanie, 161, 178, 179, 185–86, 205, 262n20, 265n70

Erinnerungsarbeit (memory-work), 18–19, 67, 123, 137, 181–82, 256n41. *See also* digging; memory
Erinnerungspolitik (politics of memory), 17–19. *See also* memory: public cultures of
Europahaus, 75, 77
everyday life: history of. *See Alltagsgeschichte*

federal belt, 35
Federal Republic of Germany (FRG): national identity, 55, 122–23, 127–32, 149–51, 205; political parties, 93, 249n79; *die Wende* (political transition), 19–22. *See also* education; generational relations; Germany; memory: public cultures of
feminist methods and politics, 11, 81, 143, 147, 235n75, 249n79
fieldnotes, 23, 107, 235n77, 252n1
film, 81, 140–41, 146, 257n50, 257n51
Fischer-Defoy, Christine, 92–93, 94, 126, 128, 147, 151–52
Flanzbaum, Hilene, 258n53
Flierl, Bruno, 261n17
footprints: of buildings, 46–47, 91, 115–16
Förderkreis zur Errichtung eines Denkmals für die Ermordeten Juden Europas. *See* Memorial Association
Foster, Norman, 35
Foucault, Michel, 94–95, 259n62
Foundation of the Memorial to the Murdered Jews of Europe (Stiftung Denkmal für die ermordeten Juden Europas), 261n12
Frank, Dieter Robert, 97
Freud, Sigmund, 12, 99
Frevert, Ute, 177, 230n12, 255n20
Friedrichstadt. *See* southern Friedrichstadt
Friedrichstraße: development of, 6, 37

Galinski, Heinz, 201
Gedenkstätten (memorial museums), 81–83, 88–89, 206, 267n21; hypnotic quality, 111–14, 119; international networks, 86, 146–47, 259n67; terror pedagogy, 145, 150. *See also* memory: public cultures of
Gehry, Frank, 36
Gemäldegalerie (Painting Gallery), 34, 43

generational relations: "1968 generation," 79–81, 84, 86, 93, 141, 210–11, 257n50; "1979 generation," 90, 93; anxiety over younger generations, 20, 81, 259n72; first and subsequent generation relations, vi, vii–viii, 15, 22, 35, 79–81, 86–87, 150–52, 166–67, 181, 208–12, 224; older generations, 73, 81, 86–87, 244n19; and silence, 79, 86, 208–11. *See also* ghosts; guilt; postmemory; returning

geo-ethnography, 11, 24

geopolitics, 20–21. *See also* normalization

German Democratic Republic (GDR): memorials, 85; Museum for History, 7

German Historical Museum, 7, 129, 136

Germania, 40–41

Germany: German-Jewish relations, 21, 126, 150–51, 154–60, 162–64, 173–74, 176–77, 188; national identity, 17–18, 20, 39–40, 55–57, 103, 122–23, 127–32, 149–51, 189–90, 205. *See also* Federal Republic of Germany; German Democratic Republic

Gerz, Jochen, 172

Geschichtswerkstätten (history workshop movement), 65, 90, 94, 124

Gestapo: headquarters, 63–64, 69–71, 76, 245n8

Gestapo Terrain (Gestapo Gelände): becomes Topography of Terror, 97; calls for memorial, 72–73, 81–82; calls for museum, 73–75, 86–88; discovery of, 63–65; forgetting of, 75–80, 245n31; Let's Dig operation, 94–97; memorial competition, 81–82, 90–92; naming of, 80; perpetrator/victim debates, 123–32; preservation, 132–34; stories of, 80–82; urban renewal plans, 71–72. *See also* Topography of Terror

ghosts, 9–10, 12–13, 15, 23, 224–25

Giard, Luce, 11

Goldhagen, Daniel, 201

Gordon, Avery, 9, 204

Greens *(Die Grünen)*, 68, 93, 243n9, 249n79

Gropius, Walter, 42, 237–38n31

guilt: collective, 76, 124, 171, 177–79, 181, 203

Habermas, Jürgen, 129–30, 188

Halbersztadt, Jerzy, 18

Halbwachs, Maurice, 14, 135, 233n49

Hansaviertel, 42

Hartman, Geoffrey, 142, 211

Hassemer, Volker, 87, 103

haunting, 12–17, 23–24, 79–80, 151, 154–60, 196, 224–25

hauntology, 12, 232–33n36

Heidegger, Martin, 43, 188, 265n72

Heimat, 81, 257–58n51

Henderson, Fiona, 236n3

Herf, Jeffrey, 20, 21, 237n20

Hesse, Klaus, 113, 137, 144–45, 204–5

Heydrich, Reinhard, 71, 76

Hillgruber, Andreas, 129–30, 255n18

Hilmer, Heinz, 34

Himmler, Heinrich, 71

Hirsch, Marianne, 15, 233n54, 258n55, 258n56, 268n47

Historians' Debate (Historikerstreit), 87–88, 129–30, 254–55n17, 258–59n61

historic preservation, 59–61, 132–34, 256n35

historic site *(Ort)*, 9, 22, 90, 123, 126, 252n2; as authentic place, 208–12; as site of perpetrators, 131–43

history: presentation of, 143–45; re-creation of, 6–8, 33, 194

history workshop movement. *See Geschichtswerkstätten*

Hitler, Adolf, 40–41, 174–78

Hoffmann-Axthelm, Detleff, 91, 239n52

Hoheisel, Horst, 99–101

Holocaust: Americanization, 140–42, 258n53; denial, 122, 124, 138–40, 151, 260n73; interpretations of, 87–88, 127–30, 174–75, 254–55n17, 258–59n61, 263n40; memorials, 82–86, 90–92, 155–60, 162, 168–72, 176–80, 246n42; significance of, 161–62; tourism, 22, 140–41, 141–42, 189–90, 213–14, 215–19; unrepresentability of 142, 202, 211, 218, 258n58

Holocaust (miniseries), 141, 257n51

Holocaust Memorial: competitions, 161, 170–72, 253n8; construction of, 168;

debates about, 1–3, 9, 17–18, 21–22, 162–68, 186–88, 189–90, 261n17; designs for, 168–72, 176–80; funding, 170, 263n33; site of, 174–76, 263n35; tourism, 197–98

home: revisiting, 13, 14–15

Horn, Rebecca, 171, 177

Hoss, Christiana, 93, 94, 146

Hotel Adlon, 36

Hotel Prinz Albrecht, 71, 74, 75

Howell-Ardila, Deborah, 41–42

Huyssen, Andreas, 8, 218, 231n13, 231n15, 231n16

hypervisibility, 7–8, 202–4, 224

IBA (Internationale Bauaustellung) (International Building Exhibition movement), 45, 50, 69–72, 76

identity: collective, 17; historic, 6–8; individual, 16–17; national, 122–23, 127–32, 149–51

imprint: buildings, 46–47, 91, 115–16; of death, 208

INFOBOX, 27, 235n1

Initiativkreis gegen den Schlußstrich (Initiative against Drawing a Final Line with the Past), 1–3, 19, 229n2

Inselstadt (island city), 53, 69

intentionalism, 175, 178

internationale Begegnungsstätte (international youth centers of encounter), 82–83, 90, 136, 147, 248n71

Internet, 53, 215–17, 228

Jackob-Marks, Christine, 166, 171

Jaeckel: Eberhard, 174

Jewish Museum: controversy, 9; design of, 198–201, 219–23, 268–69n49; as memorial, 170; in memory district, 7, 22, 149, 196, 201–2; tourism, 216–17

"Jewish question," 21, 129

Jews: memorials to, 21–22, 123–27, 173–74. *See also* Holocaust Memorial

Jobst, Gerhard, 42

Johnson, Philip, 6, 26

Kelley, Jeff, 57, 125, 183

Kernd'l, Alfred, 133

Kewenig, Wilhelm, 86

Kiez (neighborhood), 44, 45

Kirsch, Jan-Holger, 178

Kleihues, Josef Paul, 46

Kohl, Helmut, 20, 128–29, 172, 261n17, 263n36

Kollhoff, Hans, 49, 239n52

Koshar, Rudy, 57, 232n23, 232n27

Kracauer, Siegfried, 31

Kraft, Rudolf, 189–90

Kramer, Jane, 56, 124

Kreuer, Willy, 42

Kreutzner, Gabrielle, 140

Kreuzberg, 69, 75, 77, 82

Kuckhoff, Adam, 114

Kuftinec, Sonja, 16

Kulturforum. *See* Cultural Forum

Lacy, Suzanne, 183

Lammert, Norbert, 150

Lampugnani, Vittorio Magnago, 48–49, 239n52

landscape, 9–11, 64–68, 95–97, 243n6; ghosts of, 9–10, 64–65, 72, 117, 175–76; as material marker, 9, 11, 39, 91, 94–97, 103, 133–34, 194–95; as palimpsest, 43n7, 67–68; preservation, 133–34; stories, 67–68, 80–82

Lang, Nikolaus, 91–92

Lange, Gustav, 242n2

Lehrter Bahnhof, 35

Let's Dig, 94–97

Libeskind, Daniel: Holocaust Memorial, 172; Jewish Museum, 22, 170, 198, 201, 219; views of, 50, 240n78

Lifton, Robert Jay, 210

Liss, Andrea, 15, 212

Loewy, Hanno, 22–23, 79, 80, 84, 122, 127, 150–51, 205, 209

London: architecture, 43–44

Lowenthal, David, 132

Lustgarten, 59–61, 242n2

Lustiger, Arno, 206

Lutz, Thomas, 137, 149–50, 202

Mahnen (admonishment), 21–22

Mahnmal, 73, 82–86, 125

Maier, Charles, 129

mapping: Topography of Terror, 134–37

Marcuse, Harald, 90

Marcuse, Peter, 55

marketing: New Berlin, 5–6, 37–39, 51–55, 193–95. *See also* Partners for Berlin; Schaustelle Berlin

Marlene Dietrich Platz, 34

Martin Gropius Bau: building of, 74; haunting of, 64–65; museum proposals, 73, 75, 88, 250n90; restoration, 63–66, 67, 68–69, 108

Martiny, Anke, 136–37

materiality, 11, 13–14, 75–80; of landscape, 67–68, 94, 117, 133–34; of place, 10, 208; staging the city, 31–51, 194–96; as trace, 9, 11, 41, 49, 209, 214. *See also* aura; authenticity; historic site; imprint; place; trace

Mayer, Margit, 55

McDowell, Linda, 11, 43

Memorial Association (Förderkreis zur Errichtung eines Denkmals für die Ermordeten Juden Europas), 163, 170–71, 172–80, 260n5, 262n20. *See also* Perspective for Berlin

Memorial for the Murdered Jews of Europe. *See* Holocaust Memorial

Memorial Museum of German Resistance, 12

memorials: to National Socialism victims, 82–86, 246n42; of perpetrators, 88–90, 103, 205. *See also* Holocaust Memorial

memory: authenticity, 212–14; national, 204–5; politics of, 17–19; postmemory, 15–16, 113, 150, 211–18, 219–23, 258n55, 258n56; public cultures of, 20–22, 80–90, 103; remembering the future, 39, 40, 55–57; as scene (*Schauplatz*), 10–11, 102; social memory, 8–11, 13–14, 17–19; traumatic recall, 16, 142, 210. *See also Aufarbeitung der Vergangenheit*; *Betroffenheit*; normalization; places of memory; *Vergangenheitsbewältigung*

memory district: construction of, 7–8, 22; marketing, 53; planning of, 200–202;

role of, 123, 149, 196–97, 202–4; tourism, 197–200

memory industry, 63, 80–81

memory-work. *See Erinnerungsarbeit*

Merz, Gerhard, 242n2

Mies van der Rohe, Ludwig, 42, 237–38n31

Ministry Gardens, 174

modernism, 41, 51

modernity: crisis of, 9

Moldenschardt, Heiner, 88–89

monumentalism, 40–41

Morris, Leslie, 142, 258n58

Morsch, Günter, 196–97, 206, 212–13

Müller-Rehm, Klaus, 42

Muratore, Giorgio, 35

Museum for History (GDR), 7

Museum Island (Museumsinsel), 36, 236n9

Museum of Contemporary Art, 36

Museum of Industrial Arts and Crafts, 74, 75

Museum of Prehistory and Early History, 69, 75, 245n28

museums: concentration camps, 206–7; as memorial, 83, 204–7; politics of, 87–89

Mussolini, Benito, 40–41

Nachama, Andreas, 64–65, 79, 88–89, 91, 134, 188, 224, 242n3

narratives, 11, 23, 47–48

national identity, 122–23, 127–32, 149–51

nationalism, 56–57

national memory, 204–5

National Socialism: architecture of, 40–41, 48–49, 237n20; government headquarters, 63–64, 69–71, 75; history exhibits, 105; legacies, 17–18; Schutzstaffel (SS, storm troopers), 63–64, 69–71, 76, 105, 245n28; Sicherheitsdienst (SD, security services), 64, 71, 76, 245n28; social memories, 20. *See also* Gestapo Terrain; Holocaust; Topography of Terror

Naumann, Michael, 148, 172, 177

neo-Nazis, 139

neotraditionalism, 44–45, 47–49, 240n69

Neue Gessellschaft für bildende Kunst (New Society for the Arts), 184

Neue Wache memorial, 130, 206, 263n36

New Berlin: Cold War, 41–43; construction
of, 31–39; Hitler's vision, 40–41; marketing
of, 5–6, 51–55, 193–95; postunification,
43–55; tourism, 225–28

New German Cinema, 141, 257n50,
257–58n51

Nolte, Ernst, 129

Nora, Pierre, 135

normalization, 6, 128–29, 253–54n14, 254n17

nostalgia, 15, 38–39, 48, 56–57

open wound. *See* wound

Ort der Täter (site of perpetrators), 121,
123, 131, 252n2. *See also* historic site;
perpetrators

Palace of the Republic, 7, 59

Palestinians, 15–16

Pariser Platz, 35–36

Partners for Berlin, 32, 52–53, 193, 240n87,
240–41n88

past: construction of, 10–11, 13–14, 51

Pei, I. M., 7

Pelt, Robert Jan van, 41

Perlman, Michael, 39, 218

perpetrators: desktop perpetrators *(Schreibtischtäter)*, 63–64, 111–12, 123, 244n12;
documentary approach, 137–45; site of,
88–90, 103, 121–23, 149–50; social identity,
127–32, 150–51, 205

Perspective for Berlin, 123–27, 163, 172,
253n5. *See also* Memorial Association

Philharmonic concert hall, 34, 43

photographs, 1, 23, 46–47, 112–14, 143–45

Piano, Renzo, 34

Pile, Steve, 9, 24, 194, 224, 235n78

place, 8–11, 231n14, 232n26; authenticity, 197,
208, 212–15, 267n28; as human imprint,
208; as object, 47; and performance, 14–17,
101, 155–56, 167, 183–84, 223–24, 228; as
"real," 9, 183–84, 218; regimes of, 11–12; as
scene, stage, 8, 10–12, 31–39, 193–95; sense
of place, 252n1; as testimony, 208; as trace,
210–12; as witness, survivor, meta-physical

subject, 4, 13, 208–12. *See also* haunting;
imprint; materiality; temporality

place making, 8–9, 16, 18–19, 66–67, 196; and
emotions, 101, 144–46, 151, 224. *See also*
haunting; landscape; materiality; place

places of memory, 9–12, 21, 130; Holocaust
Memorial, 17, 164, 187; Sachsenhausen
concentration camp, 207; Topography of
Terror, 103; tourist attractions, 214–19,
223. *See also* imprint

planning. *See* city planning

political education, 89–90

political parties: Federal Republic of Germany
(FRG), 93, 249n79

politics: of architecture, 41; of museums,
87–89

postmemory, 15–16, 113, 150, 211–18, 219–23,
258n55, 258n56

postmodernism, 36, 48–51, 194, 239n58

postnationalism, 21, 122–23, 130

Potsdamer Platz, 6, 25–28, 34, 35, 46, 235n1,
236n6

preservation: Topography of Terror, 132–34

Prinz-Albrecht-Palais, 71, 73, 75, 76–77, 96,
243–44n11

Prinz-Albrecht-Straße, 65, 69–71, 225, 244n26

property developers, 44, 239n50

Prussia exhibition (1981), 63–64, 69, 72, 73,
79, 81

public art. *See* art

public space, 17–18, 50, 187–88

Puvogel, Ulrike, 246n42

Rau, Johannes, 56

regimes of place, 11–12

Reichstag: renovation, 35

Reitz, Edgar, 141

remembering the future, 39–57

returning: rituals of, 14–17

reunification: of Germany, 20, 21, 43–45

Richter, Gerhard, 232n27, 242n5

Roma, 126, 128, 188, 261n17, 262n20

Roman Empire, 40

Rose: Romani, 261n17

Rosenfeld, Gavriel, 42

Rosh: Lea, 123, 126, 162–64, 167, 173, 175–76, 260n6

Rossi, Aldo, 6, 37, 49

rubble: as "Nazi disease," 41, 76–78; as postwar forgetting, 63, 65–66, 75–79, 94–96, 114, 117–19

Rückreim, Ulrich, 177

ruins, 33, 37, 63, 65, 107, 116–20, 192

Rürup, Reinhard, 76, 121, 131, 132–33, 135, 201, 205, 209, 250n101

Sachsenhausen Concentration Camp: forced labor, 41; funding, 206, 267n25; as historical site, 22; Memorial Museum, 9, 206–7, 212–15, 268n37

Sanders, Andreas, 105, 113, 121, 137, 138, 145, 146, 150, 198, 201–2, 210, 215

Sattler, Christoph, 34

Schama, Simon, 10

Scharoun, Hans, 34, 43

Schaustelle Berlin (Showcase Berlin), 33, 193–94, 195, 219–223

Schindler's List (film), 141

Schinkel, Karl Friedrich, 60, 73, 76, 236n9, 242n2

Schliesser, Wilhelm, 42

Schlusche, Günter, 17, 178, 187, 188

Schmidt, Helmut, 129, 253–54n14

Schnock, Frieder, 156–60, 167, 179, 180–86

Schoenberner, Gerhard, 91, 93

School of Industrial Arts and Crafts (former Gestapo headquarters), 69, 74–75, 76

Schröder, Gerhard, 56, 123, 149, 172, 203, 261n17

Schroder, Richard, 261–62n18

Schulz: Hagen, 87

Schulze-Rohr, Jochen, 173

self: identity, 16–17

sense of place, 252n1

Serra, Richard, 171, 172, 183

Siegmann, Gerhard, 42

Sievers, Johannes, 76–77

Sinti, 126, 128, 188, 261n17, 262n20

site of perpetrators (Ort der Täter). See perpetrators

Social Democratic Party (SPD), 20, 123, 149–50, 253–54n14

Socialist Unity Party (SED), 85

social memory, 8–11, 13–14, 17–19

Sontag, Susan, 142

Sony building, 6, 34, 236n6

southern Friedrichstadt, 73–75

SPD. See Social Democratic Party

specters. See ghosts

Speer, Albert, 40, 174

Spuren. See trace

Stadtbild Berlin, 59–60

Stalinallee, 42, 225, 237n30

state library (Staatsbibliothek), 34, 43

Stelter, Roland, 75–76, 88

Stiege, Rudolf, 86

Stih, Renata, 156–60, 166–67, 179, 180–86

Stimmann, Hans, 44, 45–46, 48, 50, 239n51, 240n71

Strieder, Peter, 239n52

Strom, Elizabeth, 55

Sturken, Marita, 13, 266n15

Szeemann, Harald, 176–78, 179

Tacheles, 36–37

temporality: as archaeology, 9–10; architectural fragments, 33, 39, 49, 193–95; awakenings, 101, 155–56, 167, 228; chronotope, 10, 193; history, 6–8, 33, 38, 50, 143–45, 194; the new/old, 33, 38, 40–45, 52, 55, 194–95; nostalgia, 15, 31, 38–39, 48, 50, 56–57; past in presence/present, 5–7, 33, 50–51, 101, 194, 228; recovery myths, 47–48; remembering the future, 39–40, 55–57; as ritual returns, 6, 12–17, 208–12; urban renewal, 33–39, 63–72; utopianism, 5, 194. See also ghosts; haunting; landscape; place

"terror pedagogy," 89, 145, 150

testimony, 208–9, 267n30

Thierse, Wolfgang, 261n17

topography: meaning of, 134–35

Topography of Terror: documentation, 137–45, 147; establishment of, 20–21, 66–67, 97, 102–3; future of, 145–52,

226–27; International Documentation Center, 7, 104–5, 148–50, 259n71; international significance, 136–37, 146–47; mapping, 134–37; national role, 148–51; as open wound, 97–102, 134; as place of memory, 21, 103; plans for, 7, 22, 104–5, 131–32, 199, 250–51nn101–6; role of, 103, 205; rubble heaps, 89, 117–18, 252n10; sense of place, 107–19, 252n1; as site of perpetrators, 88–90, 103, 121–23, 131, 149–50; tourism, 118, 121, 197–98, 200, 217–18, 223–24, 225–27. *See also* Gestapo Terrain

Torok, Maria, 224–25, 232n22, 235n79

tourism: Cold War tourism, 26, 116–17; construction sites, 31–33, 193–94; dark, 214–19; Holocaust Memorial, 197–98; Holocaust tourism, 22, 140–41, 189–90, 213–14; Internet guides, 215–17; memory district, 197–202; places of memory, 214–19; Topography of Terror, 118, 121, 197–98, 200, 217–18, 223–24, 225–27

trace: Derridean, 11, 13–14; Foucauldian, 94–95; historical, 94–95, 222; humans as, 210; as material *(Spuren)*, 9, 11, 13–14, 95, 197, 208–14

transition: moments of, 19–22

traumatic recall, 16, 142, 210

Troost, Paul Ludwig, 40

Tuan, Yi-Fu, 133

Ulbricht, Walter, 42

Ungers, O. M., 6

Unter den Linden, 36

Vasudevan, Alex, 241n95, 265n3

Vergangenheitsbewältigung (mastering the National Socialist past), 8, 230–31n12

victims: memorials to, 126–27; myth of Germans as, 130, 255n30; social identity, 127–32

violence: and the nation-state, 9, 12, 66, 103, 132, 151, 206–7; photographs of, 144; and place, 9, 218, 224; representations of,

112–14, 131–32, 144. *See also* ghosts; witness; wound

Waigel, Theo, 136

Wannsee Villa Memorial Museum, 71, 185, 257n44

Ward, Janet, 194

Weimar period: cosmopolitanism, 53–54; marketing of Berlin, 38, 45; modernism, 51; re-creation of, 194

Weinmiller, Gesine, 172

Weißler, Sabine, 92

Weizsäcker, Richard von, 73, 82, 86, 244n19

Weltstadt (world-class city), 26, 38, 42–43, 53–54

Wende (political change), 19–22

Wenders, Wim, 34

Wenzel, Jürgen, 91–92

Westerwelle, Guido, 56

West Germany. *See* Federal Republic of Germany

Widmer, Caroline, 202

Wilcken, Dagmar von, 169

Williams, Rhodri, 222

Wilson, Elizabeth, 15, 57

Winkler, Heinrich August, 122–23

witness: bearing witness to violent pasts, 22, 208–9, 224; landscape as, 67; place, 210–11

wound: healing, 266n15; national, 11, 18, 134; open wound, 11, 21, 99–102, 232n29; Topography of Terror as open wound, 21, 67, 97–99, 134; weeping, 208–11, 232n29

Yad Vashem, 125, 142, 162–63

Young, James, 91, 111, 117, 165–66, 167, 170, 187, 210, 261n11

young people: attitudes of, 151–52

Zelizer, Barbie, 142

Zeughaus, 7

Zeugnis (evidence), 197, 208–14

Zifonun, Dariuš, 83, 90, 248n70

Zumthor, Peter, 7, 22, 104–5, 109, 148, 148–50

Karen E. Till is senior lecturer of geography at Royal Holloway, University of London, and codirector of the Space and Place Research Collective at the Institute of Global Studies, University of Minnesota.